Preparing Teachers for Inclusive Education in China

Focusing on the competence of teachers that underpins inclusive education seeking equal access to education for special needs children, this title examines teacher competence cultivation based on examples in China and excellent international experience.

To give a clear picture of the context of inclusive education in China, the author first clarifies the relevant concepts and reviews the evolving policies and practices embodied in the "Learning in Regular Classrooms" (LRC) program. The study then constructs an analytical model of four key indicators that help evaluate the competence of teachers in inclusive education. Based on analysis of the influencing factors of teacher competence, the book elucidates how these factors work to determine teacher competence. Drawing on international experience, especially pre-service teacher cultivation in the US and in-service training in China, it introduces three major cultivation models and feasible suggestions and strategies to improve the competence of teachers in inclusion.

This book will benefit researchers, professionals, and policymakers interested in inclusive education, special education, and teacher education.

Wang Yan is Professor and Doctoral Supervisor at the Faculty of Education, Beijing Normal University, China. Her research and publications focus on special education, inclusive education, and teacher training.

Preparing Teachers for Inclusive Education in China

Wang Yan

LONDON AND NEW YORK

This book is sponsored by "Jingshi Xuepai (BNU School of Thought)" Educational Series Project

First published in English 2024
by Routledge
4 Park Square, Milton Park, Abingdon, Oxon OX14 4RN

and by Routledge
605 Third Avenue, New York, NY 10158

Routledge is an imprint of the Taylor & Francis Group, an informa business

© 2024 Wang Yan

The right of Wang Yan to be identified as author of this work has been asserted in accordance with sections 77 and 78 of the Copyright, Designs and Patents Act 1988.

All rights reserved. No part of this book may be reprinted or reproduced or utilised in any form or by any electronic, mechanical, or other means, now known or hereafter invented, including photocopying and recording, or in any information storage or retrieval system, without permission in writing from the publishers.

Trademark notice: Product or corporate names may be trademarks or registered trademarks, and are used only for identification and explanation without intent to infringe.

British Library Cataloguing-in-Publication Data
A catalogue record for this book is available from the British Library

ISBN: 978-1-032-55934-6 (hbk)
ISBN: 978-1-032-55938-4 (pbk)
ISBN: 978-1-003-43298-2 (ebk)

DOI: 10.4324/9781003432982

Typeset in Times New Roman
by Newgen Publishing UK

Contents

List of Figures	*vi*
List of Tables	*viii*
Introduction	1
1 Overview of the Development of the LRC Program in China	17
2 Analysis of the Policies for Development of the LRC Program	46
3 Structural Analysis of the Competence of Teachers in Inclusive Education	76
4 Research into the Competence of Chinese Teachers in Inclusive Education and Its Influencing Mechanism	118
5 International Experience in Cultivation of the Competence of Teachers in Inclusive Education	191
6 Research into the Training of the Competence of Teachers in Inclusive Education	247
7 Action Research into the Improvement of the Competence of Teachers in Inclusive Education	303
Appendix: Interview Outline	*328*
Index	*329*

Figures

1.1	Trends in Number of LRC Students vs Enrollment, 2001–2019	30
1.2	Change in Proportion of LRC Students in Total Number of Students Enrolled in Special Education, 2001–2019	32
1.3	Number of LRC Students in Primary School Sector by Disability Category, 2001–2019	33
1.4	Number of LRC Students in Junior High School Sector by Disability Category, 2001–2019	35
1.5	Changes in Number of LRC Students in Primary and Junior High School Sectors, 2001–2019	37
1.6	Changes in Number of LRC Students in Primary School Sector, 2001–2019	38
1.7	Changes in Number of LRC Students in Junior High School Sector, 2001–2019	39
3.1	Conceptual Framework of Competence of Teachers in Inclusive Education	90
3.2	Research Approach	91
3.3	Scree Plot	104
3.4	Structural Model of 'Scale of Teacher Competence in Inclusive Education'	107
4.1	Average Scores of Competence of Teachers in Inclusive Education and Its Dimensions	129
4.2	Competence of Teachers in Inclusive Education by Region	131
4.3	Competence of Teachers in Inclusive Education by Age	131
4.4	Competence of Teachers in Inclusive Education by Number of Years Teaching	132
4.5	Competence of Teachers in Inclusive Education by Experience of Teaching LRC Students	132
4.6	Competence of Teachers in Inclusive Education by Professional Title	133
4.7	JD–R Model with New Dimensions of Personal Resources and Job Crafting	155

List of Figures   vii

4.8 Model of Intermediary Effects of School Climate on
Competence of Teachers in Inclusive Education via
Occupational Stress and Teacher Agency   162
4.9 Model of Intermediary Factors for the Competence of
Teachers in Inclusive Education   163
4.10 Model to Improve Competence of Teachers in
Inclusive Education   171
6.1 Multi-level and Multi-dimensional Full-coverage
Training Network   291
7.1 Path to Improve Inclusive Education Competence of Teachers
in Case Study School   325

Tables

2.1	Some Policy Documents Concerning the LRC Program	49
2.2	Some Policy Documents Concerning Cultivation of Competence of Teachers of the LRC Program in Inclusive Education	63
2.3	Some Policy Documents Concerning In-service Training of Competence of Teachers of the LRC Program in Inclusive Education	70
3.1	Requirements on Inclusive Education Competence in Chinese Standards for Teachers	80
3.2	Demographic Characteristics of Interviewees	93
3.3	Prediction Scale for Inclusive Education Competence of Teachers (n=34)	98
3.4	Basic Information on Respondents (n=1,703)	101
3.5	Item Loading Matrix Table for Exploratory Factor Analysis	105
3.6	Internal Consistency Test Results of All Dimensions of 'Scale of Teacher Competence in Inclusive Education'	108
4.1	Sampling Information	121
4.2	Demographics of Samples (n=1,676)	122
4.3	Multiple Comparisons of Four Dimensions of Competence of Teachers in Inclusive Education	130
4.4	Correlation Analysis of School Climate, Competence of Teachers in Inclusive Education, and Their Dimensions (n=1,676)	157
4.5	Correlation Analysis of Teachers' Occupational Stress, Competence in Inclusive Education, and Their Dimensions (n=1,676)	158
4.6	Correlation Analysis of Teacher Agency, Teacher Competence in Inclusive Education, and Their Dimensions (n=1,676)	159
4.7	Abstract of Multiple Regression Analysis of Influence of the Three Factors on Teacher Competence in Inclusive Education	160
4.8	Assessment of Model Fit	161

List of Tables ix

4.9	Direct and Mediating Effects of School Climate on Competence of Teachers in Inclusive Education via Occupational Stress and Teacher Agency	163
5.1	Basic Information of International Teachers' Inclusive Education Competence Cultivation Programs (2010–2019)	204
6.1	Information on Participants	251
6.2	Some Examples of Coding Process	253
6.3	Basic Information on Respondents	273
6.4	Some Examples of Coding Process	275
7.1	Basic Information on Interviewees in Action Planning Phase	308
7.2	Basic Information on Interviewees in Evaluation Phase	308
7.3	Data Coding	310

Introduction

Education is an eternal undertaking, and teaching is a sacred profession! Education is essential to every country, while good teachers assure quality education.

With regard to inclusive education, children with disabilities are allowed to enroll in ordinary schools in their communities on the premise of equality and non-discrimination, and are provided with corresponding support and assistance to receive the best possible public education. Inclusive education not only refers to the form of placement and strategy of special education, but also represents an educational idea that promotes the common development of typically developing children and children with special needs. Teacher competence in inclusive education is one of the key factors to improve the quality of inclusive education.

Today's world sees highly developed social civilization and the popularization of education. The quality of education received by a country's children with special needs is not only of great significance to their development, but is also turning into an important factor to measure the overall quality of the country's educational development and even the entire social civilization level. Thus, great importance should be attached to it. The course of development of special education in China was marked by the initial establishment of special schools for children with sensory impairments, the subsequent formation of various educational institutions for children with disabilities, the emergence and then the deepened implementation of ideas, concepts, and principles such as "returning to the mainstream," "normalization," "integration," and "least restricted environment," the gradual emergence of the recognition of the disadvantages of segregated education, and finally the emergence and widespread practice of the concept of "inclusive education," which advocates breaking down the barriers between general education and special education. This clearly reveals that inclusive education is subverting the educational model of segregated special education, and leads the development of special education.

Although the aim of meeting the educational needs of school-age children with special needs as soon as possible is different from the background

DOI: 10.4324/9781003432982-1

2   *Introduction*

and prerequisites of Western inclusive education, the practice of "Learning in Regular Classrooms" (LRC) that began in China in the 1980s coincides with the idea of inclusive education. Children with special needs in China thus gained access to regular schools. As a result, the enrollment rate of special needs children in China was improved most efficiently in the shortest span of time. It was of strategic significance to the popularization of compulsory education for children and adolescents in China, considered by academic circles to be the primary form of the practice of Western inclusive education in China. Although, given basic national conditions, early LRC practice was a local exploration made by special education staff, the LRC program has been constantly improved toward the essence of inclusive education thanks to the increasing influence of international practice. So far, it has been increasingly aligned with the characteristics of international inclusive education.

The *National Special Education Promotion Plan (2014–2016)* issued by the Ministry of Education and other state agencies in January 2014 points out: "Work should be done to comprehensively promote inclusive education so as to ensure that every child with disability can gain access to appropriate education."[1] This marks the direction for the future development of special education in China. The *Regulations on Education for Individuals with Disabilities* revised in 2017 regards promotion of inclusive education as an important legislative principle, highlighting the vital role of regular schools in the education of individuals with disabilities. This is the first time that the concept and principle of inclusive education[2] have been confirmed legally after the *Compulsory Education Law of the People's Republic of China* (PRC) listed LRC as an approach to education for the disabled in China. According to *China Education Modernization 2035*, released by the State Council of the PRC in February 2019, it is critical to improve special education, promote the universal attendance of school-age children and adolescents with disabilities, comprehensively advance inclusive education, and boost the combination of medicine and education.

As soon as the LRC program was initiated, relevant policies were formulated to promote the cultivation of the competence of teachers in inclusive education. For example, the *Several Opinions on the Development of Special Education* was jointly issued by the State Education Commission and seven other state agencies in 1989. It clearly states that "relevant professional courses in regular secondary normal schools and preschool teacher training schools in various regions may appropriately add the content of special education according to local needs; and normal colleges and universities should add elective courses in special education in a planned way." In a series of policy documents issued thereafter, regulations and requirements were made on the addition of special education-related content to teacher training. Among them, the *Law of the PRC on the Protection of Persons with Disabilities* (2008), which has the highest level of legal effect, stipulates that "regular normal colleges and universities should offer special education courses or teach relevant contents, so that general teachers can master necessary special education knowledge." The *Opinions on Strengthening the Development of Special Education Teaching Force*, jointly promulgated by the Ministry of Education and the State Commission Office of Public Sectors Reform in 2012, suggested reforming the training model and supporting normal colleges and other institutions of higher learning generally to offer special education courses in normal majors for cultivating the education and teaching ability of normal majors to guide students with disabilities to study in regular classrooms, and for the first time stipulated that "special education-related content should be included in the teacher qualification examination." Afterwards, the relevant requirements were highlighted in the *National Special Education Promotion Plan (2014–2016)*, the *Second Special Education Enhancement Plan (2017–2020)*, the *Regulations on Education for Individuals with Disabilities* revised in 2017, and the *Special Education Development and Improvement Action Plan during the 14th Five-Year Plan Period*. It can be seen that with the in-depth development of the concept and practice of inclusive education, China has paid ever more attention to the cultivation of the competence of teachers in inclusive education, and gradually included it in the relevant national development plans and policies.

Inevitable Trend of Special Education–Inclusive Education

Inclusive education was a brand-new educational idea formally established in the *Salamanca Statement* adopted by UNESCO at the World Conference on Special Needs Education held in Spain in 1994. It maintains that "regular schools should admit all children without regard to their physical, intellectual, social, emotional, linguistic or any other conditions. They should also provide high-quality support and service for their equal participation in social life."[3] Compared with segregated education, inclusive education is not only a form and strategy of education for children with special needs, but also an educational idea imbued with humanism that promotes the common development of special needs children and their typically developing peers. Based on the Western values of equality, freedom, and diversity, it unequivocally opposes discrimination and exclusion, reflects humanism and educational equity, and advocates consciously eliminating the materialization, domestication, alienation, and other negative influences imposed on children by "unfair competition," while maintaining people's self-esteem and self-confidence with "educational tolerance" and "developmental diversity."[4] So far, inclusive education has not only changed the concept and development model of special education, but also prompted countries to reflect profoundly on overall educational goals and functions, and has readjusted overall educational value orientation and educational positioning.[5] It has also promoted the reform of the entire education system and added new content to general education.

Many countries and regions in the world have successively promulgated a series of relevant laws and regulations that have created a "law-based" policy environment for the development of inclusive education. It is emphasized that regular schools are open to all children, and must admit all students to receive

4   *Introduction*

education together, regardless of the degree of their learning difficulties and disabilities; and teaching should meet the abilities and needs of all students, including those with disabilities. Examples include in the US *Public Law 94–142*, the *Individuals with Disabilities Education Act* (1997), the *No Child Left Behind Act* (2001), the *Individuals with Disabilities Education Improvement Act* (2004), and the *Every Student Succeeds Act* (2015); in the UK the *Warnock Report* (1978); and in Sweden the *Education Act* (1985) and the *Education Act* (2010). Under the guidance of these laws and regulations, inclusive education in developed countries has made great achievements. For example, 40 percent of children with autism in the US spend more than 80 percent of their study time in regular classrooms of regular schools, while 65.6 percent of children with developmental delays spend more than 80 percent of the time in regular classrooms of regular schools.[6] The number of special needs students in special education schools dropped from 2 percent in 1978 to 1.15 percent in 1996.[7] In the 1990s, 99 percent of students with disabilities in Sweden were admitted to regular schools, and only 1 percent of students with moderate and severe disabilities were enrolled in special education schools.[8] In Taiwan of China, most children with disabilities are enrolled in regular classrooms in regular schools (about 80 percent).[9] Inclusive education has become the direction of development of special education in developed countries or regions, and the traditional segregated special education system is gradually disintegrating.

As for developing countries, although the implementation of inclusive education is relatively slow, and segregated special education schools still exist and are tasked with educating the disabled, all of them are actively exploring inclusive education on the basis of their own national conditions. A typical example is Thailand. In 2004, only 390 schools in the country implemented the small-scale experimental program of inclusive education; by the end of 2005, the number of such schools had expanded to 2,000; as of 2008, the number had reached 5,000, with the children benefitting accounting for 35.13 percent of all children with disabilities. Inclusive schools enroll most children with disabilities in Thailand.[10] It can be seen that the development of inclusive education is an irresistible trend.

Urgent Demand for Quality Improvement of the LRC program

The "Learning in Regular Classrooms" (LRC) program is designed to enroll children with disabilities in nearby regular schools. It is a significant strategy for the development of special education in China, and also an educational innovation made by Chinese educators, with international inclusive education practice as a reference and based on the reality of China.[11] It was first mentioned in the *Notice on the Printing and Distribution of the Teaching Plan of Full-time Schools (Classes) for the Retarded*, issued by the former State Education Commission in 1987. At the first national conference on special education work held in 1988, a development model of special education was first proposed: "Take a certain number of special education schools as the backbone, and a large number of special education classes and LRC program as the main body." The LRC program was designed to increase the enrollment rate of children with disabilities, which is very different from the inclusive education practice geared to the ideas of freedom, equality, and diversity; but it does not conflict with the concept of inclusive education in essence and gradually shows some attributes and characteristics of inclusive education. In recent years, the concept of "inclusive education" has appeared in relevant national documents, and some provinces and cities have taken the lead in promoting inclusive education for children with disabilities. For examples, Beijing launched the *Action Plan for Inclusive Education in Beijing Primary and Secondary Schools* in 2013; Xinjiang Uygur Autonomous Region set up the "Xinjiang Inclusive Education Support and Guarantee System Construction Project" in 2012; Shanghai rolled out the *Action Plan for Special Education (2014–2016)*, with a general goal of "improving the special education system, promoting the combination of medicine and education, implementing inclusive education, providing quality services, and driving intensive development"; Jiangsu Province released the *Phase II Special Education Promotion Plan* in 2017, initiating the construction of an inclusive education resource center with integrated functions of education, rehabilitation and service, and issued the *Guiding Opinions on Strengthening the Construction of Inclusive Education Resource Centers in Regular Schools* in 2018, involving inclusive education positioning, personnel, outlay, equipment, curriculum, and management mechanism;[12] and Guangzhou, Shenzhen, and other places have also introduced their own special education promotion plans, highlighting their support plans for the LRC program and inclusive education in combination with the actual development of special education in the region. The promulgation and implementation of these policies show that China's educational administration has fully recognized the idea of inclusive education, and the LRC program has developed from the initial form of inclusive education to the best practice of inclusive education in China.

In the past 30 years or more, great achievements have been made. First of all, the LRC program enables children with various disabilities to enroll in nearby regular schools, providing universal access to compulsory education for individuals with disabilities in a relatively economical way and at a faster speed.[13] This rapidly increased the enrollment rate of children with disabilities, and solved the contradiction between the high demand of children and teenagers with disabilities for enrollment and the insufficient number of special education schools.[14] According to the *Educational Statistics Yearbook of China*, there were 47,200 children and teenagers with disabilities in school. Thanks to the launch of the experimental LRC program in 1987, the total number of children and adolescents with disabilities in school increased rapidly, and hit 211,400 in 1994. As the *Trial Measures for the Development of the LRC program* was issued by the State Education Commission in 1994, the total enrollment of children and adolescents with disabilities reached 295,600 in 1995, an increase of 84,200 or 40 percent in one year, setting a record in the development history of special education in China.[15] According to the

6   *Introduction*

2020 Statistical Communique of the PRC on the Development of Educational Undertakings, there were 435,800 students enrolled under the LRC program, accounting for 49.47 percent of special education students. The LRC program has become the main form of arrangement for special needs children to receive education in China. Moreover, it has changed mainstream society's perception of and attitude toward the disabled, and promoted the understanding and acceptance of disabled by people from all walks of life, resulting in a higher degree of social civilization. In the meantime, the LRC program has promoted the transformation of educators' educational ideas, so that the leaders and teachers of regular schools can re-understand and rethink the function and value of education, and further boost the reform of basic education.

Much headway has been made in China's LRC program, but the quality of the corresponding education and teaching is still poor. According to some researches, the quality of education, the status of personal development, and the realization of their potential in the regular educational environment are not ideal for children with disabilities.[16] "Just being seated in regular classrooms" and "just being mixed in regular class" are still the reality for most children with disabilities receiving education in regular schools.[17] In most cases, teachers in regular schools only support the ideal of inclusive education in concept and principle, but still adopt traditional segregated education in actual teaching practice. Now inclusive education is being promoted in an all-round way, it is more urgent to crack the major task of improving the quality after expanding the scale.

Teacher Competence Underpins Development of Inclusive Education

Implementation of inclusive education requires a strong support system. In the development process of the LRC program for over three decades, a preliminary support system has been set up, and effective management experience accumulated. The *National Special Education Promotion Plan (2014–2016)* promulgated in 2014 makes specific and practical stipulations on the support and guarantee system for the LRC program in the aspects of school environment construction, funding guarantee, the development of the teaching force, education management, education, and teaching. Among them, the development of the teaching force is undoubtedly a key area. In 2020, the Ministry of Education issued the *Guidelines on Enhancing Implementation of the LRC Program in Compulsory Education* (hereinafter referred to as the *Guidelines*), proposing to improve teachers' professional ability in special education.

Teachers' practice is the only way to realize education reform and development. Whether from the general concept of education, or from the specific content, methods, approaches, and other practices of education, reform must begin with the improvement of teachers' professional competence, and be carried out with every teacher's effort.[18] Therefore, teachers' professional competence and development have a close bearing on the smooth implementation of inclusive education. For teachers, professional competence mainly refers to

Introduction 7

the basic qualifications and abilities required for them to engage in education and teaching activities. It shows the quality of contemporary teachers, which is the premise for them to gain recognition for their professionalization and professional status.[19] Numerous studies at home and abroad have shown that, relative to other factors such as class size, class structure, physical environment, and student background, teacher competence plays a more important role in students' academic performance.[20,21]

In the context of inclusive education, the admission of children with disabilities has brought unprecedented challenges to teachers' teaching and class management. Students with disabilities may encounter great problems in adaptation to study and life due to their various physical or mental development obstacles. For examples, some have poor learning ability, unable to effectively participate in classroom teaching; some lack social skills, thus having difficulties in fostering normal relationship with teachers and classmates; and some with severe disabilities have serious problems in their self-life and emotional management behaviors. Therefore, teachers should make timely adjustments and changes to adapt to the new class ecology caused by the entry of students with disabilities. Furthermore, the original knowledge structure of teachers needs to be supplemented and adjusted, that is, they need to learn the concept, knowledge, and skills of inclusive education to meet the educational needs of all students, including those with disabilities.

With the further implementation and research of the LRC program in China, our understanding of the factors influencing the quality improvement of LRC practice has become increasingly comprehensive. According to relevant research, the overall quality of the LRC program is affected by government support, the improvement of the management system of the LRC program, the degree of acceptance of regular schools, the degree of support of parents for the schooling of children with disabilities, the degree of financial support, the necessary knowledge and skill level of teachers, the number of times that teachers accept teaching tour guidance, the degree of satisfaction of teachers with the workload and pay, and the support of resource rooms and special education resource centers for LRC practice.[22] Other research has found that "teachers' lack of necessary knowledge and skills" ranks among the top three factors affecting the quality of the LRC program, and is the main difficulty in the current operation of the LRC program.[23] These problems further demonstrate the importance of primary and secondary school teachers in improving the quality of LRC practice. A high-quality teaching force for inclusive education is expected to play a key role in improving the quality of LRC practice in China.

Although the cultivation of inclusive education competence of regular primary and secondary school teachers has been stressed in relevant policies since the late 1980s, the pre-service professional education and in-service training received by most of our primary and secondary school teachers rarely involve inclusive education, and they also lack professional support and guidance in practical work, so that, in practice, they have poor professional competence in

8 *Introduction*

this regard, and cannot meet the needs of inclusive education. According to a 2006 survey of 137 normal colleges and universities, only 19 were offering or had ever offered compulsory or elective courses in special education—and this was on a small scale, neither systematic nor scientific.[24] Even in the *Curriculum Standards for Teacher Education* for primary and secondary schools issued by the Ministry of Education in 2011, there is no special curriculum related to inclusive education. When educational equity is involved in courses such as *Pedagogy* or *Introduction to Pedagogy*, some views of inclusive education appear randomly in classroom teaching.[25] Research[26] on the syllabus of six representative normal colleges and universities in China reveals that their courses related to inclusive education and special education are elective, which have strong flexibility and greater freedom in the aspects of content, implementation, and evaluation. The objective and orientation of the courses are not in line with the actual role of general teachers for the LRC program. In addition, investigation of and research into the training status of LRC program teachers show that fewer than half of the teachers had received relevant training, and 70 percent of the teachers who had received relevant training just attended "short training classes," "lectures" and other similar forms instead of systematic pre-service training.[27] It is therefore clear that the relevant content of inclusive education is still lacking in the cultivation of teachers (pre-service and in-service trainings) in China.

In brief, the development of inclusive education has necessitated new requirements for regular primary and secondary school teachers. In the face of increasing differences due to the entry of students with disabilities into regular classrooms, teachers need to truly understand the significance of inclusive education from the perspectives of social development, national interests, and individual development, correctly judge the various difficulties of the students in time, and provide them with effective and professional help and support. Therefore, it is necessary for teachers to correctly understand and respect the differences among students, truly embrace all children, and adopt effective education and teaching strategies to help students with difficulties remove their obstacles, and meet students' personalized learning needs, so as to ensure that all children can receive high quality education. At this point, if the training of teacher competence in inclusive education is not in place, the quality of the teaching force cannot be guaranteed, thus affecting the quality of inclusive education.

In view of the contemporary significance of the development of inclusive education, and the requirements for the competence of teachers in inclusive education, this book focuses on the cultivation (also including "training") of the inclusive education competence in teacher education in China, analyzes the development of the LRC program and the policy evolution concerning inclusive education competence cultivation in teacher education, and explores the characteristics and trends of the development. A tool is developed to evaluate the development level and characteristics of primary and secondary school teachers' inclusive education competence so as to explore the factors that

Introduction 9

influence the competence and their mechanism of action, and build a model for improving the competence. Both international and domestic experience in the cultivation of the competence of teachers in inclusive education is analyzed, and case studies are presented to put forward strategies for improving teacher competence in inclusive education and building a strong teaching force for better development of inclusive education in China.

The following concepts are covered in this book.

Teachers

This refers to full-time teachers engaged in class education and teaching in regular primary and secondary schools.

LRC Program Teachers

The teaching force of the LRC program includes class teachers, resource teachers, and itinerant tutors. Today, special education school teachers in the places where the LRC program is carried out serve as the resources teachers and itinerant tutors. Therefore, LRC program teachers in this book, in particular, refer to the regular primary and secondary school teachers who work for the LRC program.

Inclusive Education

In a broad sense, inclusive education refers to the definition in UNESCO's 2005 *Guidelines for Inclusion: Ensuring Access to Education for All*:

> Inclusion is seen as a process of addressing and responding to the diversity of needs of all learners through increasing participation in learning, cultures and communities, and reducing exclusion within and from education. It involves changes and modifications in content, approaches, structures and strategies, with a common vision which covers all children of the appropriate age range and a conviction that it is the responsibility of the regular system to educate all children.[28]

In a narrow sense, it means that children with disabilities are allowed to study together with typically developing children in regular schools, and receive high-quality, equal education suitable for their own characteristics with no discrimination in the same environment. This book adopts a narrow concept.

LRC Program

This refers to the placement of students with disabilities in regular schools to receive education, playing a major role in China's special education system. It is somewhat similar in form to the Western integration of children with

10 Introduction

disabilities into the mainstream of education, but has Chinese characteristics in terms of the starting point, guiding ideology, and implementation methods.[29] In actual studies, researchers usually compare and distinguish between LRC program and inclusive education, or even mix them. When it comes to the relationship between the two, there are three typical viewpoints in current research. One viewpoint holds that the LRC program in China is a product of complete indigenization, which cannot be treated in the same way as inclusive education, although they have something in common. The second viewpoint argues that inclusive education is the same as China's LRC program since the latter is carried out under the influence of international special education theories, such as the return to or integration into the mainstream of education.[30] The third viewpoint concludes that the LRC program is a combination of Western inclusive education and special education in China, a pragmatic model of inclusive education.[31] No matter which viewpoint is taken, it is acknowledged that the two are a form of education that places special needs children and typically developing children together, but the LRC program is only in the initial stage of the implementation of inclusive education, and is a practical and inclusive education with Chinese characteristics. In its development process, China's LRC program has been increasingly influenced by inclusive education, and tends to develop into a full and effective form of inclusive education. Some researchers believe that "inclusive education is the goal and vision of future educational development in China. It guides LRC practice with more democratic, notary values and brand-new theoretical system while LRC program is a bridge and process leading to inclusive education."[32] Therefore, this book equates China's LRC program with inclusive education, and uses the term flexibly according to the context, without making specific differentiation and discussion.

Competence of Teachers in Inclusive Education

The Chinese word *suyang* (competence) has a synonymous interpretation of *suzhi* (quality) in the *Cihai* Chinese dictionary. According to Zhang Hui, *suyang* is synonymous with *suzhi*, which refers to the characteristic properties, including knowledge and skills, that determine a person's behavioral habits and mode of thinking.[33] Professional competence refers to the special qualities for a certain job or occupation. For teachers, it mainly refers to their basic qualifications and abilities to engage in educational and teaching activities.[34]

With the promotion of the LRC program, the educational objects have changed, so the teachers' original knowledge structure needs to be supplemented and adjusted. After receiving pre-service training, teachers basically have the ability to educate typically developing children, but lack the ability to teach special needs children in the same regular classroom. In this book, the competence of teachers in inclusive education refers to their understanding, knowledge, skills, and other qualities related to inclusive education to meet the needs of all children, including special needs children. Some studies call it "the competence of general education teachers for the LRC program."

Introduction   11

Children with Special Needs

In a broad sense, children with special needs refers to all kinds of children who are significantly different from typically developing children in various aspects, such as intelligence, sense organs, emotion, physical body, behaviors and verbal ability. Their development level is lower or higher than that of typically developing peers. And children who have committed minor offenses are also included in the category of children with special needs. In the narrow sense, they only refer to children with disabilities, that is, children with various defects in physical and mental development, also known as "defective children" and "disabled children."[35] This book adopts the concept in the narrow sense, and uses the terms "children with special needs" or "disabled children" flexibly, depending on the context.

Children with Special Educational Needs

This term refers to children with a variety of special educational needs due to individual differences. These needs involve psychological development, physical development, learning, life, and other aspects, which are higher or lower than those of typically developing children for a long time or for a certain period of time, not only for a developing defect, but also for the ability, social factors, and other aspects that affect learning.

Cultivation of Competence of Teachers in Inclusive Education

This term refers to the cultivation and training of inclusive education competence for teachers in the process of teacher education, including pre-service cultivation, induction training, and in-service training. This book mainly adopts the terms pre-service cultivation of the competence of teachers in inclusive education and in-service training of the competence of teachers in inclusive education respectively according to different needs of expression.

This book comprises seven chapters. Chapter 1 gives an overview of the development of the LRC program. From the perspective of the development of equal access to education, it explores the characteristics and significance of the development of the LRC program in different stages on the Chinese mainland, and based on the changes of development indicators of the LRC program, completes the "data profiling" reflecting the development of the LRC program. Chapter 2 deals with the policy evolution of the LRC program. Starting from the macro policy of the LRC program carried out on the Chinese mainland and the policy concerning the cultivation and training of teachers, it sorts out the relevant policies through value analysis and further explores their characteristics. Chapters 3 and 4 focus on the empirical research into the competence of teachers in inclusive education. Chapter 3 develops a scale to evaluate the competence of teachers in inclusive education. Based on the theories of teacher competence and domestic and foreign

12 *Introduction*

research on the competence of teachers in inclusive education, a theoretical model is constructed for Chinese the competence of teachers in inclusive education. Then, a scale survey is conducted, and through exploratory factor analysis and confirmatory factor analysis, the composition of the competence of teachers in inclusive education is studied. Chapter 4 tries to analyze the development level and characteristics of the competence of teachers in inclusive education in China through investigation. It also finds out the main variables affecting the competence of teachers, explores their mechanism of action, and establishes a mechanism model of these factors, in order to find a key strategy to improve competence. Chapter 5 rolls out research into the international experience in cultivation of the competence of teachers in inclusive education to explore its characteristics and regular patterns from the mode of cultivation and projects. Chapter 6 revolves around research into the training of the competence of teachers in inclusive education. Based on the current situation of the competence of teachers in inclusive education and the training of competence presented by local interview data, a qualitative research method is adopted to present the regional experience in training of the competence of teachers. Chapter 7 focuses on the action research for the improvement of the competence of teachers in inclusive education. Based on the factors influencing the competence of teachers in inclusive education, their mechanism of action, experience in cultivation and training of the competence of teachers, and theories on teachers' professional development, this chapter finds out the "evidence" of a typical school's efforts made to improve its the competence of teachers in inclusive education through action research, and explores the process and strategies of improving the competence of teachers.

Unless specified, the policies and data mentioned in this book mainly refer to those from the China's mainland, excluding those from China's Taiwan, Hong Kong, and Macao.

Notes

1 *Guanyu zhuanfa jiaoyubu deng bumen teshu jiaoyu tisheng jihua (2014–2016) de tongzhi* 关于转发教育部等部门特殊教育提升计划(2014–2016年)的通知. Zhongguo zhengfu wang中国政府网, 2014. www.gov.cn/zwgk/2014–01/20/content_2570527.htm.
2 Wang, Daquan 王大泉. "Xin xiuding 'canjiren jiaoyu tiaoli' de linian yu zhidu chuangxin" 新修订《残疾人教育条例》的理念与制度创新. *Chinese Journal of Special Education* 中国特殊教育 no. 6 (2017): 3–6, 12.
3 Booth, T., and Ainscow, M. *From Them to Us: An International Study of Inclusion in Education*. London: Psychology Press, 1998.
4 Fang, Junming 方俊明. "Ronghe jiaoyu: dangdai teshu jiaoyu fazhan de biyou zhi lu 融合教育:当代特殊教育发展的必由之路." *Chinese Social Sciences Today* 中国社会科学报 (Beijing), Dec. 15, 2009.
5 Fang, Junming 方俊明. "Ronghe jiaoyu yu jiaoshi jiaoyu" 融合教育与教师教育. *Journal of East China Normal University* (Educational Sciences) 华东师范大学学报(教育科学版) no. 3 (2006): 37–42, 49.

6 *Digest of Education Statistics.* National Center for Education Statistics, 2019. https://nces.ed.gov/programs/digest/d19/tables/dt19_204.60.asp.

7 Huang, Zhicheng 黄志成, and Wang, Wei 王伟. "Yingguo quanna jiaoyu yanjiu de xianzhuang" 英国全纳教育研究的现状. *Studies in Foreign Education* 外国教育研究 no. 3 (2002): 13–16.

8 Persson, B. "Exclusive and Inclusive Discourses in Special Education Research and Policy in Sweden." *International Journal of Inclusive Education* 7, no. 3 (2003): 271–280.

9 Wu, Wudian 吴武典. "Cong teshu ertong de jiaoyu anzhi tan teshu jiaoyu de fazhan—taiwan de jingyan yu xingsi" 从特殊儿童的教育安置谈特殊教育的发展——台湾的经验与省思. *Chinese Journal of Special Education* 中国特殊教育 no. 3 (1997): 15–21.

10 Hu, Yichao 胡毅超. "Zouxiang quanna: taiguo quanna jiaoyu shijian yanjiu" 走向全纳：泰国全纳教育实践研究, 40. Shanghai: East China Normal University, 2009.

11 Piao, Yongxin 朴永馨. *Teshu jiaoyu cidian* 特殊教育辞典, 91. Beijing: Huaxia Publishing House, 2014.

12 "Jiangsu sheng guifan ronghe jiaoyu ziyuan zhongxin jianshe 江苏省规范融合教育资源中心建设." *China Education News* 中国教育报 (Beijing), Jan. 15, 2019.

13 See note 12 above, 58.

14 Xiao, Fei 肖非. "Zhongguo de suiban jiudu: lishi xianzhuang zhanwang" 中国的随班就读：历史·现状·展望. *Chinese Journal of Special Education* 中国特殊教育 no. 3 (2005): 3–7.

15 Zhao, Xiaohong 赵小红. "Jin 25 nian zhongguo canji ertong jiaoyu anzhi xingshi bianqian—jian lun suiban jiudu zhengce de fazhan" 近25年中国残疾儿童教育安置形式变迁——兼论随班就读政策的发展. *Chinese Journal of Special Education* 中国特殊教育 no. 3 (2013): 23–29.

16 Qian, Lixia 钱丽霞, and Jiang, Xiaoying 江小英. "Dui woguo suiban jiudu fazhan xianzhuang pingjia de wenjuan diaocha baogao" 对我国随班就读发展现状评价的问卷调查报告. *Chinese Journal of Special Education* 中国特殊教育 no. 5 (2004): 2–6.

17 Guan, Wenjun 关文军. "Ronghe jiaoyu xuexiao canji xuesheng ketang canyu yanjiu" 融合教育学校残疾学生课堂参与研究, 8. Beijing: Doctoral dissertation of Beijing Normal University, 2016.

18 Zhang, Zhengzhi 张正之, Li, Min 李敏, and Zhao, Zhongjian 赵中建. "You biaozhun toushi jiaoshi zhuanye suyang—jian ping meiguo jiaoshi zige renzheng biaozhun zhong yunhan de jiaoshi zhuanye suyang" 由标准透视教师专业素养——兼评美国教师资格认证标准中蕴含的教师专业素养. *Global Education* 全球教育展望 31, no. 8 (2002): 18–21.

19 Ye, Lan 叶澜. "Xin shiji jiaoshi zhuanye suyang chutan" 新世纪教师专业素养初探. *Educational Research and Experiment* 教育研究与实验 no. 1 (1998): 41–46, 72.

20 Sanders, W. L., and Horn, S. P. "Research Findings from the Tennessee Value-Added Assessment System (TVAAS) Database: Implications for Educational Evaluation and Research." *Journal of Personnel Evaluation in Education* 12, no. 3 (1998): 247–256.

21 Savolainen, H. "Responding to Diversity and Striving for Excellence: The Case of Finland." *Prospects* 39, no. 3 (2009): 281–292.

22 Zhai, Haizhen 翟海珍. "Teshu jiaoyu xuyao ertong suiban jiudu zhiliang yingxiang yinsu he duice" 特殊教育需要儿童随班就读质量影响因素和对策. *Journal of Shanxi Coal-Mining Administrators College* 山西煤炭管理干部学院学报 23, no. 4 (2010): 101–102.

14 *Introduction*

23 Wang, Zhu 王洙, Yang, Xijie 杨希洁, and Zhang, Chong 张冲. "Canji ertong suiban jiudu zhiliang yingxiang yinsu de diaocha" 残疾儿童随班就读质量影响因素的调查. *Chinese Journal of Special Education* 中国特殊教育 no. 5 (2006): 3–13.

24 Wang, Haiping 汪海萍. "Putong shifan yuanxiao teshu jiaoyu kecheng kaishe qingkuang de diaocha" 普通师范院校特殊教育课程开设情况的调查. *Chinese Journal of Special Education* 中国特殊教育 no. 12 (2006): 13–17.

25 Wang, Juan 王娟, and Wang, Jiayi 王嘉毅. "Woguo zhiqian jiaoshi jiaoyu zhong quanna jiaoyu de xianzhuang ji duice yanjiu" 我国职前教师教育中全纳教育的现状及对策研究. *Chinese Journal of Special Education* 中国特殊教育 no. 12 (2009): 3–6, 56.

26 Feng, Yajing 冯雅静, Li, Aifen 李爱芬, and Wang, Yan 王雁. "Woguo putong shifan zhuanye ronghe jiaoyu kecheng xianzhuang de diaocha yanjiu" 我国普通师范专业融合教育课程现状的调查研究. *Chinese Journal of Special Education* 中国特殊教育 no. 1 (2016): 9–15, 29.

27 Ma, Hongying 马红英, and Tan, Heping 谭和平. "Shanghai shi suiban jiudu jiaoshi xianzhuang diaocha" 上海市随班就读教师现状调查. *Chinese Journal of Special Education* 中国特殊教育 no. 1 (2010): 60–63, 82.

28 Zhou, Mansheng 周满生. "Quanna jiaoyu: gainian ji zhuyao yiti" 全纳教育：概念及主要议题. *Educational Research* 教育研究 342, no. 7 (2008): 16–20.

29 See note 14 above.

30 Deng, Meng 邓猛, and Zhu, Zhiyong 朱志勇. "Suiban jiudu yu ronghe jiaoyu—zhongxifang teshu jiaoyu moshi de bijiao" 随班就读与融合教育——中西方特殊教育模式的比较. *Journal of Huazhong Normal University* (Humanities and Social Sciences) 华中师范大学学报(人文社会科学版) no. 4 (2007): 125–129.

31 Ibid.

32 Li, La 李拉. "Dangqian suiban jiudu yanjiu xuyao chengqing de jige wenti" 当前随班就读研究需要澄清的几个问题. *Chinese Journal of Special Education* 中国特殊教育 no. 11 (2009): 3–7.

33 Zhang, Hui 张辉. "Xin kecheng linian xia zhongxue huaxue jiaoshi zhuanye suyang de fazhan yanjiu" 新课程理念下中学化学教师专业素养的发展研究, 73. Beijing: Capital Normal University, 2007.

34 Zhang, Huanting 张焕庭. *Jiaoyu cidian* 教育辞典, 753–754. Nanjing: Jiangsu Education Publishing House, 1989.

35 See note 12 above, 1.

References

Booth, T., and Ainscow, M. *From Them to Us: An International Study of Inclusion in Education*. London: Psychology Press, 1998.

Deng, Meng 邓猛, and Zhu, Zhiyong 朱志勇. "Suiban jiudu yu ronghe jiaoyu—zhongxifang teshu jiaoyu moshi de bijiao" 随班就读与融合教育——中西方特殊教育模式的比较. *Journal of Huazhong Normal University* (Humanities and Social Sciences) 华中师范大学学报(人文社会科学版) no. 4 (2007): 125–129.

Digest of Education Statistics. Washington, DC: National Center for Education Statistics, 2019. https://nces.ed.gov/programs/digest/d19/tables/dt19_204.60.asp.

Fang, Junming 方俊明. "Ronghe jiaoyu yu jiaoshi jiaoyu" 融合教育与教师教育. *Journal of East China Normal University* (Educational Sciences) 华东师范大学学报(教育科学版) no. 3 (2006): 37–42, 49.

Fang, Junming 方俊明. "Ronghe jiaoyu: dangdai teshu jiaoyu fazhan de biyou zhi lu 融合教育:当代特殊教育发展的必由之路." *Chinese Social Sciences Today* 中国社会科学报 (Beijing), Dec. 15, 2009.

Feng, Yajing 冯雅静, Li, Aifen 李爱芬, and Wang, Yan 王雁. "Woguo putong shifan zhuanye ronghe jiaoyu kecheng xianzhuang de diaocha yanjiu" 我国普通师范专业融合教育课程现状的调查研究. *Chinese Journal of Special Education* 中国特殊教育 no. 1 (2016): 9–15, 29.

Guan, Wenjun 关文军. "Ronghe jiaoyu xuexiao canji xuesheng ketang canyu yanjiu" 融合教育学校残疾学生课堂参与研究, 8. Beijing: Doctoral dissertation of Beijing Normal University, 2016.

Guanyu zhuanfa jiaoyubu deng bumen teshu jiaoyu tisheng jihua (2014–2016) de tongzhi 关于转发教育部等部门特殊教育提升计划（2014–2016年）的通知. Zhongguo zhengfu wang中国政府网, 2014. www.gov.cn/zwgk/2014–01/20/content_2570 527.htm.

Hu, Yichao 胡毅超. "Zouxiang quanna: taiguo quanna jiaoyu shijian yanjiu" 走向全纳：泰国全纳教育实践研究, 40. Shanghai: East China Normal University, 2009.

Huang, Zhicheng 黄志成, and Wang, Wei 王伟. "Yingguo quanna jiaoyu yanjiu de xianzhuang" 英国全纳教育研究的现状. *Studies in Foreign Education* 外国教育研究 no. 3 (2002): 13–16.

"Jiangsu sheng guifan ronghe jiaoyu ziyuan zhongxin jianshe 江苏省规范融合教育资源中心建设." *China Education News* 中国教育报 (Beijing), Jan. 15, 2019.

Li, La 李拉. "Dangqian suiban jiudu yanjiu xuyao chengqing de jige wenti" 当前随班就读研究需要澄清的几个问题. *Chinese Journal of Special Education* 中国特殊教育 no. 11 (2009): 3–7.

Ma, Hongying 马红英, and Tan, Heping 谭和平. "Shanghai shi suiban jiudu jiaoshi xianzhuang diaocha" 上海市随班就读教师现状调查. *Chinese Journal of Special Education* 中国特殊教育 no. 1 (2010): 60–63, 82.

Persson, B. "Exclusive and Inclusive Discourses in Special Education Research and Policy in Sweden." *International Journal of Inclusive Education* 7, no. 3 (2003): 271–280.

Piao, Yongxin 朴永馨. *Teshu jiaoyu cidian* 特殊教育辞典, 91. Beijing: Huaxia Publishing House, 2014.

Qian, Lixia 钱丽霞, and Jiang, Xiaoying 江小英. "Dui woguo suiban jiudu fazhan xianzhuang pingjia de wenjuan diaocha baogao" 对我国随班就读发展现状评价的问卷调查报告. *Chinese Journal of Special Education* 中国特殊教育 no. 5 (2004): 2–6.

Sanders, W. L., and Horn, S. P. "Research Findings from the Tennessee Value-Added Assessment System (TVAAS) Database: Implications for Educational Evaluation and Research." *Journal of Personnel Evaluation in Education* 12, no. 3 (1998): 247–256.

Savolainen, H. "Responding to Diversity and Striving for Excellence: The Case of Finland." *Prospects* 39, no. 3 (2009): 281–292.

Wang, Daquan 王大泉. "Xin xiuding 'canjiren jiaoyu tiaoli' de linian yu zhidu chuangxin" 新修订《残疾人教育条例》的理念与制度创新. *Chinese Journal of Special Education* 中国特殊教育 no. 6 (2017): 3–6, 12.

Wang, Haiping 汪海萍. "Putong shifan yuanxiao teshu jiaoyu kecheng kaishe qingkuang de diaocha" 普通师范院校特殊教育课程开设情况的调查. *Chinese Journal of Special Education* 中国特殊教育 no. 12 (2006): 13–17.

Wang, Juan 王娟, and Wang, Jiayi 王嘉毅. "Woguo zhiqian jiaoshi jiaoyu zhong quanna jiaoyu de xianzhuang ji duice yanjiu" 我国职前教师教育中全纳教育的现状及对策研究. *Chinese Journal of Special Education* 中国特殊教育 no. 12 (2009): 3–6, 56.

16 *Introduction*

Wang, Zhu 王洙, Yang, Xijie 杨希洁, and Zhang, Chong 张冲. "Canji ertong suiban jiudu zhiliang yingxiang yinsu de diaocha" 残疾儿童随班就读质量影响因素的调查. *Chinese Journal of Special Education* 中国特殊教育 no. 5 (2006): 3–13.

Wu, Wudian 吴武典. "Cong teshu ertong de jiaoyu anzhi tan teshu jiaoyu de fazhan— taiwan de jingyan yu xingsi" 从特殊儿童的教育安置谈特殊教育的发展——台湾的经验与省思. *Chinese Journal of Special Education* 中国特殊教育 no. 3 (1997): 15–21.

Xiao, Fei 肖非. "Zhongguo de suiban jiudu: lishi xianzhuang zhanwang" 中国的随班就读：历史·现状·展望. *Chinese Journal of Special Education* 中国特殊教育 no. 3 (2005): 3–7.

Ye, Lan 叶澜. "Xin shiji jiaoshi zhuanye suyang chutan" 新世纪教师专业素养初探. *Educational Research and Experiment* 教育研究与实验 no. 1 (1998): 41–46, 72.

Zhai, Haizhen 翟海珍. "Teshu jiaoyu xuyao ertong suiban jiudu zhiliang yingxiang yinsu he duice" 特殊教育需要儿童随班就读质量影响因素和对策. *Journal of Shanxi Coal-Mining Administrators College* 山西煤炭管理干部学院学报 23, no. 4 (2010): 101–102.

Zhang, Huanting 张焕庭. *Jiaoyu cidian* 教育辞典, 753–754. Nanjing: Jiangsu Education Publishing House, 1989.

Zhang, Hui 张辉. "Xin kecheng linian xia zhongxue huaxue jiaoshi zhuanye suyang de fazhan yanjiu" 新课程理念下中学化学教师专业素养的发展研究, 73. Beijing: Capital Normal University, 2007.

Zhang, Zhengzhi 张正之, Li, Min 李敏, and Zhao, Zhongjian 赵中建. "You biaozhun toushi jiaoshi zhuanye suyang—jian ping meiguo jiaoshi zige renzheng biaozhun zhong yunhan de jiaoshi zhuanye suyang" 由标准透视教师专业素养——兼评美国教师资格认证标准中蕴含的教师专业素养. *Global Education* 全球教育展望 31, no. 8 (2002): 18–21.

Zhao, Xiaohong 赵小红. "Jin 25 nian zhongguo canji ertong jiaoyu anzhi xingshi bianqian—jian lun suiban jiudu zhengce de fazhan" 近25年中国残疾儿童教育安置形式变迁——兼论随班就读政策的发展. *Chinese Journal of Special Education* 中国特殊教育 no. 3 (2013): 23–29.

Zhou, Mansheng 周满生. "Quanna jiaoyu: gainian ji zhuyao yiti" 全纳教育：概念及主要议题. *Educational Research* 教育研究 342, no. 7 (2008): 16–20.

1 Overview of the Development of the LRC Program in China

Providing equal access to quality education has been a long-term target of China's basic education reform, and also taken as the value basis for the development of basic education policies. Since the founding of the People's Republic of China (PRC) in 1949, the basic education development strategy of China has experienced several waves of changes, with its focus shifting from "giving priority to efficiency" to "giving priority to efficiency with due consideration to fairness," and then to "equitable and balanced development of education." The "Learning in Regular Classrooms" (LRC) program is an important approach to provide equal access to quality education for children with disabilities. In response to the changes in national demands for educational equity and the policy environment in different periods, the LRC program has gone through a continuous evolution in its policy and practice.

Overview of Development Stages of the LRC Program

Origin of the LRC Program (1949–1987)

In the early years of the PRC, the demand for talent from all walks of society surged, resulting in an urgent call for all-round improvement in national quality. Hence, to provide universal access to basic education and improve the quality of basic education became a major task for education development in this period. When it comes to special education, providing universal education for the disabled and increasing the enrollment rate of children with disabilities were set as the main development goals. Due to the limited accommodation of special education schools at that time, some children with disabilities were admitted to regular schools, a pioneering practice implemented in many areas. Gradually, a formal system for children with disabilities to learn in regular classrooms was established, hereinafter referred to as the LRC program.

DOI: 10.4324/9781003432982-2

18 *Overview of the Development of the LRC Program in China*

Pioneering LRC Practice to Meet Practical Demand

In the early days of the PRC, a large number of education-related policy documents were promulgated in accordance with the principle set by *The Common Program of the Chinese People's Political Consultative Conference* adopted on September 30, 1949. It stated:

> The culture and education of the People's Republic of China shall be New Democratic-national, scientific and popular. The main tasks of the People's Government in cultural and educational work shall be the raising of the cultural level of the people, the training of personnel for national construction work, the eradicating of feudal, comprador and fascist ideology and the developing of the ideology of service to the people ... in order to meet the extensive requirements of revolutionary and national construction work, universal education shall be carried out ... . All this is to be done in a planned and systematic manner.

It provided an objective guarantee for the public's equal right to education.

Based on a series of education-related policy documents and practices, a socialist education system took shape, with a highlight of universal education. According to the *Decision on Reforming School System* issued by the Government Administration Council of China in October 1951, comprehensive basic education would be provided for children in their primary education stage, and the people's governments at all levels would set up special education schools for children, adolescents, and adults with physical disabilities, including the deaf, dumb, and blind. It was the first time that special education was formally incorporated into China's education system and children with disabilities were included in the scope of educatees. After that, the *Interim Regulations for Primary Schools (Draft)* and the *Interim Regulations for Secondary Schools (Draft)* were promulgated, requiring the use of a fair assessment with equal opportunities as a screening method for admission. With ability as the screening criterion, regardless of gender, ethnicity, or religious belief, every student had the opportunity to obtain admission qualifications through hard work. Therefore, the equality of educational opportunities was ensured to a certain extent. In the meantime, institutional mechanisms for education of various types at all levels were established to promote universal education and the equitable principle of the right to education for all, reflecting the national concern for equity at the starting point of education.

In this context, to provide compulsory education for all children with special educational needs became the primary task for special education development. Although the *Decision on Reforming the Academic System* fundamentally changed the charitable nature of education for individuals with disabilities by incorporating it into China's education system, various forms of secondary, higher, and technical education remained priorities in educational development due to a severe lack of resources, and the development of education for individuals with disabilities was still marginalized. In 1948, there were only 42 schools for the blind and deaf in China, with only 2,380 students and 360 faculty members; by 1966, the number of special education schools for the blind and deaf in China had increased to 226, with 22,800 students (not including those in Hong Kong and Taiwan).[1] Obviously, these special education schools could not meet the demand of so many children with disabilities for admission. Therefore, how to provide more educational opportunities for children with special needs became an urgent issue to be solved nationwide. Without no other options, a pioneering form of special education emerged in some areas, such as the Daba Mountain area, in the 1950s—admitting children with disabilities into regular schools.[2] In the 1970s, deaf students with certain hearing ability were transferred to regular schools.[3] In the language environment of regular schools, they were encouraged to practice speaking and improve their speaking ability. These non-governmental, private initiatives were often launched out of the compassion, love, and conscience of front-line teachers and principals for children with disabilities, who enrolled them and provided individual coaching to them.[4]

Although these initial attempts were not made in consideration of the rights of children with disabilities, but to fulfil the educational development tasks proposed in the national education policies, they also laid a practical foundation for the subsequent development of the LRC system and the realization of educational equity for individuals with disabilities.

Establishment of LRC System

China's launch of reform and opening up in 1978 resulted in an urgent need for large numbers of personnel for socialist construction work. Thus, the top priority in educational work was given to the task of improving the national quality and providing compulsory education for all, including the disabled. In 1985, the *Decision of the Central Committee of the Communist Party of China on the Reform of the Education System* was promulgated at the first national conference on educational work after the Reform and Opening-up Program was initiated. It defined the implementation of nine years' compulsory education as a basic task in educational development and reform of the educational system, established the principle of local hierarchical management of basic education, and required efforts to develop preschool education as well as special education for the blind, deaf, dumb, disabled, and other so-called retarded children. As stipulated by Article 9 of the *Compulsory Education Law of the PRC* enacted in July 1986, "Local people's governments at various levels shall establish primary and junior high schools at such locations that children and adolescents can attend schools near their homes. Local people's governments shall establish special education schools (classes) for children and adolescents who are blind, deaf-mute or retarded." As of 1988, there were only 504 special education schools for the blind, deaf-mute, and so-called retarded children nationwide, with a total enrollment of over 52,000 students.[5] However,

20 Overview of the Development of the LRC Program in China

according to the data from the first national sample survey of disabled population in 1987, the number of children with disabilities in China was up to 8.17 million by 1986, of which about 6.25 million were school-age children, and about 2.8 million school-age children with disabilities had not been enrolled.[6] Despite the significantly rapid increase in the number of special education schools, there was still a long way to go toward achieving the goal of providing access to nine years' compulsory education for all school-age children with disabilities.

There was an urgent need to blaze a new trail to enroll special needs children. Thus, the existing LRC practice was gradually taken as an important means to improve the education for individuals with disabilities. According to the *Opinions on Several Issues Concerning the Implementation of the Compulsory Education Law* issued by the State Education Commission and other departments in 1986, the people's governments at various levels should attach importance to compulsory education for children with disabilities, such as the blind, deaf-mute, and so-called retarded, and solve the problem of their admission in a step-by-step manner, and those children who have disabilities but did not hinder normal learning should be absorbed into regular primary and secondary schools. This marked the formal recognition of LRC practice as a form of compulsory education for children and adolescents with disabilities in China. From then on, active explorations were made on LRC practice. In 1987, experimental research into LRC practice was carried out, covering 15 counties and cities across the country, to explore suitable local LRC approaches. In December of the same year, the former State Education Commission pointed out in the *Notice on the Printing and Distribution of the Teaching Plan of Full-time Schools (Classes) for the Retarded* (Draft for Solicitation of Comments):

> In the process of providing universal primary education, most mildly retarded children have been admitted into regular schools to learn in regular classrooms. This form is conducive to the interaction between mentally retarded children and typically developing children. It is a feasible way to solve the problem of mildly retarded children's enrollment in areas where schools (classes) for the retarded have not yet been established, especially in rural areas.

The notice clearly used the term "learning in regular classrooms" for the first time, affirmed its positive significance, and established the LRC system.

Stemming from the practical need of increasing the enrollment rate of children with disabilities, LRC practice is the result of spontaneous exploration for a solution, rather than the result of purposeful design based on the concept of equal access to education for the disabled. However, the goal of universal compulsory education for the disabled itself implies the pursuit of the value concept of equal access to education, and the resulting LRC system also maintains this value concept. From a practical perspective, LRC practice guarantees some disabled children's opportunities to receive education, and makes

Overview of the Development of the LRC Program in China   21

it possible for children with disabilities and their typically developing peers to enjoy equity in educational opportunities and quality of education.

Exploration of the LRC Program and Establishment of Its Dominant Position (1988–2000)

From the mid-1980s to the beginning of the 21st century, issues concerning educational equity, such as uneven allocation of educational opportunities and resources, came to the fore. Promoting the overall balanced and coordinated development of education became an important task in China, and special education was also on the list of educational development. For various reasons, special education had become the weakest part of universal primary education, and the national enrollment rate of blind and deaf school-age children was less than 6 percent. In this context, increasing the enrollment rate of children and adolescents with disabilities became a major goal for the development of special education, so development of the LRC program began to accelerate.

In 1988, the first national conference on special education work was held in Beijing. Based on the achievements in previous LRC practice, a new model of education for children and adolescents with disabilities was first proposed: insisting on multiple forms of schooling, with a certain number of special education schools as the backbone and a large number of special education classes and the LRC program as the main body.[7] The *Several Opinions on the Development of Special Education* was also adopted at the conference, advocating the development of the LRC program and special education classes, proposing that local education departments should make full use of existing regular primary schools to enroll children with disabilities, while admitting children with disabilities who have greater learning difficulties into special education classes attached to primary schools. At this point, the dominant position of the LRC program was established. From then on, China continued to carry out large-scale LRC experiments in many places. In 1989, the former State Education Commission entrusted Beijing, Hebei, Jiangsu, Heilongjiang, Shanxi, Shandong, Liaoning, and Zhejiang provinces and cities to conduct LRC tryouts for children and adolescents with visual impairment and intellectual disability; in 1992, the Commission also entrusted Beijing, Jiangsu, Heilongjiang, and Hubei provinces and cities to carry out LRC pilot projects for children and adolescents with hearing impairment and speech impairment. Since May 1990, the State Education Commission had also held nationwide, provincial, or municipal live meetings or seminars in Jiangsu, Hebei, Heilongjiang, Beijing, Shandong, and other areas on LRC issues for children and adolescents with visual impairment, hearing impairment, speech impairment, and intellectual disability.[8]

In 1993, the Central Committee of the Communist Party of China (CPC) and the General Office of the State Council, PRC promulgated the *Outline for Reform and Development of Education in China*, a programmatic document

22 Overview of the Development of the LRC Program in China

for education reform in the 1990s and into the next century. It set the educational goal of the 1990s, that is to make compulsory nine years' universal education and eradicate illiteracy among young adults, and pointed out the need to "improve the quality of education and emphasize the effectiveness of schooling." In terms of special education, it stipulated that governments at various levels should take education for the individuals with disabilities as a part of national education, and develop education for individuals with disabilities in a variety of forms, such as running separate special education schools or admitting them into regular schools. Under this guidance, the LRC program was gradually promoted nationwide, with the aim of universal education for individuals with disabilities. In May 1994, the Department of Basic Education of the former State Education Commission held a national conference on the LRC program in Yancheng City, Jiangsu Province, listing the duties that the government, regular schools, and special education schools should perform in implementation of the LRC program, and emphasizing the need to comprehensively promote the development of the LRC program. This marks a new development stage of the LRC program in China, from separate explorations by disability category and region to national overall promotion. In July of the same year, based on the content of the conference, the State Education Commission issued the *Trial Measures for the Development of the LRC Program*, clearly positioning LRC practice as a major form of universal compulsory education for children and adolescents with disabilities in China, affirming the effectiveness of the LRC program and its positive significance to both special education and general education. It also required efforts to attach great importance to and actively carry out the LRC program, and set various standards for LRC practice nationwide.

Subsequently, the *Regulations on Education for Individuals with Disabilities* enacted in 1994 and the *Law of the PRC on the Protection of Persons with Disabilities* in 1996 set the enrollment of children with disabilities as a criterion to evaluate the work for nine years' compulsory universal education. The *Implementation Plan on Compulsory Education for Children and Adolescents with Disabilities during the Ninth Five-Year Plan Period* promulgated in 1996 stated: "The LRC program should be widely carried out, and special education classes be set up in townships," and "A pattern of compulsory education for children and adolescents with disabilities should be formed with LRC program and special education classes as the main body and special education schools as the backbone."

Quality Improvement Stage of the LRC Program (since 2001)

With the advent of the 21st century, China's "two basic tasks" (to make nine years' compulsory education universal and to eliminate illiteracy among young and middle-aged adults) had been mostly completed. Due to the imbalance in local economic and cultural development levels, the negative effects of the urban–rural dual structure and the key school system began to surface, and

Overview of the Development of the LRC Program in China 23

there were large disparities in the conditions and development levels of education among regions, urban and rural areas, schools, and groups. In response to this situation, the focus of education development was shifted to realization of educational equity, improvement of educational quality, and promotion of the balanced development of compulsory education while continuing to expand the enrollment.

In 2004, the *10th Five-Year Plan and the Development Plan Toward 2015 for the Education Sector* first proposed adherence to the principles of equity and justice in the development of socialist education, and that education for the vulnerable should be given more attention. This marks a new stage of China's education in which "equity and justice" is the core value orientation. Subsequently, several new important policy documents touched on the concept of "equal access to education," continuously enriched its connotation, and listed various measures to constantly promote educational equity. For example, the report delivered at the 17th National Congress of the CPC in October 2007 regarded educational equity as an important foundation for social equity, and called for efforts to optimize the educational structure and promote balanced development of compulsory education, including "achieving equity in education" into the national development strategy. The *Outline of China's National Plan for Medium and Long-term Education Reform and Development (2010–2020)* issued in 2010 set "promoting equity" and "improving quality" as the guidelines for education development between 2010 and 2020, and required great efforts to solve the issue of unbalanced education development. Ensuring educational opportunities and quality for children and adolescents with disabilities became one of the important methods to promote the balanced development of compulsory education. The *Compulsory Education Law of the PRC*, amended in 2006, the *Opinions on Further Promoting Balanced Development of Compulsory Education* promulgated by the State Council in 2012 and many other policy documents clearly pointed out the priority of developing special education at the compulsory education stage and guaranteeing equal access to compulsory education for special groups. Thanks to the national support for special education development, the LRC program saw rapid development in both scale and quality, showing changes in the direction of development and practice characteristics.

Development Toward Inclusive Education

Since the beginning of the 21st century, the connotation of the LRC program had been further enriched by greater integration into inclusive education, as evidenced by various policy documents that advocated the development of the LRC program toward inclusive education. For example, *the Minutes of National Conference on the Exchange of Experiences in LRC Practice* issued by the Department of Basic Education in 2003 stated: "The LRC program is to implement compulsory education for children with disabilities in the general education system, making full use of general education resources,"

24   Overview of the Development of the LRC Program in China

and "this form breaks the tradition of separating general education from special education, and promotes the integration of the two systems." It also affirmed the decisive role of the LRC program in the enrollment of children and adolescents with disabilities as well as its significant role in promoting their social integration and changing their educational ideas. Furthermore, it pointed out that the LRC program would be the main form of compulsory education for children and adolescents with disabilities and the key task of special education in the future. In 2014, the *Program for Promoting Special Education (2014–2016)* was promulgated, clarifying the concept of "inclusive education" for the first time. It pointed out that in the next three years work should be done to comprehensively promote inclusive education and explore an inclusive education model suitable for China's reality, so as to ensure that every child with disability can gain access to appropriate education, marking the fact that China's special education had entered into a new stage of development with the concept of "inclusion" as the core value. The *Regulations on Education for Individuals with Disabilities* revised in 2017 endorsed the concept of inclusive education and the basic principles of its implementation for the first time. It stipulated:

> Education for individuals with disabilities shall improve the quality of instruction, actively promote inclusive education, and adopt general education approach or special education approach in accordance with the categories of disabilities and their abilities of receptivity, while giving priority to general education approach ... school-age children and adolescents with disabilities who are able to receive general education but need special support in school life shall, according to their physical conditions, attend regular schools near the places of their residence for receiving compulsory education that are furnished with appropriate resources and conditions and designated within specific regions by the administrative departments of education under the people's governments at the county level.

Several subsequent policy documents contain similar statements to guide the development of the LRC program toward inclusive education.

Some economically developed provinces and cities have taken the lead in exploring the full implementation of inclusive education. For example, Beijing issued the *Action Plan for Inclusive Education in Beijing Primary and Secondary Schools* in 2013, carrying out six major projects: the guiding project of special support education centers, the main project of the LRC program, the auxiliary project for delivering education to home, the preschool special education service project, the special education teacher team building project, and the social support project for special education. This action plan also proposed that in about three years, 100 compulsory education schools in the districts and counties should be supported to establish model resource rooms with complete software and hardware, 20 municipal model schools for inclusive education should be created, 60 rehabilitation resource centers for children with special educational needs should be established, and a modern comprehensive special education system in line with the status of the capital should be built.[9] In 2016, the Department of Education of Zhejiang Province issued a notice on the *13th Five-Year Plan of Zhejiang Province for Development of Special Education*, proposing the goal of normalizing inclusive education. Corresponding specific measures were also put forward in the notice, that is promoting the integration of special education and general education, launching the LRC program in preschools and senior high schools, admitting all children with mild disabilities to regular primary and secondary schools to learn in regular classrooms therein; continuing to promote the construction of resource rooms to have at least one resource room in each township (neighborhood) and 1,000 model resource rooms in the province; expanding the implementation of "special education schools + satellite classes" to have 100 such "satellite classes" in the province.[10] These pioneering regions have provided valuable practical experience for the all-round promotion of inclusive education nationwide. However, there is still a long way to go before the goal of inclusive education is truly realized, and efforts will still be needed for a long time.

In recent years, several policy documents have been issued in succession, closely linking the future development of education with inclusive education. For example, specific requirements on the future development of inclusive education are listed in *China's Education Modernization 2035* released in February 2019, that is to achieve universal access to basic public education services by 2035; improve special education, promote universal attendance of school-age children and adolescents with disabilities, and comprehensively advance inclusive education. In June 2020, the Ministry of Education of China promulgated the *Guidelines on Enhancing Implementation of the LRC Program in Compulsory Education*, making comprehensive deployment of the LRC program in China for the first time. It clearly puts forward the requirements of adhering to the integration of general education and special education, improving education quality, achieving fair and quality development of special education, and promoting better integration of children and adolescents with disabilities into social life. It also gives corresponding guidance to solve the serious problems of inadequate working mechanism, imperfect supporting conditions, and the low professional level of teachers and tutors for special education. These policy documents specify the goals and practical approaches for the future development of the LRC program, and the priority given to the program has further strengthened its dominant position.

Emphasis on Development of Supporting System

Under the guidance of inclusive education thinking, the LRC program also aims to achieve equity in the educational process and results for children and adolescents with disabilities by improving its own quality.

With the advent of the 21st century, China has attached greater importance to the quality of the LRC program as well as the development of its supporting

26 *Overview of the Development of the LRC Program in China*

system while continuing to scale it up. In 2001, a national conference on the exchange of experience in LRC practice was held in Beijing, jointly organized by the Department of Basic Education under the Ministry of Education and the China Disabled Persons' Federation. For the first time, it proposed to establish a supporting system for the LRC program, and required pilot work of establishing the supporting system in 100 counties (districts) nationwide. After the conference, the *Minutes of National Conference on the Exchange of Experience in LRC Practice*, the *Circular on the Work of Pilot Counties (Districts) for Establishing a Supporting System for the LRC Program* and other documents were issued to guide the implementation of the requirements put forward at the conference. In 2004 and 2010, conferences were held in Nanjing and Shanghai respectively to share experience in development of the supporting system for the LRC program, so as to promote and deepen the development of the system.

During this period, priority was given to the construction of resource rooms and resource centers, and the establishment of supporting networks for the LRC program. On the one hand, it was required to provide professional support for LRC practice through increasing financial investment and establishing resource rooms in regular schools and resource centers in each area. On the other hand, the establishment of supporting networks was required to ensure reasonable management over LRC practice and the building of a competent teaching team. Counties (districts) were required to form two kinds of supporting networks. One kind links the county (district) education bureau, township central schools, and the schools that implement LRC program to exercise overall management. The other kind connects the county (district) teaching and research office (or special education schools, special education centers), teaching and research personnel, township central schools (backbone school teachers), and teachers at LRC sites to give teaching and research guidance. Meanwhile, the supporting networks actively promoted the functional transformation of special education schools, and undertook the task of guiding, inspecting, training, and consulting on the LRC sites in their respective area, so as to provide support for LRC practice in various aspects.

In June 2004, experts were organized by the Department of Basic Education under the Ministry of Education to make a survey of LRC practice in the pilot counties (districts) in six provinces. The results show that, during the year, the pilot work in all provinces went smoothly, some valuable experience schemes had been formed, the number of LRC students had increased, a large number of new resource rooms had been set up, and unique local LRC practice models had also been created in accordance with local conditions; but there was still an imbalance in the development of the LRC program.[11] From then on, further practical explorations on the development of supporting system for the LRC program were launched in various areas. By the promulgation of *The Program for Promoting Special Education* in 2014, increasing the number of LRC students, strengthening the construction of special education resource rooms, and building barrier-free facilities remained key tasks for developing the supporting system.

Recent years have seen more concerns of the Chinese government about the support for the LRC program. Several education-related normative documents of the State Council called for efforts to strengthen the support for the LRC program, and the effectiveness level of such policies was increased. From the specific contents of the work for development of the supporting system, the following characteristics are presented. The first is the shift of focus from previous construction of special education resource centers to the quality improvement of the resource centers. For example, the *Circular of the General Office of the State Council on Further Strengthening the Control of Dropouts and Improving the Level of Consolidation of Compulsory Education* issued in 2017 proposed to improve the conditions of special education schools, equip them with professional teachers, and bring into play the role of special education resource centers to improve the quality of the LRC program in regular schools. The *Guidelines on Enhancing Implementation of the LRC Program in Compulsory Education* issued in June 2020 provides instructions on the work of improving the supporting system for LRC practice from two aspects: strengthening the construction of resource rooms and bringing into play the role of resource centers. In terms of strengthening the construction of resource rooms, it proposed that schools that accept more than five students with disabilities should set up special resource rooms and equip them with necessary educational, teaching and rehabilitation training facilities and equipment as well as resource teachers and professionals. With regard to the role of resource centers, it called for accelerated construction to make each province, municipality, and county have special education resource centers at corresponding levels, the gradual improvement of the working mechanism and the reasonable allocation of itinerant tutors, and gave instructions on the work assigned to resource centers.

The second is the priority given to the development of the LRC program in poverty-stricken areas and rural areas. Compared with the economically developed areas, poverty-stricken areas and rural areas see slow development of the LRC program. On the basis of consolidating existing achievements, priority was given to the development of the supporting system for the LRC program in the relatively underdeveloped areas. For example, the *13th Five-year Plan for Education* issued by the State Council in 2017 proposed to improve the supporting policy system for the LRC program, focus on supporting LRC practice in regular primary and secondary schools in poverty-stricken areas and rural areas, and implement inclusive education.

The third is the emphasis on further strengthening financial support and increasing the support for students with disabilities to attend school. For example, the *Opinions of the State Council on Accelerating the Process of Building a Well-off Society for the Disabled* issued in 2015 proposed to promote inclusive education and establish a supporting system for the LRC program. It also stipulated:

28 *Overview of the Development of the LRC Program in China*

All localities should increase support for children with disabilities to attend school, and actively promote free education for the disabled at the senior high school stage; first subsidize the students with disabilities and children of people with disabilities who meet the standards of the financial aid policies for students; and establish and improve the subsidy policies on special school supplies, educational training, transportation fees and other expenses for students with disabilities.

The *Circular of the State Council on Further Improving the Funding Guarantee Mechanism for Urban and Rural Compulsory Education* issued in 2016 clearly stipulates that LRC students should be subsidized at the same rate of 6,000 yuan per year as students in special education schools. The General Office of the State Council issued the *Opinions on Further Adjusting and Optimizing Structure to Improve Efficiency in the Use of Educational Appropriations* in 2018 and *the Circular on the Issuance of the Reform Scheme on the Division of Common Financial Authority and Expenditure-related Responsibilities between the Central and Local Governments in the Field of Basic Public Services* in 2019. Both point out that public funds for compulsory education of LRC students should be separately approved to ensure targeted appropriation to the schools (teaching sites). The *Measures for the Administration of Special Education Subsidy Funds* promulgated in 2021 requires the provision of subsidies to support regular primary and secondary schools that enroll a large number of students with disabilities, and provides for the specific use of such funds. The subsidy funds for the LRC program should be specifically used for the following three purposes: first, to renovate the barrier-free facilities of special education schools and regular schools with a large number of LRC students; second, support schools that assume the functions of special education resource centers (including education centers for autistic children) and regular schools with special education resource rooms to install necessary facilities and equipment; and, third, support regular primary and secondary schools to create an inclusive cultural environment to promote inclusive education.

Development of the LRC Program Still Needs Long-term Practical Explorations

Despite the policy provisions on the specific content and the direction of development of the supporting system for the LRC program, LRC practice in China is still far from enough to meet the requirements on its development stipulated in relevant policies. From the perspective of policy text itself, the related policies are mostly presented in the form of "guidelines," "decisions," and "circulars," often using such terms as "concern," "should," and "encourage," so their binding force and feasibility are insufficient.[12] In terms of financial funding, China has not yet established a regular funding mechanism for the LRC program, and the total financial input in this regard is insufficient, but characterized by structural imbalance.

Overview of the Development of the LRC Program in China   29

Relatively speaking, the economically developed regions in eastern China see better development of the LRC program, while the central and western regions just have limited special funds and lack of regular appropriations to the program, and there are still many regular schools that have never received special funding support for LRC practice.[13] Although investment in special education, mainly coming from central state finance, has increased significantly since 2007, most of the funds were used for the construction of special education schools. In 2010 and 2011, the Chinese government invested a total of 4.1 billion yuan to support the construction and expansion of special education schools in the central and western regions, while the sum actually used for LRC practice was fairly limited.[14]

What is more, there are still many schools that have not yet built resource rooms, and many areas lack resource centers. However, the resource rooms and centers that have been established in some areas face low usage and difficulty in performing their functions. This phenomenon even appears in Beijing, Shanghai, Jiangsu, and Hangzhou with their relatively better development of the LRC program. Due to the serious shortage of equipment and facilities, the difficulties in allocating sufficient full-time special education teachers, and the unclear positioning and functions of the resource rooms and centers in policy documents, these resource rooms and centers only serve a limited number of schools, and it is difficult to give full play to their functions.[15] With regard to human resources, there is a lack of professional teachers and a low level of professional development. LRC program teachers lack professional thinking and possess weak professional knowledge and ability, especially in the active acquisition and utilization of support or resources. Coupled with the fact that the current cultivation and training mechanism for inclusive education teachers is not sound, these teachers find it hard to meet the actual needs in professionalism.[16,17] Therefore, long-term practical exploration under the guidance of state policies is needed in the future to deal with the above-mentioned practical problems, and promote the development of the LRC program toward high-quality inclusive education.

Overview of Changes in Group Composition of LRC Students

With the development of the LRC program, the composition of LRC students is changing accordingly. Based on education statistics released by the Ministry of Education of China from 2001 to 2019, we make an analysis of the changes in the composition of LRC students by disability category and school sector.

Change in Overall Number of LRC Students

As shown in Figure 1.1, the number of LRC students and enrollment presented an overall upward trend during 2001–2019; however, they followed different patterns of change. The annual enrollment of LRC students showed a continuous, slow increase between 2001 and 2019, reaching a peak of 70,900 in

30 *Overview of the Development of the LRC Program in China*

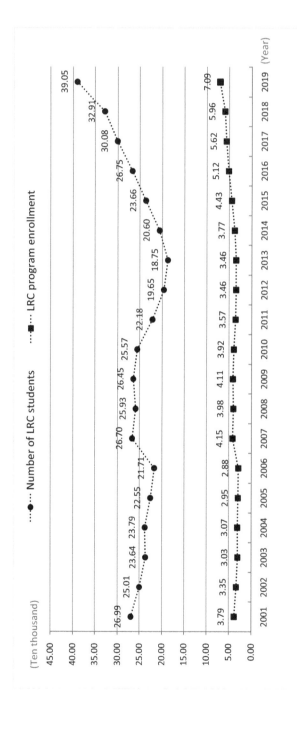

Figure 1.1 Trends in Number of LRC Students vs Enrollment, 2001–2019.

Source: 2001–2019 "Education Statistics" released by the Ministry of Education. Please see also: www.moe.gov.cn/.

2019, about 1.87 times that of 2001. The number of students enrolled in the LRC program showed a fluctuating downward trend between 2001 and 2013, dropping to a low of about 187,500 in 2013; it declined year by year from 2001 to 2006, began to have a significant increase in 2007, about 22.98 percent over the previous year, but declined again between 2010 and 2013; it showed a continuous upward trend between 2014 and 2019, with an average increase of 13.05 percent or so. The largest increase of 18.68 percent was recorded in 2019, bringing the total size to 390,500, about 2.08 times that of 2013.

Although the overall trend of the number of LRC students was on the rise, as shown in Figure 1.2, the proportion of LRC students in the total number of students enrolled in special education showed a decreasing trend between 2001 and 2019. The highest proportion was 69.86 percent, recorded in 2001, as against the lowest level of 49.15 percent in 2019. Since 2013, the proportion remained about 50 percent.

Changes in LRC Students by Disability Category

According to the statistics from the Ministry of Education, the LRC program only covered three categories—the blind, deaf-mute, and so-called retarded between 2002 and 2006. In 2007, four categories were covered, including visual impairment, hearing impairment, intellectual disability, and other disabilities; and in 2017, the category of "other disabilities" was specified to include speech impairment, physical disability, mental disorder, and multiple disabilities. With the development of special education and in-depth implementation of the LRC program, the disability category of LRC students became more diversified, and the range of new entrants was gradually expanding. The enrollments of LRC students vary with disability category in primary and secondary school sectors.

Changes in Number of LRC Students in Primary School Sector by Disability Category

As shown in Figure 1.3, LRC students in the primary school sector show the following notable features. First, they mainly have intellectual disability. From 2001 to 2019, LRC students with intellectual disability were far more than those with other categories of disabilities. Between 2001 and 2014, the number of LRC students with intellectual disability continued to decline significantly, from 188,482 in 2001 to 68,846 in 2013, a decrease of approximately 63.47 percent. It began to rebound in 2014 and rose to 101,682 in 2019, only 53.95 percent of the number in 2001. Second, the number of LRC students with visual impairment and hearing impairment remained relatively stable over the period 2001–2018. Among them, the number of those with hearing impairment first fell from 22,327 in 2001 to 14,469 in 2014, a decrease of 7,858, then rose rapidly to 30,907 by 2019, up 113.61 percent from 2014, reaching its highest ever level. In terms of the number of LRC students with visual impairment, it was

32 *Overview of the Development of the LRC Program in China*

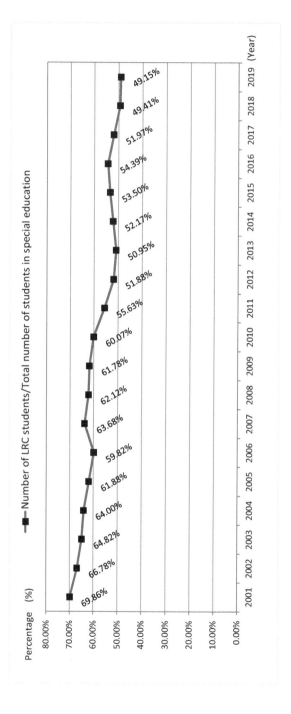

Figure 1.2 Change in Proportion of LRC Students in Total Number of Students Enrolled in Special Education, 2001–2019.

Source: 2001–2019 "Education Statistics" released by the Ministry of Education. Please see also: www.moe.gov.cn/.

Overview of the Development of the LRC Program in China 33

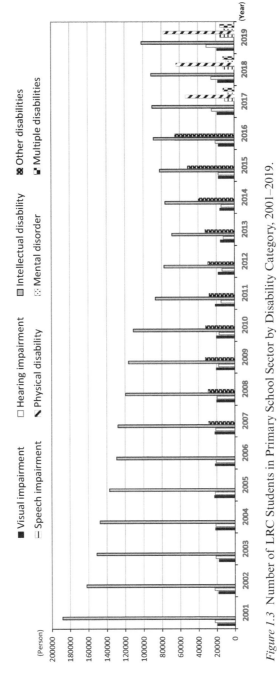

Figure 1.3 Number of LRC Students in Primary School Sector by Disability Category, 2001–2019.

Source: 2001–2019 "Education Statistics" released by the Ministry of Education. Please see also: www.moe.gov.cn/.

34 Overview of the Development of the LRC Program in China

19,694 in 2001, exceeded 20,000 in 2004, and basically stayed at 20,000–22,000 between 2004 and 2011, but declined significantly between 2011 and 2013, from 21,553 to 15,837, a decrease of about 26.5 percent. From 2014 to 2019, it rose again, but basically remained stable at around 19,000.

Third, the number of LRC students with other categories of disabilities was generally on the rise. It was relatively stable at around 30,000 between 2007 and 2013, but rose significantly from 2014 onwards, to reach 65,196 in 2016, the highest in a decade, or an increase of about 1.24 times compared to 29,101 in 2007; a growth of 32,705 compared to the figure in 2013.

Fourth, among those in the four new disability categories set in 2017, the number of LRC students with physical disability was the largest, and showed a significant upward trend, increasing to 77,862 in 2019, almost equaling the number of LRC students with "other disabilities" in 2016. It was followed by the number of those with multiple disabilities, increasing slightly from 11,889 in 2017 to 15,559 in 2019.

Changes in Number of LRC Students in Junior High School Sector by Disability Category

As shown in Figure 1.4, the changes in the number of LRC students in the junior high school sector are significantly different from those in the primary school sector. Among LRC students in the junior high school sector, those with intellectual disability still occupy a large proportion; their number was relatively stable at around 28,000 between 2001 and 2010, but decreased significantly from 2011 to the lowest level of 20,659 in 2013; it began to rebound in 2014 and grew to 34,908 in 2019, the highest level since the start of the 21st century. As for the number of LRC students with other disability categories in the junior high school sector, it began to exceed those with intellectual disability from 2014. But in 2017, the number of those with physical disability was the largest, and showed a significant upward trend, increasing to 46,439 by 2019, up by 59.39 percent from 2017.

Compared with the LRC students in the primary school sector, those in the junior high school sector have the biggest change in the number of those with visual impairment and those with hearing impairment.

As shown in Figure 1.4, the number of those with hearing impairment was relatively stable, and slightly fluctuated as the total number of LRC students, peaking at 11,993 in 2019. The trend in the number of LRC students with visual impairment in the junior high school sector differed from that in the primary school sector as it was always significantly higher than the number of those with hearing impairment. Among them, the number of those with visual impairment was relatively stable between 2002 and 2006, and began to show a significant increase in 2007, reaching a peak of 20,698 in 2011. But in 2012, it significantly dropped to 12,878, down by 26.7 percent, and then tended to increase steadily.

Overview of the Development of the LRC Program in China 35

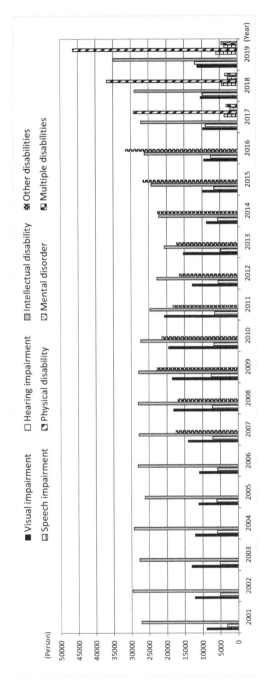

Figure 1.4 Number of LRC Students in Junior High School Sector by Disability Category, 2001–2019.

Source: 2001–2019 "Education Statistics" released by the Ministry of Education. Please see also: www.moe.gov.cn/.

36 *Overview of the Development of the LRC Program in China*

Changes in LRC Students by School Sector

Changes in Number of LRC Students in Primary and Junior High School Sectors

As shown in Figure 1.5, the changes in the number of LRC students in the primary and junior high school sectors are generally consistent. The number of LRC students in the primary school sector gradually declined from 230,503 in 2001 to 172,139 in 2006, while the number of those in the junior high school sector basically remained stable at around 48,000. Between 2007 and 2013, the number of those in the primary school sector showed a fluctuating downward trend; it began to rise significantly each year from 2014 onwards, reaching an all-time high of 271,528 in 2019. The number of those in the junior high school sector, instead, was on the rise overall, increasing at a faster rate since 2014, and also reaching a peak of 118,997 in 2019. From 2013 to 2019, the number of LRC students in the primary school sector increased by 142,020 or 1.10 percent, while that of LRC students in the junior high school sector rose by 60,971 or 1.05 percent, showing a slower pace of expansion.

Changes in Number of LRC Students by Grade

As shown in Figure 1.6, the changes in the number of LRC students in the primary school sector was generally consistent by grade. Between 2002 and 2013, the number showed a fluctuating downward trend, reaching the lowest level in 2013. Since 2014 it showed a significant upward trend, reaching a climax in 2019. Overall, there is a small disparity in the number of LRC students by grade. In particular, the largest number of LRC students is in grades 5 and 6, followed by grades 2 through 4, as against the significantly smaller number in grade 1.

As shown in Figure 1.7, the changes in the number of LRC students in grades 7–9 were consistent between 2001 and 2018, generally on the rise. The largest increase occurred from 2006 to 2007, and the average increase of those in grades 7–9 was about 49.32 percent. With a slight fluctuation between 2007 and 2014, the number of LRC students in grades 7–9 showed a continuously upward trend from 2014. In addition, the number of LRC students in grade 10 and above was significantly lower than that of those in other grades; it increased significantly from 123 to a peak of 1,350 between 2003 and 2004, and slightly fluctuated from 2006 to 2019.

Analysis of Characteristics of Changes in Composition of LRC Students

From the above analysis, the overall number of LRC students in China increased remarkably in a wider range between 2001 and 2019. A comprehensive analysis of the data shows the following characteristics of the changes in the composition of LRC students.

Overview of the Development of the LRC Program in China 37

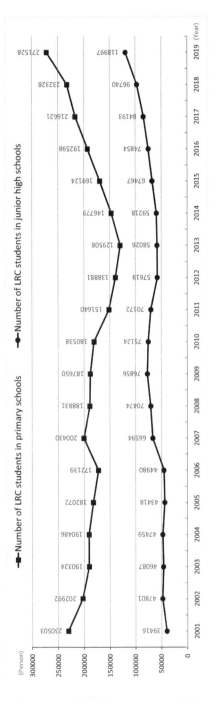

Figure 1.5 Changes in Number of LRC Students in Primary and Junior High School Sectors, 2001–2019.

Source: 2001–2019 "Education Statistics" released by the Ministry of Education. Please see also: www.moe.gov.cn/.

38 *Overview of the Development of the LRC Program in China*

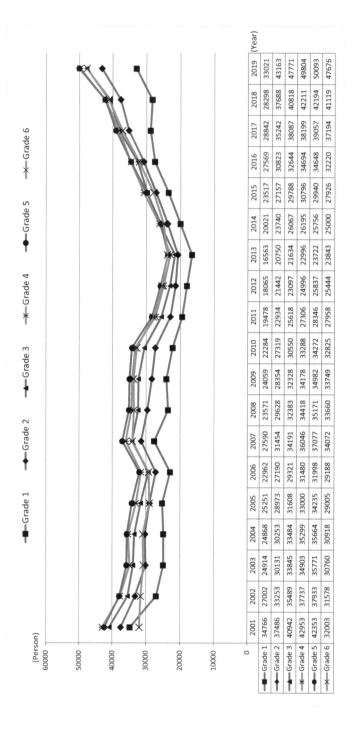

Figure 1.6 Changes in Number of LRC Students in Primary School Sector, 2001–2019.

Source: 2001–2019 "Education Statistics" released by the Ministry of Education. Please see also: www.moe.gov.cn/.

Overview of the Development of the LRC Program in China 39

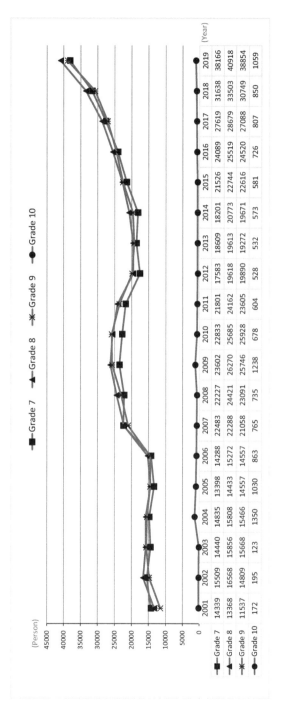

Figure 1.7 Changes in Number of LRC Students in Junior High School Sector, 2001–2019.

Source: 2001–2019 "Education Statistics" released by the Ministry of Education. Please see also: www.moe.gov.cn/.

40 *Overview of the Development of the LRC Program in China*

Expanding Number, Decreasing Proportion

Although both LRC students and annual enrollments of the LRC program are increasing, the proportion of LRC students in the special education students has been declining. Based on recent research findings and practical experience in special education, we attribute the decreasing proportion to the scale expansion and quality improvement of special education schools as well as the quality problems of the LRC program itself. On the one hand, increasing policy-based support for the construction of special education schools since 2007 has resulted in fast growth in the number of special education schools as well as the number of students in special education schools. When the denominator becomes larger, the share of the numerator decreases. On the other hand, the difficulty in ensuring the quality of the LRC program may be one of the important reasons. Relevant available research findings show that the education provided for children with special educational needs in regular schools is not satisfactory because school administrators and teachers predominantly subscribe to the medical view of disability, and the policy support and resources for the LRC program are insufficient. This results in the return to special education schools of some children who would otherwise be enrolled in regular classes.[18,19] In the meantime, with greater capacity and professionalism, special education schools have become the first choice for more families of children with special needs.

However, the decreasing proportion does not represent a shaking of the dominant position of the LRC program, but rather a reflection of the development of special education and the program into a new stage. Due to the difficulties and problems that have arisen in the development process in recent years, the public has held more rational attitude toward the LRC program. From initial disapproval due to a lack of understanding to the gradual acceptance and active support for the program, they now begin to recognize it in a rational and cautious manner, and call for the higher educational quality of the program.

Wider Range of Disability Categories with Higher Degrees of Disability

With the development of the LRC program, the number of disability categories of LRC students has increased from three to seven, while the number of LRC students with intellectual disability in primary and secondary school sectors has shown a significant decline. Despite the rise after 2014, there is still a large gap compared to the figure at the beginning of the 21st century. In contrast, the number of LRC students in other disability categories continues to rise, which may result from the development of medical care and special education in China. The development of diagnostic and assessment techniques for children with disabilities gives rise to more accurate diagnostic results and specific categorization of special needs children. By disability category, the number of LRC students with multiple disabilities and mental disorder has gradually risen in the past two years, which reflects the gradual increase in the number of students with moderate to severe disabilities enrolled in regular schools. This trend has also been shown in a survey of LRC students in several regions of China. According to the survey, 60 percent of the respondents are mildly impaired, 36.4 percent moderately impaired, and 3 percent severely impaired; children with autism account for 49.7 percent, followed by those with hearing impairment (25.5 percent) and those with intellectual disability (11.5 percent).[20]

The wider range of LRC students, in fact, results from China's emphasis on the realization of educational equity and the promulgation of policies to guarantee special needs children equal access to education, even a zero rate rejection rate, as well as the greater accommodation capacity of regular schools for LRC students. Previously, the accommodation capacity of regular schools for LRC students was poor because teachers lacked competence in inclusive education and regular schools had limited conditions. According to a 2018 survey of preschool teachers' attitudes toward inclusive education, 47.76 percent of them had a "disapprove" attitude.[21] A 2013 survey of rural primary school students' attitudes toward acceptance of LRC classmates showed that they were more willing to accept those with visual impairment and intellectual disability, and the key to acceptance depended on whether the special needs classmates had good personalities and behavioral habits.[22] With the advent of the 21st century, the Chinese government has not only attached importance to the scale expansion of the LRC program but also given more attention to the improvement of educational quality by establishing the supporting system and strengthening the building of a competent teaching team. As a result, the acceptance of children with special educational needs by teachers in regular schools has increased in recent years. For example, a 2019 survey concerning attitudes toward inclusive education on the Chinese mainland showed that the attitudes of general education teachers, LRC students' teachers, and special education teachers had changed from negative and conservative to positive and supportive; so had the attitudes of parents of typically developing students and those of students with special educational needs.[23] Moreover, the ability of schools to meet the educational needs of children with disabilities has been improved. For example, a survey by Yu Suhong on the LRC program of 300 regular schools in Shanghai showed that some of them had made a series of adjustments in management systems, teaching and research activities, individualized education, inclusive education, and home-school cooperation in order to guarantee the smooth implementation of the LRC program.[24]

Imbalanced Development of LRC Program among Different School Sectors

Generally speaking, the LRC program has made much headway in various school sectors in China, but has shown imbalanced development, as evidenced by the slower pace of expansion of the number of LRC students in the secondary school sector. The development of the LRC program in the secondary school sector lags behind that in the primary school sector, and LRC students

42 *Overview of the Development of the LRC Program in China*

in the primary school sector often encounter many problems in gaining access to secondary school education. This issue has been touched on in much of the research on LRC students by disability category. For example, research into the status of hearing-impaired LRC students reveals that there are problems with educational thinking and goals, the slow development of language instruction and insufficient follow-up educational services.[25]

According to the results of research into the status of LRC students with intellectual disability, most primary schools fail to transfer the relevant files of LRC students to their secondary schools, and their secondary school teachers also fail to create "growth files" for them due to their heavy workload and pressure from enrollment quotas, and thus lack measures to supervise, check and evaluate the academic performance of the LRC students. The acceptance of students with intellectual disability by regular secondary schools is fairly low, and teachers' attention to and guidance of them are more casual, resulting in lower educational quality.[26] Some researchers have also studied the factors influencing special needs children's attendance in regular classes. The results show that the policy of "two exemptions and one subsidy" (exemptions from school fees and textbook fees, and subsidy for living expenses of boarding students) has reduced the burden of family expenses for children with disabilities in compulsory education, but the average annual education expenditure for children with disabilities in regular secondary schools and secondary vocational schools is 3,931 yuan per year, which is unaffordable for many poor families, thus reducing the likelihood for children with disabilities to attend these schools.[27] Various measures should be taken in future to address the above problems and promote the development of the LRC program in the secondary school sector.

Notes

1 Piao, Yongxin 朴永馨. *Teshu jiaoyu xue* 特殊教育学, 41–42. Fuzhou: Fujian Education Press, 1995.
2 Hua, Guodong 华国栋. "Canji ertong suiban jiudu xianzhuang ji fazhan qushi" 残疾儿童随班就读现状及发展趋势. *Educational Research* 教育研究 no. 2 (2003): 65–69.
3 Zhang, Ningsheng 张宁生. "Shilun longtong 'yitihua' jiaoyu anzhi de xinli tiaojian—yige youguan jiakuai canji ertong ruxue de keti" 试论聋童"一体化"教育安置的心理条件 —— 一个有关加快残疾儿童入学的课题. *Journal of Liaoning Normal University* 辽宁师范大学学报 no. 1 (1990): 43–45.
4 Huang, Zhicheng 黄志诚. *Quanna jiaoyu* 全纳教育, 269. Shanghai: Shanghai Educational Publishing House, 2004.
5 Deng, Pufang 邓朴方. "Deng pufang tongzhi zai zhongguo canjiren lianhehui diyici quanguo daibiao dahui shang de baogao" 邓朴方同志在中国残疾人联合会第一次全国代表大会上的报告. *China Statistical Yearbook on the Work for Persons with Disabilities* 中国残疾人事业年鉴 (2002): 21–25.
6 Li, Rongshi 李荣时. "Zhongguo canji ertong renkou de xianzhuang yu duice yanjiu" 中国残疾儿童人口的现状与对策研究. *Chinese Journal of Population Science* 中国人口科学 no. 4 (1990): 1–5.

Overview of the Development of the LRC Program in China 43

7 Piao, Yongxin 朴永馨. *Teshu jiaoyu cidian* 特殊教育辞典, 36. Beijing: Huaxia Publishing House, 1996.

8 "Quanguo canji ertong shaonian suiban jiudu gongzuo huiyi jiyao" 全国残疾儿童少年随班就读工作会议纪要. *Modern Special Education* 现代特殊教育 no. 6 (1994): 7–8.

9 *Beijing shi tuijin ronghe jiaoyu cujin jiaoyu gongping* 北京市推进融合教育促进教育公平. Jiaoyubu guanwang 教育部官网, 2013. www.moe.gov.cn/jyb_xwfb/moe_1946/s7097/201307/t20130718_154322.html.

10 *Zhejiang sheng teshu jiaoyu 'shisanwu' fazhan guihua de tongzhi* 《浙江省特殊教育"十三五"发展规划》的通知. Zhejiang sheng jiaoyuting guanwang 浙江省教育厅官网, 2016. http://jyt.zj.gov.cn/art/2016/10/20/art_1532994_27483884.html.

11 Li, Tianshun 李天顺. "Shenru chijiu di kaizan canji ertong shaonian suiban jiudu gongzuo" 深入持久地开展残疾儿童少年随班就读工作. *Modern Special Education* 现代特殊教育no. 12 (2014): 5–8.

12 Huang, Chunchun 黄春春, and Tang, Ruqian 唐如前. "Suiban jiudu zhichi baozhang tixi wenti ji duice" 随班就读支持保障体系问题及对策. *Journal of Hunan University of Science and Engineering* 湖南科技学院学报no. 4 (2018): 132–134.

13 Tian, Zhilei 田志磊, Zhang, Mei 张眉, Guo, Nan 郭楠, and Zhong, Weiping 钟未平. "Ronghe jiaoyu linian xia de teshu jiaoyu caizheng: lishi xianzhuang ji weilai" 融合教育理念下的特殊教育财政: 历史、现状及未来. *Education Research Monthly* 教育学术月刊 no. 1(2015): 35–49.

14 See note 13 above.

15 Peng, Xiaguang 彭霞光. "Suiban jiudu zhichi baozhang tixi jianshe chutan" 随班就读支持保障体系建设初探. *Chinese Journal of Special Education* 中国特殊教育 no. 11 (2015): 3–7.

16 Li, La 李拉. "Zhuanye hua shiye xia de suiban jiudu jiaoshi: kunjing yu chulu" 专业化视野下的随班就读教师：困境与出路. *Theory and Practice of Education* 教育理论与实践 no. 23 (2012): 34–36.

17 Wang, Yan 王雁, Huang, Lingling 黄玲玲, Wang, Yue 王悦, and Zhang, Lili 张丽莉. "Dui guonei suiban jiudu jiaoshi ronghe jiaoyu suyang yanjiu de fenxi yu zhanwang" 对国内随班就读教师融合教育素养研究的分析与展望. *Teacher Education Research* 教师教育研究 no. 1 (2018): 26–32.

18 Yang, Xijie 杨希洁. "Dangqian teshu jiaoyu fazhan ruogan tedian ji wenti de sikao" 当前特殊教育发展若干特点及问题的思考. *Chinese Journal of Special Education* 中国特殊教育 no. 8 (2019): 8–13.

19 Fu, Wangqian 傅王倩, and Xiao, Fei 肖非. "Suiban jiudu ertong huiliu xianxiang de zhixing yanjiu" 随班就读儿童回流现象的质性研究. *Chinese Journal of Special Education* 中国特殊教育 no. 3 (2016): 3–9.

20 Yang, Xijie 杨希洁. "Suiban jiudu xuexiao canji xuesheng fazhan zhuangkuang yanjiu" 随班就读学校残疾学生发展状况研究. *Chinese Journal of Special Education* 中国特殊教育 no. 7 (2010): 3–10.

21 Zhao, Hong 赵红, and Xu, Li 徐莉. "Ronghe jiaoyu beijing xia youjiao gongzuozhe dui teshu ertong taidu de diaocha" 融合教育背景下幼教工作者对特殊儿童态度的调查. *Journal of Teacher Education* 教师教育学报 no. 1 (2018): 32–40.

22 Jiang, Xiaoying 江小英, and Wang, Jing 王婧. "Nongcun xiaoxuesheng dui suiban jiudu tongban jiena taidu de diaocha baogao" 农村小学生对随班就读同伴接纳态度的调查报告. *Chinese Journal of Special Education* 中国特殊教育 no. 12 (2013): 10–18.

44 *Overview of the Development of the LRC Program in China*

23 Gao, Li 高利. "Zhongguo dalu diqu ronghe jiaoyu taidu yanjiu jinzhan ji qishi" 中国大陆地区融合教育态度研究进展及启示. *Journal of Suihua University* 绥化学院学报 no. 7 (2019): 19–23.

24 Yu, Suhong 于素红. "Shanghai shi putong xuexiao suiban jiudu gongzuo xianzhuang de diaocha yanjiu" 上海市普通学校随班就读工作现状的调查研究. *Chinese Journal of Special Education* 中国特殊教育 no. 4 (2011): 3–9.

25 Yan, Yanjun 闫艳军, and Yuan, Huijie 袁慧洁. "Long'er suiban jiudu cuizai de xiangguan wenti yu duice" 聋儿随班就读存在的相关问题与对策. *Chinese Scientific Journal of Hearing and Speech Rehabilitation* 中国听力语言康复科学杂志 no. 2 (2007): 46–48.

26 Liu, Hongyun 刘红云, and Dong Xingfang 董兴芳. "Zhizhang suiban jiudu xuesheng xiao sheng chu zhuanxian jiaoyu cunzai weiti yu jiejue celue" 智障随班就读学生小升初转衔教育存在问题与解决策略. *Modern Special Education* 现代特殊教育 no. 5 (2014): 49–51.

27 Hou, Jingjing 侯晶晶. "Woguo canji ertong suiban jiudu de yingxiang yinsu yanjiu" 我国残疾儿童随班就读的影响因素研究. *Educational Research and Experiment* 教育研究与实验 no. 5 (2015): 49–57.

References

Deng, Pufang 邓朴方. "Deng pufang tongzhi zai zhongguo canjiren lianhehui diyici quanguo daibiao dahui shang de baogao" 邓朴方同志在中国残疾人联合会第一次全国代表大会上的报告. *China Statistical Yearbook on the Work for Persons with Disabilities* 中国残疾人事业年鉴 (2002): 21–25.

Fu, Wangqian 傅王倩, and Xiao, Fei 肖非. "Suiban jiudu ertong huiliu xianxiang de zhixing yanjiu" 随班就读儿童回流现象的质性研究. *Chinese Journal of Special Education* 中国特殊教育 no. 3 (2016): 3–9.

Gao, Li 高利. "Zhongguo dalu diqu ronghe jiaoyu taidu yanjiu jinzhan ji qishi" 中国大陆地区融合教育态度研究进展及启示. *Journal of Suihua University* 绥化学院学报 no. 7 (2019): 19–23.

Hou, Jingjing 侯晶晶. "Woguo canji ertong suiban jiudu de yingxiang yinsu yanjiu" 我国残疾儿童随班就读的影响因素研究. *Educational Research and Experiment* 教育研究与实验 no. 5 (2015): 49–57.

Hua, Guodong 华国栋. "Canji ertong suiban jiudu xianzhuang ji fazhan qushi" 残疾儿童随班就读现状及发展趋势. *Educational Research* 教育研究 no. 2 (2003): 65–69.

Huang, Chunchun 黄春春, and Tang, Ruqian 唐如前. "Suiban jiudu zhichi baozhang tixi wenti ji duice" 随班就读支持保障体系问题及对策. *Journal of Hunan University of Science and Engineering* 湖南科技学院学报 no. 4 (2018): 132–134.

Huang, Zhicheng 黄志诚. *Quanna jiaoyu* 全纳教育, 269. Shanghai: Shanghai Educational Publishing House, 2004.

Jiang, Xiaoying 江小英, and Wang, Jing 王婧. "Nongcun xiaoxuesheng dui suiban jiudu tongban jiena taidu de diaocha baogao" 农村小学生对随班就读同伴接纳态度的调查报告. *Chinese Journal of Special Education* 中国特殊教育 no. 12 (2013): 10–18.

Li, La 李拉. "Zhuanye hua shiye xia de suiban jiudu jiaoshi: kunjing yu chulu" 专业化视野下的随班就读教师：困境与出路. *Theory and Practice of Education* 教育理论与实践 no. 23 (2012): 34–36.

Li, Rongshi 李荣时. "Zhongguo canji ertong renkou de xianzhuang yu duice yanjiu" 中国残疾儿童人口的现状与对策研究. *Chinese Journal of Population Science* 中国人口科学 no. 4 (1990): 1–5.

Li, Tianshun 李天顺. "Shenru chijiu di kaizan canji ertong shaonian suiban jiudu gongzuo" 深入持久地开展残疾儿童少年随班就读工作. *Modern Special Education* 现代特殊教育no. 12 (2014): 5–8.

Liu, Hongyun 刘红云, Dong Xingfang 董兴芳. "Zhizhang suiban jiudu xuesheng xiao sheng chu zhuanxian jiaoyu cunzai weiti yu jiejue celue" 智障随班就读学生小升初转衔教育存在问题与解决策略. *Modern Special Education* 现代特殊教育no. 5 (2014): 49–51.

Peng, Xiaguang 彭霞光. "Suiban jiudu zhichi baozhang tixi jianshe chutan" 随班就读支持保障体系建设初探. *Chinese Journal of Special Education* 中国特殊教育 no. 11 (2015): 3–7.

Piao, Yongxin 朴永馨. *Teshu jiaoyu xue* 特殊教育学, 41–42. Fuzhou: Fujian Education Press, 1995.

Piao, Yongxin 朴永馨. *Teshu jiaoyu cidian* 特殊教育辞典, 36. Beijing: Huaxia Publishing House, 1996.

Tian, Zhilei 田志磊, Zhang, Mei 张眉, Guo, Nan 郭楠, and Zhong, Weiping 钟未平. "Ronghe jiaoyu linian xia de teshu jiaoyu caizheng: lishi xianzhuang ji weilai" 融合教育理念下的特殊教育财政: 历史、现状及未来. *Education Research Monthly* 教育学术月刊 no. 1 (2015): 35–49.

Wang, Yan 王雁, Huang, Lingling 黄玲玲, Wang, Yue 王悦, and Zhang, Lili 张丽莉. "Dui guonei suiban jiudu jiaoshi ronghe jiaoyu suyang yanjiu de fenxi yu zhanwang" 对国内随班就读教师融合教育素养研究的分析与展望. *Teacher Education Research* 教师教育研究 no. 1 (2018): 26–32.

Yan, Yanjun 闫艳军, and Yuan, Huijie 袁慧洁. "Long'er suiban jiudu cuizai de xiangguan wenti yu duice" 聋儿随班就读存在的相关问题与对策. *Chinese Scientific Journal of Hearing and Speech Rehabilitation* 中国听力语言康复科学杂志 no. 2 (2007): 46–48.

Yang, Xijie 杨希洁. "Suiban jiudu xuexiao canji xuesheng fazhan zhuangkuang yanjiu" 随班就读学校残疾学生发展状况研究. *Chinese Journal of Special Education* 中国特殊教育 no. 7 (2010): 3–10.

Yang, Xijie 杨希洁. "Dangqian teshu jiaoyu fazhan ruogan tedian ji wenti de sikao" 当前特殊教育发展若干特点及问题的思考. *Chinese Journal of Special Education* 中国特殊教育 no. 8 (2019): 8–13.

Yu, Suhong 于素红. "Shanghai shi putong xuexiao suiban jiudu gongzuo xianzhuang de diaocha yanjiu" 上海市普通学校随班就读工作现状的调查研究. *Chinese Journal of Special Education* 中国特殊教育 no. 4 (2011): 3–9.

Zhang, Ningsheng 张宁生. "Shilun longtong 'yitihua' jiaoyu anzhi de xinli tiaojian–yige youguan jiakuai canji ertong ruxue de keti" 试论聋童"一体化"教育安置的心理条件 —— 一个有关加快残疾儿童入学的课题. *Journal of Liaoning Normal University* 辽宁师范大学学报 no. 1 (1990): 43–45.

Zhao, Hong 赵红, and Xu, Li 徐莉. "Ronghe jiaoyu beijing xia youjiao gongzuozhe dui teshu ertong taidu de diaocha" 融合教育背景下幼教工作者对特殊儿童态度的调查. *Journal of Teacher Education* 教师教育学报 no. 1 (2018): 32–40.

2 Analysis of the Policies for Development of the LRC Program

Educational policy analysis serves as a bridge between educational theory and practice. Through an analysis of the policies concerning the LRC program, we can get a glimpse of the internal logic and developmental clues of the formulation and implementation of the policies, and better understand the connotations of the LRC program and its significant role in the all-round development of Chinese children and adolescents with disabilities. To improve the quality of the LRC program, the key is to improve the quality of the corresponding teaching force. Therefore, this chapter will also analyze the policies related to the cultivation and training of the LRC program teachers' competence in inclusive education. In view of the uniformity of terms used in this book, LRC program teachers mentioned in this chapter refer to teachers who are responsible for the education and teaching of various special education classes attached to regular schools, and those who are responsible for the education and teaching of regular classes that embrace students with disabilities, excluding resource teachers and itinerant tutors. The teaching force for the LRC program comprises class teachers, resource teachers, and itinerant tutors.

Basis of Policy Analysis

Under China's social system, the CPC Central Committee and governments at all levels have played an important leading role in the development of education, and the national policy impetus has always been a great boon for the development of the LRC program. Therefore, analysis of the policies for the LRC program is helpful to better understand its developmental context in China as well as the difficulties in its development.

The premise of analyzing the policies for the LRC program is to understand the basic concept and connotations of educational policy. The policies for the LRC program constitute an organic part of China's educational policy system. Educational policy is generally understood as a purposefully organized and dynamic development process, which is the action basis and criterion set by political entities such as political parties and governments to coordinate the internal and external relations of education in order to achieve certain

DOI: 10.4324/9781003432982-3

educational goals and tasks in a certain historical period.[1] Educational policy is, in essence, an organic part of national public policy, and its connotations also reflect the essential attribute of public policy. From the perspective of the attributes of public policy, the subject of educational policy is the government department that enjoys public authority, and the policy process is marked by value selection by the decision maker. The fundamental purpose is to coordinate and balance the conflicts between interests and values in various aspects, and to distribute educational interests in society. The LRC policy bears these essential characteristics of educational policy.

Research into educational policy started late in China, and the unified educational policy analysis model has not taken shape so far, but there are several kinds of widely recognized educational policy analysis frameworks for reference. According to the different fields of questions that policy analysis aims to answer, policy analysis includes three dimensions: factual analysis, value analysis, and normative analysis.[2] Factual analysis refers to the factual judgment made on policies and activities to answer the question of "what" or "how"; value analysis is to judge the value of policy activities and answer questions such as "what is expected" and "why are the interests distributed in this way" behind policy decisions; and normative analysis is to make normative judgment and command judgment on policy activities, and answer the questions of "what should be" and "how it should be." If educational policy is regarded as a dynamic structure, it can be regarded as the result of the interaction and dynamic change in the outer layer, the middle layer, and the core layer from the perspective of structural change.[3] The core layer refers to the educational policies directly related to people; the middle layer covers all kinds of educational policies, laws, and regulations formulated by the state and education authorities at all levels; and the outer layer includes the national macro-political, economic and cultural policies directly or indirectly related to educational policy, as well as the ideology, customs, traditions, and values of the society. It is recommended to look at the dynamic characteristics of educational policy in the aspects of the pathway, approach, and dynamics of its changes from the above three-layer structure perspective. In addition, if viewed from its essence, educational policy is to coordinate various conflicting educational interests, which is "value-loaded." Based on this, educational policy analysis can adopt a three-dimensional framework, covering three dimensions: value analysis, content analysis, and process analysis.[4] Among them, value analysis mainly answers the value criterion of educational policy, content analysis mainly deals with the goal, means, and object of educational policy, and process analysis focuses on all the formal stages of educational policy from designation to implementation and evaluation. After reviewing various educational policy analysis frameworks, some researchers have pointed out that the current Western policy analysis framework is not fully applicable to China's policy environment, and it often ignores the important role of the policy subject and its value. Therefore, an analysis model of the subjective value of educational policy has been put forward.[5] It proposes to analyze the

48 *Analysis of the Policies for Development of the LRC Program*

value demands and choices of educational policy subjects such as the state, the ruling party, the government, non-political social organizations, individuals, and families, as well as the value conflicts among different subjects and their significance in educational policy. No matter from what perspective, it is believed that educational policy not only includes the text, but also involves a whole dynamic process. At the same time, they all emphasized that the value of educational policy should be underlined, and the analysis framework of educational policy contains three basic dimensions: policy value, policy content, and policy process.

Today, there are a large number of policies related to the LRC program in China. By content and focus, these policies can be divided into macro and micro categories. The macro policies focus on the overall development of the LRC program, involving its overall development concept, objectives, and organizational forms, while the micro policies usually focus on the development of certain aspects required by the LRC program, such as the cultivation and training of teachers. Although the micro policies also involve the development concept, goals, organizational forms, and other content, they are basically specific regulations on specific fields under the guidance of the macro policies.

This chapter will make an analysis of the macro policies concerning the LRC program as well as the micro policies related to the cultivation and training of the teachers for the program. It adopts a comprehensive analysis framework based on value analysis and factual analysis to better explain the internal logic changes behind the existing macro policy texts and their changes.

Analysis of Macro Policies Concerning LRC Program

Since the founding of the PRC, more than 30 important policy texts concerning the LRC program have been issued in China. The specific content is shown in Table 2.1.

Value Analysis: Shift of Priority from Efficiency to Fairness

From its original aspiration of addressing the enrollment problem of children with disabilities to the present practice of implementing inclusive education, the LRC program has undergone significant changes in its core value orientation and policy content. Since 1987, when the State Education Commission officially put forward the concept of "Learning in Regular Classrooms" in the *Notice on the Printing and Distribution of the Teaching Plan of Full-time Schools (Classes) for the Retarded* (Draft for Solicitation of Comments), the content related to the LRC program in relevant policies has always touched on "improving the enrollment rate of the children with disabilities." According to the *Notice Regarding Several Opinions on the Development of Special Education*, after the founding of the PRC, special education, especially the education of children and adolescents with disabilities, has become the weakest link in universal primary education in China. In order to solve this problem, multiple

Table 2.1 Some Policy Documents Concerning the LRC Program

Date of promulgation	Title	Promulgators	Relevant content (excerpts)
Sep. 11, 1986	Opinions on Several Issues Concerning the Implementation of the Compulsory Education Law	The State Education Commission, etc.	X. Compulsory Education for Children with Disabilities (31) In the course of implementing compulsory education, the people's governments at various levels shall attach importance to the compulsory education for the blind, deaf-mute, mentally retarded and other disabled children.
Dec. 30, 1987	Notice on the Printing and Distribution of the Teaching Plan of Full-time Schools (Classes) for the Retarded	The State Education Commission	II. In the process of achieving universal primary education, most mildly retarded children have been enrolled in local regular primary schools.
Sep. 3, 1988	Five-Year Work Outline for the Cause of Disabled Persons in China (1988–1992)	The State Planning Commission, etc.	42. We will continue to run schools in various forms. 45. Basic education for persons with disabilities should be incorporated into the nine-year compulsory education as one of the tasks of universal primary education in all regions.
May 4, 1989	Notice on Several Opinions on the Development of Special Education	The State Education Commission, etc.	6. We should run schools in various forms to speed up the development of special education. 7. Layout of special education. □
Dec. 28, 1990	Law of the PRC on the Protection of Disabled Persons	The National People's Congress	Article 22 (Methods of General Education): Institutions of general education shall provide education to disabled persons who are capable of receiving general education.
Jul. 21, 1994	Trial Measures for the Development of the LRC Program	The State Education Commission	I. General Provisions 1. Thoroughly implement the *Compulsory Education Law of the PRC* and the *Law of the PRC on the Protection of Disabled Persons* … 2. LRC program is conducive for disabled children and adolescents to enter the schools nearby …

(*Continued*)

Table 2.1 (Continued)

Date of promulgation	Title	Promulgators	Relevant content (excerpts)
Aug. 23, 1994	Regulations on Education for Individuals with Disabilities	The State Council	Article 17 School-age children and adolescents with disabilities may receive compulsory education in the following forms according to relevant conditions.
May 9, 1996	Implementation Plan on Compulsory Education for Children and Adolescents with Disabilities during the Ninth Five-Year Plan Period	The State Education Commission, etc.	III. Main Measures 1. LRC program shall be implemented widely. 2. Regular preschool education institutions and preschool classes attached to regular primary schools shall actively enroll disabled children in regular classes, and set up classes for disabled children according to needs.
Aug. 3, 1998	Several Opinions on the Consolidation and Improvement Work after Acceptance Check of the Realization of "Two Basically" Goal	The Ministry of Education	8. Vigorously develop the special education undertakings. The work of providing synchronous compulsory education for disabled and typically developing children and adolescents should be included in the consolidation and improvement plan.
Dec. 2, 1998	Interim Regulations for Special Education Schools	The Ministry of Education	Article 12 Special education schools shall accept disabled children and adolescents who are approved by the administrative department of education to apply for transfer to other schools … Article 14 Students who can study in regular classes in regular schools after examination shall apply to the administrative department of education for transfer …
Oct. 19, 2001	Opinions on Further Promoting the Reform and Development of Special Education during the 10th Five-Year Plan Period	The Ministry of Education, etc.	8. Further strengthen guidance for special classes and LRC program in regular schools, and strive to improve the quality of teaching. 17. Strive to improve school conditions and provide a good educational environment for students with disabilities.

Feb. 19, 2003	Circular on the Work of Pilot Counties (Districts) for Establishing Supporting System for the LRC Program	The Ministry of Education	I. Purpose Establish a supporting system for the LRC program to make it more scientific, standardized and institutionalized.
Jun. 29, 2006	Compulsory Education Law of the PRC	The National People's Congress	Article 19. Local people's governments at or above the county level shall, according to needs, set up corresponding schools (classes) for the implementation of special education to provide compulsory education for school-age children and adolescents with visual, hearing, speech, and mental disabilities.
Feb. 15, 2008	Key Work Points of the Department of Basic Education of the Ministry of Education in 2008	The Ministry of Education	6. Establish and implement the Scientific Outlook on Development in an all-round way, and promote the sustainable, coordinated and healthy development of various undertakings of basic education. 23. Prepare for the fourth National Conference on Special Education Work, launch the construction projects of special education schools …
May 7, 2009	Opinions on Further Accelerating the Development of Special Education	The Ministry of Education, etc.	II. Improving the Mechanism to Ensure Special Education Funds IV. Strengthening the Development of Special Education Teachers, and Improving the Professional Level of Teachers
Jan. 29, 2010	Main Work Points of the Ministry of Education in 2010	The Ministry of Education	13. Care and support for special education. We should improve the special education system.
May 5, 2010	Outline of China's National Plan for Medium and Long-Term Education Reform and Development (2010–2020)	The State Council	Chapter 10 Special Education 29. Improve special education system. By 2020, every prefecture, prefecture-level city, and every county that has more than 300,000 residents and a large number of disabled children shall have at least one special education school.

(*Continued*)

Table 2.1 (Continued)

Date of promulgation	Title	Promulgators	Relevant content (excerpts)
Jan. 8, 2011	Regulations on Education for Individuals with Disabilities (revised in 2011)	The State Council	Article 17 School-age disabled children and adolescents may, according to conditions, receive compulsory education in the following forms. Article 21 Regular schools shall, in accordance with relevant national regulations, enroll school-age disabled children and adolescents who can adapt to regular classes …
Jan. 10, 2011	Key Work Points of the Ministry of Education in 2011	The Ministry of Education	12. The right of disabled children and adolescents to education shall be guaranteed.
Feb. 2, 2012	Key Work Points of the Ministry of Education in 2012	The Ministry of Education	32. Care and support for special education. We should formulate policies and measures for regular schools to accept disabled students to learn in regular classes.
Jan. 22, 2013	Main Work Points of the Ministry of Education in 2013	The Ministry of Education	21. Support special education. We will continue to implement major programs of special education.
Jan. 8, 2014	Program for Promoting Special Education (2014–2016)	The Ministry of Education, etc.	1. The overall objective. We will comprehensively promote inclusive education so that every disabled child can receive appropriate education. 2. Main measures.
Jan. 24, 2014	Key Work Points of the Ministry of Education in 2014	The Ministry of Education	III. Reform the Way of Resource Allocation and Vigorously Promote Educational Equity 29. Care and support for special education.
Jan. 12, 2015	Key Work Points of the Ministry of Education in 2015	The Ministry of Education	37. Care and support the development of special education. The *Program for Promoting Special Education (2014–2016)* shall be thoroughly implemented.

Jan. 27, 2016	Guidelines on the Construction of Special Education Resources in Regular Schools	The Ministry of Education	Special education resource rooms provide key support for disabled children and adolescents to study in regular schools, and play an irreplaceable role in improving the popularization of special education.
May 11, 2016	Guiding Opinions on Accelerating the Development of Education in Central and Western China	The State Council	(7) Protect the right of disabled persons to education. Focusing on universal compulsory education for children and adolescents with disabilities, we will expand total resources for special education, raise the proportion of disabled people receiving education ...
Feb. 1, 2017	Regulations on Education for Individuals with Disabilities (revised)	The State Council	Article 17 School-age disabled children and adolescents shall accept general education in nearby regular schools if they can adapt to the study and life of regular schools ...
Apr. 26, 2017	Notice on Doing a Good Job in Enrollment of Children and Adolescents with Disabilities in Compulsory Education	The Ministry of Education	III. "One person, One Scheme" Educational Placement IV. Strengthen the guarantee for relevant conditions. We will make overall plans for the construction of resource rooms for special education at the district and county level ...
Jul. 17, 2017	Program for Promoting Special Education: Phase II (2017–2020)	The Ministry of Education, etc.	I. Basic principles II. Key Tasks III. Main Measures
Feb. 6, 2018	Main Work Points of the Ministry of Education in 2018	The Ministry of Education	26. Do a good job in special education. The *Program for Promoting Special Education: Phase II (2017–2020)* shall be fully implemented.
Feb. 22, 2018	Notice on Enrollment of Regular Primary and Secondary Schools in 2018	The Ministry of Education	(2) Ensure the enrollment of different groups as a whole.
Feb. 22, 2019	Key Work Points of the Ministry of Education in 2019	The Ministry of Education	14. Doing a good job in special education.

(*Continued*)

Table 2.1 (Continued)

Date of promulgation	Title	Promulgators	Relevant content (excerpts)
Feb. 23, 2019	China's Education Modernization 2035	The State Council	IV. Equal access to basic public education services shall be achieved.
Jun. 17, 2020	2020 Guidelines on Enhancing Implementation of the LRC Program in Compulsory Education	The Ministry of Education	Full text.
Apr. 10, 2021	Administrative Measures for Special Education Grant Funds	The Ministry of Finance, etc.	Article 4 The grant funds shall cover the independent special education schools and regular primary and secondary schools that enroll a large number of disabled students.
Jul. 18, 2021	The 14th Five-Year Plan for the Protection and Development of Persons with Disabilities	The State Council	5. Improve the education system for persons with disabilities. We will promote the all-round development of children and adolescents with disabilities.

forms of schooling were encouraged; the existing primary schools across the country should actively recruit the children with disabilities who can learn in regular class; special education classes should be set up to absorb children with disabilities who have greater learning difficulties in regular class to increase the enrollment rate of children with disabilities as much as possible. The *Trial Measures for the Development of the LRC Program* issued by the State Education Commission in 1994 contains detailed provisions on the work of the LRC program, clearly pointing out its nature and significance but still emphasizing its important role in improving efficiency of enrollment. The *Implementation Plan on Compulsory Education for Children and Adolescents with Disabilities during the Ninth Five-Year Plan Period* issued by the State Education Commission and China Disabled Persons' Federation in 1996 set a target for the enrollment rate of children and adolescents with disabilities during the Ninth Five-Year Plan period, and established a pattern of compulsory education for children and adolescents with disabilities, with the LRC program and special education classes as the main body and special education schools as the backbone. The reason for selecting the LRC program and special education classes as the main body instead of special education schools is that the LRC program has performed outstandingly in improving the enrollment rate, and has proven to be an effective means to achieve the development goal of education for the disabled.

The most important function of the LRC program is to ensure the enrollment of children with disabilities. The situation of giving priority to efficiency did not change until the advent of the 21st century. In the new century, the imbalance between regions, urban and rural areas, and groups in education development under the guidance of the market economic system has gradually emerged. As the biggest supplier, demander, and beneficiary of education in China, the government needs through policies to offset the negative influence brought by the marketization of education, provide a good environment for the education system to promote the equitable development of education, and ensure the public nature of education. The value concept of national education development turned to "giving priority to efficiency with due consideration to fairness," and then gradually began to highlight "equal access to education." Accordingly, the new policies concerning the LRC program talked much about the issues of right and quality.

In 2001, the General Office of the State Council of China put forward the *Opinions on Further Promoting the Reform and Development of Special Education during the 10th Five-Year Plan Period* jointly formulated by the Ministry of Education and eight other state agencies. It regards the protection of the right of individuals with disabilities to receive education as an important embodiment of the superiority of the socialist system. Then, the LRC program was not judged in terms of efficiency but positioned from the perspective of guaranteeing the right to education and the equal access to education for children and adolescents with disabilities. Thus, the subsequent policy texts concerning the LRC program underlined "fairness" and "quality" and took the program

56 *Analysis of the Policies for Development of the LRC Program*

as an approach for the government to reflect the public nature of education and realize the fairness of education. The *Compulsory Education Law of the PRC* amended in 2006 clearly states that regular schools shall accept school-age children and adolescents with disabilities who have the ability to receive general education. But at the time, the right to learn in regular classrooms was still enjoyed by a small number of individuals with disabilities. The *Key Points of Work of the Ministry of Education in 2010* proposed to effectively change the concept and practice of simply measuring the development effect and work performance by enrollment rate, development scale, and development speed, and promote the people-oriented, comprehensive, coordinated, and sustainable development of education. Under the guidance of new ideas, caring for and supporting special education and expanding the scale of the LRC program and special education classes in regular schools became important measures to comprehensively improve the quality of education and promote the equality of education. Subsequently, the *Promotion Plan* issued in 2014 and the *Notice on Doing a Good Job in Enrollment of Children and Adolescents with Disabilities in Compulsory Education* issued by the General Office of the Ministry of Education in 2017 successively proposed to promote inclusive education in an all-round way, and formulated an educational placement program for disabled children in line with the principle of "full coverage and zero rejection." The LRC program is not only a form of educational placement, but also regarded as an educational right for children and adolescents with disabilities. However, the *Regulations on Education for Individuals with Disabilities* amended in 2017 still stresses that children with special needs cannot be enrolled in regular schools unless they meet the basic conditions for admission to a general education school. The current practice of "zero rejection" actually points to the enrollment of *all* children and adolescents with disabilities; there is still a long way to go before the full realization of zero rejection in the LRC program.

Content Analysis: The Connotations of the LRC Program Gradually Enriched

With the change in value concept in policies, there appears significant changes in object, objective, and means of the LRC program.

Object: Scope Expanding Gradually

With regard to the scope of objects, the LRC program first admitted qualified children with disabilities, but gradually tended to accept all children with disabilities unconditionally. The early documents mostly made clear the degree of disability of the children to be admitted to the LRC program, mainly including the blind, deaf, and mentally disabled children, and adolescents with relatively mild disabilities who could adapt to education and teaching in regular schools. Specific provisions can be found in the *Five-Year Program of Work for the Cause of Persons with Disabilities in China (1988–1992)*. The *Trial Measures for the Development of the LRC Program* issued by the State Education

Commission in 1994 loosened the requirements for the degree of disability, no longer limited to children and adolescents with the above three categories of disabilities. The *Interim Regulations of the Ministry of Education for Special Education Schools* issued in 1998 clearly proposed that some children with disabilities could, after approval, transfer from special education schools to the LRC program in regular schools.

The *Circular on the Work of Pilot Counties (Districts) for Establishing Supporting System for the LRC Program* issued in 2003 first stated that it is the obligation and responsibility of every regular primary and secondary school to accept eligible children and adolescents with disabilities to learn in regular classrooms, and it should not refuse them for any reason. However, this circular made no detailed description of the admission threshold, resulting in the fact that the LRC program is still the right of a small number of individuals with disabilities. The *Promotion Plan* in 2014 further proposed that the greatest possible number of students with disabilities should be arranged to attend the LRC program in regular schools, which means that the LRC program has become the primary choice of educational placement for children with disabilities, and the scope of disabled children who can attend the LRC program was further expanded. The *Guiding Opinions on Accelerating the Development of Education in Central and Western China* issued by the State Council in 2016 called for support for secondary vocational schools to actively enroll students with disabilities. The *Notice on Doing a Good Job in Enrollment of Children and Adolescents with Disabilities in Compulsory Education* issued by the General Office of the Ministry of Education in 2017 put forward the concept of "full coverage and zero rejection," and stressed that priority should be given to children and adolescents with disabilities to receive compulsory education in nearby or designated regular schools with adequate conditions.

Objective: Turning to Improvement of Quality and Realization of Equal Access to Education

In terms of its objective, the LRC program gradually shifted its focus from the pursuit of efficiency and scale expansion to the pursuit of equity and quality improvement. In 1987 when the concept of "learning in regular classrooms" was first put forward, the purpose of encouraging the LRC program was to solve the "enrollment problem of mildly retarded children." From then on until the end of the 1990s, the development objective of the LRC program prescribed in relevant policies was mostly to expand its scale and improve the enrollment rate of children with disabilities. A change took place in 2001 when the *Opinions on Further Promoting the Reform and Development of Special Education during the 10th Five-Year Plan Period* was issued. It clearly proposed to further strengthen the guidance for special education classes and the LRC program in regular schools, and strive to improve the quality of teaching. At this point, the objective of the LRC program changed significantly, and began to focus on quality improvement.

58 *Analysis of the Policies for Development of the LRC Program*

In response to this trend, the Chinese Ministry of Education issued the *Circular on the Work of Pilot Counties (Districts) for Establishing Supporting System for the LRC Program* in 2003, which clearly stated that the goal of the LRC program during this period was to enroll children with disabilities in regular primary and secondary schools smoothly, and enable them to finish school with good results through establishing a supporting system for the program. For a long time after that, the objective of the LRC program stated in relevant policy texts emphasized the quality improvement of the program, but policies with higher effectiveness level still take "expanding the scale of the LRC program" as the main objective. In 2014, the Ministry of Education and six other state agencies jointly promulgated the *Program for Promoting Special Education*, clearly proposing to promote inclusive education in an all-round way, improve the popularization level, strengthen the guarantee for the conditions, and improve the quality of education and teaching. From then on, the LRC program formally entered a new stage with the overall improvement of quality as the primary goal. The revised *Regulations on Education for Individuals with Disabilities* and the *Program for Promoting Special Education: Phase II (2017–2020)* issued in 2017 emphasize the support and guidance for the LRC program to improve its quality. The *China's Education Modernization 2035* plan, issued in 2019, lists the realization of equal access to basic public education services as one of the 10 strategic tasks for the future. It clearly calls for "doing a good job in special education" and "comprehensively promoting inclusive education." It indicates that long-term exploration will be made to improve the quality of the LRC program.

Means: Emphasizing Support Guarantee and Preferential Policy Compensation

With the advent of the 21st century, policies concerning the LRC program emphasized the realization of educational equity for individuals with disabilities by strengthening the construction of the supporting system and setting up preferential policies to compensate for disadvantaged groups. On the one hand, the education quality of children with disabilities was improved mainly by means of establishing a supporting system for the LRC program. The establishment of resource rooms, resource centers, and the system of itinerant guidance was the major task of the establishment of the supporting system, as shown in the *Opinions on Further Promoting the Reform and Development of Special Education during the 10th Five-Year Plan Period*. The *Program for Promoting Special Education: Phase II (2017–2020)* promulgated in 2017 still laid stress on the construction of resource rooms, and made more detailed provisions in this regard. It also proposed to promote the development of the LRC program by strengthening the management mechanism and teaching force.

In the process of promoting inclusive education, the government actively promoted the transformation of special education schools into an integral part of inclusive education to provide support for the LRC program. Since it was proposed in the *Opinions on Further Accelerating the Development of*

Special Education in 2009 and the *Outline of China's National Plan for Medium and Long-term Education Reform and Development* in 2010 to basically establish one special education school in every city (prefecture) and county with a population of more than 300,000, the number of special education schools has been growing rapidly, from 1,531 in 2001 to 2,192 in 2019, a 43.17 percent increase, according to education statistics. Thanks to the size expansion and quality improvement of special education schools, it is possible to rely on them to support local children with disabilities to learn in regular classrooms. Subsequently, the *Program for Promoting Special Education: Phase II (2017–2020)* further proposed to "support special education schools to establish special education resource centers for providing special education guidance and support. Districts and counties that do not have special education schools shall build special education resource centers by integrating related resources with regular schools that can afford them."

On the other hand, efforts were made to achieve the educational equality of children with disabilities through various preferential policies and other compensatory means. The most common approach is to encourage children with disabilities to attend school on time by providing direct financial assistance to their families. It was clearly pointed out in the *Circular on the Work of Pilot Counties (Districts) for Establishing Supporting System for the LRC Program* issued in 2003 that relevant departments should increase the capital input for the LRC program, including regular and institutionalized input, and project input such as "free compulsory education project" and "poor students' grant project." The *Outline of China's National Plan for Medium and Long-term Education Reform and Development* released in 2010 proposed to increase financial support for disabled students from poor families and gradually implement free senior high school education for students with disabilities. The *Program for Promoting Special Education* promulgated in 2014 not only emphasized the need to provide direct financial support for the families of disabled children learning in regular classrooms, but also required compensation for the staff of the LRC program, so as to attract high-caliber teachers to improve the quality of the program. It also stressed that "teachers who are responsible for the teaching and management of disabled students in regular schools shall be given a preference in performance evaluation"; and "work and transportation subsidies shall be provided to relevant medical personnel who offer medical and educational services." The importance of financial subsidies was emphasized in subsequent policy documents regarding the LRC program, especially the provision of the outlay for the LRC program students and the preferential salaries for the staff members. The *Notice on Doing a Good Job in Enrollment of Children and Adolescents with Disabilities in Compulsory Education* issued by the Ministry of Education in 2017 stated that, on the basis of "two exemptions and one subsidy," the subsidy level should be increased to ensure the smooth enrollment of children with disabilities.

In addition to the above economic compensation, relevant policy documents also proposed to provide additional tutoring and support for children and

60 *Analysis of the Policies for Development of the LRC Program*

adolescents with disabilities who are taught by means of courses delivered at home or distance education, and offer counseling and other family services to their parents or other guardians; and to provide compensation through "environmental transformation." Specific provisions can be found in the *Regulations on Education for Individuals with Disabilities* revised in 2017. The *Program for Promoting Special Education: Phase II (2017–2020)* also pointed out that regular institutions of higher learning that enroll disabled students should carry out necessary barrier-free environment transformation, and provide disabled students with support and assistance in both study and living.

Process Analysis: Transformation from Bottom-up to Top-down Practice

Viewing the evolution of LRC policies, the whole process is not linear, but reflects diversified characteristics in the pathway, approach, and dynamics of policy change. In terms of the pathway of policy change, from the 1980s when the LRC concept was put forward, to the 1990s, LRC policies were revised in line with the change in educational policy and special education policy of China. At first, universal compulsory education was taken as the most important goal, which determined that the main goal set in LRC policies was to improve the enrollment rate of disabled children by expanding the scale of the LRC program. Later, the educational policy turned to educational equity, causing the changes of LRC policy to emphasize the improvement of LRC quality and the realization of educational equity for disabled children. The applicable objects and development means of the LRC program also changed accordingly.

But after entering the 21st century, LRC policies began to put an emphasis on the standardization and development of the LRC system through building a high-quality teaching force, establishing a supporting system, and improving the management mechanism, which in turn promoted reform of the overall layout of special education. Take the establishment of a supporting system for the LRC program as an example. Special education schools were required to actively transform their functions from simple educational placement to multi-functional educational institutions that integrate placement, education, and teaching, and LRC program support services. Moreover, the LRC program was oriented toward inclusive education to promote the general education sector to cooperate in the reform, and further impose influence on the overall planning of China's educational policy. As a result, the development goal of the LRC program gradually turned into one of the goals of national educational development.

From the perspective of the approach of policy change, LRC policies were formulated mainly through innovation, and then led to the reform of national educational policy. This finds full expression in the development of the innovative LRC program based on China's reality.

However, the LRC program mainly adopts the way of gradual development toward inclusive education, as evidenced by the coexistence of general education and special education. Existing LRC policies mainly come from the special education sector, which have very limited binding effect on the general education system, and the general education sector's contribution to the LRC program has proven very small.

The LRC program mainly advocates and promotes the gradual transformation of functions, the reallocation of resources and cooperation between special education and general education, rather than restructuring. However, the main battlefield of the LRC program for its development toward inclusive education is inevitably in general education schools, which must shoulder the due responsibilities and actively promote the transformation of general education to inclusive education.

From the perspective of dynamics, the policy change of the LRC program is the result of natural evolution and rational construction. Natural evolution refers to the gradual change in educational policy along its own internal logic. Rational construction means that the change in educational policy is closely related to the value tendency and interest demands of policy makers.[6] On the one hand, LRC policies have changed in line with the internal logic of gradually realizing the equality and quality improvement of education for children with disabilities. On the other hand, the change has always been closely related to the change in the educational development concept of China. The change in the value orientation of policy makers is the deep driving force for the change of the LRC program. All-round development of the LRC program toward inclusive education is the result of the rational construction of education for the disabled by policy makers based on rational thinking, and also the product of the efforts made by the state to coordinate, standardize, and guide various interest groups related to the LRC program.

Analysis of Cultivation Policy for the LRC Program

The pre-service cultivation stage is seen as the starting point of the professional development of teachers, and the cognition of occupational identity and professionalism of teachers began to take shape in this stage. It is of great significance to improve the competence of teachers in inclusive education in the cultivation stage for them to successfully cope with the inclusive classroom in the future. The *Five-Year Work Outline for the Cause of Disabled Persons in China (1988–1992)*, promulgated by the former State Planning Commission and other state agencies and forwarded by the State Council in 1988, defined LRC program the competence of teachers in inclusive education, but only emphasized that teachers should have basic knowledge and skills of special education. Both the *Law on the Protection of Disabled Persons* and the *Regulations on Education for Individuals with Disabilities* have provisions on the cultivation of inclusive education competence of regular normal university students, forming an important basis for the formulation of relevant policies thereafter. With the urgent need for the quality improvement of the LRC program in the 21st century, the cultivation of the competence of teachers in

62   *Analysis of the Policies for Development of the LRC Program*

inclusive education attracted more and more attention. As shown in Table 2.2, a number of policies issued in the past decade or more require regular normal colleges and universities to set up special education-related courses, and propose to include the content of special education into the teacher qualification examination, and cultivate teachers with the ability to teach children with disabilities learning in regular classrooms.

Cultivation Aiming to Improve Competence of Teachers in Inclusive Education

Since 1988 when relevant provisions on the cultivation of LRC program teachers first appeared in the policy text, it has been proposed that teachers prepared for the LRC program should master the basic knowledge and skills of special education on the basis of having relevant competence of general education. Later, a number of state policies required imparting necessary knowledge and skills of special education in the process of teacher cultivation. This is manifested in the *Law of the PRC on the Protection of Disabled Persons* promulgated in 1990 and the *Trial Measures for the Development of the LRC Program* issued in 1994. The *Curriculum Standards for Teacher Education* (for trial implementation) issued by the Ministry of Education in 2011 added a module of "development and learning of special needs children" to the preschool teacher education section. Special education-related content became compulsory content of preschool teacher cultivation, and the cultivation of inclusive education competence began to cover all preschool teachers. During this period, LRC program teachers were required to possess both general education competence and special education competence. However, no clear explanation was found on the exact qualification for a LRC program teacher.

Since then, more and more policy texts have emphasized in the sections related to preservice cultivation that teachers should have competence in inclusive education, and the connotations for the competence also began to change. Teachers were required to master the basic knowledge and skills of special education, and form the concept of inclusive education, and improve their educational and teaching ability for the LRC program. Specific provisions can be found in the *Opinions on Strengthening the Development of Teaching Force for Special Education* issued in 2012, the *Program for Promoting Special Education* promulgated in 2014, and the *Guidelines on Enhancing Implementation of the LRC Program in Compulsory Education* released in 2020.

In general, the current cultivation of LRC program teachers mainly relies on the existing major setup and curriculum system, and is realized by adding some special education-related courses or contents in the curriculum of normal colleges and comprehensive universities.

Gradually Expanding Subjects of Cultivation

From the expression of the policy content, the cultivation subjects of LRC program teachers have gradually shifted from secondary normal schools to

Table 2.2 Some Policy Documents Concerning Cultivation of Competence of Teachers of the LRC Program in Inclusive Education

Date of promulgation	Title	Promulgators	Relevant contents (excerpts)
May 4, 1989	Several Opinions on the Development of Special Education	The State Education Commission, etc.	III. Leadership and Management 18. Strengthen the development of teaching contingent. Special education contents may be appropriately added to the professional courses of regular secondary normal schools and preschool teacher training schools in light of local needs....
Dec. 28, 1990	Law of the PRC on the Protection of Disabled Persons	The National People's Congress	Chapter 3 Education Article 25 Regular normal schools shall offer curricula or lectures on special education so that teachers in general education may have some necessary knowledge of special education.
Dec. 29, 1991	Outline of the Eighth Five-Year Plan for the Cause of Disabled Persons in China (1991–1995)	The State Planning Commission, etc.	III. Main Tasks, Targets and Measures for the Period of the Eighth Five-Year Plan
May 12, 1992	Plan on Implementation of Compulsory Education for Disabled Children and Adolescents during the Eighth Five-Year Plan Period	The State Education Commission, etc.	III. Major Measures (3) Strengthen the training of teachers and administrators.
Jul. 21, 1994	Trial Measures for the Development of the LRC Program	The State Education Commission	V. Teacher Training 21. ...Regular secondary normal schools should offer special education courses in stages and batches to ensure the source of LRC program teachers.

(Continued)

Table 2.2 (Continued)

Date of promulgation	Title	Promulgators	Relevant contents (excerpts)
Aug. 23, 1994	Regulations on Education for Individuals with Disabilities	The State Council	Chapter 5 Teachers Article 41 Normal colleges and universities shall offer compulsory or elective special education courses for disabled persons in a planned way …
May 9, 1996	Implementation Plan on Compulsory Education for Children and Adolescents with Disabilities during the Ninth Five-Year Plan Period	The State Education Commission, etc.	III. Main Measures 4. Development of Teaching Contingent
Oct. 19, 2001	Opinions on Further Promoting the Reform and Development of Special Education during the 10th Five-Year Plan Period	The Ministry of Education, etc.	11. Regular normal colleges (schools) and preschool teacher training schools (majors) should offer special education courses or lectures in a planned way …
Apr. 24, 2008	Law of the PRC on the Protection of Disabled Persons	The Standing Committee of the National People's Congress	Chapter 4 Education Article 28 Regular normal colleges shall offer special education courses or teach relevant contents so that regular teachers can master necessary knowledge of special education.
May 7, 2009	Opinions on Further Accelerating the Development of Special Education	The Ministry of Education, etc.	16. Encourage and support normal and comprehensive institutions of higher learning at all levels to offer special education majors or courses.
Oct. 8, 2011	Curriculum Standards for Teacher Education	The Ministry of Education	I. Curriculum Objectives and Setting for Pre-service Education for Kindergarten Teachers
Sep. 20, 2012	Opinions on Strengthening the Development of Teaching Force for Special Education	The Ministry of Education, etc.	2. Strengthen the training of special education teachers.

Jan. 8, 2014	Program for Promoting Special Education (2014–2016)	The Ministry of Education, etc.	Colleges and universities are encouraged to offer special education courses in normal majors …
May 11, 2016	Guiding Opinions on Accelerating the Development of Education in Central and Western China	The State Council	Expand the training scale of special education majors in colleges and universities, and encourage normal majors in colleges and universities to offer special education courses.
Feb. 1, 2017	Regulations on Education for Individuals with Disabilities (revised)	The State Council	Chapter VI Teachers Article 44. Regular normal schools and colleges and comprehensive universities with teacher education majors shall offer special education courses …
Jul. 17, 2017	Program for Promoting Special Education: Phase II (2017–2020)	The Ministry of Education, etc.	3. Main measures (5) Strengthen the development of professional special education teachers.
Jun. 17, 2020	Guidelines on Enhancing Implementation of the LRC Program in Compulsory Education	The Ministry of Education	12. Do a good job in teacher training and cultivation.

institutions of higher learning, and relevant provisions on the subject of cultivation have gradually become clear. The *Several Opinions on the Development of Special Education* issued in 1989 required regular secondary normal schools, preschool teacher training schools, and normal colleges and universities to increase the content of special education in curriculum. Since it was proposed in the *Outline of the Eighth Five-Year Plan for the Cause of Disabled Persons in China* in 1991 that "special education courses should be provided in normal schools and colleges at all levels," the "regular normal schools and colleges" mentioned in policy documents refer to all kinds of normal schools and colleges at all levels, and various kinds of normal schools and colleges are no longer listed separately therein. The above policies confine the subject of the cultivation to regular secondary normal schools, preschool teacher training schools, and normal colleges and universities, basically determining the main source of LRC program teachers in China. In the late 1990s, secondary normal schools encountered a survival crisis due to the disappearance of secondary normal school-related policy, the pressure of their students brought by higher requirement on the educational background of teacher candidates, and the loss of outstanding junior middle school students caused by the expansion of university and senior middle school enrollment, so they gradually stepped out of the historical stage of education.[7] In this context, the cultivation subject gradually became higher normal schools and colleges. The *Opinions on Further Accelerating the Development of Special Education*, issued in 2009, first proposed to "encourage and support normal schools and colleges at all levels as well as comprehensive universities to set up special education programs or provide special education courses." Subsequently, the *Opinions on Strengthening the Development of Teaching Force for Special Education* issued in 2012 pointed out that normal schools and colleges and teacher education programs in other institutions of higher learning should generally offer special education courses. A number of subsequent policies have relevant provisions consistent with this.

In general, the task of cultivating LRC program teachers mainly falls on the teacher education programs of normal colleges or comprehensive universities, and the cultivation mode remains semi-open. In addition, the *Implementation Measures for Certification of Teacher Education Programs in Regular Institutions of Higher Learning (Interim)* issued by the Ministry of Education in 2017 proposed that all kinds of teacher education courses should conform to teachers' professional standards and teacher education curriculum standards, but the "development and learning of special needs children" was only added into the curriculum of pre-service preschool teacher education, and no relevant provisions were made for teacher education courses in the compulsory education stage. Therefore, the number of compulsory education teacher cultivation units that pay attention to the cultivation of inclusive education competence in accordance with the above policy requirements is very small, and needs to be increased in the future.

Gradually Standardized and Enforced Cultivation Approach

Since 1989 when *Several Opinions on the Development of Special Education* proposed to add special education-related content in the professional courses of normal schools and colleges at all levels, the cultivation of teachers' inclusive education competence mainly relied on adding special education-related content into the curriculum system of general teacher education. The *Trial Measures for the Development of the LRC Program* released in 1994 made further provisions, requiring secondary normal schools to offer special education courses "by stages and in batches" to ensure the source of new teachers for the LRC program, but how to do it "in batches" and "by stages" specifically was not explained in the document. According to the *Opinions on Further Promoting the Reform and Development of Special Education during the 10th Five-Year Plan Period* issued in 2001, special education knowledge can be popularized through lectures in addition to special education courses. During the period from 2001 to 2008, no relevant provisions on cultivation of LRC program teachers were found in the policy texts, and the relevant expressions in the *Law on the Protection of Disabled Persons* revised in 2008 were exactly the same as those in the original version promulgated in 1990. This shows that the discussion of the issue of teacher cultivation was relatively stagnant during the period. In the aforementioned policy texts, words such as "elective," "added content" and "lecture" are used in the provisions regarding the cultivation approach. The provisions related to special education mainly appear in the form of additional content instead of being systematically included in the teacher cultivation program. Moreover, the policy texts often use words such as "successively carrying out," "should," and "in a planned way," so the relevant provisions are not mandatory and operable, unable to arouse sufficient attention of the cultivation units to truly implement them.

The *Curriculum Standards for Teacher Education* (for trial implementation) issued in 2011 required including relevant content of education for special needs children into the curriculum system of preschool teacher education as a curriculum module, ushering in a new development period for the cultivation of LRC program teachers. At present, this change only appears in the preschool education stage, but the vast majority of LRC students are found in the compulsory education stage. Thus, it is necessary to actively promote the improvement of relevant policies on the cultivation of LRC program teachers in the compulsory education stage. Then, the *Program for Promoting Special Education* issued in 2014 put forward that special education-related content should be included in the teacher qualification examination, which forces teacher cultivation institutions to strengthen the cultivation of teacher candidates' inclusive education competence. It can be seen that the cultivation approach of LRC program teachers is gradually being standardized and enforced.

68 *Analysis of the Policies for Development of the LRC Program*

Suggestions on Policies Concerning Cultivation of LRC Program Teachers

According to the results of the policy analysis on the cultivation of LRC program teachers, cultivation policies can be improved in the following aspects: First, the cultivation of the competence of teachers in inclusive education should be included in the relevant policies regarding general education or development of teaching force. Among relevant policies formulated since the initiation of reform and opening-up in China in the late 1970s, more than 10 policies concerning the pre-service cultivation of the competence of teachers in inclusive education mainly came from the special education sector, and few policies from the general education sector involved this content, which greatly limits and weakens the scope and intensity of implementation of the policies. However, teacher cultivation for the LRC program is related to the reform of the entire teacher cultivation system. It is difficult to achieve the expected effect only by relying on the policies from the special education sector, which is also the main reason that the implementation of the current policy is blocked and the influence of the policy is limited. In future, it is advisable to include the requirements of general teachers' pre-service cultivation of inclusive education competence into relevant policies concerning educational development or development of the teaching force by dint of the reform of teacher education.

Second, it is encouraged to shift the "cultivation of special education knowledge and skills" to the "cultivation of inclusive education competence." From the perspective of policy expression, content concerning the inclusive education competence of LRC program teachers basically involves "special education courses," "basic knowledge and skills of special education," and "educational and teaching ability to guide disabled students to learn in regular classrooms." The knowledge of special needs children and the skills to educate them are only part of the competence of teachers in inclusive education. The inclusive education concept, inclusive environment adjustment, curriculum adjustment, and other content should also be included in relevant policies. In future, it is advised to directly use the term "competence in inclusive education," and make specific provisions on the cultivation content and methods from the perspective of inclusive competence.

Third, it is necessary to increase LRC program teacher cultivation units, make evidence-based decisions, and promulgate more detailed and specific regulations. According to our investigation on the setting of primary education courses in 22 normal schools and colleges, only five offer courses related to inclusive education. Moreover, existing policies lack specific provisions on the nature, content, teaching force, and funding guarantee of special education-related courses offered by regular normal schools and colleges. Some studies have found that even in the schools that have added special education courses in the general teacher cultivation program, there are still problems such as lack of unified core norms and guidance.[8] Since the current scale and quality of pre-service cultivation of LRC program teachers are not satisfactory, it is critical to launch an open teacher education model in future, and make requirements

Analysis of the Policies for Development of the LRC Program

in policies that all teacher cultivation units should include competence in inclusive education into the cultivation content, and increase practice bases to assist all kinds of schools and colleges to cultivate teachers with competence in inclusive education. In addition to increasing cultivation units, evidence-based decisions should also be made to explore appropriate course content and cultivation models through expert demonstration and field research, and more detailed and specific provisions should be made on specific cultivation methods and quality standards of cultivation units in national policies.

Analysis of Training Policy for LRC Program Teachers

When a special needs child is placed in a regular class, the teachers of this class will automatically become LRC program teachers. Therefore, the identity of LRC program teachers always changes dynamically with the entry and transfer of special needs children. How to help this kind of teacher smoothly complete identity transformation through in-service training, and meet the requirements of educational and teaching ability in response to the change in work, and how to improve their inclusive education competence through in-service training are all the focuses in the development of the teaching force for the LRC program. Similar to the cultivation of LRC program teachers, the training of such teachers was first stipulated in the *Five-Year Work Outline for the Cause of Disabled Persons in China (1988–1992)*. The *Trial Measures for the Development of the LRC Program* promulgated in 1994 contains detailed provisions on the training of LRC program teachers, basically establishing an in-service training system for LRC program teachers. Since the beginning of the new century, more than 10 policy documents have involved the relevant contents of in-service training for the LRC program, as shown in Table 2.3. Over time, the provisions on the training units, methods, and content in the policy texts become more specific and operable. The training system for LRC program teachers has been gradually improved and standardized, which provides a strong guarantee for the smooth development of the LRC program.

Long-term Goal to Build Specialized Teaching Force for the LRC Program

The early training for the LRC program was only provided for subject teachers of the classes with special needs children.

The *Five-Year Work Outline for the Cause of Disabled Persons in China (1988–1992)* clearly stated that "teachers in regular schools shall be given special education training according to the needs of mixed schools and mixed classes." The *Trial Measures for the Development of the LRC Program* promulgated in 1994 specifically described the object and form of the LRC program. With the subsequent promotion of the LRC program to improve its quality, it was no longer enough to provide training only for the subject teachers, and it was gradually required to provide training for the entire teaching force involved in the LRC program. The *Opinions on Further Accelerating the Development of Special*

Table 2.3 Some Policy Documents Concerning In-service Training of Competence of Teachers of the LRC Program in Inclusive Education

Date of promulgation	Title	Promulgators	Relevant contents (excerpts)
Sep. 3, 1988	Five-Year Program of Work for the Cause of Persons with Disabilities in China (1988–1992)	The State Planning Commission, etc.	IV. Measures 43. Strengthen the training of special education teachers.
May 12, 1992	Plan on Implementation of Compulsory Education for Disabled Children and Adolescents during the Eighth Five-Year Plan Period	The State Education Commission, etc.	III. Main Measures (3) Strengthen the training of teachers and administrators.
Jul. 21, 1994	Trial Measures for the Development of the LRC Program	The State Education Commission	V. Teacher Training 21. Local administrative departments of education at various levels shall include in their plans the training of regular teachers for children and adolescents with visual, hearing, speech, and intellectual disabilities …
Oct. 19, 2001	Opinions on Further Promoting the Reform and Development of Special Education during the 10th Five-Year Plan Period	The Ministry of Education, etc.	10. Vigorously strengthen the cultivation and training of special education teachers.
Feb. 9, 2003	Minutes of National Conference on the Exchange of Experiences in LRC Practice	The Ministry of Education, etc.	(2) Fourth, continue to strengthen the capacity for implementation of the LRC program. (3) The management and guidance network of provinces, prefectures (cities) and counties should be formed …
Feb. 19, 2003	Circular on the Work of Pilot Counties (Districts) for Establishing Supporting System for the LRC Program	The Ministry of Education	II. Pilot Content 5. Two networks should be formed at the county (district) level. 10. Strengthen the professional training of LRC program teachers, and provide materials, consultation, and guidance for them.

Date	Policy	Issued by	Relevant content
May 7, 2009	Opinions on Further Accelerating the Development of Special Education	The Ministry of Education, etc.	IV. Strengthen the development of special education teachers, and improve the professional level of teachers.
Oct. 8, 2011	Curriculum Standards for Teacher Education (For Trial Implementation)	The Ministry of Education	Include the module of "education for special needs children" into the in-service teacher education curriculum.
Sep. 20, 2012	Opinions on Strengthening the Development of Teaching Force for Special Education	The Ministry of Education, etc.	3. Carry out training for all special education teachers.
Jan. 8, 2014	Program for Promoting Special Education (2014–2016)	The Ministry of Education, etc.	Promote local governments to determine post requirements for LRC program teachers, teachers who go to students' home to give instruction, and rehabilitation trainers.
Jan. 20, 2016	Guidelines for the Construction of Special Education Resource Classrooms in Regular Schools	The General Office of the Ministry of Education	List "carrying out general education teacher training" as one of the main functions of resource rooms. VIII. Standardized Management (4) Provide guidance for evaluation.
Feb. 1, 2017	Regulations on Education for Individuals with Disabilities (revised)	The State Council	Chapter VI. Teachers Article 26 The administrative departments of education at the county level shall strengthen guidance on the implementation of compulsory education for disabled children and adolescents.
Jul. 17, 2017	Program for Promoting Special Education: Phase II (2017–2020)	The Ministry of Education, etc.	III. Main Measures (5) Strengthen the development of specialized teaching force for special education.
Jun. 17, 2020	2020 Guidelines on Enhancing Implementation of the LRC Program in Compulsory Education	The Ministry of Education	12. Do a good job in teacher training and cultivation.

72 *Analysis of the Policies for Development of the LRC Program*

Education issued in 2009 proposed that the training for teachers engaged in special education work in regular schools, children's welfare institutions, or other institutions, and itinerant tutors in special education schools should be strengthened. Later, the *Program for Promoting Special Education* issued in 2014 and the *Guide to the Construction of Special Education Resource Rooms in Regular Schools* released in 2016 also included resource teachers into the scope of the training objects.

At present, the purpose of the training is not only to improve the professional ability of LRC program teachers to meet the practical needs, but also to build a specialized teaching force to improve the quality of the LRC program.

Formation of Multi-level Network of Training Subjects

The complex teaching force of the LRC program comprises regular school teachers who directly provide the education and teaching for LRC students, resource teachers, and itinerant tutors who provide support for the LRC program, involving multiple institutions. This complexity results in the complex composition of the training subjects.

The *Trial Measures for the Development of the LRC Program* promulgated in 1994 stipulated that local administrative departments of education at all levels should be responsible for the training of LRC program teachers, and provide pre-service and in-service training for them. The *Minutes of National Conference on the Exchange of Experiences in LRC Practice* and the *Circular on the Work of Pilot Counties (Districts) for Establishing Supporting System for the LRC Program* issued in 2003 made an overall and detailed deployment of the training and teaching research work for LRC program teachers. It was proposed to "form management and guidance network at provincial, prefectural and county levels, especially the network based on county." According to the specific content of the two documents, the basic thinking of the training for LRC program teachers changed as follows: First, the single-subject structure of administrative departments of education at all levels changed into a complex that embraces the administrative departments of education, central schools, special education schools, special education centers, and other institutions. In this way, various resources can be utilized efficiently. Second, a multi-level, multi-institution network was formed for the integration of management and training for the LRC program. Taking county-level special education schools and special education resource centers as the main positions of the training is helpful to provide more targeted training according to the actual needs of each area.

Subsequent policies concerning the training of LRC program teachers were adjusted and enriched on the basis of the above content. For example, the *Opinions on Further Accelerating the Development of Special Education*, issued in 2009, required special education colleges, other relevant colleges, and professional institutions to participate in the training work. The training work showed a trend of cooperation among colleges and universities, governments,

Analysis of the Policies for Development of the LRC Program 73

and schools, aiming at training teachers with both theoretical competence and practical ability. The *Program for Promoting Special Education: Phase II (2017–2020)* further stipulated in detail the training units for different types of teachers. This helps lighten the training task of special education schools at the county level and further optimize the training network.

Gradually Systematized and Institutionalized Training Approaches

Compared with the cultivation of LRC program teachers, the training work is more comprehensive and rich in form and supportive work. There are diversified training forms and increasing training opportunities under the trend of the standardization and institutionalization of the training. The *Plan on Implementation of Compulsory Education for Disabled Children and Adolescents during the Eighth Five-Year Plan Period* released in 1992 required the provision of both pre-service training and in-service training for LRC program teachers, and also proposed that the education schools for disabled children and adolescents should provide short training for them. The *Trial Measures for the Development of the LRC Program* proposed for the first time to set up training bases, and advocated training in various forms. The *Minutes of National Conference on the Exchange of Experiences in LRC Practice* issued in 2003 advocated planned training to regularize and institutionalize the work. Although several subsequent policy documents touch on the training of LRC program teachers, only the *Opinions on Strengthening the Development of Teaching Force for Special Education* issued in 2012 first proposed that training should be provided for all LRC program teachers. The *Guidelines on Enhancing Implementation of the LRC Program in Compulsory Education* issued in 2020 that basically covers the main forms of the training not only emphasizes centralized short-term training at all levels and of various types, but also advocates the integration of training and regular professional development activities.

Since the beginning of the 21st century, the Chinese government has adopted various supportive measures to improve the quality of the training of LRC program teachers. The *Opinions on Further Promoting the Reform and Development of Special Education during the 10th Five-Year Plan Period* issued in 2001 proposed that the Ministry of Education should compile the training materials for LRC program teachers. It was expected to provide a basis for the determination of training content through the preparation of unified training materials, so as to alleviate the problem of uneven training levels in different regions. The *Minutes of National Conference on the Exchange of Experiences in LRC Practice* issued in 2003 clearly required that management of the educational and teaching work of LRC program teachers should be strengthened, and that district and county-level teaching and research sections should conduct research, guidance and training, and counseling on the LRC practice in the region. Similar expressions also appeared in the *Guidance for the Development of Special Education Resource Teachers in Regular Schools* issued

74 *Analysis of the Policies for Development of the LRC Program*

by the Ministry of Education in 2016, which pointed out that "special education guidance centers or special education schools within the region should strengthen the professional guidance and evaluation of resource rooms, and regularly assign special personnel to provide training and professional support for resource teachers."

Suggestions on Policies Regarding Training of LRC Program Teachers

According to the analysis results, policies regarding the training of LRC program teachers can be improved in the following aspects.

First, it is necessary to promote the training of the LRC program to cover all general education teachers. At present, training is still mainly provided for teachers who have already become itinerant tutors, not covering all teachers. As the enrollment of LRC students gradually increases, more general education teachers will become LRC program teachers in the future, so every general education teacher should be prepared for this challenge. Thus, it is advisable to provide all general education teachers with training for the LRC program, so as to reserve professionals for the future LRC practice.

Second, it is critical to integrate the training content from the perspective of inclusive education competence. The existing training-related policies mainly limit the training content to special education knowledge and skills. However, inclusive education competence is not completely equivalent to special education knowledge and skills, nor is it a simple superposition of general education competence and special education competence. It also includes the concept of inclusive education, curriculum adjustment in inclusive environment, and other aspects. The simple supplementing of some special education knowledge and skills is far from enough to prepare teachers to deal with the inclusive classroom. In future, policy makers should make overall plans on the content and form of the training for LRC program teachers from the perspective of overall inclusive education competence.

Third, it is significant to include the content of in-service training for improving inclusive education competence of teachers in regular schools in more policy documents from the general education sector. Among the existing training policy documents for LRC program teachers, only the *Curriculum Standards for Teacher Education* (for trial implementation) comes from the general education sector, while all the rest are from the special education sector. The general education sector pays little attention to the inclusive education competence training for LRC program teachers. The main position of the LRC program should be in general education schools. In view of the insufficient support from the general education sector, the actual implementation effect of the policy documents from the special education sector is greatly reduced. In future, the content of in-service training of general teachers' inclusive education competence should be included into more policy documents from the general education sector, so as to strengthen the binding force on the general education sector.

Notes

1 Sun, Miantao 孙绵涛. *Jiaoyu zhengce xue* 教育政策学, 10. Wuhan: Wuhan University of Technology Press, 1997.
2 Liu, Fuxing 刘复兴. *Jiaoyu zhengce de jiazhi fenxi* 教育政策的价值分析, 5–6. Beijing: Educational Science Publishing House, 2003.
3 Shao, Zebin 邵泽斌, and Zhang, Letian 张乐天. "Jiaoyu zhengce: yige jiegou zhuyi de fenxi shijiao" 教育政策：一个结构主义的分析视角. *Theory and Practice of Education* 教育理论与实践 no. 11 (2007): 14–18.
4 Meng, Weiqing 孟卫青. "Jiaoyu zhengce fenxi: jiazhi neirong yu guocheng" 教育政策分析：价值、内容与过程. *Journal of Modern Education* 现代教育论丛 no. 5 (2008): 38–41.
5 Wang, Ning 王宁. "Jiaoyu zhengce zhutixing jiazhi fenxi kuangjia yanjiu—yi zhongguo guojia zhuxue daikuan wei shili" 教育政策主体性价值分析框架研究——以中国国家助学贷款为实例. Wuhan: Huazhong University of Science and Technology, 2011.
6 See note 3 above.
7 Liu, Xiufeng 刘秀峰. "Huihuang yu xiaoshi: zhongdeng shifan jiaoyu fazhan de huisu yu fansi" 辉煌与消逝：中等师范教育发展的回溯与反思. *Research on Educational Development* 教育发展研究 37, no. 10 (2017): 56–62.
8 Feng, Yajing 冯雅静. "Woguo guanyu putong jiaoshi teshu jiaoyu suyang peiyang de zhengce zhichi" 我国关于普通教师特殊教育素养培养的政策支持. *Chinese Journal of Special Education* 中国特殊教育 no. 3 (2017): 28–31.

References

Feng, Yajing 冯雅静. "Woguo guanyu putong jiaoshi teshu jiaoyu suyang peiyang de zhengce zhichi" 我国关于普通教师特殊教育素养培养的政策支持. *Chinese Journal of Special Education* 中国特殊教育 no. 3 (2017): 28–31.
Liu, Fuxing 刘复兴. *Jiaoyu zhengce de jiazhi fenxi* 教育政策的价值分析, 5–6. Beijing: Educational Science Publishing House, 2003.
Liu, Xiufeng 刘秀峰. "Huihuang yu xiaoshi: zhongdeng shifan jiaoyu fazhan de huisu yu fansi" 辉煌与消逝：中等师范教育发展的回溯与反思. *Research on Educational Development* 教育发展研究 37, no. 10 (2017): 56–62.
Meng, Weiqing 孟卫青. "Jiaoyu zhengce fenxi: jiazhi neirong yu guocheng" 教育政策分析：价值、内容与过程. *Journal of Modern Education* 现代教育论丛 no. 5 (2008): 38–41.
Shao, Zebin 邵泽斌, and Zhang, Letian 张乐天. "Jiaoyu zhengce: yige jiegou zhuyi de fenxi shijiao" 教育政策：一个结构主义的分析视角. *Theory and Practice of Education* 教育理论与实践 no. 11 (2007): 14–18.
Sun, Miantao 孙绵涛. *Jiaoyu zhengce xue* 教育政策学, 10. Wuhan: Wuhan University of Technology Press, 1997.
Wang, Ning 王宁. "Jiaoyu zhengce zhutixing jiazhi fenxi kuangjia yanjiu—yi zhongguo guojia zhuxue daikuan wei shili" 教育政策主体性价值分析框架研究——以中国国家助学贷款为实例. Wuhan: Huazhong University of Science and Technology, 2011.

3 Structural Analysis of the Competence of Teachers in Inclusive Education

Research into Competence of Teachers in Inclusive Education

Analysis of General Composition of Teacher Competence

Teacher competence refers to the sum of a series of professional qualities that make teachers competent in education and teaching. Many researchers have conducted in-depth studies on the composition of teacher competence. Lin Chongde and his colleagues studied the competence composition of primary and secondary school teachers by means of questionnaires. They hold that teacher competence should cover five dimensions that interact with each other: professional ideal, knowledge level, educational concept, teaching monitoring ability, and teaching behavior and strategy, among which teaching monitoring ability is in the core position of teacher competence. Based on this, a model of teacher competence was established.[1] Then they further summarized teacher competence in three aspects: teacher's ethics, knowledge, and ability. According to Ye Lan, teacher competence should cover the following three aspects. The first aspect is the educational concept accordant with the spirit of the times. This is the rational fulcrum of teachers' professional behavior, which is embodied in the education view, view about students, and view about educational activities. The second is the multi-layer composite knowledge structure, including the basic knowledge of contemporary science and humanities, as well as the solid foundation of instrumental disciplines and proficient skills; knowledge and skills of one or two specialized subjects; and educational subject knowledge. The third involves the responsibilities and rights entrusted to teachers by society, including communication ability, management ability, and educational research ability.[2] They can be summarized in the composition of teacher competence of educational concept, subject-related knowledge and skills, and other general abilities. A research finding indicates that "teachers do need to master the technical dimension of teaching, but their profession involves more than that. Issues such as reflection, emotions, beliefs, disposition, agency, professional values, etc. are key in developing as a teacher along with robust knowledge."[3] Arnon and Reichel once summarized the main viewpoints in a study of teacher competence composition: "There are two major categories

DOI: 10.4324/9781003432982-4

that comprise perceptions of an ideal teacher: first, personal qualities; and second, knowledge of the subject taught as well as didactic knowledge."[4]

Based on the views of different researchers, it can be found that although there are some differences in understanding of teacher competence composition, they all show strong consistency, that is, they all define it from the knowledge, skills, and educational concept (attitude and psychology) necessary for teachers to be competent in teaching.[5] The *Professional Standards for Primary School Teachers* (for trial implementation) and the *Professional Standards for Secondary School Teachers* (for trial implementation) issued in 2012 both provide for the competence of teachers from three aspects: professional concept and teachers' ethics, professional knowledge, and professional ability, indicating that a consensus has been reached on the understanding of teacher competence composition.

The general composition of teacher competence is the basis for further exploring teacher competence in inclusive education. With the advancement of the LRC program, teachers of regular primary and secondary schools have their work tasks changed due to the admission of special needs children, so their original knowledge structure needs to be supplemented and adjusted accordingly. After systematic pre-service training, teachers are basically equipped with the ability to educate typically developing children, but they lack the ability to educate special needs children, that is, they lack the ability to implement inclusive education. This research only focuses on the qualities that should be underlined and possessed by teachers in the context of inclusive education, that is the concept, knowledge, and skills that teachers should possess in order to meet the needs of all children, including special needs children. The general composition of teacher competence provides an analytical framework for exploring the composition of and connotations for teacher competence in inclusive education.

Requirements for Inclusive Education Competence in National Professional Standards for Teachers

In some European and American countries with a high level of inclusive education, the professional standards for teachers clearly reflect the role and quality requirements of teachers engaged in inclusive education, and the provisions on the inclusive education competence of teachers are comprehensive and detailed.

In the US, there are two standards for teacher competence. One is the *InTASC Model Core Teaching Standards* set up by the Interstate Teacher Assessment and Support Consortium (InTASC) for beginning teachers; and the other is the standards developed for experienced teachers by the National Board for Professional Teaching Standards (NBPTS).[6] The *InTASC Model Core Teaching Standards*, revised in 2011, contains 10 standards in total that fall into four categories: the Learner and Learning, Content Knowledge, Instructional Practice, and Professional Responsibility. Each standard is described from three

78 *Structural Analysis of the Competence of Teachers*

aspects: performances, essential knowledge, and critical dispositions. Except for the two standards in the category of "Content Knowledge," which do not involve knowledge and skills for teaching special needs students, the other eight standards all mention the knowledge, performances, and dispositions that teachers should possess to educate diverse learners such as special needs children. For examples, in terms of knowledge, "the teacher understands students with exceptional needs, including those associated with disabilities and giftedness, and know how to use strategies and resources to address these needs," and "the teacher understands how to prepare learners for assessments and how to make accommodations in assessments and testing conditions, especially for learners with disabilities and language learning needs," and so on. With regard to performances, "the teacher creates developmentally appropriate instruction that takes into account individual learners' strengths, interests, and needs, and that enables each learner to advance and accelerate his/her learning," and "the teacher prepares all learners for the demands of particular assessment formats and makes appropriate accommodations in assessments or testing conditions, especially for learners with disabilities and language learning needs," and so on. As for dispositions, "the teacher respects learners' differing strengths and needs and is committed to using this information to further each learner's development," and "the teacher respects learners' diverse strengths and needs and is committed to using this information to plan effective instruction."[7]

In 2009, the European Agency for Development in Special Needs Education issued the *Key Principles for Promoting Quality in Inclusive Education: Recommendations for Policy Makers*,[8] laying out seven key principles. Two of them involve demands on teachers: widening participation to increase educational opportunity for all learners; developing personalized learning approaches for all learners, where the learner sets, records, and reviews their own learning goals in collaboration with their teachers and families, and is helped to develop a structured way of learning independently in order to take control of their own learning; cooperative teaching, where teachers take a team approach; and education and training in inclusive education for all teachers. In 2012, the European Agency for Development in Special Needs Education and its members issued the *Profile of Inclusive Teachers*,[9] putting forward requirements on competence of all teachers in inclusive settings. For example, in the dimension of "attitudes and beliefs," the profile states: "Inclusive education is about societal reform," "learner diversity is to be respected, valued and understood," "on some occasions, particular learning difficulties require responses based upon adaptations to the curriculum and teaching approaches," and "inclusive education requires all teachers to work in teams." In the dimension of "knowledge and understanding," it says: "Inclusive education is an approach for all learners, not just those who are perceived to have different needs and may be at risk of exclusion from educational opportunities," "inclusive teaching as based on a collaborative working approach," and "multi-agency working models where teachers in inclusive classrooms co-operate with other experts and staff from a range of different disciplines," and so on. In the "skills and abilities" dimension, it indicates: "Coping strategies that prepare teachers to challenge non-inclusive attitudes and to work in segregated situations," "identifying the most appropriate ways of responding to diversity in all situations," and "collaboratively problem solving with other professionals," and so on. The standards fully reflect the *Key Principles for Promoting Quality of Inclusive Education: Recommendations for Practice.*

The Chinese professional standards for secondary, primary, and preschool teachers issued in 2012 also reflect the requirements on the inclusive education competence of teachers, as shown in Table 3.1. Suzanne Carrington and her partners analyzed the professional teaching standards of China and Australia, and found that the two countries put forward requirements on the core values that teachers need to have in inclusive settings, such as giving equal treatment to each student, and valuing student diversity and individualized learning needs.[10] However, compared with the teachers' standards in Europe and America, the standards for primary and secondary school teachers in China have far fewer requirements on the competence of teachers in inclusive education. For example, in the dimension of "professional concept and teachers' ethics," the concept of inclusive education is only reflected in the equal treatment of students, respect for their personality, respect for individual differences and other aspects, but other content seldom mirrors the requirements of inclusive education on the professional quality of primary and secondary school teachers. In particular, the concept of inclusive education is lacking in the educational and teaching attitudes.[11] In the dimensions of "professional knowledge" and "professional ability," the knowledge and skills of inclusive education for addressing the special needs of the LRC program students are rarely touched upon.

Composition of and Connotations for Competence of Teachers in Inclusive Education

What inclusive education competencies should teachers possess? Scholars have basically adopted two ways of thinking to answer this question. One is to analyze the overall competence that teachers should possess, while the other only pays attention to the competencies related to inclusive education that should be supplemented and adjusted after special needs children enter the class, not involving subject knowledge and teaching skills. Although there are some differences in the understanding of the composition and connotation of the competence of teachers in inclusive education, most of them focus on teachers' concept (or attitude), quality, knowledge, and ability.

Analysis of Composition of and Connotations for Competence of Teachers in Inclusive Education in the US

By analyzing research into teacher competence in inclusive education in the US, we found the competence items under three basic dimensions, that is professional value, professional knowledge, and professional ability.[12] Among them, the teacher competence in inclusive education under the dimension of professional

80   *Structural Analysis of the Competence of Teachers*

Table 3.1 Requirements on Inclusive Education Competence in Chinese Standards for Teachers

Standards for Inclusive Education Competence	Professional Standards for Preschool Teachers (For Trial Implementation)	Professional Standards for Primary School Teachers (For Trial Implementation)	Professional Standards for Secondary School Teachers (For Trial Implementation)
View of difference, view of equality Understand needs and strategies	Respect individual difference, and treat every child equally. Actively understand and meet the different needs conducive to children's physical and mental development, and grasp the characteristics of physical and mental development of children with special needs as well as educational strategies and methods for them.	Respect individual difference, and treat every pupil equally. Actively understand and meet the different needs conducive to the physical and mental development of pupils, and grasp the physical and mental development characteristics and law of pupils of different ages and with special needs.	Respect individual difference, and treat every secondary school student equally. Actively understand and meet the different needs of secondary school students.
Provide suitable education for every student	—	Respect the laws of education and physical and mental development of pupils, and provide suitable education for every pupil.	Respect the laws of education and physical and mental development of secondary school students, and provide suitable education for every secondary school student.
Cooperation	In the spirit of teamwork, cooperate and communicate with colleagues, and maintain effective communication with students' parents.	In the spirit of teamwork, cooperate and communicate with colleagues, and maintain effective communication with students' parents.	In the spirit of teamwork, cooperate and communicate with colleagues, and maintain effective communication with students' parents.
Individualized instructional plan	—	Formulate reasonable individualized and collective educational and teaching plans for pupils.	—

Source: Notice of the Ministry of Education on Issuance of the "Professional Standards for Preschool Teachers (For Trial Implementation)," the "Professional Standards for Primary School Teachers (For Trial Implementation)," and the "Professional Standards for Secondary School Teachers (For Trial Implementation)" www.moe.gov.cn/srcsite/A10/s6991/201209/t20120913_145603.html.

value covers six areas. First, advocate the concept of inclusive education. It is firmly believed that inclusive education is the fundamental guarantee for the realization of equal educational opportunities and human rights. Second, adhere to the principle of equal access to education. A truly inclusive education should be democratic and fair to all students. Third, promote individual morality and values. Values and morality are the embodiment of the basic quality of an individual, determining a teacher's behavior. Fourth, correct the attitude toward the diversity of learners. In an inclusive classroom, the coexistence of students with different types of disabilities is a reflection of the diversity of learners. Students with disabilities are also educational resources and wealth, and teachers should learn to treat different students from a professional perspective, and treat everyone equally. Fifth, attach importance to the natural development of students' personality and nature. Teachers should teach students according to their aptitude and adopt appropriate teaching methods for students with different characteristics, and have certain expectations of learning achievements for disabled students, just like that for typically developing students. Sixth, lifelong learning is a personal responsibility. Teachers should take the current inclusive education work as the basis for further learning and development, realize the importance of lifelong learning, and constantly promote personal professional development. The items under the dimension of professional knowledge are put forward based on the knowledge needed in the process of inclusive education, paying particular attention to the practical guidance knowledge of inclusive education. There are many items under the dimension of professional ability that reflect the high requirements for teachers' professional ability. Two kinds of professional ability are highlighted. One is cooperative teaching ability. The appropriate application of cooperative teaching can help teachers better integrate disabled students into the classroom, and promote the development of individual cooperative ability. The other is differentiated teaching ability. Differentiated teaching can ensure that students with different characteristics (including students with disabilities) are provided with targeted learning opportunities in inclusive settings.

Analysis of Composition of and Connotations for Competence of Teachers in Inclusive Education in China

The teachers' concept of (or attitude toward) inclusive education refers to the understanding of inclusive education and teachers' thinking and attitude toward various elements in education and teaching in inclusive settings. The concept not only directly affects the teaching behavior of teachers, but also imposes indirect influence on the nature and quality of future education. Teachers' views about inclusive education play a decisive role in its implementation. Some people even think that it is the key to the success of inclusive education.[13] In terms of concept, teachers should recognize the idea of inclusive education, that is, humans' pursuit of freedom and equal human rights, "emphasize participation, reject exclusion," and accept the value and significance of inclusive education. Moreover, teachers should hold the attitude of sincere acceptance, respect each child's giftedness and needs, accept the differences and diversity of students, and establish non-utilitarian, equal, and positive educational values, a democratic opportunity view, a process view, a student evaluation view, a cooperative teaching view, and so on.[14]

Teachers should have the knowledge and skills related to inclusive education, which is the core of implementing inclusive education and ensuring the smooth start of education and teaching. With regard to knowledge, teachers should master the knowledge related to inclusive education, including: the development history and trends of inclusive education, relevant laws and regulations, the definition, classification, and physical and mental characteristics of special needs children, the learning characteristics and instructional strategies of special needs children, the behavior management of special needs children, and early detection and diagnosis of special needs children. It is even proposed that teachers of a particular class should at least have the basic knowledge related to the special needs children in the class. With regard to ability, teachers should have the ability to communicate with special needs children, for example using sign language and braille, the ability to evaluate special needs children, the ability to develop and implement individualized education plans, the ability in differentiated teaching, the ability to adjust curriculum, the ability to cooperate with parents, colleagues, and professionals, the ability to implement cooperative teaching, and the ability in environment establishment.

Some researchers have determined the core items of teacher competence in inclusive education in China through making content analysis, comparing teachers' professional standards, and consulting with front-line teachers and special education teachers in colleges and universities for confirmation. There are three items in the dimension of knowledge: "definition, classification, and physical and mental characteristics of children with disabilities," "learning and behavioral characteristics of children with disabilities," and "laws and policies related to special education." There are eight items in the dimension of professional skills: "differentiated teaching ability," "multielement," "objective identification and evaluation ability," "communication and exchange ability," "curriculum adjustment ability," "ability in cooperating with parents, colleagues and professionals," "ability in implementation of cooperative teaching," "ability in creation of harmonious environment," and "self-development and reflection ability." There are two items in the dimension of attitude: "recognizing the value and significance of inclusive education" and "accepting the differences and diversity of students."[15]

Characteristics of the Composition of and Connotations for the Competence of Teachers in Inclusive Education

Comprehensive Regulations on Competence of Teachers in Inclusive Education

After analyzing foreign research on the competence in inclusive education that teachers should possess, as well as teachers' professional standards, we found that the requirements for the competence of teachers in inclusive education are not only what researchers expect, but are embodied in the professional standards of teachers, and distributed in various aspects of professional standards. For example, in the InTASC standards, there are five relevant items in "performances" and "dispositions" respectively, and six items in "knowledge." Some studies analyzed the research on teacher competence in inclusive education in the US and summed up the characteristics reflected in the dimensions of professional value, professional knowledge, and professional ability:[16] strengthening the theoretical leading role of professional value; emphasizing the essence of "inclusion," and attaching importance to practical knowledge; and highlighting the important core status of professional ability. There are six items in the dimension of professional value and professional knowledge respectively, and nine items in the dimension of professional ability. Another example is the *Key Principles for Promoting Quality in Inclusive Education: Recommendations for Practice* issued by the European Agency for Development in Special Needs Education in 2010, which requires that teachers should be equipped with the skills, knowledge, and understanding that will give them the confidence to deal effectively with a range of learner needs, and they should also value and show commitment to meeting a broad range of outcomes and maintain high expectations for all learners. There are also regulations and requirements in the dimensions of professional knowledge and professional ability.

"Disability" Is Incorporated into Concept of Diversity and Pluralism

In the US, Europe, and other countries, the object of inclusive education not only refers to disabled children, exceptional children, and other special needs children, but also includes a large number of vulnerable children who are very different from mainstream society in terms of race, language, family, and social background. According to the InTASC standards, "diverse learners are those who, because of gender, language, cultural background, differing ability levels, disabilities, learning approaches, and/or socioeconomic status, may have academic needs that require varied instructional strategies to ensure their learning," and "diversity is inclusive of individual differences (e.g., personality, interests, learning modalities, and life experiences), and group differences (e.g., race, ethnicity, ability, gender identity, gender expression, sexual orientation, nationality, language, religion, political affiliation, and socio-economic background)." The *Common European Principles for Teacher Competences and Qualifications* states that teachers should be able to meet the individual needs of different learners in an inclusive manner and need to understand their social, cultural, and historical context.[17] In this way, "disability," like race, language, family background, and other characteristics, belongs to the category of "diversity and pluralism," which is something that every teacher should actively and naturally accept and pay attention to, rather than treat it as an abnormal state. Therefore, the development of inclusive education is an important boon for realization of educational equality for all.

84   *Structural Analysis of the Competence of Teachers*

"Supplementary" Requirements of "General Education Competence and Special Education Competence" for Chinese Teachers

At the beginning of the LRC program, the cultivation of teachers' inclusive education competence was advocated in relevant policies. Then, relevant policy documents were successively issued to emphasize the supplementing of basic knowledge and skills of special education for teachers from the perspectives of teacher preparation and professional development, in order to meet the challenges to education and teaching after students with disabilities enter the class.

Some researchers believe that implementation of inclusive education requires teachers to develop inclusive attitudes, values, and expectations, and establish a democratic view of education. At the present stage, teachers should first have the knowledge, skills, and dispositions to educate special needs children.[18] Some studies hold that inclusive education requires teachers to have a brand new educational concept, as well as knowledge and ability of both general education and special education.[19] Other researchers analyzed the inclusive education competence that teachers should possess from four dimensions—knowledge, skills, ability, and attitude; or from the dimensions of professional concept, knowledge, and ability; or from the dimensions of knowledge, skills, and attitude. Some researchers discuss the structure of the overall quality that teachers should have from the perspective of inclusive education, and put forward four key systems: professional concept, professional intelligence, professional feelings, and professional norms.[20]

The above "supplementary" requirements of "general education competence and special education competence" for teachers are basically consistent with the most common practice in foreign countries at the beginning of the implementation of inclusive education: to train teachers of regular schools in basic aspects of special education. It is also consistent with the development of the LRC program in China, because the main objects of the Chinese LRC program are various kinds of disabled children. Therefore, the supplementing of teachers' special education competence was highlighted in both the formulation of and research into relevant policies in China.

However, the development of inclusive education has long gone beyond the practice of "supplementing" the competence of teachers with some basic knowledge and skills in special education. With the increasing influence of international inclusive education, China's LRC program is no longer simply to place disabled children in regular schools, but has begun to seek quality improvement toward the essence of inclusive education. The *Program for Promoting Special Education (2014–2016)* required promoting inclusive education in an all-round way so that every disabled child can gain access to appropriate education. The *Regulations on Education for Individuals with Disabilities* revised in 2017 took the promotion of inclusive education as an important legislative principle, confirming the concept and principle of inclusive education for the first time at the legal level. Inclusive education is not only aimed at children with disabilities, but also focuses on and understands the difficulties faced by all children, especially those who are vulnerable, marginalized, and excluded from education. Teachers' assistance should be given not only to disabled children in the traditional special education sector, but also to the large numbers of children with learning, behavioral, and emotional difficulties who are commonplace in regular schools. Therefore, the core characteristic of a teacher is to correctly recognize and respect differences among students, truly embrace all children, and adopt effective educational strategies to help students in difficulties remove obstacles and meet their personalized learning needs, so as to ensure that all children can receive high-quality education.

In understanding Chinese the competence of teachers in inclusive education, the following breakthroughs should be made.

First, it is to break the biased understanding that the competence of teachers in inclusive education means competence in special education, and to deepen and enrich the composition of and connotations for the competence of teachers in inclusive education. The inclusive education competence of teachers is not unchanged, but is gradually deepened and enriched with the progress of human society and people's requirements for better quality of education. Therefore, the competence of teachers in inclusive education has dynamic attributes and characteristics. Considerations should be given to the development and changes in two aspects. First, China's LRC program is becoming increasingly inclusive, and making its way onto the stage of inclusive education. Second, the practical features of the LRC program in China are far apart from the inclusive education in developed countries such as the US, and they even vary greatly in different regions of China. Obviously, in understanding the competence of teachers in inclusive education, we can neither copy that in developed countries, nor stick to the research results of a certain period of time. We should, taking into account the latest development of international inclusive education and the actual development of inclusive education in China, deepen and enrich the competence of teachers in inclusive education. In particular, existing research in China has mostly constructed the model of teacher competence in inclusive education through theoretical analysis, logic deduction, foreign and domestic comparison, and reference to the advanced ideas of foreign countries. Future research needs to be based on the theories of teachers' professional development and inclusive education as well as the reality of China's LRC program, follow the scale compilation standards, have both top-down theoretical construction and bottom-up practice testing, and systematically construct the model of teacher competence in inclusive education so as to make it reasonable and well-founded. Based on research, scientific answers should be given to what ideas, attitudes, ethics, beliefs, and morals should be included in the competence of teachers in inclusive education, and what kind of knowledge and ability should be possessed to break through the limitation of "special education knowledge and ability." For example, "differentiated teaching ability," a requirement in common competence, is considered by domestic and foreign researchers as

86   *Structural Analysis of the Competence of Teachers*

one of the essential skills for the implementation of inclusive education.[21,22] However, it is necessary to further probe into whether teachers' differentiated teaching ability is the same as the original differentiated teaching ability after special needs children enter regular classes. Fortunately, some domestic researchers have analyzed the basic elements of differentiated teaching ability, and the elements of differentiated teaching ability specifically required by the LRC program, and thus made clear the structure of differentiated teaching ability for the LRC program.[23] That teachers have the ability to cooperate with professionals in teaching design, curriculum planning, and learning is also a requirement of the US and other developed countries for teachers to implement inclusive education.[24] However, China's supportive system for the LRC program is far less satisfactory than that of developed countries, and regular schools lack professional support from special education teachers, relevant service providers, and linguistic experts. How should "cooperative ability" be reflected in the competence of teachers in inclusive education? It is necessary to dig deep and enrich the inclusive education competence that teachers should have.

Second, it is necessary to clarify in the professional standards of teachers that the competence of teachers in inclusive education is an integral part of their professional competence. The experience of countries that have taken the lead in implementing inclusive education tells us that it is an irresistible trend to reflect the characteristics and requirements of inclusive education in the professional standards of teachers, which is not only conducive to ensuring that all beginning teachers have the basic awareness and ability of inclusive education, but also can promote the formation of a teacher education system with the purpose of training competent teachers for inclusive education. In the InTASC standards of the US, specific requirements on teachers in the education of special needs students are clearly stipulated, so that teachers can clearly know their roles and responsibilities in inclusive education. For example, while pointing out that teachers are required to cooperate with other professionals in teaching, the standards further specify the types of professionals, including special educators, relevant service providers, language learning specialists, librarians, and so on. For another example, in terms of teaching plan, the standards clearly point out specific content that teachers need to consider in differentiated teaching, that is, how to choose appropriate teaching strategies, what kind of adjustments to make, and what kind of resources and textbooks to choose. In the professional standards of teachers in China, the demand for the competence of teachers in inclusive education has already appeared, but there is a huge gap with the provisions of the above-mentioned countries in terms of the scope, quantity, and specific degree of the items involved in the competence in inclusive education. To this end, we should make it clear in the professional standards of teachers that meeting the normal and special learning needs of all students is the legal duty of teachers, and make specific provisions on the basic theory, knowledge, and ability of inclusive education that teachers should have. In other words, relevant provisions on the inclusive education competence of teachers should be fully reflected in three dimensions: professional concept and ethics, professional knowledge, and professional ability.

Third, it is critical to strengthen the development of the teaching force for inclusive education, and clarify the inclusive education competence of teachers at different levels. In the concrete practice of inclusive education, due to the complexity and diversity of difficulties encountered by students, the support required will involve different professional fields and professional levels. In this respect, the experience of countries that have implemented inclusive education is mostly to build a pyramid-shaped inclusive teacher system.[25] At the bottom of the pyramid are the largest number of teachers with the basic skills of inclusive education, and they refer to all the teachers of every school. The middle of the pyramid consists of teachers who have mastered the advanced skills of inclusive education, and only a small number of teachers in each school qualify. At the top of the pyramid are the smallest number of experts with more specialized inclusive education skills, often shared not by each school but by several schools. According to the concept put forward by Chinese researchers, LRC program teachers are not a single type of teachers, but a group and a collection of multi-level professionals with different professional backgrounds.[26] The teachers of inclusive education in China also form a multi-level structure. One part includes subject teachers who undertake inclusive education teaching in regular schools. Due to the admission of special needs children, subject teachers should take into account all the children in the inclusive class in their daily work. The second part comprises resource teachers who provide multi-disciplinary and multi-major special education and guidance for special needs children in inclusive classes as well as training for other teachers. The third part consists of itinerant tutors from special education schools or special education resource centers with broader knowledge, skills, and rich experience in inclusive education; they are responsible for supervision over inclusive education work and teacher training in the schools in a designated area. They intervene in school education when necessary, provide professional assessment and intervention for children with difficulties, and offer professional guidance and consultation to teachers. There is no doubt that they all need to have ability in both general education and special education.[27] But their different identities also determine their different tasks and scopes. It also requires the difference between their professional qualities, especially the stratification of inclusive education competence. According to the practical work experience of some researchers,[28] resource teachers need to love inclusive education, be career-minded and proficient in general education, have received special education training, have practical experience in special education, and be familiar with the work of resource rooms. In terms of professional ability, it is the basic skill of resource teachers to make individualized education plan for students with special needs. The development, application, and integration of resources are the basic content of resource teachers' work, including the integration of both human resources and material resources. For example, itinerant tutors should be divided into

88   *Structural Analysis of the Competence of Teachers*

professional teachers for hearing-impaired, visually impaired, and mentally impaired children respectively, rehabilitation trainers, and psychotherapists according to their professional background and division of tasks. They should provide higher-level professional support and rehabilitation training for special needs children, and at the same time give guidance and consultation services to other teachers. In view of this, it is necessary to build a multi-level inclusive education teaching force by category.

Construction of Structural Model of Competence of Teachers in Inclusive Education

The professional competence of LRC program teachers mentioned in this section refers to regular school teachers' competence for LRC practice, which is a part of their overall professional competence. It is equivalent to the inclusive education competence of LRC program teachers. For the construction of the structural model of the competence of teachers in inclusive education, top-down theoretical construction is needed, that is, a conceptual framework of the theoretical model of the competence of teachers in inclusive education should be formed through literature analysis and based on relevant theories. Qualitative interviews with LRC program teachers should be conducted in their schools to explore the elements of the competence of teachers in inclusive education. Meanwhile, a bottom-up practice test is needed to test the constructed theoretical model using a quantitative research method, so as to develop an evaluation tool of the competence of teachers in inclusive education with high reliability and validity. By combining qualitative research with quantitative research and obtaining multiple data sources through various methods, the composition of competence in inclusive education can be comprehensively and truly reflected, the model of the competence of teachers in inclusive education can be systematically constructed, and a standardized and scientific evaluation tool of the competence of teachers in inclusive education can be worked out.

Research Framework and Approach

Theoretical Sources Analysis of Composition of Competence of Teachers in Inclusive Education

A competency model contains all the competency characteristics required to complete a specific task on a specific position. Teacher competency refers to the professional knowledge, skills, and values that teachers have for implementation of successful teaching.

Mainly there are two kinds of theoretical model of competency: the iceberg model and the onion model.[29] The iceberg model of competency involves five types of competency: motives, traits, self-concept characteristics, knowledge, and skills. Knowledge refers to the information possessed by an individual in a specific field, the ability to discover information, and whether he can guide his behavior with knowledge. Skills mean the ability to perform specific physical or mental tasks. Self-concept refers to an individual's attitude, values, or self-image. Traits refer to an individual's physiological characteristics and consistent response to a situation or information. Motives refer to the intrinsic motivation of an individual's behavior. According to the iceberg model, knowledge and skills are visible, most likely to change; motives and traits are more hidden, deeper in the personality structure, not easily accessible; and self-concept is somewhere in between. The onion model is evolved on the basis of the iceberg model, which is another angle to explain the iceberg model. It is a structure that encapsulates competency characteristics from the inside out. The core is individual potential characteristics such as motives and traits; the outer layer is self-concept, attitude, and values; and the outmost layer is knowledge and skills. Knowledge and skills are easy to develop and evaluate, while it is hardest to develop core characteristics.

When using the theoretical model of competency to guide the construction of the model of the competence of teachers in inclusive education, we not only need to pay attention to inclusive education knowledge and skills, but also should explore in-depth characteristics such as attitudes and values that will not be changed by external influences but play a key role in individual behavior and performance.

Conceptual Framework of Components of Competence of Teachers in Inclusive Education

The Chinese professional standards for teachers put forward requirements for teacher quality from three dimensions: professional concept and teacher's ethics, professional knowledge, and professional ability. The *InTASC Model Core Teaching Standards* of the US contain 10 standards in four fields, each of which has requirements in performances, knowledge, and dispositions. The European profile of inclusive teachers presents four core values along with the associated areas of teacher competence that are made up of three elements: attitudes, knowledge, and skills. When Chinese researchers probe into the composition of the competence of teachers in inclusive education, they either discuss it from the theoretical level, or carry out empirical research. Some studies analyze the professional quality and existing problems of LRC program teachers from the perspectives of professional concept, professional knowledge, and professional ability.[30] Some researchers track, observe and record the educational and teaching activities of LRC program teachers, and summarize 33 indicators of these teachers from four aspects: knowledge, skills, ability, and attitude.[31] Although there are some differences in the understanding of the composition of the competence of teachers in inclusive education, most researchers focus on teachers' professional concept (or attitude) and quality, professional knowledge, and professional ability. Therefore, a conceptual framework showing the composition of the competence of teachers

90 *Structural Analysis of the Competence of Teachers*

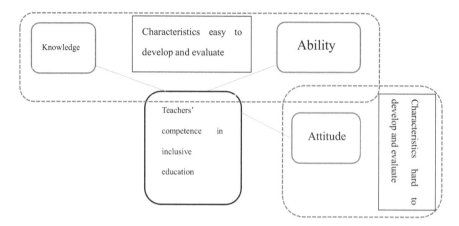

Figure 3.1 Conceptual Framework of Competence of Teachers in Inclusive Education.

in inclusive education is formed, covering attitude, knowledge, and ability, as shown in Figure 3.1.

Research Approach

Focusing on LRC program teachers, this research follows the scale compilation standard, and through top-down theoretical construction and bottom-up practice testing, systematically constructs a model of the competence of teachers in inclusive education. Based on the above research objective, the research approach is shown in Figure 3.2.

Preliminary Qualitative Research Stage—Preparation of Scale to Evaluate Competence of Teachers in Inclusive Education

Purpose, Method, and Data Analysis Technique of Research

In this research, qualitative data were obtained by interview survey to make in-depth exploration of LRC program teachers' competence in inclusive education, and prepare a scale to evaluate their competence in inclusive education (to construct a theoretical model of the competence of teachers in inclusive education).

Interview survey is a social investigation method in which visitors collect survey data and information by talking with interviewees in a planned way.[32] This research adopts brainstorming group interviews and semi-structured individual interviews.

Technically, the analysis of interview data is based on Kvale's exposition of the objectivity of interview survey.[33] To avoid personal bias and form inter-subjective knowledge, we worked simultaneously and cooperatively through

Structural Analysis of the Competence of Teachers 91

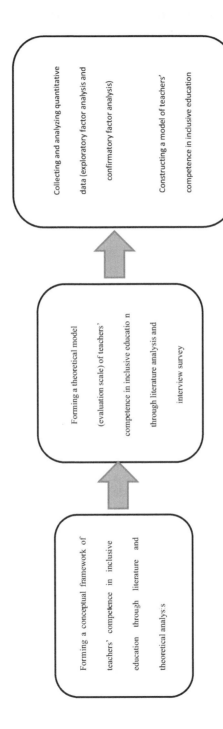

Figure 3.2 Research Approach.

92 *Structural Analysis of the Competence of Teachers*

mutual discussion, recursive negotiation, mutual comment, and exchange verification. This approach helps to generate reliable information about the interview data. Since these data have been systematically cross-verified, avoiding the influence of individual bias, it is possible to achieve inter-subject verifiability and repeatability as much as possible.

Research Process

We chose primary and junior middle schools in Beijing to explore the professional quality of LRC program teachers. In order to achieve this goal, group interview and individual interview were conducted respectively. The group interviews were arranged in a more natural dialogue environment (in the school). Through discussion and brainstorming, various viewpoints on the required professional competence were obtained from LRC program teachers. A thematic analysis was carried out on these data (that is, viewpoints), and a conceptual framework of the thematic analysis was derived from the aforementioned literature analysis. The key words "attitude," "knowledge," and "skills" repeatedly appeared in the process of group interviews. Interestingly, group interviewees also mentioned "actively getting support." This key phrase prompted us to conduct further individual interviews focusing on "actively getting support" (similar to "agency") so as to explore the professional competence of LRC program teachers.

First, we conducted two one-hour group interviews. The first group interview was made in a primary school in Chaoyang District with five LRC program teachers. The second group interview was conducted in a junior middle school in Haidian District with 10 LRC program teachers. Both schools are research cooperators for the researchers. The primary school in Chaoyang District is a demonstration school of LRC practice, while the junior middle school in Haidian District is just a regular school with an LRC program. Based on gender and teaching experience, we asked the leaders of the two schools to recommend 12 teachers to participate in the interviews. The interviewees were teachers who accepted our invitation and were willing to receive the interviews. The demographic characteristics of the interviewees are shown in Table 3.2. Based on the differences shown by the interviewees in LRC practice, we attempted to have an in-depth understanding of the interviewees' different views on competence in inclusive education. In other words, we tried to select the teachers with strong differences among the samples, so as to obtain the maximum variation in the samples.

Second, we conducted one-hour individual interviews. Invitations for individual interviews were sent to teachers who had participated in the group interviews. Three teachers accepted the invitation, two from the school in Chaoyang District and one from the school in Haidian District. Among the two teachers from Chaoyang District, one has rich experience in LRC practice, while the other has just average experience in this regard. The teacher from Haidian District has relatively little experience in LRC practice. In

Table 3.2 Demographic Characteristics of Interviewees

District	Number of participants	Number of years teaching			Gender	
		Less than 3 years	5–10 years	More than 15 years	Female	Male
Chaoyang	5	2	1	2	4	1
Haidian	10	5	3	2	7	3

order to further enrich the data, we also interviewed two administrators from Haidian District and former Xuanwu District respectively. The administrator from Haidian District has witnessed the success of the LRC program in many schools in the district, while the one from former Xuanwu District has only begun to pay attention to LRC program in recent years.

Research Results

In the group interviews, the interviewees mainly discussed what are the key professional qualities of LRC program teachers. And this content is highly consistent with our research topic: "What are the core professional qualities of LRC program teachers?" Inspired by the conceptual framework of the existing literature, we analyze and present the interview data in a thematic manner. First, we briefly analyze the topics of attitude, knowledge, and skills, as these are well covered in the existing literature. We focus on the discussion of the fourth topic, which is the teachers' ability to actively get support, namely teacher agency. We believe that this could be an important complement to the identified professional qualities of LRC program teachers.

POSITIVE ATTITUDE

The positive attitude toward LRC students can be clearly seen from the interview data. All interviewees believe that positive attitude is a significant professional quality of LRC program teachers. In the group interview, when faced with the question of "what is important to a competent LRC program teacher," one teacher gave the following answer:

> I think the most important thing is to be kind to students with special needs. Personally, I will include special needs students in our class activities instead of excluding or ignoring them. They have the same right to education as typically developing students. I will also ask my students to treat them kindly and not discriminate against them.

In the group interview, this view was recognized by other interviewees. "Don't give up on anyone," one of the interviewees added. Another interviewee

94 *Structural Analysis of the Competence of Teachers*

concluded: "No matter what the teachers do in an inclusive classroom, they should take into account the special needs of the students." According to the framework put forward by Eagly and Chaiken, the above positive feelings for special needs students and strong tendency of the teachers to help the students can be coded as "feelings," or the "emotional aspect" of teachers' attitudes, or as "behavioral tendency" or "behavioral aspect" of teachers' attitudes.[34] The interviewees also mentioned the positive attitude and strong belief in the LRC program. They believe that the LRC program can "boost students' confidence" and "create a friendly learning environment and an inclusive community for students with intellectual, hearing, and physical disabilities." To refer again to the framework of Eagly and Chaiken, the above description of LRC program teachers can be coded as "beliefs," or the "cognitive aspect" of teachers' attitudes.[35]

NECESSARY KNOWLEDGE

In addition to positive attitude, many interviewees also mentioned the importance of necessary knowledge, including "understanding the theory of special education," "grasping the latest national policies and local regulations concerning inclusive education," "understanding the psychological, physical and educational needs of every child," and "knowing how to carry out and evaluate LRC practice." Based on Western literature, the above description is consistent with the knowledge dimension of LRC program teachers.[36,37]

KEY SKILLS

Besides positive attitude and necessary knowledge, the interviewees also touched on the various skills needed for LRC practice. In the group interview, an experienced teacher commented:

> Teachers need to teach both special and regular students in the class. To meet different needs of the students, teachers' instructional design needs to be more strategic. Organization of group activities in the classroom and beyond also requires skills. We need to think about how to engage special needs students in learning and cultural activities, and should also consider how to get other students to genuinely accept special needs students.

According to Fisher and Bocala, these skills can be coded as "the ability to meet differences, identify students' learning characteristics, and adjust, differentiate, and modify teaching methods."[38,39] When asked "what skills will you need to develop in the future," a beginning teacher said:

> I find it very challenging to teach special needs students in the class. One of the students is very emotional. She would burst into tears in class. At first she scared me and I didn't know what to do. I think this is an absolutely

important skill for me and for every LRC program teacher. We need to know how to respond appropriately to students' emotional problems.

In accordance with Idol's classification, the above description can be coded as "student norms and class management."[40] Other important skills cited by teachers in group interviews include "working with the community on extra-curricular activities," "working with resource teachers and mental health teachers to promote student development," and "communicating with parents about the past and current situation of special needs students." According to the available literature, these skills can be coded as "cooperative skills."[41,42]

ABILITY TO ACTIVELY GET SUPPORT

Interestingly, many interviewees mentioned the importance of seeking resources in the group interviews. This is the key focus of our analysis. Let us give consideration to the following examples:

Every teacher will encounter difficulties and problems in LRC practice. This prompts us to actively seek support, for example, from experts, leaders, and resource teachers. We have formed a discussion group for the LRC program to hold regular discussions. We discuss the problems and needs we encounter. If we can't solve the problems on our own, we'll take LRC program teacher training courses, or seek help from special education center.

When asked further about seeking support, two teachers added:

I agree with that. LRC program teachers need all kinds of support. We need to do our best to seek support from leaders, students' parents, and community. The ability of teachers to get support is critical.

Teachers' sense of responsibility plays an important role in LRC practice. What I mean is that we need to actively carry out the LRC program. When we can't solve a problem, we have to think hard, work hard to seek assistance.

The above interviews seem to indicate that it is important to seek support and assistance in a positive way and from a variety of sources. In addition, these interviews are consistent with Western literature and practice. The InTASC required teachers to gain access to resources to support special needs students' learning.[43] Similarly, Tomlinson holds that seeking a variety of different material resources is a necessary skill for teachers to cope with students' special needs.[44] In five of the nine districts surveyed by Bocala et al., teachers are required to seek support and resources within schools and to work with other professionals, family members, and community members with various backgrounds, to help and serve special needs students.[45] Therefore, as a required skill, seeking support is nothing new. In our data, it is striking that

96 *Structural Analysis of the Competence of Teachers*

in group interviews seeking support was repeatedly mentioned. This shows that seeking support is a key skill in China. With this in mind, we set out to conduct individual interviews to explore teachers' understanding of seeking support.

When asked if it is important to actively seek support, all interviewees responded in an unequivocal affirmative. For example, the administrator of the education department in Xuanwu District emphasized the importance of seeking support: "It is particularly important that in-service teachers seek advice and resources to support LRC practice. 'To do' and 'to wait' yield completely different results. If teachers expect better results, they can't wait for help. Instead, they have to be very active in seeking support." This description shows that seeking support requires active effort and personal input. There are individual differences in the degree of effort and commitment, which produce completely different results in LRC practice.

When asked the question of how you understand the ability to seek support compared to other professional competencies, interviewees pointed out that they lacked the ability to seek support, and believed that the ability to seek support is more important than attitude, knowledge, and skills. For example, one primary school teacher described it this way:

> Given the prevailing conditions, I think the ability to seek support is more important than attitude, knowledge, and skills. For example, our local education department organizes regular training for LRC program teachers. The trainers are experts in this field who share with us the background knowledge, research progress, and policy guidelines of the LRC program. They also tell us how to teach in the classroom. We are all interested in the training. However, there are limited opportunities and time to communicate with experts. In most cases, we have to do it ourselves. Teachers need motivation to learn and put it into practice. We have to discover information for ourselves, such as how to get knowledge and support.

This teacher seemed to place more emphasis on individual efforts to seek support.

When the interviewees were asked to provide cases in which they sought support, they told us of their efforts in seeking various resources to help special needs students. An experienced junior middle school teacher provided a case in point:

> There are different kinds of support. Sometimes, the support comes from our school, but more often it depends on ourselves. For example, our school is very supportive of the development of school-based textbooks for special needs students. We've been doing this for years. I am responsible for the compilation of Chinese textbooks. The school only provides policy support, so I have to seek substantive support. I have to study on my own, looking for online resources and reading a lot of literature and materials.

When asked about the reasons behind the important role of seeking support in LRC practice, an administrator from the education department of Haidian District explained:

> When it comes to the LRC program, many schools lack resources and teachers. Not all schools have resource rooms and resource teachers. In this context, teachers must rely on their subjectivity and agency to meet the special needs of students. Teachers must keep in mind that it is important to seek support and develop the ability to seek support.

This description is consistent with the view of the administrator from former Xuanwu District education department:

> Right now, the supportive system is not sound. Few resources are available. Teachers must act as both leader and master of the LRC program. For example, when you're hungry, you need to go out and forage instead of waiting for food. When food is scarce, no one will provide food. You have to find something to eat!

Echoing the views of the administrators, the teachers revealed that support from external systems is "inadequate," "limited," and "minimal." These interviews fully reflect the imperfection of the supportive system for the LRC program in China at present, helping us understand the necessity for seeking support against such a background. When the support available is limited, teachers need to seek it out. "Teacher agency" refers to a kind of positive and dynamic function, which is manifested as teachers plan, initiate, and carry out conscious actions to promote LRC practice. This agency requires teachers, under the guidance of their deeply rooted teaching epistemology, to take control of his or her professional practice.[46] It also requires teachers to have the ability to critically shape their own responses to the context of problems.[47] Our data suggest that agency is embodied in the action and initiation of the LRC program. More specifically, agency is the ability of LRC program teachers independently to seek support under a specific social structure and organizational framework, and this ability is not subject to a specific social structure and organizational framework.

According to Eagly and Chaiken, agency is a behavioral tendency, and therefore can be defined as the "behavioral aspect" of attitudes.[48] At the same time, as described in Western literature, the agency to seek support can be regarded as a necessary skill.[49,50,51] Given the lack of support for the LRC program in China, it is not surprising that the teachers' ability (agency) to seek support emerged as an important topic in our interview. Therefore, we assume that teachers' ability to seek and obtain support is the fourth dimension of teachers' professional competence.

In the preliminary qualitative research, we found that the four dimensions of the competence of teachers in inclusive education, namely attitude, knowledge, skills, and ability to get support, form a complex structural model. Taking

98 *Structural Analysis of the Competence of Teachers*

them as the basic structural dimensions of the competence of teachers in inclusive education, opinions were screened from the interview data and, combined with existing literature analysis results and related items, a scale for the evaluation of the competence of teachers in inclusive education was prepared as shown in Table 3.3. It is a five-point Likert scale, ranging from 1 (strongly disagree), 2 (disagree), 3 (neutral), 4 (agree) to 5 (strongly agree).

To verify this hypothetical model, we carried out the following research.

Table 3.3 Prediction Scale for Inclusive Education Competence of Teachers (n=34)

Dimension	Item description
Professional attitude	1.All the disabled students should receive education equally as typically developing students. 2.The LRC program makes disabled students more confident. 3.I have confidence in teaching the disabled students in my class well. 4.The LRC program has a positive effect on the social communication ability of disabled students. 5.The LRC program is conducive to reducing social discrimination against the disabled. 6.Disabled students can make academic progress in regular class. 7. The LRC program makes teachers pay more attention to individual differences among students. 8.The LRC program is conducive to the overall reform and quality improvement of the school.
Professional knowledge	9.I am familiar with the national policies and regulations on LRC program. 10.I know the basic principles and methods of educating disabled students. 11.I'm acquainted with the policies and measures such as the rules and management system for the LRC program formulated by the local administrative department. 12.I understand the psychological and behavioral characteristics of my disabled students. 13.I know the educational evaluation methods for my disabled students. 14.I am familiar with the practical measures for the LRC program. 15.I understand the theory of inclusive education.
Professional skills	16.Ordinary students and disabled students can help and learn from each other in the class. 17.I can carry out stratified teaching for disabled students in my class. 18.I can cooperate with other teachers or professionals in teaching students with disabilities. 19.I can give flexible assignments and use evaluation methods for disabled students. 20.I can adjust the teaching objectives and requirements according to the characteristics of disabled students. 21.I can use group discussion and cooperative learning methods to help disabled students.

Structural Analysis of the Competence of Teachers 99

Table 3.3 (Continued)

Dimension	Item description
	22. I can provide individualized tutoring service to meet the learning needs of disabled students.
	23. I can conduct effective behavioral management over disabled students.
	24. I can harmonize the relationship between ordinary and disabled students.
	25. I can help disabled students through effective cooperation with their parents.
	26. I can cooperate effectively with community personnel to help disabled students.
Ability to get support	27. I can take the initiative to get assistance from parents of disabled students to educate their children.
	28. I can obtain support from administrators at all levels for implementation of the LRC program.
	29. I can take the initiative to seek guidance and help from special school teachers.
	30. I'm able to establish contacts with relevant professionals and obtain their guidance and services (such as medical treatment, speech correction, and so on).
	31. I can collect and utilize a variety of teaching and learning materials to help disabled students.
	32. I can make use of resource rooms to help disabled students.
	33. I'm able to mobilize community resources to support my teaching.
	34. I have access to relevant equipment to support my teaching.

Exploration and Verification of Composition of Competence of Teachers in Inclusive Education

According to this qualitative study, we constructed a four-dimension model, and compiled related items. Among the four dimensions, professional attitude shows how teachers view the impact of the LRC program on students with disabilities, professional development of teachers, schools and social development, with eight items in total. In the dimension of professional knowledge, the teachers' grasp of relevant policies and regulations, theoretical knowledge, and practical knowledge related to LRC practice is investigated with seven items. In the dimension of professional skills, the specific performance of LRC program teachers in setting teaching objectives, implementing teaching content, and evaluating teaching effects according to the characteristics of disabled students is investigated with a total of 11 items. In the dimension of the ability to get support, the ability of LRC program teachers to seek and obtain support is examined with eight items.

100 *Structural Analysis of the Competence of Teachers*

Objective, Respondents, and Methods of Research

The scale to evaluate the competence of teachers in inclusive education was verified for the construction of a structural model of teacher competence in inclusive education.

A large sample survey was used to obtain quantitative research data from the completed scale for evaluation of the competence of teachers in inclusive education. SPSS20.0 and Mplus6 were used for data processing. The main statistical methods included factor analysis and reliability analysis.

A total of 1,761 primary and secondary school teachers who had undertaken the LRC program were selected in a convenient sampling method in various districts of Beijing. In the scale distribution and collection, one way was to distribute, fill in, and collect the scale sheets in the in-service training class of the teachers. The other way was to contact the relevant responsible person of each district to assist in sending out and collecting the scale sheets. Among the 1,761 LRC program teachers, 78 were from Chaoyang District, 165 from Dongcheng District, 192 from Fangshan District, 271 from Haidian District, 413 from Shunyi District, 181 from Shijingshan District, and 449 from Xicheng District. Another 12 teachers did not fill in the relevant information. Before data analysis, 1,761 scale sheets were preliminarily sorted out to delete extreme data. Firstly, 38 scale sheets with full marks (that is, 5 points) in each item were deleted. Secondly, eight scale sheets with 10 or more missing items were excluded. When the number of missing values is less than 10, the method of linear trend at point was used to replace the missing values.[52] Thirdly, the mean total score and standard deviations of the remaining 1,715 scale sheets were calculated, and the 12 scale sheets whose total score was three standard deviations lower than the mean were excluded. After the extreme data were deleted, there remained 1,703 scale sheets, accounting for 96.7 percent of the total. Table 3.4 lists the basic information about the 1,703 respondents.

SPSS20.0 for Windows software was used to randomly divide 1,703 valid scale sheets into two groups with a proportion of about 50 percent. The homogeneity test of the two groups in 34 items did not significantly ($p>0.05$) indicate that the two groups of data have a good homogeneity. One group of sample data from 820 scale sheets was used for item analysis and exploratory factor analysis, to revise and improve the theoretical model of the scale, and to preliminarily construct a theoretical model for the scale of the professional qualities of teachers in special education schools. The other group of sample data from 883 scale sheets was used for confirmatory factor analysis and reliability analysis to verify the constructed structural model of the competence of teachers in inclusive education, that is, to determine the structure of the formal scale.

Structural Analysis of the Competence of Teachers   101

Table 3.4 Basic Information on Respondents (n=1,703)

Variable	Level	Number	Ratio
Gender	Male	263	15.4%
	Female	1,408	82.7%
	Missing ones	32	1.9%
School sector	Primary school	1,193	70.0%
	Junior middle school	510	30.0%
Title	Junior or below	565	33.2%
	Medium grade	908	53.3%
	Senior	137	8.1%
	Missing ones	93	5.5%
Educational background	Junior college education or below	131	7.7%
	Bachelor	1,506	88.5%
	Master	38	2.2%
	Missing ones	28	1.6%
Subject	Chinese, math, foreign language	1,078	63.3%
	Other subjects	550	32.3%
	Missing ones	75	4.4%
Number of years teaching LRC students	Less than 3 years	674	39.6%
	3–5 years	196	11.5%
	6–10 years	255	15.0%
	11–15 years	57	3.4%
	Over 15 years	70	4.1%
	Missing ones	451	26.5%
Total number of LRC students taught	Less than 5	1,451	85.2%
	6–10	159	9.3%
	11–15	52	3.1%
	Over 15	41	2.4%
Class tutor of LRC students or not	Yes	578	33.9%
	No	1,091	64.1%
	Missing ones	34	2.0%
Accumulated time of the LRC program training received	None	1,242	72.9%
	Less than one month	271	15.9%
	More than one month	190	11.2%

Research Results

Item Analysis

The performance indexes of the item test were obtained through item analysis, and the items meeting the requirements were selected according to the indexes to improve the effectiveness of the scale. In the item analysis of this research, five criteria were used to analyze the items, namely, critical ratio, item-total correlation, reliability testing, communalities, and factor loading.

102 *Structural Analysis of the Competence of Teachers*

CRITICAL RATIO

The scores earned by each respondent on each item were added up respectively, and the resulting sums were ranked from high to low. The total scores ranking at 27 percent in the top-down and bottom-up sequence respectively (148 points and 120 points) were used as the critical values, and the respondents were divided into high-score and low-score groups. Independent Samples T-Test was used to calculate the difference between the high-score and low-score groups in the mean of each item. Generally, the standard t statistic value of a critical ratio is set to 3.000. If the t statistic value is less than 3.000, it means that the degree of discrimination of the item is poor. The t value of each item in the scale is above 3.000, indicating that each item has a good degree of discrimination.

ITEM–TOTAL CORRELATION COEFFICIENT

The higher the item–total correlation coefficient, the higher the homogeneity between the item and the whole scale, and the closer the psychological trait or potential behavior to be measured. If the item–total correlation coefficient is not significant, or it is low (less than 0.400), it indicates that the homogeneity between the item and the whole scale is not high. In this scale, the item–total correlation coefficient is above 0.400, indicating a high homogeneity between the items and the whole scale.

RELIABILITY TESTING

Reliability testing is conducted to see the change in the reliability coefficient of the whole scale after some items are deleted. If the overall reliability coefficient of the scale is higher than the original reliability coefficient after an item is deleted, the attributes or psychological trait to be measured by this item may be different from those to be measured by other items, which means that this item is not highly homogenous with others. Therefore, this item can be deleted during item analysis. After four items in this scale (items 1, 28, 30, and 32) are deleted, the overall reliability coefficient of the scale reaches 0.953, which is higher than the original 0.952.

COMMUNALITY

Communality reveals the amount of variation that the item can explain a common trait or attribute. The higher the communality value, the greater the degree to which the psychological trait can be measured. If the communality value of the item is lower, it means that the degree of psychological trait that can be measured by the item is smaller, so it can be deleted. In the item analysis, the overall scale is set as a factor. If the communality value is lower than 0.200, it indicates that the relationship between the item and the common factor is

Structural Analysis of the Competence of Teachers 103

not close. Except for items 28 and 30, all the other 32 items in the scale have an amount of variation higher than 0.200.

FACTOR LOADING

Factor loading shows the degree of relationship between item and common factor. The higher the factor loading of an item, the closer the relationship between the item and the common factor. If the factor loading of an item is less than 0.45, this indicates that the relationship between the item and the common factor is not close. Except for items 28 and 30, the relationship between each of the other 32 items and the common factor is higher than 0.450.

According to the item analysis results, items 28, 30, 32, and 1 should be deleted. However, according to the hypothesis of the scale structure, the researchers believe that the above items constitute an important part of teachers' "professional attitude" and "ability to get support." In addition, the statistics of critical ratio and item–total correlation for items 28 and 30 all reached the standards, while items 32 and 1 also reach the standards in critical ratio, item–total correlation, communalities, and factor loading. Therefore, after item analysis, all 34 items in the original scale are included in factor analysis.

Factor Analysis

Exploratory Factor Analysis   In order to clarify the factor structure of the scale, SPSS20.0 for Windows software was used for exploratory factor analysis of the formal scale. The common factors were extracted via principal component analysis and orthogonal rotation. The KMO statistic for sampling adequacy is 0.955, and the Bartlett's sphericity test statistic reaches 17,229.977 (df=561, p<0.001), indicating that the data are very suitable for factor analysis. Factor extraction was carried out without limiting the number of extraction factors, and the number of factors was determined according to the following criteria: (1) the eigenvalues of factors are greater than 1; (2) the factor solution must conform to the steep ramp test, as shown in Figure 3.4; (3) the item loading for each factor is greater than 0.4; (4) the extracted factors explain at least 3 percent of the total variation before rotation; (5) each factor contains at least three items. In addition, the items with high loading on two factors are screened according to the principle of maximum loading and the theoretical conception. On the basis of the above criteria and in combination with the theoretical conception of the scale, this exploration process was repeated many times, and six items were excluded successively until the accumulation rate of variation and the number of factors extracted tended to be stable, and the items contained in each factor were close to the pre-designed items. Finally, a four-factor structural model of the competence of teachers in inclusive education was worked out. The eigenvalues of the four factors are all greater than 1, and the cumulative variance interpretation rate reaches 61.322 percent, as shown

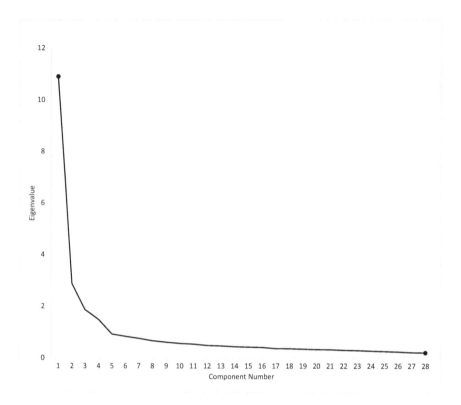

Figure 3.3 Scree Plot.

in Figure 3.3 and Table 3.5. The remaining 28 items have a large loading on the corresponding factors, ranging from 0.445 to 0.824, as shown in Table 3.5.

According to the above analysis results, the items' factor attribution and contents are as follows. The first factor extracted includes eight items from no. 1 to no. 8, which reflect the teachers' understanding of the educational rights of disabled students, the LRC program, and the significance of LRC practice to disabled students, teachers, schools, and social development. It is designated as "professional attitude." The second factor extracted includes eight items from no. 16 to no. 25, which reflect the skills of LRC program teachers in curriculum adjustment, flexible evaluation, differentiated teaching, and cooperation. It is designated as "professional skills." The third factor extracted includes six items from no. 10 to no. 15, which reflect the knowledge of LRC program teachers in relevant policies and regulations, inclusive education theory, physical and mental characteristics of disabled students, and practical measures for educating disabled students. It is designated as "professional knowledge." The fourth factor extracted includes six items from no. 28 to no. 34, which reflect the teachers' initiative to seek or obtain the main resources in LRC practice

Table 3.5 Item Loading Matrix Table for Exploratory Factor Analysis

Item	Item loading				
	Factor 1	*Factor 2*	*Factor 3*	*Factor 4*	*Communality*
5	.824				.728
2	.822				.731
4	.821				.732
6	.695				.630
1	.691				.509
3	.685				.651
8	.593				.571
7	.445				.437
21		.781			.689
19		.757			.656
20		.687			.640
25		.666			.533
18		.655			.639
23		.621			.540
22		.608			.550
16		.521			.496
11			.776		.707
14			.757		.740
13			.757		.698
10			.734		.666
12			.651		.621
15			.621		.549
33				.781	.702
29				.771	.642
30				.734	.568
34				.711	.616
28				.654	.452
32				.637	.477
Eigenvalue	10.914	2.891	1.876	1.489	
Contribution rate	38.978	10.326	6.701	5.318	61.322

(also a kind of teacher agency). It is designated as teachers' "ability to get support."

Confirmatory Factor Analysis Confirmatory Factor Analysis (CFA) is a statistical method that makes reasonable assumptions about the relationship between potential variables and observed variables based on certain theories, and carries out statistical test on such assumptions. There are usually two modes of CFA. One is pure confirmatory analysis, that is, only one model is used to fit sample data, and the model is rejected or accepted according to the analysis results. The other is model selection analysis, that is, after several models are put forward, compare the advantages and disadvantages of each model in fitting the sample data and decide which model is the most desirable.[53]

106 *Structural Analysis of the Competence of Teachers*

This research adopts the first mode. Mplus6 software was used to verify the structural model of the competence of teachers in inclusive education obtained through exploratory factor analysis. Before the CFA, the normal distribution of the remaining variables (items) after the exploratory factor analysis was tested first, and the results showed that all variables presented significant negative skewed distribution. Huang Fangming pointed out that when the absolute value of kurtosis is greater than 25, it will have sufficient influence on the maximum likelihood method.[54] In addition, non-random sampling will also affect the data estimation of the maximum likelihood method.[55] Therefore, the CFA adopts the robust maximum likelihood estimator, an estimation method that does not require the normal distribution of hypothetical variables, to estimate the data.[56] For the selection of fit index, Boomsma, McDonald and Ho suggested using chi-square value ($\chi2$), root mean square error of approximation (RMSEA) and 90 percent confidence interval, comparative fit index (CFI), and standardized root mean square residual (SRMSR).[57,58] The chi-square value is the main model fit index, and a significant chi-square value is obtained under a certain degree of freedom, representing the mismatch between the observation matrix and the theoretical estimate matrix.[59] However, the scholar Rigdon held that the $\chi2$ statistic is usually not helpful when using real-world data to evaluate theoretical models since it is greatly affected by the estimated parameters and sample number.[60] The most suitable sample number of $\chi2$ test is 100 to 200.[61] So, $\chi2/df$ is usually adopted instead. The results of CFA showed that $\chi2/df$ was 3.779, CFI was 0.908, RMSEA was 0.056 (90 percent confidence interval 0.053–0.059), and SRMSR was 0.051. When $\chi2/df$ is between 2.0 and 5.0, the model is acceptable.[62] The value of CFI greater than 0.9 is acceptable, and the values of SRMR and RMSEA less than 0.08 are acceptable.[63] In short, the model constructed in this research has a good fit with the data, as shown in Figure 3.4.

In addition, the factor loading indicates the degree to which the item reflects the potential variable, and a sufficiently large factor loading indicates that the item has satisfactory structural validity. According to Tabachnica and Fidell, the factor loadings of the scales developed by social science researchers are not too high, which may be limited by the nature of measurement, the influence of external interference and measurement errors, and even the controversy over whether the nature of constructs is formative or reflective. When the factor loading is 0.71, it means that the factor can explain 50 percent of the total variance of the observed variable (squared loading), which is a very ideal condition; when the factor loading is 0.63, it means that the factor can explain 40 percent of the total variation of the observed variable, which is a very good condition. When the factor loading is 0.55, it means that this factor can explain 30 percent of the total variation of the observed variable, which is a good condition; and when the factor loading is 0.45, it means that this factor can explain 20 percent of the total variation of the observed variable, which is a normal condition.[64] Moreover, the sample size should be taken into account when selecting the standard of factor loading. If the sample size is

Structural Analysis of the Competence of Teachers 107

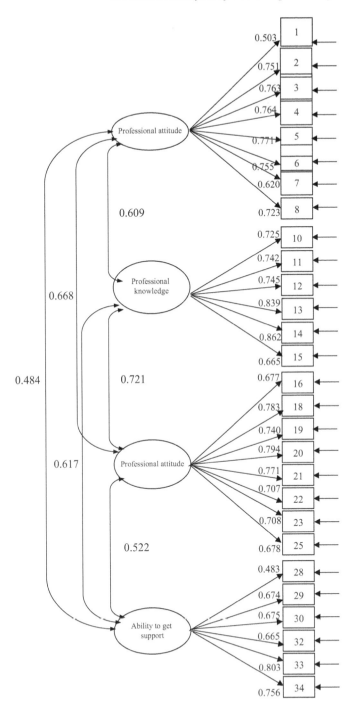

Figure 3.4 Structural Model of 'Scale of Teacher Competence in Inclusive Education.'

108 *Structural Analysis of the Competence of Teachers*

small, the selected standard of factor loading should be higher. If the sample size is large, the selected standard of factor loading should be lower. According to Chen Shunyu's study, if the sample size is 350, the selected standard of factor loading should not be lower than 0.30.[65] In view of the specific factor loadings in Figure 3.3 and the total number of respondents in this research, we believe that the structural model of the *Scale of Teacher Competence in Inclusive Education* has ideal factor loadings.

In brief, the results of factor analysis show that the model is reasonable, and the fit degree is acceptable. That is, the structural model of the competence of teachers in inclusive education is a multidimensional model composed of four factors.

RELIABILITY ANALYSIS

Test reliability refers to the degree of consistency or reliability of test results. For a scale with a good reliability coefficient, the reliability coefficient of the total scale should be above 0.80. If it is between 0.70 and 0.80, the scale is still acceptable. If it is a subscale, its reliability coefficient should be above 0.70. If its reliability coefficient is between 0.60 and 0.70, it is acceptable. If the internal consistency coefficient of a subscale is below 0.60 or the reliability coefficient of a total scale is below 0.80, it is advisable to revise the scale or add or delete some items.[66] In the *Scale of Teacher Competence in Inclusive Education*, the internal consistency reliability coefficients of the four dimensions are all above 0.80, and the internal consistency reliability coefficient of the total scale is above 0.90. Therefore, the reliability of the scale of teacher competence in inclusive education in this research is high, as shown in Table 3.6.

Analysis and Discussion

Existing research on the composition of teacher competence mainly have three orientations. One is a theoretical orientation, that is, researchers construct the structural dimensions of teacher competence by theoretical analysis based on the existing research findings and corresponding theories. The second is empirical orientation, that is, the researchers investigate respondents on teacher competence, and then adopt certain statistical analysis methods to analyze the survey data so as to get the structural dimensions. The third is comprehensive

Table 3.6 Internal Consistency Test Results of All Dimensions of 'Scale of Teacher Competence in Inclusive Education'

	Professional attitude	*Professional knowledge*	*Professional skills*	*Ability to get support*	*Professional competence*
α coefficient	0.887	0.891	0.902	0.834	0.939

Structural Analysis of the Competence of Teachers 109

orientation, which combines theoretical analysis and empirical technology. Firstly, theoretical analysis is made to construct the structural dimensions of teacher competence, and then empirical methods are adopted to test and revise them. In this research, the structural model of teacher competence in inclusive education is analyzed in a comprehensive orientation.

Based on analysis of the structural model of the scale of teacher competence in inclusive education, we constructed a four-factor model of teacher competence in inclusive education, including professional attitude, professional knowledge, professional skills, and ability to get support. Its major difference with previous models is that it has another factor besides attitude, knowledge, and skills, namely the ability to get support.

International experience tells us that implementation of inclusive education needs a strong supportive system. A teacher cannot be and also does not need to be an expert in inclusive education. It is also impossible for inclusive education to rely solely on teachers of regular classes. In order to meet the diverse needs of students in the class, especially to provide appropriate education for special needs children, there must be special education teachers, related professionals and resource rooms, auxiliary equipment, and other material resources and professional support and services.

Chinese researchers have pointed out that there are many theoretical perplexities and practical problems in implementation of the LRC program that need to be actively explored and solved by teachers from the perspective of professional development, so as to acquire practical wisdom.[67] However, there have been many deficiencies in building the supportive system for LRC practice.[68,69] This is the main reason why the quality of the LRC program is not high. In our interviews, LRC program teachers stressed the necessity of actively seeking assistance. Therefore, when the support provided is limited, it is critical for teachers to have the ability to "seek and obtain support." At the same time, if good resources and support are placed in front of an "indifferent" teacher, they also cannot play a role. This also gives expression to the importance of teachers' ability to seek and obtain support from another perspective, and highlights that the ability to seek and obtain support is a deep-seated feature of the teacher competence model, that is, the component of "initiative" or "agency." Therefore, the teachers' ability to get support (also a kind of agency) becomes the fourth factor parallel to attitude, knowledge, and skills, which is an independent factor in teacher competence in inclusive education.

What is more, the scores of all items in this research are higher than the theoretical median, and generally tend to be high. On the one hand, this may be related to social approval effect and self-value protection. As the scale of teacher competence in inclusive education is a self-reporting test, the answers to the items often reflect people's good subjective wishes, just like other similar tests. Perhaps lie detection factors should be set in the test to control it, but some studies have found that this cannot solve the fundamental problem.[70] Some researchers hold that behavior rating scales generally adopt others' evaluation, that is, a third party who is familiar with the respondent evaluates him or her according to the results of long-term observation. If the superior or subordinate who knows the respondent gives the answers, the social approval effect may be controlled to a certain extent, which may be a solution to the problem.[71] Another researcher proposed to add a validity item to each subscale in the research of teacher competency. The respondents evaluate themselves on the competency characteristics and qualities, and the scores obtained are taken as the criterion scores. Then, the correlation between the score of each subscale and its corresponding validity item score is calculated to judge the validity of each subscale and the entire test.[72] This might also be a solution to the problem. On the other hand, the five-point Likert scale was adopted in this research, which easily resulted in the phenomenon of evaluation mean tending toward the middle. Due to the influence of the "Doctrine of the Mean" advocated by traditional Chinese culture, the respondents may tend to choose "uncertain" and other options. Perhaps a six-point Likert scale can avoid this phenomenon.

Notes

1 Lin, Chongde 林崇德, Shen, Jiliang 申继亮, and Xin, Tao 辛涛. "Jiaoshi suzhi de goucheng jiqi peiyang tujing" 教师素质的构成及其培养途径. *Journal of the Chinese Society of Education* 中国教育学刊 no. 6 (1996): 16–22.
2 Ye, Lan 叶澜. "Xin shiji jiaoshi zhuanye suyang chutan" 新世纪教师专业素养初探. *Educational Research and Experiment* 教育研究与实验 no. 1 (1998): 41–47.
3 Bradford, K., Pendergast, D., and Grootenboer, P. "What Is Meant by 'Teacher Quality' in Research and Policy: A Systematic, Quantitative Literature Review." *Education Thinking* 1, no. 1 (2021): 57–76.
4 Arnon, S., and Reichel, N. "Who Is the Ideal Teacher? Am I? Similarity and Difference in Perception of Students of Education Regarding the Qualities of a Good Teacher and of Their Own Qualities as Teachers." *Teachers and Teaching: Theory and Practice* 13, no. 5 (2007): 441–464.
5 Ma, Chaoshan 马超山, and Zhang, Guichun 张桂春. "Jiaoshi suzhi jiegou moxing chutan" 教师素质结构模型初探. *Journal of Liaoning Normal University* 辽宁师范大学学报 no. 4 (1989): 33–36.
6 Feng, Yajing 冯雅静, Zhu, Nan 朱楠, and Wang, Yan 王雁. "Meiguo guojiaxing jiaoshi zhuanye biaozhun zhong ronghe jiaoyu xiangguan yaoqiu tanxi" 美国国家性教师专业标准中融合教育相关要求探析. *Teacher Education Research* 教师教育研究 28, no. 4 (2016): 121–128.
7 Interstate Teacher Assessment and Support Consortium (InTASC). *InTASC Model Core Teaching Standards: A Resource for State Dialogue.* Washington, DC: Council of Chief State School Officers, 2011. www.ccsso.org/sites/default/files/2017–11/InTASC_Model_Core_Teaching_Standards_2011.pdf.
8 European Agency for Development in Special Needs Education. *Key Principles for Promoting Quality in Inclusive Education: Recommendations for Policy Makers.* Odense: European Agency for Development in Special Needs Education, 2009. www.european-agency.org/sites/default/files/key-principles-for-promoting-quality-in-inclusive-education_key-principles-EN.pdf.

Structural Analysis of the Competence of Teachers   111

9 European Agency for Development in Special Needs Education. *Profile of Inclusive Teachers*. Odense: European Agency for Development in Special Needs Education, 2012. www.european-agency.org/sites/default/files/Profile-of-Inclusive-Teachers.pdf.

10 Carrington, S., Saggers, B., Adie, L., et al. "International Representations of Inclusive Education: How Is Inclusive Practice Reflected in the Professional Teaching Standards of China and Australia?." *International Journal of Disability, Development and Education* 62, no. 6 (2015): 556–570.

11 Gao, Li 高利, Zhu, Nan 朱楠, and Lei, Jianghua 雷江华. "Zhongxiaoxue yu teshu jiaoyu jiaoshi zhuanye biaozhun de bijiao ji qishi" 中小学与特殊教育教师专业标准的比较及启示. *Chinese Journal of Special Education* 中国特殊教育 216, no. 6 (2018): 23–27.

12 Zhou, Dan 周丹, and Wang, Yan 王雁. "Meiguo ronghe jiaoyu jiaoshi suyang goucheng ji qishi" 美国融合教育教师素养构成及启示. *Comparative Education Review* 比较教育研究 39, no. 3 (2017): 89–95.

13 Hodkinson, Alan. "Inclusive and Special Education in the English Educational System: Historical Perspectives, Recent Developments and Future Challenges." *British Journal of Special Education* 37, no. 2 (2010): 61–67.

14 Wang, Yan 王雁, Huang, Lingling 黄玲玲, Wang, Yue 王悦, and Zhang, Lili 张丽莉. "Dui guonei suiban jiudu jiaoshi ronghe jiaoyu suyang yanjiu de fenxi yu zhanwang" 对国内随班就读教师融合教育素养研究的分析与展望. *Teacher Education Research* 教师教育研究 30, no. 1 (2018): 26–32.

15 Feng, Yajing 冯雅静. "Suiban jiudu jiaoshi hexin zhuanye suyang yanjiu" 随班就读教师核心专业素养研究. *Chinese Journal of Special Education* 中国特殊教育 no. 1 (2014): 4–9, 23.

16 See note 12 above.

17 European Commission. *Common European Principles for Teacher Competences and Qualifications*. Brussels: European Commission, 2009. www.cedefop.europa.eu/fi/news-and-press/news/common-european-principles-teacher-competences-and-qualifications.

18 Hao, Zhenjun 郝振君, and Lan, Jijun 兰继军. "Lun quanna jiaoyu yu jiaoshi suzhi" 论全纳教育与教师素质. *Chinese Journal of Special Education* 中国特殊教育 no. 7 (2004): 2–5.

19 Wang, Meiping 王美萍, and Hu, Pingfan 胡平凡. "Quanna jiaoyu linian xia de jiaoshi suzhi jiqi peiyang" 全纳教育理念下的教师素质及其培养. *Forum on Contemporary Education* 当代教育论坛 no. 9 (2008): 88–90.

20 Meng, Wanjin 孟万金. "Quanna jiaoyu linian xia jiaoshi zhuanye suzhi ji zhuanyehua biaozhun yanjiu" 全纳教育理念下教师专业素质及专业化标准研究. *Chinese Journal of Special Education* 中国特殊教育 no. 5 (2008): 13–17.

21 Andrews, J., and Lupart, J. *The Inclusive Classroom: Educating Exceptional Children*, 15–16. Nelson: Nelson College Indigenous, 2000.

22 Hua, Guodong 华国栋. *Teshu xuyao ertong de xinli yu jiaoyu* 特殊需要儿童的心理与教育, 110–112. Beijing: Higher Education Press, 2004.

23 Li, Zehui 李泽慧, and Zhou, Min 周珉. "Dui suiban jiudu jiaoshi chayi jiaoxue nengli goucheng de fenxi" 对随班就读教师差异教学能力构成的分析. *Chinese Journal of Special Education* 中国特殊教育 no. 1 (2009): 25–33.

24 McCormick, L., Noonan, M. J., Ogata, V., et al. "Co-teacher Relationship and Program Quality: Implications for Preparing Teachers for Inclusive Preschool Settings." *Education and Training in Mental Retardation and Developmental Disabilities* (2001): 119–132.

112 *Structural Analysis of the Competence of Teachers*

25 Shen, Weihua 沈卫华. "Quanna: weilai jiaoshi zhuanye fazhan de zhongyao keti" 全纳:未来教师专业发展的重要课题. *Educational Science Research* 教育科学研究 no. 6 (2010): 70–73.

26 Li, La 李拉. "Lun suiban jiudu jiaoshi duiwu de zhuanyehua" 论随班就读教师队伍的专业化. *Theory and Practice of Education* 教育理论与实践 34, no. 17 (2014): 21–23.

27 Zhu, Nan 朱楠, and Wang, Yan 王雁. "'Fuhexing' teshu jiaoyu jiaoshi de peiyang—jiyu fuhexing de neihan fenxi" "复合型"特殊教育教师的培养——基于复合型的内涵分析. *Teacher Education Research* 教师教育研究 27, no. 6 (2015): 39–44.

28 Sun, Quanhong 孙全红. "Ronghe jiaoyu beijing xia ziyuan jiaoshi jianshe yu ziyuan jiaoshi zhuanye fazhan" 融合教育背景下资源教室建设与资源教师专业发展. *Modern Special Education* 现代特殊教育 no. 17 (2016): 28–29.

29 Xu, Jianping 徐建平. "Jiaoshi shengrenli moxing yu ceping yanjiu" 教师胜任力模型与测评研究. Beijing: Beijing Normal University (doctoral thesis), 2004.

30 Li, La 李拉. "Zhuanyehua shiye xia de suiban jiudu jiaoshi: kunjing yu chulu" 专业化视野下的随班就读教师：困境与出路. *Theory and Practice of Education* 教育理论与实践 32, no. 23 (2012): 34–36.

31 See note 23 above.

32 Jing, Lingling 荆玲玲. *Shehui yanjiu fangfa* 社会研究方法, 106. Harbin: Harbin Engineering University Press, 2016.

33 Kvale, S. *Interviews: An Introduction to Qualitative Research Interviewing*, 326. Thousand Oaks: Sage Publications, 1996.

34 Eagly, A. H., and Chaiken, S. *The Psychology of Attitudes*, 1–21. Orlando: Harcourt Brace Jovanovich College Publishers, 1993.

35 Ibid.

36 Bocala, C., Morgan, C., Mundry, S., et al. "Do States Have Certification Requirements for Preparing General Education Teachers to Teach Students with Disabilities? Experience in the Northeast and Islands Region. Issues & Answers." *Regional Educational Laboratory Northeast & Islands* no. 9, 2010.

37 See note 7 above.

38 Fisher, D., Frey, N., and Thousand, J. "What Do Special Educators Need to Know and Be Prepared to Do for Inclusive Schooling to Work?" *Teacher Education and Special Education* 26, no. 1 (2003): 42–50.

39 See note 36 above.

40 Idol, L. "Toward Inclusion of Special Education Students in General Education: A Program Evaluation of Eight Schools." *Remedial and Special Education* 27, no. 2 (2006): 77–94.

41 See note 37 above.

42 See note 36 above.

43 See note 37 above.

44 Tomlinson, C. A. *How to Differentiate Instruction in Mixed-ability Classrooms*, 16–20. Bergen: Pearson Education, 2001.

45 See note 36 above.

46 Campbell, E. "Teacher Agency in Curriculum Contexts." *Curriculum Inquiry* 42, no. 2 (2012): 183–190.

47 Emirbayer, M., and Mische, A. "What Is Agency?" *American Journal of Sociology* 103, no. 4 (1998): 962–1023.

48 See note 34 above.

49 See note 36 above.

50 See note 37 above.

51 See note 44 above.

52 Wu, Minglong 吴明隆. *Wenjuan tongji fenxi shiwu—SPSS caozuo yu yingyong* 问卷统计分析实务——SPSS操作与应用, 99. Chongqing: Chongqing University Press, 2010.

53 Hou, Jietai 侯杰泰, Wen, Zhonglin 温忠麟, and Cheng, Zijuan 成子娟. *Jiegou fangcheng moxing jiqi yingyong* 结构方程模型及其应用, 154–165. Beijing: Educational Science Press, 2004.

54 Huang, Fangming 黄芳铭. *Jiegou fangcheng moshi: lilun yu yingyong* 结构方程模式：理论与应用, 228. Beijing: China Taxation Publishing House, 2005.

55 Ibid, 121.

56 Wang, Jichuan 王济川, Wang, Xiaoqian 王小倩, and Jiang, Baofa 姜宝法. *Jiegou fangcheng moxing: fangfa yu yingyong* 结构方程模型：方法与应用, 59. Beijing: Higher Education Press, 2011.

57 Boomsma, A. "Reporting Analyses of Covariance Structures." *Structural Equation Modeling* no. 7 (2000): 461–483.

58 McDonald, R. P., and Ho, M.-H. R. "Principles and Practice in Reporting Structural Equation Analyses." *Psychological Methods* no. 7 (2002): 64–82.

59 See note 53 above, 147.

60 Rigdon, E. E. "A Necessary and Sufficient Identification Rule for Structural Models Estimated in Practice." *Multivariate Behavioral Research* 30, no. 3 (1995): 359–383.

61 Wu, Minglong 吴明隆. *Jiegou fangcheng moxing—AMOS de caozuo yu yingyong* 结构方程模型——AMOS的操作与应用, 41. Chongqing: Chongqing University Press, 2009.

62 See note 53 above, 156.

63 See note 53 above, 155–161.

64 Qiu, Haozheng 邱皓政, and Lin, Bifang 林碧芳. *Jiegou fangcheng moxing de yuanli yu yingyong* 结构方程模型的原理与应用, 101. Beijing: China Light Industry Press, 2009.

65 See note 52 above, 200.

66 Wu, Minglong 吴明隆. *SPSS tongji yingyong shiwu—wenjuan fenxi yu yingyong tongji* SPSS统计应用实务——问卷分析与应用统计, 109. Beijing: Science Press, 2003.

67 Peng, Xiaguang 彭霞光. "Zhongguo canji ertong suiban jiudu xianzhuang he weilai fazhan jianyi"中国残疾儿童随班就读现状和未来发展建议. *Modern Special Education* 现代特殊教育 no. 9 (2012): 19–21.

68 Qing, Sulan 卿素兰, and Liu, Zaihua 刘在花. "Nongcun teshu ertong suiban jiudu zhichi xitong de diaocha yanjiu" 农村特殊儿童随班就读支持系统的调查研究. *Chinese Journal of Special Education* 中国特殊教育 no. 11 (2007): 3–8, 24.

69 Peng, Xiaguang 彭霞光. "Suiban jiudu zhichi baozhang tixi jianshe chutan" 随班就读支持保障体系建设初探. *Chinese Journal of Special Education* 中国特殊教育 no. 11 (2014): 3–7.

70 See note 29 above.

71 Shi, Xueyun 石学云. *Teshu jiaoyu jiaoshi shengrenli yanjiu* 特殊教育教师胜任力研究, 89. Beijing: Educational Science Publishing, 2012.

72 See note 29 above, 53.

114 *Structural Analysis of the Competence of Teachers*

References

Andrews, J., and Lupart, J. *The Inclusive Classroom: Educating Exceptional Children.* Nelson: Nelson College Indigenous, 2000.

Arnon, S., and Reichel, N. "Who Is the Ideal Teacher? Am I? Similarity and Difference in Perception of Students of Education Regarding the Qualities of a Good Teacher and of Their Own Qualities as Teachers." *Teachers and Teaching: Theory and Practice* 13, no. 5 (2007): 441–464.

Bocala, C., Morgan, C., Mundry, S., et al. "Do States Have Certification Requirements for Preparing General Education Teachers to Teach Students with Disabilities? Experience in the Northeast and Islands Region. Issues & Answers." *Regional Educational Laboratory Northeast & Islands* no. 9 (2010): 10–11.

Boomsma, A. "Reporting Analyses of Covariance Structures." *Structural Equation Modeling* no. 7 (2000): 461–483.

Bradford, K., Pendergast, D., and Grootenboer, P. "What Is Meant by 'Teacher Quality' in Research and Policy: A Systematic, Quantitative Literature Review." *Education Thinking* 1, no. 1 (2021): 57–76.

Campbell, E. "Teacher Agency in Curriculum Contexts." *Curriculum Inquiry* 42, no. 2 (2012): 183–190.

Carrington, S., Saggers, B., Adie, L., et al. "International Representations of Inclusive Education: How Is Inclusive Practice Reflected in the Professional Teaching Standards of China and Australia?." *International Journal of Disability, Development and Education* 62, no. 6 (2015): 556–570.

Eagly, A. H., and Chaiken, S. *The Psychology of Attitudes.* Orlando: Harcourt Brace Jovanovich College Publishers, 1993.

Emirbayer, M., and Mische, A. "What Is Agency?" *American Journal of Sociology* 103, no. 4 (1998): 962–1023.

European Agency for Development in Special Needs Education. *Key Principles for Promoting Quality in Inclusive Education: Recommendations for Policy Makers.* Odense: European Agency for Development in Special Needs Education, 2009. www.european-agency.org/sites/default/files/key-principles-for-promoting-quality-in-inclusive-education_key-principles-EN.pdf.

European Agency for Development in Special Needs Education. *Profile of Inclusive Teachers.* Odense: European Agency for Development in Special Needs Education, 2012. www.european-agency.org/sites/default/files/Profile-of-Inclusive-Teachers.pdf.

European Commission. *Common European Principles for Teacher Competences and Qualifications.* Brussels: European Commission, 2009. www.cedefop.europa.eu/fi/news-and-press/news/common-european-principles-teacher-competences-and-qualifications.

Feng, Yajing 冯雅静. "Suiban jiudu jiaoshi hexin zhuanye suyang yanjiu" 随班就读教师核心专业素养研究. *Chinese Journal of Special Education* 中国特殊教育 no. 1 (2014): 4–9, 23.

Feng, Yajing 冯雅静, Zhu, Nan 朱楠, and Wang, Yan 王雁. "Meiguo guojiaxing jiaoshi zhuanye biaozhun zhong ronghe jiaoyu xiangguan yaoqiu tanxi" 美国国家性教师专业标准中融合教育相关要求探析. *Teacher Education Research* 教师教育研究 28, no. 4 (2016): 121–128.

Fisher, D., Frey, N., and Thousand, J. "What Do Special Educators Need to Know and Be Prepared to Do for Inclusive Schooling to Work?" *Teacher Education and Special Education* 26, no. 1 (2003): 42–50.

Gao, Li 高利, Zhu, Nan 朱楠, and Lei, Jianghua 雷江华. "Zhongxiaoxue yu teshu jiaoyu jiaoshi zhuanye biaozhun de bijiao ji qishi" 中小学与特殊教育教师专业标准的比较及启示. *Chinese Journal of Special Education* 中国特殊教育 216, no. 6 (2018): 23–27.

Hao, Zhenjun 郝振君, and Lan, Jijun 兰继军. "Lun quanna jiaoyu yu jiaoshi suzhi" 论全纳教育与教师素质. *Chinese Journal of Special Education* 中国特殊教育 no. 7 (2004): 2–5.

Hodkinson, Alan. "Inclusive and Special Education in the English Educational System: Historical Perspectives, Recent Developments and Future Challenges." *British Journal of Special Education* 37, no. 2 (2010): 61–67.

Hou, Jietai 侯杰泰, Wen, Zhonglin 温忠麟, and Cheng, Zijuan 成子娟. *Jiegou fangcheng moxing jiqi yingyong* 结构方程模型及其应用. Beijing: Educational Science Press, 2004.

Hua, Guodong 华国栋. *Teshu xuyao ertong de xinli yu jiaoyu* 特殊需要儿童的心理与教育. Beijing: Higher Education Press, 2004.

Huang, Fangming 黄芳铭. *Jiegou fangcheng moshi: lilun yu yingyong* 结构方程模式：理论与应用. Beijing: China Taxation Publishing House, 2005.

Idol, L. "Toward Inclusion of Special Education Students in General Education: A Program Evaluation of Eight Schools." *Remedial and Special Education* 27, no. 2 (2006): 77–94.

Interstate Teacher Assessment and Support Consortium (InTASC). *InTASC Model Core Teaching Standards: A Resource for State Dialogue.* Washington, DC: Council of Chief State School Officers, 2011. www.ccsso.org/sites/default/files/2017–11/InTASC_Model_Core_Teaching_Standards_2011.pdf.

Jing, Lingling 荆玲玲. *Shehui yanjiu fangfa* 社会研究方法. Harbin: Harbin Engineering University Press, 2016.

Kvale, S. *Interviews: An Introduction to Qualitative Research Interviewing.* Thousand Oaks: Sage Publications, 1996.

Li, La 李拉. "Zhuanyehua shiye xia de suiban jiudu jiaoshi: kunjing yu chulu" 专业化视野下的随班就读教师：困境与出路. *Theory and Practice of Education* 教育理论与实践 32, no. 23 (2012): 34–36.

Li, La 李拉. "Lun suiban jiudu jiaoshi duiwu de zhuanyehua" 论随班就读教师队伍的专业化. *Theory and Practice of Education* 教育理论与实践 34, no. 17 (2014): 21–23.

Li, Zehui 李泽慧, and Zhou, Min 周珉. "Dui suiban jiudu jiaoshi chayi jiaoxue nengli goucheng de fenxi" 对随班就读教师差异教学能力构成的分析. *Chinese Journal of Special Education* 中国特殊教育 no. 1 (2009): 25–33.

Lin, Chongde 林崇德, Shen, Jiliang 申继亮, and Xin, Tao 辛涛. "Jiaoshi suzhi de goucheng jiqi peiyang tujing" 教师素质的构成及其培养途径. *Journal of the Chinese Society of Education* 中国教育学刊 no. 6 (1996): 16–22.

Ma, Chaoshan 马超山, and Zhang, Guichun 张桂春. "Jiaoshi suzhi jiegou moxing chutan" 教师素质结构模型初探. *Journal of Liaoning Normal University* 辽宁师范大学学报 no. 4 (1989): 33–36.

Meng, Wanjin 孟万金. "Quanna jiaoyu linian xia jiaoshi zhuanye suzhi ji zhuanyehua biaozhun yanjiu" 全纳教育理念下教师专业素质及专业化标准研究. *Chinese Journal of Special Education* 中国特殊教育 no. 5 (2008): 13–17.

McCormick, L., Noonan, M. J., Ogata, V., et al. "Co-teacher Relationship and Program Quality: Implications for Preparing Teachers for Inclusive Preschool Settings."

116   *Structural Analysis of the Competence of Teachers*

Education and Training in Mental Retardation and Developmental Disabilities (2001): 119–132.

McDonald, R. P., and Ho, M.-H. R. "Principles and Practice in Reporting Structural Equation Analyses." *Psychological Methods* no. 7 (2002): 64–82.

Peng, Xiaguang 彭霞光. "Zhongguo canji ertong suiban jiudu xianzhuang he weilai fazhan jianyi" 中国残疾儿童随班就读现状和未来发展建议. *Modern Special Education* 现代特殊教育 no. 9 (2012): 19–21.

Peng, Xiaguang 彭霞光. "Suiban jiudu zhichi baozhang tixi jianshe chutan" 随班就读支持保障体系建设初探. *Chinese Journal of Special Education* 中国特殊教育 no. 11 (2014): 3–7.

Qing, Sulan 卿素兰, and Liu, Zaihua 刘在花. "Nongcun teshu ertong suiban jiudu zhichi xitong de diaocha yanjiu" 农村特殊儿童随班就读支持系统的调查研究. *Chinese Journal of Special Education* 中国特殊教育 no. 11 (2007): 3–8, 24.

Qiu, Haozheng 邱皓政, and Lin, Bifang 林碧芳. *Jiegou fangcheng moxing de yuanli yu yingyong* 结构方程模型的原理与应用. Beijing: China Light Industry Press, 2009.

Rigdon, E. E. "A Necessary and Sufficient Identification Rule for Structural Models Estimated in Practice." *Multivariate Behavioral Research* 30, no. 3 (1995): 359–383.

Shen, Weihua 沈卫华. "Quanna: weilai jiaoshi zhuanye fazhan de zhongyao keti" 全纳:未来教师专业发展的重要课题. *Educational Science Research* 教育科学研究 no. 6 (2010): 70–73.

Shi, Xueyun 石学云. *Teshu jiaoyu jiaoshi shengrenli yanjiu* 特殊教育教师胜任力研究. Beijing: Educational Science Publishing, 2012.

Sun, Quanhong 孙全红. "Ronghe jiaoyu beijing xia ziyuan jiaoshi jianshe yu ziyuan jiaoshi zhuanye fazhan" 融合教育背景下资源教室建设与资源教师专业发展. *Modern Special Education* 现代特殊教育 no. 17 (2016): 28–29.

Tomlinson, C. A. *How to Differentiate Instruction in Mixed-ability Classrooms.* Bergen: Pearson Education, 2001.

Wang, Jichuan 王济川, Wang, Xiaoqian 王小倩, and Jiang, Baofa 姜宝法. *Jiegou fangcheng moxing: fangfa yu yingyong* 结构方程模型：方法与应用. Beijing: Higher Education Press, 2011.

Wang, Meiping 王美萍, and Hu, Pingfan 胡平凡. "Quanna jiaoyu linian xia de jiaoshi suzhi jiqi peiyang" 全纳教育理念下的教师素质及其培养. *Forum on Contemporary Education* 当代教育论坛 no. 9 (2008): 88–90.

Wang, Yan 王雁, Huang, Lingling 黄玲玲, Wang, Yue 王悦, and Zhang, Lili 张丽莉. "Dui guonei suiban jiudu jiaoshi ronghe jiaoyu suyang yanjiu de fenxi yu zhanwang" 对国内随班就读教师融合教育素养研究的分析与展望. *Teacher Education Research* 教师教育研究 30, no. 1 (2018): 26–32.

Wu, Minglong 吴明隆. *SPSS tongji yingyong shiwu—wenjuan fenxi yu yingyong tongji* SPSS统计应用实务——问卷分析与应用统计. Beijing: Science Press, 2003.

Wu, Minglong 吴明隆. *Jiegou fangcheng moxing—AMOS de caozuo yu yingyong* 结构方程模型——AMOS的操作与应用. Chongqing: Chongqing University Press, 2009.

Wu, Minglong 吴明隆. *Wenjuan tongji fenxi shiwu—SPSS caozuo yu yingyong* 问卷统计分析实务——SPSS操作与应用. Chongqing: Chongqing University Press, 2010.

Xu, Jianping 徐建平. "Jiaoshi shengrenli moxing yu ceping yanjiu" 教师胜任力模型与测评研究. Beijing: Beijing Normal University (doctoral thesis), 2004.

Ye, Lan 叶澜. "Xin shiji jiaoshi zhuanye suyang chutan" 新世纪教师专业素养初探. *Educational Research and Experiment* 教育研究与实验 no. 1 (1998): 41–47.

Zhou, Dan 周丹, and Wang, Yan 王雁. "Meiguo ronghe jiaoyu jiaoshi suyang goucheng ji qishi" 美国融合教育教师素养构成及启示. *Comparative Education Review* 比较教育研究 39, no. 3 (2017): 89–95.

Zhu, Nan 朱楠, and Wang, Yan 王雁. "'Fuhexing' teshu jiaoyu jiaoshi de peiyang—jiyu fuhexing de neihan fenxi" "复合型"特殊教育教师的培养——基于复合型的内涵分析. *Teacher Education Research* 教师教育研究 27, no. 6 (2015): 39–44.

4 Research into the Competence of Chinese Teachers in Inclusive Education and Its Influencing Mechanism

Research Design

Among various factors that affect the quality of inclusive education, teachers play a key role in the schooling of children with special educational needs. Increasing research across the globe focuses on the role of teachers in inclusive education. Specifically, Chinese scholars Ma Hongying and Tan Heping held that the competence of teachers to understand and teach students with disabilities is a critical factor in ensuring the success of inclusive education.[1] Hannu Savolainen, a professor at the University of Jyväskylä in Finland, found out in his research that the competence of teachers outdoes other factors such as class size, class structure, physical environment, and student background in affecting students' academic performance.[2] There are also research findings showing that mastery of relevant professional skills is an important predictor for successful implementation of inclusive education,[3] and the fundamental guarantee for teachers to meet the special educational needs of every student with disability.[4] According to some research findings, general education teachers lack special education knowledge and skills, and the resulting difficulties and restrictions have formed a bottleneck hindering improvement in the quality of the LRC program in China. It can be seen that whether primary and secondary school teachers are competent for inclusive education is the key to improving the quality of inclusive education. Therefore, the issue concerning how to deepen teachers' thinking on inclusive education and sharpen their competence has been brought to public attention. What are the key factors that affect the improvement of teacher competence in inclusive education? How do these factors act on it? In the course of probing these issues, we have made an in-depth analysis of these factors, found out the fundamental engine for improving the competence of teachers in inclusive education from the perspective of their professional development, come up with an effective way for continuous improvement of their competence, and constructed a model to improve their competence.

DOI: 10.4324/9781003432982-5

Research Approach

Beginning with an overview of the current state of LRC program teachers (hereinafter referred to as "the teachers"), this research reveals a scale investigation on the level of their competence in inclusive education, and finds out the specific situation of their knowledge, attitudes, skills, and ability to get support for inclusive education. Based on the investigation results and document analysis, we try to make clear the relationship between the competence of teachers in inclusive education and three factors—teacher agency, school climate for inclusive education, and occupational stress—and work out how these factors act on each other so as to find out their mechanism of action on the competence of teachers in inclusive education, and finally construct a model to improve the competence.

First of all, this research adopts the reliable and effective *Scale of Teacher Competence in Inclusive Education* to evaluate the level of competence of teachers in China, as well as the dimensions of competence—teachers' knowledge, attitudes, skills, and ability to get support for inclusive education—and analyze the differences between these dimensions.

Secondly, it gives an analysis of the difference in competence by region, demographic factors (gender, age), occupational characteristics (years of teaching experience, professional title, school sector, subject, experience of teaching LRC students, category of students' disabilities, class tutor or not) and educational factors (major, educational background, and training experience).

Thirdly, it probes the relationship between the competence of teachers in inclusive education and three factors—teacher agency, school climate for inclusive education, and occupational stress.

Finally, it explores how these three factors act on the competence of teachers in inclusive education. On this basis, it aims to make clear their mechanism of action on the competence of teachers in inclusive education, and construct a model to improve competence after analyzing the results of empirical research.

Research Scheme

Respondents

SAMPLE AND PROCEDURES

Convenience sampling was used to enlist respondents (teachers of LRC students) by region. To take account of the political and economic development level, the development of inclusive education, the representativeness of the sample size and other factors in different regions, the sampling method was in time adjusted to obtain the most authentic, reliable, and effective sample data.

120 *Research into the Competence of Chinese Teachers*

SURVEY PROJECT

Regional Division According to relevant state stipulations on administrative division, China comprises eight administrative regions: North China, Central China, East China, South China, Northwest China, Northeast China, Southwest China, and the Region of Hong Kong, Macao, and Taiwan.

North China includes Beijing, Tianjin, Hebei, Shanxi, and Inner Mongolia. East China covers Shanghai, Jiangsu, Zhejiang, Shandong, Anhui, Jiangxi, and Fujian. Northeast China comprises Liaoning, Jilin, and Heilongjiang. Central China is made up of Hubei, Hunan, and Henan. South China consists of Guangdong, Guangxi, and Hainan. Southwest China covers Sichuan, Chongqing, Guizhou, Yunnan, and Tibet. Northwest China includes Shaanxi, Gansu, Xinjiang, Qinghai, and Ningxia.

Sampling Based on Provinces or Municipalities Directly under the Central Government Giving an overall consideration to various aspects, we selected 139 schools with LRC students in six provinces/municipalities (Beijing, Shanghai, Jiangxi, Guangdong, Sichuan, Yunnan) in four regions—North China, East China, South China, and Southwest China—to issue our scale sheets. A total of 2,130 scale sheets were retrieved, including 1,676 that were effective, accounting for 78.69 percent of the total. The specific information is shown in Table 4.1.

To ensure the validity of the scale data, we did a relatively strict screening of the scale sheets retrieved. If the following situations were to appear in the scale sheet, it would be deemed ineffective and discarded. First, there is too much information missing in the scale. If more than three questions are not given an answer, or more than two personal basic information items are not provided in the scale, it would be discarded. Second, if the answering method shown in the scale is obviously regular, it would be discarded. For example, the same answer to each question is chosen or answers are given in a wavy pattern. Third, if several different subjects are given the same answer in the scale, it would be discarded.

Issuance of Scale Sheets In the specific operation, administrators of local education departments or special education research centers were entrusted to issue and retrieve most of the scale sheets on site. A small proportion of the scales were electronic, issued by local special education research centers' administrators through WeChat, QQ, and other channels. A total of 1,233 scale sheets were issued to groups of teachers on site. Of those, 1,095 were effective, making up 88.81 percent of the total. Of the 897 electronic scales, 581 were effective, accounting for 64.77 percent of the total.

Basic Information of Samples A total of 1,676 teachers were selected as respondents to our surveys. The basic information collected mainly covers their gender, age, years of teaching experience, professional title, school sector, subject, experience of teaching LRC students, category of students' disabilities,

Table 4.1 Sampling Information

Sampling region	North China	East China		South China	Southwest China		Total
Province/ municipality	*Beijing*	*Shanghai*	*Jiangxi*	*Guangdong*	*Sichuan*	*Yunnan*	
City	Beijing	Shanghai	Nanchang	Guangzhou	Chengdu	Kunming	6
District	Haidian	Changning	Xihu	Liwan, Yuexiu	Wuhou	Wuhua	7
Number of schools	45	19	19	24	8	24	139
Issuance time (2018)	Early November	May	Mid July	October	Late July	Late June	6
Number of effective scale sheets	434	111	146	466	383	136	1,676

Note: To maintain the balance of data in various regions, the Sichuan data adopted are 50 percent of the original data, randomly chosen.

122 *Research into the Competence of Chinese Teachers*

Table 4.2 Demographics of Samples (n=1,676)

Item		Number	Percentage (%)
Gender	Male	244	14.56%
	Female	1,432	85.44%
School sector	Primary school	1,237	73.81%
	Secondary school	439	26.19%
Age	21–30 years	377	22.49%
	31–40 years	663	39.56%
	41–50 years	545	32.52%
	51–60 years	91	5.43%
Number of years teaching	0–2 years	183	10.92%
	3–10 years	472	28.16%
	11–20 years	711	42.42%
	Over 20 years	310	18.50%
Number of years teaching LRC students	0–2 years	817	48.75%
	3–10 years	528	31.50%
	11–20 years	272	16.23%
	Over 20 years	59	3.52%
Major	Teaching-training	1,453	86.70%
	Others	223	13.30%
Subject	Basic subjects	883	52.68%
	Others	793	47.32%
Highest level of education	Junior college education or below	246	14.68%
	Bachelor or above	1,430	85.32%
Professional title	Not provided	207	12.3%
	Not graded	94	5.61%
	Third-grade	177	10.56%
	Second-grade	546	32.58%
	First-grade	538	32.10%
	Senior grade	114	6.80%
Category of the LRC students' disabilities	Single category	645	38.48%
	Multiple categories	1,031	61.52%
Having received training or not	Ever	1,101	65.69%
	Never	575	34.31%
Teacher identity	Class tutor	971	57.94%
	Non-class tutor	705	42.06%

being class tutor or not, major, educational background, and training experience, as shown in Table 4.2.

Research Instruments

This research mainly involves four variables: the competence of teachers in inclusive education, teacher agency, occupational stress, and school climate for inclusive education, with four scales as instruments.

SCALE OF TEACHER COMPETENCE IN INCLUSIVE EDUCATION

We measured teacher competence in inclusive education with a 28-item scale proposed by Wang Yan et al in 2015.[5] It covers four dimensions. The first dimension, comprising eight items, covers teachers' professional attitudes toward the influence of the LRC program on the growth of students with disabilities, the professional development of teachers, and the development of schools and society. The second dimension, consisting of six items, includes teachers' professional knowledge about policies, regulations, theories, and practices regarding LRC program. The third dimension, made up of eight items, covers teachers' professional skills in the planning, implementation and assessment of teaching to address the individual needs of students with disabilities. The final dimension, represented through six items, includes teacher agency for seeking and acquiring various forms of support to serve students with disabilities. A five-point Likert scale is used, ranging from 1 (strongly disagree), 2 (disagree), 3 (neutral), 4 (agree) to 5 (strongly agree), with higher scores indicating higher levels of teacher competence in inclusive education. The validity analysis result of this scale reveals that the average internal consistency coefficient of the four dimensions—ability to get support, professional knowledge, professional skills, and professional attitude is 0.928, 0.943, 0.941, and 0.925 respectively, all above 0.90, and their split-half reliability coefficient is 0.903, 0.934, 0.915, and 0.904 respectively, all above 0.90. The overall internal consistency coefficient of the scale reaches 0.967, and the overall split-half reliability coefficient is up to 0.880, indicating that this scale has good structural validity. An acceptable level of model fit ($\chi2/df$=4.902; CFI=0.972; GFI=0.939; AGFI=0.919; NFI=0.965; IFI=0.972; TLI=0.965; RMSEA=0.048; SRMR=0.0393; and RMR=0.038) was achieved for the measurement model. Therefore, this scale can be used for follow-up research.

SCALE OF LRC PROGRAM TEACHERS' AGENCY

We measured the agency of LRC program teachers with a 17-item scale proposed by Zhou Dan et al in 2019.[6] It covers two dimensions—self-efficacy in teaching and constructive participation. The coefficient of correlation between the two dimensions and the total score is between 0.792 and 0.980, showing a high correlation and demonstrating the sound structural validity of this scale. The internal consistency reliability coefficients of self-efficacy in teaching and constructive participation are 0.897 and 0.926 respectively, and their split-half reliability coefficient is 0.840 and 0.869 respectively. The overall internal consistency coefficient of this scale reaches 0.945, and the overall split-half reliability coefficient is up to 0.820, indicating the satisfactory internal consistency and reliability of this measurement instrument. An acceptable level of model fit ($\chi2/df$=4. 936; CFI=0.978; GFI=0.968; AGFI=0.951; NFI=0.972; IFI=0.978; TLI=0.969; RMSEA=0.048; SRMR=0.0331; RMR=0.024;) was achieved for the measurement model. Therefore, this scale can be used for follow-up research.

124 *Research into the Competence of Chinese Teachers*

SCALE OF TEACHERS' OCCUPATIONAL STRESS

We measured the teachers' occupational stress with a 22-item scale proposed by Li Qiong et al in 2011.[7] It covers five dimensions: workload stress (six items), stress from academic performance (five items), stress from social and school evaluation (four items), stress from professional development (four items), and stress from students' problem behaviors (three items). The Cronbach's alpha coefficients of each dimension therein and the whole scale are between 0.72 and 0.90, and the test–retest reliability coefficient is between 0.86 and 0.92, showing satisfactory internal consistency reliability. Considering the difference in occupational stress between LRC program teachers and ordinary teachers, we made some adjustments on the items, and carried out confirmatory factor analysis. After MI correction, an acceptable level of model fit ($\chi2/df=4.905$; CFI=0.981; GFI=0.975; AGFI=0.956; NFI=0.976; IFI=0.981; TLI=0.971; RMSEA=0.048; SRMR=0.0296; and RMR=0.033;) was achieved for the measurement model. Therefore, this scale can be used for follow-up research.

SCALE OF SCHOOL CLIMATE FOR INCLUSIVE EDUCATION

We measured the school climate for inclusive education with a scale proposed by Schaefer J. in 2010.[8] The internal consistency reliability coefficient of the scale is 0.807. Since the original scale is in English, we had it translated and revised in five steps. First, translate the original scale. One special education expert, one PhD candidate in special education, and one PhD candidate in English major were invited to independently complete the literal translation of the original items according to their own understanding. Second, integrate the three translations to form the first draft of the Chinese version, which was then proofread by one PhD candidate in special education and one special education expert. After discussion, the first Chinese version of the scale was formed. Third, complete the second draft of the Chinese version by revising the first Chinese version in conformity with Chinese expression, and reviewing the content of the first draft in accordance with the specification for the use of professional terms to make its linguistic expression concise and smooth and the meaning of its items clear and accurate. Fourth, revise the second draft through back-translation to complete the third draft. Fifth, special education experts were invited again to evaluate all items in the third draft. After revision for model fit, the final Chinese scale comprises 9 items in two dimensions— principal support (5 items) and school-wide inclusive practices (4 items). According to the result of its validity analysis, its overall internal consistency reliability coefficient and split-half reliability coefficient are 0.968 and 0.887 respectively. With regard to its two dimensions, their internal consistency reliability coefficient is 0.946 and 0.954 respectively, and their split-half reliability coefficient 0.837 and 0.927 respectively. The nine items can explain 79.895 percent of the total variance. The coefficient of correlation between each item and the overall scale/each dimension is between 0.756 and 0.952, showing a high correlation and demonstrating the sound structural validity of this scale.

After confirmatory factor analysis and MI correction, an acceptable level of model fit ($\chi2/df$=4.855; CFI=0.995; GFI=0.987; AGFI=0.972; NFI=0.994; IFI=0.995; TLI=0.992; RMSEA=0.048; SRMR=0.0111; and RMR=0.009) was achieved for the measurement model. Therefore, this scale can be used for follow-up research.

Research Methods

The research methods adopted in this chapter mainly include scale survey and literature analysis.

SCALE SURVEY

Scale survey is the main method of this research. Used to collect both quantitative data and qualitative data, it boasts wide survey scope, high efficiency, standardization and anonymity, more real and objective research conclusions, and convenient sorting and categorization of research results. There are two kinds of scales for descriptive and explanatory purposes respectively. The former is to estimate as accurately as possible a certain attribute of the population or the status quo of a certain phenomenon while the latter is to check whether there is some relationship between variables. Both are involved in this research.

LITERATURE ANALYSIS

As for the literature analysis, some literature materials available are studied to find out the nature and status of the research object, and draw one's own views therefrom.

Development Status and Characteristics of Competence of Teachers in Inclusive Education

Research into Status of Competence of Teachers in Inclusive Education

Inclusive education requires teachers to acquire relevant thinking, knowledge, and skills to meet the educational needs of all students, including those with disabilities, in regular classrooms. According to the existing research on the status of the competence of teachers in inclusive education from the perspectives of concept, knowledge, and skills, the competence differs in different periods and regions.

Status of Teachers' Thinking on Inclusive Education

Teachers' thinking on education not only has a direct impact on their educational behaviors but also indirectly affects the nature and quality of future education. With regard to inclusive education, their thinking involves the

126   *Research into the Competence of Chinese Teachers*

understanding of inclusive education as well as their views and attitudes toward various elements of education and teaching in the context of inclusive education. In the research into teachers' thinking on inclusive education, most researchers make scale surveys and conduct interviews to know teachers' views and attitudes toward the LRC program.

According to a survey of 368 teachers in regular primary schools by Liu Chunling et al. in 2000, 98 percent of these teachers hold that children with special needs and typically developing children are equal in personality, and 95.8 percent of them argue that special needs children should be given equal rights to education with typically developing children. But at the same time, 39.6 percent of them hold a negative (19.1 percent) or skeptical (20.5 percent) attitude about whether regular school teachers can accept children with special needs; 82.6 percent of them think that special needs children will make teachers lack a sense of accomplishment, and 81.8 percent of teachers have a desire to teach special needs children, but are worried about their competence.[9] Through a comparative study in 2000, Wei Xiaoman and Yuan Wende found that, compared with special education teachers, regular primary and secondary school teachers have a negative attitude toward the LRC program.[10] Deng Meng investigated the attitudes toward inclusive education of 223 teachers who have participated in the LRC program in Wuhan, and found that their overall attitudes toward inclusive education involve the pros and cons of inclusive education and the advantages of special education schools. Among the 223 teachers, 39.74 percent and 31.33 percent strongly or relatively agree with the advantages of inclusive education, indicating their positive attitude toward inclusive education, but 49.46 percent and 29.88 percent of them strongly or relatively agree with the advantages of special education schools. In other words, if choices are given, they would support special needs students to attend special education schools. This shows that although most teachers are in favor of inclusive education, most of them are more willing to choose special education schools to teach special needs students.[11] As shown in a survey of regular primary school teachers by Zeng Yaru in 2007, teachers' attitudes toward the LRC program are generally positive, but still in the initial stage toward a mature positive attitude.[12]

According to the survey of LRC program teachers by Ma Hongying and Tan Heping in 2010, teachers had a rational identification with the LRC program, and generally accepted special needs students.[13] However, a survey of inclusive education in primary schools by Wang Hongxia et al in 2011 reveals that teachers and school leaders still had reservations about the development of inclusive education, that is, it depends on various factors such as students' disabilities and environment.[14] A survey by Zhang Yuhong and Gao Yuxiang in 2014 shows that teachers, students, and parents had negative attitudes toward inclusive education, among which teachers' attitude was most negative.[15] As revealed in a survey by Zhao Hong and Xu Li in 2018 of kindergarten teachers who carried out inclusive education in Guilin City, 58.21 percent of teachers "agreed" or "strongly agreed" that "inclusive education enables special needs children and their typically developing peers to promote each other," and 62.69 percent of teachers "agreed" or "strongly agreed" that "inclusive education effectively promotes the improvement of the social communication ability of children with special needs," which shows that most preschool educators agreed with the role of inclusive education. However, only 26.87 percent of teachers were willing to admit children with special needs into kindergartens.[16] A survey of 592 teachers of LRC students in Nanjing City by Xiong Qi et al in 2019 reveals that the average score of the teachers' attitudes toward inclusive education was 2.70, slightly higher than the theoretical median of 2.5 points. The scores for the four dimensions were as follows: 3.51 for inclusive values, 2.49 for placement method, 2.35 for children's rights and 2.12 for teachers' workload.[17] According to Gao Li's summary of the research on the attitudes toward inclusive education on the Chinese mainland in 2019, all the attitudes of general education teachers, LRC students' teachers, and special education teachers had shown a change from a passive, conservative attitude to active support, so did the attitudes of the parents of both typically developing students and special needs students.[18]

In general, teachers' attitudes toward inclusive education have changed with its development, and vary in different regions. In the early stage of the LRC program, their attitudes were negative due to lack of understanding; as the concept of inclusive education was promoted, it was accepted by most of them, and their attitudes turned positive; and when they are required to improve the quality of inclusive education and are faced with difficulties in practice, they are cautious about the development but with a rational identification of inclusive education.

Status of Teachers' Knowledge and Skills for Inclusive Education

To deal with the challenges of inclusive education and ensure a smooth process in teaching LRC students, teachers should possess relevant knowledge and skills. Existing research on the status of their knowledge and skills for inclusive education were mostly undertaken by the investigation method.

According to some research findings, many general education teachers disapproved of the LRC program, arguing that LRC students' learning ability is poor, and they themselves are somewhat incapable of teaching those students due to the lack of professional knowledge and skills for special education.[19] Teachers in regular schools lacked the basic knowledge of special education;[20] they had poor theoretical understanding of inclusive education;[21] and they had no idea of the learning characteristics and educational needs of special children, and were unable to carry out classroom teaching and give extracurricular guidance for them.[22] The mathematics teachers of LRC students generally had poor knowledge and skills for special education, not to mention a rational structure or a wide range of knowledge and skills.[23] According to a survey by Tan Heping and Ma Hongying in 2010, 69 percent of teachers felt a lack of special education knowledge, while 81.5 percent revealed their lack of special education skills.[24] A survey by Zhang Yuhong et al in 2014 shows that teachers of LRC students lacked the awareness of actively using support from various aspects, and the utilization rate was also low.[25] According to a survey by Du Lingyu in 2018, teachers had a greater need for training of knowledge and skills. As for the teachers of LRC students with more years of teaching experience, they were poor in knowledge but proficient in skills.[26]

As revealed in a survey by Wei Shouhong et al. in 2018, the level of teachers' study of the inclusive education curriculum and teaching adjustment was below the middle level; they got the highest score in assignment adjustment, followed by teaching adjustment, goal adjustment, and evaluation adjustment, while that in textbook adjustment was the lowest. The failure in the study of the inclusive education curriculum and teaching adjustment was one of the main reasons for the difficulty of regular primary school teachers in implementing inclusive education.[27] According to a survey of primary and secondary school teachers' implementation of inclusive education in Beijing, 59.06 percent of the teachers were confident in designing appropriate teaching goals based on the characteristics of the students with disabilities; 61.43 percent said they were capable of organizing appropriate teaching activities; 62.34 percent had confidence in choosing a suitable teaching method; 68.27 percent argued that they could provide meaningful demonstration and guidance for the learning of students with disabilities; 66.33 percent believed that they were flexible in implementation of evaluation according to the age, ability, and curriculum characteristics of the students with disabilities; 60.19 percent showed their confidence in flexibly designing evaluation content and methods based on the characteristics of the students with disabilities; and 64.44 percent were confident in using appropriate materials and support for evaluation.[28] As shown in a survey of curriculum adjustment carried out by 202 primary school teachers of LRC students in Beijing City via a self-compiled *Scale of Curriculum Adjustment by Teachers of LRC Students*, the overall score of the teachers' curriculum adjustment was 3.67 points, slightly higher than the middle level; the scores of their curriculum adjustment in process and evaluation were both 3.68 points; and that of their curriculum goal adjustment was 3.63 points.[29]

To sum up, teachers in China lack the knowledge and skills for inclusive education, and are especially poor in active acquisition and utilization of support and resources.

As for these surveys, most of them featured a limited sampling scope, just in the researchers' schools or areas. No nationwide sampling example was found. They ignored the impact resulting from regional differences in the development of inclusive education and other factors.

Although interview and observation methods were adopted in the existing research, the scale survey method still dominated, and mixed research design was rarely used to explore this issue. Therefore, in future research into the status of teacher competence in inclusive education, more attention should be given to comprehensive application of various research methods.

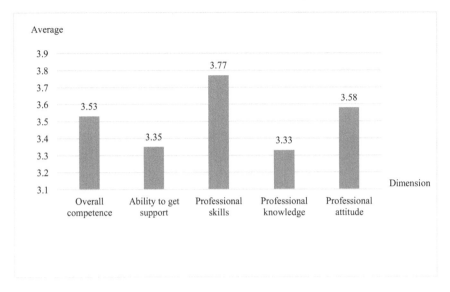

Figure 4.1 Average Scores of Competence of Teachers in Inclusive Education and Its Dimensions.

Level of Competence of Teachers in Inclusive Education

Current Status of Competence of Teachers in Inclusive Education

After making an analysis of the scale data on the inclusive education competence of 1,676 teachers, we found that the average of teachers' self-reported scores for each dimension of competence is between 3.33 and 3.77. The current overall level of competence of teachers in inclusive education in China scores 3.53, between "uncertain" and "relatively agree" options. This shows that the overall level is not high. The order of the dimensions by score from high to low is as follows: professional skills, professional attitude, ability to get support, and professional knowledge. Details are shown in Figure 4.1.

The result of our repeated-measures analysis of variance shows great differences among the four dimensions ($F = 310.704$, $p < 0.001$). The score for professional skills is significantly higher than those of the other three dimensions; and that of professional attitude far exceeds those of professional knowledge and ability to get support. The score for professional knowledge is the lowest. Details are shown in Table 4.3.

This result is basically consistent with a previous survey of 1,703 primary and secondary school teachers' competence in inclusive education in Beijing. The order of the dimensions by score from high to low in this survey is as follows: professional skills, professional attitude, professional knowledge, and

130 *Research into the Competence of Chinese Teachers*

Table 4.3 Multiple Comparisons of Four Dimensions of Competence of Teachers in Inclusive Education

Dimension	M	SD	F	P	Comparison results			P
					(I)	(J)	Mean difference (I-J)	
Ability to get support	3.35	0.87	310.704	0	Professional skills	Professional attitude	0.189*	0
Professional skills	3.77	0.75			—	Professional knowledge	0.439*	0
Professional knowledge	3.33	0.84			—	Ability to get support	0.419*	0
Professional attitude	3.58	0.84			Professional attitude	Professional knowledge	0.249*	0
—	—	—	—	—	—	Ability to get support	0.229*	0

Note: p<0.05.

ability to get support; and the scores for the former two are much higher than those for the latter two.[30]

Status of Competence of Teachers in Inclusive Education by Factor

To analyze the difference in the competence of teachers in inclusive education resulting from different factors (region, demographic factors, occupational characteristics, and educational factors), we made comparisons (t-test and one-way analysis of variance) on the averages of the competence by factor.

REGIONAL FACTOR

By region, the competence of teachers in inclusive education differs greatly in terms of overall competence, professional attitude, professional knowledge, professional skills, and ability to get support ($F(3,1672) = 16.805$, $p < 0.001$); $F(3,1672) = 9.377$, $p < 0.001$; $F(3,1672) = 8.401$, $p < 0.001$; $F(3,1672) = 38.185$, $p < 0.001$; $F(3,1672) = 6.128$, $p < 0.001$). After post hoc checks, we found that in terms of the ability to get support, teachers in North China, East China, and Southwest China scored significantly higher than those in South China. With respect to professional skills, knowledge, attitudes, and overall competence, teachers in North China outdid those in East China, Southwest China, and South China. This shows that teachers in South China left behind those in other regions in terms of the ability to get support, and teachers in North China outperformed those in other regions in all dimensions. Details are shown in Figure 4.2.

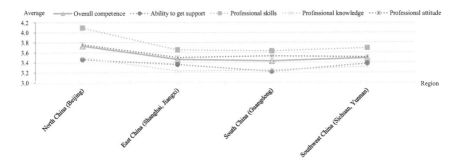

Figure 4.2 Competence of Teachers in Inclusive Education by Region.

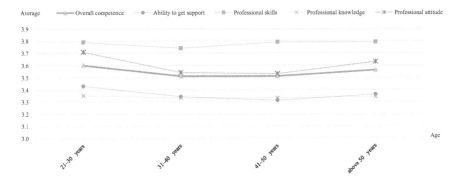

Figure 4.3 Competence of Teachers in Inclusive Education by Age.

INDIVIDUAL FACTORS

Gender By gender, the competence of teachers in inclusive education differs significantly in the ability to get support and professional knowledge ($F(1,1675) = 2.860, p < 0.05; F(1,1675) = 1.428, p < 0.01$). Male teachers far outdid females in these two dimensions. In terms of overall competence in inclusive education, males also outperformed females.

Age By age, the teachers' scores in professional knowledge hold steady, but those in overall competence, professional attitude, skills, and ability to get support first show a decline and then slowly rise, and those in professional attitude present a sharp turn ($F(3,1672) = 3.966, p < 0.01$). After post hoc checks, we found that in terms of professional attitude, teachers aged 21–30 far outperformed those in the 31–40 and 41–50 age groups. Details are shown in Figure 4.3.

132 *Research into the Competence of Chinese Teachers*

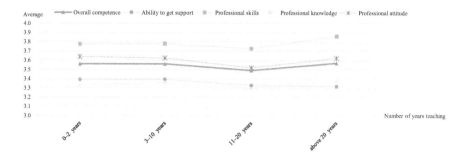

Figure 4.4 Competence of Teachers in Inclusive Education by Number of Years Teaching.

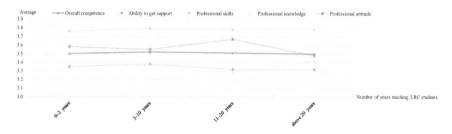

Figure 4.5 Competence of Teachers in Inclusive Education by Experience of Teaching LRC Students.

OCCUPATIONAL CHARACTERISTICS

Teaching Experience   By age, teachers' scores in overall competence, professional attitude, knowledge, and skills first show a gradual decline and then slowly rise, but those in the ability to get support present a continuous slow decline. Teachers with 11–20 years of teaching experience score the lowest, except in the ability to get support. Details are shown in Figure 4.4.

Experience of Teaching LRC Students   In terms of experience of teaching LRC students, teachers' scores in overall competence show a slow rise, but those in professional knowledge, skills, and ability to get support first rise and then decline. Teachers with 3–10 years' experience of teaching LRC students slightly outperformed those with less than two years and over 10 years of such experience in overall competence, professional skills, and ability to get support. But in professional attitude, teachers with 11–20 years' experience of teaching LRC students scored the highest, while the scores of those with over 20 years' experience of teaching LRC students declined; but no significant difference is found. Details are shown in Figure 4.5.

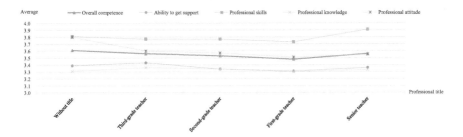

Figure 4.6 Competence of Teachers in Inclusive Education by Professional Title.

Subject By subject, the competence of teachers in inclusive education differs greatly in the ability to get support, professional skills, professional knowledge, and professional attitude ($F(1,1675) = 0.422, p \leqslant 0.05; F(1,1675) = 0.005, p \leqslant 0.05; F(1,1675) = 0.806, P<0.01; F(1,1675) = 0.012, p < 0.01; F(1,1675) = 0.042, p \leqslant 0.01$). Teachers of other subjects far outdid those of basic subjects in each dimension and in overall competence.

School Sector By school sector, teachers' scores differ significantly in professional skills ($F(1,1675) = 0.445, p \leqslant 0.01$). Teachers of junior high schools far outperformed those of primary schools. In terms of overall competence, the former also outdid the latter.

Teacher Identity By teacher identity, non-class-tutor teachers outperformed class tutors in the ability to get support and professional knowledge ($F(1,1675) = 0.305, p < 0.01. F(1,1675) = 1.090, p < 0.01$). In terms of overall competence, non-class-tutor teachers also outdid class tutors.

Professional Title By professional title from lower to higher levels, teachers' scores in the overall competence show a slow decline and then a rise. The scores of the teachers with first-grade professional titles are the lowest while those of the teachers without professional titles and the teachers with senior professional titles are higher. With regard to professional attitude, teachers with different professional titles differed greatly ($F(5, 1670) = 2.845, p < 0.05$), among whom those without a professional title far outdid those with third-grade, second-grade, first-grade, and senior professional titles. Details are shown in Figure 4.6.

EDUCATIONAL FACTORS

Educational Background By educational background, the teachers differed significantly in professional knowledge ($F(1,1675) = 0.110, p < 0.05$). Teachers with a bachelor's degree or above far outdid those holding a junior college

134 *Research into the Competence of Chinese Teachers*

diploma or below. In terms of overall competence, the former also outdid the latter.

Major By major, the teachers differed significantly in the ability to get support ($F(1,1675) = 0.014$, $p \leqslant 0.01$). After post hoc checks, we found that teachers who graduated from teacher-training majors scored much lower than those who graduated from other majors. In terms of overall competence, the latter outdid the former.

Training Experience By training experience, the teachers differed greatly in overall competence in inclusive education, professional attitude, professional knowledge, professional skills, and ability to get support ($F(1,1675) = 1.633, p < 0.001; F(1,1675) = 0.310, p < 0.01; F(1,1675) = 3.654, p < 0.001; F(1,1675) = 7.609$, $p < 0.001; F(1,1675) = 0.001$, $p < 0.001$). Teachers who had received training for special education far outperformed those without such training experience in each dimension and overall competence.

Analysis of Level of Competence of Teachers in Inclusive Education

LEVEL OF COMPETENCE OF TEACHERS IN INCLUSIVE EDUCATION IS NOT HIGH

Teacher competence in inclusive education involves the thinking, knowledge, and skills that teachers possess to meet the needs of all children, including children with special needs. Our research evaluates the level of competence via the *Scale of Teacher Competence in Inclusive Education.* This scale defines competence from four dimensions: professional attitude, professional knowledge, professional skills, and ability to get support. The research result reveals that the average of teachers' self-reported scores for each dimension of competence is between 3.33 and 3.77. The current overall level of competence of teachers in inclusive education in China scores 3.53, between the "uncertain" and "relatively agree" options. This shows that the overall level is not high. The order of the dimensions by score from high to low is as follows: professional skills, professional attitude, ability to get support, and professional knowledge. In comparison, teachers' professional skills for inclusive education are satisfactory, but there is still a lot of room for improvement in their professional attitude, ability to get support, and professional knowledge.

Teachers Have a Relatively Accepting Attitude Toward Children with Special Needs Our research findings show that teachers have a relatively accepting attitude toward children with special needs, which is basically consistent with related studies in recent years.[31,32] As mentioned above, there has been a significant shift in teachers' attitudes toward inclusive education from negative to positive and then to rational identification and prudent treatment. Generally speaking, inclusive education for children with special needs is relatively accepted by teachers at present, which is mainly attributed to two factors.

One lies in the change in policies. China has promulgated a series of policies with a focus on development of inclusive education in recent years. Under the guidance of these policies, teachers could be able to update their thinking faster and treat special needs children with a positive attitude.

Therefore, most teachers have high self-evaluation of the conceptual issues involving fairness and justice, as evidenced in our survey showing that 71.12 percent of teachers "agree" or "strongly agree" that "special needs students should receive education on an equal footing as typically developing students." On the other hand, the change and development of professional attitudes is more dependent on teachers' efforts in teaching practice. This positive attitude is gradually cultivated in their interaction with special needs children, special education and related professionals, and parents of special needs children. It is gradually promoted and formed when special needs children show positive and developmental characteristics. The integration of children with special needs into regular class may increase the workload of teachers, but it also provides opportunities for teachers' professional development and contributes to the personality development of both typically developing and special needs children. For example, 65.39 percent of teachers in our survey "agree" or "strongly agree" that the "LRC program urges teachers to pay more attention to individual differences between students," which reveals that teachers have a positive understanding of inclusive education. This is evidenced by their relatively high scores in professional attitude. At the same time, we also found that teachers showed low self-evaluation in terms of confidence in teaching special needs students. Only 39.32 percent of teachers "agree" or "strongly agree" that "I am confident to teach the special needs students in my class." This reflects that most teachers lack confidence in teaching special needs students.

Teachers Have Poor Knowledge of Inclusive Education   Our research findings show that in terms of professional knowledge, teachers have the lowest self-evaluation, scoring significantly lower than that in the other three dimensions. According to our survey data, in the following options: "I know the basic principles and methods of educating special needs students," "I have knowledge of local government's regulations, management system and other policies and measures regarding LRC students," "I understand the psychological and behavioral characteristics of the special needs students," "I know the educational evaluation methods for special needs students," "I'm familiar with the practical measures of the LRC program," and "I understand the theory of inclusive education," 47.73 percent, 41.77 percent, 46.54 percent, 36.93 percent, 41.11 percent, and 43.97 percent "agree" or "strongly agree" with them respectively.

Since the training of pre-service teachers in China generally excludes courses related to inclusive education, teachers are more dependent on post-service training to improve their professional knowledge of inclusive education. Although some of this content can also be explored and accumulated in practice, the post-service training system needs to be further improved. Among

136 *Research into the Competence of Chinese Teachers*

respondents, 34.31 percent of teachers have never received in-service training on special education. Although 65.69 percent have received such training, they lack systematic study as well as comprehensive and in-depth understanding of the professional knowledge of special education. This may be the reason for the overall low scores of teachers in terms of professional knowledge.

Teachers' Professional Skills for Inclusive Education Are Relatively Acceptable According to our survey results, teachers' scores in professional skills are significantly higher than those in professional attitude, ability to get support, and professional knowledge. A further analysis of the frequency of answers to each question in professional skills reveals that at least 60 percent of teachers selected "agree" or "strongly agree" in each question. Approximately 70 percent "agree" or "strongly agree" that "I can give assignments to and evaluate special needs students in a flexible manner," "I can help special needs students via group discussions, cooperative learning and other methods," and "I can meet the learning needs of special needs students by providing one-to-one tutoring service." However, relatively speaking, 39.80 percent and 39.38 percent of teachers "are uncertain," "disagree," or "strongly disagree" that "special needs students and their typically developing peers in the same class can help and learn from each other," and "I can effectively regulate the behaviors of special needs students." On the whole, teachers have relatively better performance with regard to professional skills for inclusive education. There may be two reasons for this. First, LRC students are generally mildly or moderately disabled,[33] and their receptive ability is relatively good, so the education and teaching strategies for typically developing children are easier to be implemented on disabled students. Second, teaching skills can be acquired and explored through daily practice, imitating other professionals or learning from other teachers.

Teachers' Ability to Get Support Is Relatively Poor As shown in our survey, fewer than 50 percent of the teachers "agree" or "strongly agree" that "I can make use of resource rooms to help special needs students," "I can enlist support from leaders at all levels for the LRC program," and "I can actively seek guidance and help from the teachers with special education schools or special education guidance (resource) centers." This shows that more than half of teachers have a poor ability to get support. The possible reason is that, compared with children with special needs, typically developing children form the main body of the class, and their educational needs will inevitably consume more of the time and energy of teachers, thereby restricting teachers' active acquisition of support for inclusive education. Although quality education has long been advocated in the field of general education, due to the influence of the elite education model in traditional culture, teachers still lay stress on the improvement of students' academic performance. In such an educational ecosystem, the all-round development of children with special needs is naturally ignored, which in turn impairs teachers' will and ability to get support. When children with special needs are just mixed into regular class, their learning needs are beyond the scope of teachers' concerns. As a result, teachers will naturally not actively seek support resources for them. For example, Boer's analysis of the inclusive education programs of 16 developing countries including China reveals that the practice of inclusive education in developing countries only increased the number of children with special needs in regular schools, but did not touch on academic participation and social participation.[34] For another example, the *Special Education Evaluation Report* (Abstract), a mid-term evaluation report required by the *Outline of China's National Plan for Medium and Long-term Education Reform and Development*, noted that the LRC program, as the main form of special education in China, is shrinking, and the quality is worrying.[35] Moreover, teachers may also fail to "act" due to the lack of access to support. This may be another reason for impairing teachers' acquisition of support.

COMPETENCE OF TEACHERS IN INCLUSIVE EDUCATION VARIES IN DIFFERENT REGIONS

The competence of Chinese teachers in inclusive education vary in different regions. Teachers in North China score higher in all dimensions of their competence in inclusive education than those in East China, South China, and Southwest China, and far outdo the latter in overall competence, professional attitude, professional knowledge, and professional skills. Teachers in South China score lower in overall competence, professional skills, and ability to get support than those in North China, East China, and Southwest China, and fall far behind the latter in the ability to get support. This may be attributed to the difference in development levels of general education, special education, and inclusive education in different regions. The unbalanced development of education is one of the main problems of China's educational cause. To effectively implement inclusive education, work should be done to improve the competence of LRC program teachers. However, the prospects for pre-service training for inclusive education in China are not good. First, only a small number of courses related to inclusive education are offered by regular teacher-training majors. Second, such courses are subject to certain limitations in terms of nature, objectives, and content.[36] Most teachers depend on in-service training and practice to develop their competence in inclusive education.

As a representative of North China, Beijing leads China in economic development. With sufficient educational resources, it boasts earlier and rapid development of special education, and also gives more attention and support in this regard. Moreover, it took the lead in China in responding to and promoting inclusive education. Since the 1990s, Beijing has promulgated, in accordance with the gist of relevant national policy, a series of documents, including the *Opinions on Further Strengthening the Implementation of the LRC Program for Disabled Children and Adolescents in the Nine-Year Compulsory Education Stage* and the *Notice on Establishment of A Supporting System for the LRC Program in all Districts and Counties of Beijing*, to provide a strong guarantee

138 *Research into the Competence of Chinese Teachers*

for inclusive education. It pioneered in China professional support models such as resource rooms and special education centers. Since 2002, special funds have been added to promote the construction of resource rooms. Beijing has carried out useful exploration and practical activities in terms of policy support, sufficient material supply, professional guidance, teacher training, and improvement of education and teaching quality for LRC students. In 2013, the General Office of the People's Government of Beijing Municipality issued the *Action Plan on Inclusive Education in Primary and Secondary Schools of Beijing*, clearly proposing to promote inclusive education, and ensure that children and adolescents with disabilities have equal rights to basic public education services. This is the first action plan on inclusive education issued in the name of a government at provincial or municipal level in China, directly promoting rapid development of inclusive education. According to a scale survey of inclusive schools in 16 districts and counties of Beijing, the overall implementation of inclusive education in Beijing is at a relatively high level, but development in various aspects is uneven.[37] In recent years, Beijing has "continuously met the educational needs of disabled children and adolescents, focused on supply-side structural reform in terms of policy support, professional support, and improvement in the social environment to actively promote the development of inclusive education." In terms of advancing inclusive education, it is absolutely necessary to develop the competence of teachers in inclusive education, an important part in the move to build the entire supporting system. The overall quality of inclusive education is a possible factor that affects the competence of teachers in inclusive education.

DIFFERENCE IN COMPETENCE OF TEACHERS IN INCLUSIVE EDUCATION BY DEMOGRAPHIC FACTORS

Male Teachers Outperform Females in Competence in Inclusive Education
Generally, male teachers outdo females in overall competence in inclusive education and each dimension of competence, in particular professional knowledge and ability to get support. This is similar to previous research. According to a survey by Li Xiu in 2016, male teachers are more active than females in recognizing the equal educational rights of children with special needs and their typically developing peers, and accepting children with special needs; and they also score higher than females in the sub-scales regarding evaluation and expectation as well as education and teaching.[38] As shown in a survey by Shi Mengliang et al. in 2017, there were significant differences between men and women in their attitudes toward related services, environmental equipment, and school support and cooperation, and male teachers generally outperformed females in dealing with these issues.[39] As for the reasons, on the one hand, the ratio of male to female teachers is unbalanced, resulting in large sample difference in comparison. On the other hand, this may be related to the personality traits of teachers of different genders. Generally speaking, males are more active than females in challenging work, and pursue

changes and challenges in their career, as evidenced in the implementation of the LRC program. Another survey by Zhang Xiaodong in 2019 reveals that 69.6 percent of primary school teachers of LRC students claimed to be under pressure at work, and female teachers felt greater stress in terms of school factors than males.[40] The teaching process is regarded as a process in which teachers implement established teaching procedures. However, when students with special needs are seated in regular classrooms, the actual educational situation is not the same as that for typically developing peers with the same teaching goals and clear teaching path. As a class proceeds as normal, some special needs students may disturb the class order due to emotional malaise, or are not interested in the teaching content, not interactive with the class at all. Teachers often find themselves falling into an uncertain situation. Such a situation is what Schon described as "low-lying wetland."[41] In an inclusive education classroom, teachers are always found in a "low-lying wetland" featuring "complexity, uncertainty, instability, uniqueness, and value conflicts." Therefore, teachers need courage to face challenges, and to flexibly adjust in the complex and changeable inclusive education environment.

Change in Competence of Teachers in Inclusive Education with Increase of Age With the increase of age, the level of teachers' overall competence in inclusive education first declines and then rises slowly, so does that of their professional attitude, knowledge, and ability to get support. Only their professional skills show little change. However, in terms of professional attitude, teachers in the 21–30 age group score significantly higher than those in the 31–40 and 41–50 age groups. Recent years have seen great efforts made by China to promote inclusive education. As stated in the *Opinions on Strengthening the Development of Special Education Teacher Teams* promulgated by the Chinese Ministry of Education in 2012, "Relevant support shall be given to normal colleges and other institutions of higher learning to generally offer special education courses in teacher-training majors to cultivate these majors' ability to educate and teach students with disabilities in regular classrooms." In response, some normal colleges offered special education courses to cultivate teacher candidates; and pre-service and in-service trainings were provided in some places to improve teachers' ability to give better guidance to LRC students. Judged by time, this may be the reason why teachers in the 21–30 age group have higher competence in inclusive education than those in other age groups. A survey of the competence in inclusive education of preschool teachers by Qi Juan in 2017 gives a similar conclusion: preschool teachers aged 25 or below hold much better attitudes toward inclusive education than those aged 36 and above.[42] Teachers aged 30 or below are basically in the first stages of their career, exploring the possibilities of their career in order to establish a stable framework.[43] Perhaps they have accepted the concept of inclusive education and new educational ideas through pre-service training.[44] Coupled with the age characteristics—"newborn calves are not afraid of tigers"—they hold a more positive attitude toward inclusive education. As for teachers in later

140 *Research into the Competence of Chinese Teachers*

age groups, their competence in inclusive education improves slowly with age, which may be attributed to the accumulation of their educational wisdom and experience in the process of interacting with special needs students.

DIFFERENCE IN COMPETENCE OF TEACHERS IN INCLUSIVE EDUCATION BY
OCCUPATIONAL CHARACTERISTICS

Change in Competence of Teachers in Inclusive Education with Increase in Years of Teaching Experience   With the increase in years of teaching experience, the level of teachers' overall competence in inclusive education first shows a gradual decline and then rises slowly, so does that of their performance in each dimension. Among teachers, those with 10–20 years of teaching experience score the lowest in overall competence and each dimension, but the difference is not significant. This trend is basically consistent with that resulting from the factor of age. One reason for this may be related to the time of the development of inclusive education in China; another reason lies in the characteristics of teachers' professional development in different stages.

Change in Competence of Teachers in Inclusive Education with Increase in Experience of Teaching LRC Students   With the increase in experience of teaching LRC students, the level of teachers' overall competence in inclusive education shows a slow rise, but that of their professional knowledge, skills, and ability to get support first shows a rise and then declines. Among teachers, those with 3–10 years' experience of teaching LRC students score slightly higher than those with less than two years or over 10 years of such experience in terms of overall competence, professional skills, and ability to get support. Although teachers' scores in professional attitude fluctuate, there is no significant difference. Teachers will gradually acquire relevant knowledge and accumulate useful experience in the process of interacting with LRC students and exploring solutions to their problems. This may be the reason why teachers with fewer than 10 years' experience of teaching LRC students score high. Teachers with 10–20 years' experience of teaching LRC students score the highest as they have witnessed the continuous promotion of inclusive education, and enjoyed the policy guarantee for implementation of the LRC program. Moreover, with the maturing of their vocation, they increasingly agree with the concept of inclusive education and become more and more active in implementation of the LRC program on the basis of more effective interactions and successful cases. Thus, they score the highest in professional attitude. Teachers with over 20 years' experience of teaching LRC students score the lowest. This might be because they lack enthusiasm and momentum at the end of their career, and grow tired of their work, developing a negative attitude.

Difference in Competence of Teachers in Inclusive Education by Subject   By subject, the competence of teachers in inclusive education differs greatly.

Teachers of other subjects (music, physical education, fine arts, and so on) far outperform those of basic subjects (Chinese, mathematics, foreign language, and so on) in overall competence and each dimension. This result may be attributed to the nature and importance of each subject. As revealed in a survey of inclusive education in 400 primary and secondary schools by Jiang Xiaoying et al. in 2016, over 70 percent of the schools evaluated special needs students in the same way as their typically developing peers, but their scores were not included in the class evaluation.[45] This brought different degrees of pressure on teachers of different subjects. Another survey by Wang Hongxia et al. in 2011 shows that more problems appeared in the inclusive education of the main subjects than that of other subjects.[46] Study of the main subjects requires students to have certain cognitive ability. However, most LRC students suffer developmental disabilities, and their cognitive ability is nowhere near as good as that of their typically developing peers. Coupled with large class size, all these factors urge teachers to focus on the learning of the majority in class. Therefore, it is inevitable for teachers to "ignore" special needs students in class, and pay little attention to the improvement of their own competence in inclusive education. In comparison with basic subjects, other subjects such as physical education and fine arts, by nature, are easier and more attractive to special needs students. Teachers of these subjects also have time and opportunities to pay attention to the performance of special needs students in class, and make corresponding adjustments to teaching strategies and methods as well as courses to meet their special needs. Thus, they outperform teachers of main subjects in competence in inclusive education.

Difference in Competence of Teachers in Inclusive Education by School Sector In terms of school sector, junior high school teachers have higher average scores than primary school teachers in terms of overall competence in inclusive education and each dimension of competence, and show significant differences in professional skills. Our design for teachers' self-evaluation of professional skills involves four items on teachers' cooperative teaching and guidance strategies, three on different aspects of individualized education plan, and one on behavior management. The result shows that junior high school teachers have higher self-evaluation of their professional skills. A survey by Xiong Qi et al. in 2019 also shows the same result: Teachers in grades seven to nine scored higher than those in grades one through six in terms of self-efficacy in teaching guidance, cooperation, and behavior management, and their scores are much higher than the latter in terms of self-efficacy in cooperation.[47] This may be attributed to LRC students' successful experience in inclusive education in primary schools, involving their will to cooperate, learning ability, and individualized education plans, as well as parents' support for and cooperation with teachers' work. These factors combined bring convenience to the work of secondary school teachers, making them more adaptable to the LRC program. Thus, they score high in self-evaluation of professional skills.

142 *Research into the Competence of Chinese Teachers*

Teacher Identity In terms of teacher identity, non-class-tutor teachers score higher than class tutors in overall competence in inclusive education, professional attitude, professional knowledge, and ability to get support, and show significant differences in the overall competence, professional knowledge, and ability to get support. This result may be attributed to the different degrees of pressure on them. According to a sampling survey of 9,697 primary and secondary school teachers across China by Zhao Fujiang et al. in 2018, class tutors are mostly teachers of basic subjects (Chinese, mathematics, and English). Among them, 49.9 percent, 28.0 percent, and 13.3 percent are Chinese-language teachers, mathematics teachers, and English teachers respectively. For class tutors, "safety responsibility" (76.7 percent), "heavy class management tasks" (65.1 percent), and "heavy workload" (64.8 percent) are the three main sources of their occupational stress.[48] Another survey by Geng Shen in 2018 reveals that class tutors lack systematic support in their work, often feeling "isolated and helpless." When faced with difficulties, the vast majority will only seek support from leaders and subject teachers. In addition, few teachers consider seeking support and help from psychological teachers, school doctors, parents, and so on.[49] Compared with other teachers, class tutors bear greater occupational stress, and face more tasks of class management and teaching, so they may spend less time and energy to improve their own competence in inclusive education. In contrast, other teachers, free from the troubles and pressures faced by class tutors, are more likely to pay attention to and think about the teaching issues concerning special needs children in the class. Therefore, other teachers outperform class tutors in the ability to get support, knowledge accumulation, and overall competence in inclusive education.

Professional Title In terms of professional title, teachers' overall competence in inclusive education shows a slow decline and then a rise as the level of their professional titles increases. Among them, those with first-grade professional titles score the lowest; those without professional title and those with senior professional titles outdo others in overall competence; and those without professional titles score significantly higher than those with professional titles. This result is attributed to the development background of the LRC program in China, as well as the complexity in developing competence in inclusive education. Thanks to the development of inclusive education in China, more young teachers have been taught the concept of inclusive education in pre-service training, and are thus willing to interact more with LRC students in class. This is just the case with teachers without professional title, most of whom have just worked at school for about one year, a case consistent with the research findings of Hwang Y. S. et al. in 2011.[50] As for teachers with senior professional titles, they have made many explorations and received relevant training in the process of professional development to acquire more knowledge and improve their skills with a more active attitude toward inclusive education.

DIFFERENCE IN COMPETENCE OF TEACHERS IN INCLUSIVE EDUCATION BY EDUCATIONAL FACTORS

Educational Background Generally speaking, teachers with a bachelor's degree or above score higher than those with a junior college diploma or below in terms of overall competence in inclusive education and each dimension, and show significant difference in professional knowledge. Educational background is an important characteristic variable of teachers, and different educational background indicates different levels of vocational training. Compared with teachers holding a junior college diploma or below, those with a bachelor's degree or above have received a higher degree of professional training and longer schooling, during which they studied more profound theories and extensive knowledge on education. However, teachers with a junior college diploma or below may have paid more attention to the study of teaching skills when they were college students. Moreover, most teachers with a junior college diploma or below are older teachers whose pre-service study may seldom have involved the concept of inclusive education. These are the possible reasons for this result.

Major Teachers without a teacher-training diploma outdo those with such a diploma in terms of overall competence in inclusive education and each dimension, and show remarkable differences in the ability to get support, which may be attributed to their different strategies for coping with teaching pressure. A survey of 222 primary school teachers of LRC students by Zhang Xiaodong in 2019 reveals the great overall stress on teachers of LRC students, a fact recognized by 69.6 percent of the respondents.[51] Attendance of special needs children in regular classrooms inevitably gives rise to greater challenges in class management, classroom teaching, and other aspects for teachers. According to a survey by Campbell in 2012, new teachers without a teacher-training diploma tend to consider the causes of problems from multiple angles in a certain way and solve them by flexible methods, while teachers holding a teacher-training diploma excel in actively probing and solving problems, and summing up experience, an advantage mainly reflected in their teaching ability.[52] The ability to get support finds expression in teacher agency in planning, launching, and carrying out conscious activities to promote the implementation of the LRC program.[53] To bring the agency into play, teachers need to critically sharpen their ability to cope with various problematic circumstances.[54] In inclusive education, teachers are faced with problems in various aspects including teaching. Teachers with no teacher-training diploma are not conservative but flexible in solving the problems, which may be a reason for this result. Moreover, the large difference in the sample size of the two sample groups may also give rise to this result.

Training Experience Teachers who have received special education training far outperform those without such training experience in terms of overall competence in inclusive education and each dimension. The professional development of teachers is a continuous process throughout their entire career. This is also the case with the improvement of their competence in inclusive education. Pre-service training is a good opportunity to shape the competence of teachers in inclusive education. However, China still lacks sound experience in cultivating teachers for inclusive education, and inclusive education courses are only available in a small number of normal colleges.[55] The development of inclusive education has enabled increasing numbers of special needs children to receive compulsory education in regular schools, but most teachers are not competent to cope with this change. Relevant laws, regulations, and policy documents in China put forward clear requirements for the cultivation of teacher competence in inclusive education. The *Law of the PRC on the Protection of Disabled Persons* promulgated in 1990 and the *Regulations on Education for Individuals with Disabilities* promulgated in 1994 and revised in 2017 requires that regular normal schools and colleges offer special education courses. Some policies even provided for the inclusion of knowledge of special education in teacher qualification examinations. However, due to the poor execution of relevant laws and regulations and the inadequate implementation of related policies, colleges and universities think little of or ignore the pre-service training of teacher competence in inclusive education, so in-service training has become an important remedy for teachers to improve their competence in this regard. Most research findings show that receiving training on inclusive education can help improve the competence of teachers in inclusive education. A survey by Wu Yang in 2017 reveals that preschool teachers who have received professional training for special education score significantly higher than those who have not received such training in terms of overall competence in inclusive education and each dimension.[56] Another survey by Qi Juan in 2017 shows that special education curriculum training has a significant impact on the attitudes and skills of preschool teachers in inclusive education.[57] As mentioned above, our survey also proves the importance of in-service training for the improvement of teacher competence in inclusive education. Among our respondents, 48.75 percent (817) of teachers have been engaged in teaching LRC students for less than two years, but only 62.67 percent (512) of teachers have ever received related training, as against 305 teachers who have not. It can be seen that even in-service training for inclusive education has not covered all teachers. Today, when the quality of basic education is pursued, great attention from all parties should be given to this point.

Theoretical Bases of Influencing Factors and Effects

Research into Factors Influencing Teacher Competence in Inclusive Education

The professional development of teachers constitutes an important part of their individual socialization, which is a dynamic process throughout their career. To realize it, they have to continuously improve their competence.

As the professional development of teachers is influenced by both external factors (social environment involving technology, culture and lifestyle, and so on, as well as school environment and family) and internal factors, it is an interactive process.[58] This is also the case with the development of teacher competence in inclusive education.

Individual Factors Influencing Teacher Competence in Inclusive Education

In comparison with the individual factors of educational background, major, teaching experience, and so on, professional psychology involving self-awareness of professional development, professional identity, achievement motivation, and self-efficacy is more closely related to the professional development of teachers.[59] In other words, by giving full play to their agency and continuously tapping their own potential, teachers can free themselves from the shackles of educational background and find a steady stream of driving force for their professional development. According to some research, agency is an important core force for teachers to change their own work and their working environment when dealing with complex educational situations,[60] and to a large extent affects teachers' working methods, job opportunities, professional interests, and teaching perspectives as well as job satisfaction and future development prospects.[61]

Foreign research on agency mainly cover the fields of philosophy, psychology, and sociology. As revealed in some research findings, agency is the ability of individuals to exercise personal control over the nature and quality of their lives,[62] generate the power of action with established purposes, and also bring about development.[63] This is reflected in the fact that individuals are driven by internal motivation and self-regulation, their actions are spontaneous and purposeful, and they are always actively participating in certain activities.[64] From the perspective of development, individuals move on a self-directed path and give meaning to their behaviors on the path. Within limited time and space, individuals make choices through their own judgments, thereby shaping themselves and the environment in which they live.

Recent years have seen much research on agency in the field of pedagogy, in particular teacher agency. Defined in a survey by Zhang Na in 2012, teacher agency refers to teachers actively exerting their inherent potential and actively leveraging external resources to improve their level of professional development and personal quality toward the professional development goals they have set in advance.[65] It is a practice of professional subjects making choices that affect their work and professional identity,[66] and also the internal driving force for professional development of teachers.[67] In the context of inclusive education, teacher agency finds expression in their active response to the implementation of the LRC program. It comprises two dimensions: self-efficacy in teaching and constructive participation.[68] The former can be seen as the soul and core of teaching in inclusive education, while the latter involves the whole teaching process. An enquiry into the professional competence in inclusive education of

146   *Research into the Competence of Chinese Teachers*

teachers in China shows that their agency is a positive predictor of their skills in inclusive education.[69] According to a survey of the role of teacher agency in their professional development in inclusive education, teachers often need to actively make explorations for the sake of professional development, and solve theoretical puzzles and practical problems arising from the development of inclusive education. In this way, they can accumulate practical wisdom and improve their professional level.[70]

With the development of inclusive education, teacher agency gradually takes on four features. First, teacher agency finds expression in their initiative. In the face of students' problem behaviors and other difficulties and crises, pro-active teachers will find out the reasons and come up with measures to meet the challenges. The second feature is related to the change in the classroom situation brought about by special needs students. Teachers should adapt themselves to the change to build a new balanced ecosystem suitable for the common growth and development of all students. Third, teacher agency is actually their immediate response capability to deal with emergencies or accidents at any time in an inclusive classroom by making decisions and giving correct guidance and help at once. Fourth, improvement of teacher agency requires a relatively long process of unremitting effort.

To meet the demand of special children for inclusive education, teachers should take the following measures. First, they should develop a special education plan based on the specific situation of special needs children to make them truly integrate into classroom study and improve the effectiveness of education. Second, they should actively give guidance to family education, and pay attention to home-school cooperation to strengthen the continuity of education. Third, they should properly handle the relationship between special needs children and their typically developing peers to form a class atmosphere of unity and friendship, as well as a good inclusive classroom atmosphere. Fourth, they should actively participate in various inclusive education-related knowledge and skill training to master the professional skills of managing special needs children and handling problems as soon as possible.

External Factors Influencing Teacher Competence in Inclusive Education

The improvement of teacher competence in inclusive education requires not only individual efforts but also support from and cooperation with collective and even social groups.[71] First of all, schools will inevitably have an explicit or implicit impact on the professional competence of teachers in terms of materials, system, and culture, and so on. Some research findings reveal that teachers are suffering a new wave of occupational stress from great classroom changes brought by educational reform on inclusive education.[72,73] These are bound to be the most direct external factors that influence the improvement of teacher competence.

SCHOOL CLIMATE

School climate reflects the quality and characteristics of school life, and gives expression to a school's guidelines, goals, values, interpersonal relationships, teaching and learning practices, and organizational structure,[74] having a relatively lasting and stable impact on the behaviors of all members, including teachers. Empirical study of organizational behaviors shows that a positive and harmonious organizational atmosphere is an important factor for relieving individual stress and anxiety, and improving work and life satisfaction, work efficiency, and labor output.

Researcher Julie Schaefer has stated that school climate for inclusive education involves the participation of special needs children in school activities, cooperation and support between general education teachers and special education teachers, the support of school principals, and school-wide inclusive practice.[75] On this basis, Chinese researcher Zhou Dan conducted an indigenized analysis and proposed a two-dimensional structure of school climate for inclusive education—principal support and school-wide inclusive practice. The former means that the principal should not only have a wealth of inclusive education knowledge, but also spread the concept of inclusive education, and provide support and guarantee for the school to carry out inclusive education; the latter refers to the school development plan formulated for inclusive education practice, preparations for teachers to accept children with special needs, and professional development activities, and so on.[76]

A survey by Zhang Lili in 2016 reveals that the school climate for inclusive education is sufficiently predictive of teacher competence in inclusive education.[77] In other words, if the climate for inclusive education of a school is more positive, the school will pay more attention to the implementation of the inclusive education concept, not only exerting a subtle impact on teachers' attitudes toward inclusive education, but also taking the initiative to provide teachers with more inclusive education training and learning opportunities to improve teachers' inclusive education knowledge level.[78,79] In addition, schools can also carry out a wealth of inclusive education and teaching activities to sharpen teachers' skills,[80] and promote the overall improvement of the competence of teachers in inclusive education.

Today, an increasing number of LRC students have brought huge challenges in education, teaching, and classroom management. A school's support, teaching equipment conditions, class size, curriculum, teaching system, teacher culture, principal's school-running ideas and management style all have an impact on the competence of teachers in inclusive education, which determines the quality of inclusive education for special needs children. In fact, the dissemination of the inclusive education concept and the tremendous changes it has caused in the field of education urgently require schools to establish a system and mechanism to improve the competence of teachers in inclusive education as soon as possible. Since teachers rely on in-service training to improve their competence in inclusive education, schools should provide a steady stream of

148 *Research into the Competence of Chinese Teachers*

motivational support for them. So, for now, building a positive and harmonious school climate for inclusive education is the most effective choice.

In short, a positive school climate for inclusive education can promote teachers' positive psychological and teaching behavior development,[81,82] so as to prepare them for the education and cultivation of all children, including special needs children.

OCCUPATIONAL STRESS

Occupational stress refers to a series of emotional or physiological negative reactions of individuals caused by certain factors at work.[83] It causes corresponding anger, anxiety, tension, depression, and other reactions. Occupational stress is usually seen as a dynamic process, involving stressors and stress results.[84] Stressors refer to the stimulus, event, or environment that causes occupational stress. It can also be the external material environment and the internal environment of the individual. Stress results refer to the responses caused by stressors.

The occupational stress of teachers is generally regarded as excessive, since the stressor threatens teachers in their work environment for a long time and continuously acts on them, causing them to produce a series of physiological, psychological, and behavioral responses.[85] Teaching has been a high-stress profession since ancient times.[86] As well as the same pressures that other professions bear, such as pressure from workload and professional prestige, teachers are also under pressure due to the occupational particularity concerning the historical responsibilities of teaching and educating students and carrying forward culture as well as student development and examination evaluation. Facing rapid social development, diversified values, and higher expectations from various parties, teachers are suffering increasing occupational stress. In addition, implementation of inclusive education requires teachers to cooperate in a highly diverse school environment, and master relevant knowledge and skills to give targeted guidance, individualized education, and differentiated teaching content according to students' different learning styles, ability levels, and learning preferences. All these have brought greater challenges and pressures on teachers.[87]

Many studies at home and abroad have shown that higher occupational stress can lead to a decrease in teachers' work efficiency and weak self-efficacy in teaching,[88,89] thereby affecting the physical and mental health of teachers. If occupational stress cannot be effectively controlled and relieved for a long time, it will readily cause extreme psychological and emotional fatigue, and eventually professional burnout, characterized by emotional exhaustion, depersonalization, and low personal accomplishment. Higher occupational stress will also affect teachers' enthusiasm for developing inclusive education, and hinder the improvement of their competence in inclusive education, a bane to their professional development.[90,91]

Among the factors that influence the competence of teachers in inclusive education, teacher agency is a significant internal factor, and school climate and occupational stress are more important external factors. However, as for how these three factors affect the improvement of the competence of teachers in inclusive education and their internal development mechanism, no research so far has provided a systematical explanation.

Theoretical Basis for Effect of Influencing Factors

Ecological Approach for Teachers' Professional Development

As a science about the "structure and function of ecosystem,"[92] ecology deals with the "whole relationship and interaction between animals and the organic and inorganic environment." According to ecological theories, no living organism exists in isolation, but survives in a certain environment and integrates with it into an overall system.[93] Therefore, ecological study focuses on the influence on the living organisms imposed by various relationships between the living organisms and the surrounding environment. The concept of ecology was first developed in the field of animals and plants, and then gradually gave birth to the sub-disciplines of human ecology, social ecology, educational ecology, and so on. Especially since the 1980s, some researchers have begun to focus on ecological analysis of educational practical problems, which has promoted the in-depth development of research on educational ecology.

As far as the teacher group is concerned, there are three main viewpoints[94] on the approach for teachers' professional development. The first is about the intellectual approach for teachers' professional development. This viewpoint lays stress on the importance of "scientific knowledge" and the "knowledge base" for the teaching profession, and holds that the professional ability of teachers is restricted by the professional knowledge and the scientific principles and technologies of pedagogy and psychology, and the competence of teachers can be ensured by mastering this professional knowledge, principles, and technologies. The second is about the practical–reflective approach for teachers' professional development. This viewpoint argues that the way for teachers to have a higher professional level is not to "accept" knowledge, but to understand their own practice through "reflection" and accumulate "practical knowledge." The third is about the ecological approach for teachers' professional development. It goes beyond the limitation in the first two viewpoints of focusing on the teachers themselves, and instead focuses on the professional background of teachers and the relationship between various factors in the professional landscape, emphasizing team cooperation and harmony, and trying to look at the professional development of teachers from a wider perspective. This viewpoint asserts that the professional growth of teachers is the result of the interaction between the individual and the environment.

150　*Research into the Competence of Chinese Teachers*

The third viewpoint is somewhat doubtful about the first two, but is actually a development of and also a further supplement to them. More importantly, the ecological approach provides a holistic, contextual, and correlative perspective to view teachers' professional development, a new path for research into teachers' professional development. To put it specifically, in the macro-research field of educational ecology, exploration is made of the relationship between the education and professional growth of teachers and the ecological environment as well as the corresponding mechanism; and in the micro-research field of educational ecology, taking teachers' professional growth as the main line amid various relationships in school, exploration is made of the cause and significance of teachers' professional growth. Therefore, the ecological approach features a logic framework of ecological environment research in which the school, administrators, teacher group, students, parents, and researchers form the main factors that result in teachers' changes in behavior, verbal expression, educational faith and thinking, self and professional identity, happiness, knowledge, teaching behaviors, and so on, finally contributing to their professional growth.

With the development of inclusive education, the ideas of inclusive education characterized by equality, pluralism, participation, and high quality have made their way into school culture and climate, and impinged on the inherent concept of teachers who thus feel an urgent need to improve their competence. The ecological approach attaches more importance to the influence of the "field" on teachers' professional development, emphasizes the role of the "groups" in the "field," and underlines the influence and stimulation brought about by the "values," "culture," and "climate" of the groups on teachers' subjective consciousness. It can be seen that the ecological approach for teachers' professional development provides a more holistic and comprehensive perspective for researchers to probe the improvement of the competence of teachers in inclusive education and the professional development path.

Dynamic Field Theory

Proposed by Kurt Tsadek Lewin, a renowned German-American psychologist, dynamic field theory is mainly used to explain the spatial field and root causes of the generation and change in individual behaviors. It consists of field theory and dynamic theory.

On the one hand, this theory is used to explain the specific space in which individual psychology and behaviors occur. According to Lewin, any kind of behavior arises from the totality of various interdependent facts that have the characteristics of a dynamic field. Dynamic field theory mainly deals with human behaviors and psychological activities based on living space or dynamic field. It asserts that in order to understand or predict behavior, individuals and their environment must be viewed as a collection of interdependent factors. The totality of these factors is known as the individual's "living space" and is expressed as follows:

$$B = f(P, E) = f(LS)$$

B represents behavior; f is function; P means personality; E refers to environment; LS stands for living space. This formula means living space comprises the person, environment, and the relationship between the person and the environment. Behavior occurs in living space, which is not only a function of personality and environment, but also a function of living space. Therefore, analysis of individual behaviors needs to be focused on the specific space–time field where the individual is located, to find the causes of the occurrence and change in the behaviors from the individual characteristics and the environment in which the individual is located.

On the other hand, dynamic field theory can also be used to explain the psychological mechanism of individual behavior dynamics. The connotation of "dynamic" includes not only its carrier but also the movement of the carrier. Only when the carrier changes and moves can dynamism be generated. Meanwhile, the nature of dynamics is positive. Lewin tends to make a relational understanding of the behavioral dynamic, attributing the essence of the dynamic of human psychology and behavior to the psychological tension system arising from the interaction of various dynamics, including humans and the environment. The generation of individual behavioral dynamics lies in the pursuit of a "steady state," that is, to achieve psychological balance. Therefore, the generating mechanism of dynamics consists in a dynamic process of clearing up imbalance and achieving balance. According to Lewin, mental processes usually arise from a tendency toward equilibrium, so do universal biological processes, as well as physical, economic or other processes. The transition from a steady state to a process, and the changes that take place during that process, can be derived from the fact that at some point the equilibrium is upset and the process toward a new equilibrium begins.

Given that the dynamic of teachers' professional development is generated in a specific field, Li Sen and Cui Youxing proposed a three-dimensional model of teachers' professional development dynamics based on Lewin's dynamic field theory. The model is composed of the teacher's subjective dynamic system, the school field dynamic system, and the social field dynamic system. Teachers' professional development dynamics is the resultant force formed by the interaction of the three to promote the professional development of teachers.[95]

A teacher's subjective dynamic system is composed of the cognitive subsystem, the affective subsystem, the will subsystem, and the conceptual subsystem, which is the carrier of a teacher's subjective dynamics. In the process of generating the subjective dynamic, teachers define and analyze problems through the cognitive subsystem; the affective subsystem is used to involve affective factors, and regulate cognitive and behavioral processes; the will subsystem is adopted to control the sustainability of problem solving; and the conceptual sub-system is leveraged to guide and regulate interaction among the subsystems. The subsystems are unified yet struggle and interact with each

152 *Research into the Competence of Chinese Teachers*

other to realize the behaviors and value orientation defined by the conceptual subsystem.

A sound school field helps to stimulate the dynamics of teachers' professional development. The school field dynamic refers to the totality of the forces that promote the professional development of teachers arising from the interaction of various components of the school, including school culture, organizational structure, rules and regulations, management, and so on. Among them, school culture is the result of school development, leading teachers' educational philosophy and also imperceptibly regulating teachers' behaviors, thus being the core force for the generation of teachers' professional development dynamics. Organizational structure is the foundation of the school, and a reasonable and complete organizational structure can stimulate the dynamics of teachers' professional development. Rules and regulations regulate the behaviors within the school, and a sound system can guarantee the generation of teachers' professional development dynamics. And management affects the development of school culture, the establishment and reorganization of organizational structures, and the formulation and improvement of rules and regulations. Therefore, management is the key to the generation of teachers' developmental dynamics.

Factors such as economy, politics, culture, technology, and population constitute the entire social system, and various subsystems interact and influence each other. The social field dynamic refers to the totality of the driving forces arising from the contradictory movements of various subsystems of society and the interaction between them. The social field influences and restricts the development of schools and teachers while its dynamic promotes school development, which in turn boosts the professional development of teachers.

To sum up, teacher agency is the main subjective dynamic factor that promotes the improvement of teacher competence in inclusive education, while the main school field dynamic factors are school climate for inclusive education and occupational stress. Based on this, consideration should be given to both the subjective needs of teachers and external support in the process of improving teacher competence in inclusive education.

Job Demands–Resources Model

Regarding the impact of job characteristics on occupation, psychologists have put forward a series of theoretical models to give explanations. Among them, the most influential is the job demands–resources model (JD–R model). The initial research was mainly used to explain the influence of individual working conditions and other factors on job burnout.[96]

With the continuous deepening of research, Arnold Bakker had incorporated work input into the model and formed a universal model theory that explains an individual's work status in which the energy loss process and the incentive process coexist.[97]

The core assumption of the JD–R model is that each occupation has unique factors that affect the physical and mental health of employees and their working conditions. All these factors can be classified as job demands and job resources. Job demands refer to factors related to the body, society, or organization at work that require continuous physical or psychological effort, mainly concerning physical and mental exhaustion; they include work-load, role conflict, emotional requirements, and so on. Job resources mean the psychological, social, or organizational resources that individuals obtain from their work, including task resources featuring job autonomy, organizational resources characterized by career development, and social resources represented by favorable interaction with colleagues.[98]

Three opinions are mainly expressed in the initial form of the JD–R model. First, any kind of occupation has its specific risk factors related to occupational stress; they fall into two types—job demands and job resources. Job demands are not always negative factors, but if individuals are required to make a lot of effort, and thus cannot rejuvenate in time, it will become a stressor and cause negative consequences. Excessive job demands or long duration may lead to health damage and cause job burnout. As energy supplements and stress relief for job demands, job resources have motivational potential. Providing individuals with the necessary job resources can motivate them to participate more actively and improve work performance.[99] However, this model pays more attention to the role of external organizational resources, and relatively ignores the role of internal resources. In the subsequent model improvement process, the connotation of job resources was expanded. In addition to organizational resources, social resources, such as superior support, colleague help, and individual resources, including self-efficacy, psychological flexibility, psychological capital, professionalism, and so on, gradually got the attention of researchers.

Second, the two types of factors have independent path mechanisms. One is the path of reduced health/energy, that is, improper work design and excessive workload may lead to excessive consumption of physical and psychological resources of individuals, causing job burnout and health problems, thereby reducing job performance or causing absenteeism and resignation. The other is the incentive path, that is, sufficient job resources may stimulate the individual's work potential to generate work engagement, organizational commitment, and other intrinsic motivations, thereby more effectively participating in work and promoting personal professional growth.[100,101]

Third, the two path mechanisms can interact, that is, the interaction of job demands and job resources also has an important impact on individual work conditions. On the one hand, job resources can buffer the impact of job demands on negative factors such as job burnout. If the job demands are too high, and there is also a lack of job resources, it is easy to cause job burnout. On the contrary, if the job resources are sufficient, even if the job demands are high, the former can offset the effects on the consequence variables such as job burnout. On the other hand, with high job demands, the motivational role of

154 *Research into the Competence of Chinese Teachers*

job resources is more significant; especially when job demands coincide with job resources, the interaction effect between the two is most obvious.

The original JD–R model only focused on the impact of job characteristics on occupational mental health, while ignoring the impact of individual-level variables. There is no doubt that good working conditions can motivate employees. However, what should be done if good working conditions do not exist? Some researchers have proposed a new concept—job crafting. This refers to a series of positive behaviors that individuals implement themselves to make their own interests, motivations, and passions consistent with their work, which change their work tasks and relationship boundaries.[102] According to Maria Tims et al., job crafting means that workers spontaneously change the job demands and resources they face in order to ensure or promote the completion of their personal (or work) goals, and the purpose is to obtain a sense of meaning and identity at work.[103] For example, teachers work out innovative teaching programs to stimulate students' learning motivation.

Job crafting highlights the agency of individuals at work. Employees can actively adjust their work according to their own abilities and preferences, rather than completely passively accepting the work assigned to them. In an organization, individual adaptivity and proactivity are displayed in two different processes. The former features the individual's response and handling of changes, while the latter results in the individual's spontaneous and active changes and response to work.[104]

Job crafting can be divided into different types from different perspectives. Among them, the classification standard of Amy Wrzesniewski and Jane E. Dutton has been widely recognized. They divide job crafting into task crafting, relational crafting, and cognitive crafting.[105] Task crafting refers to when individuals change the number, scope, and type of work tasks, such as increasing or decreasing the number of tasks, altering the nature of tasks, and changing the distribution of time and energy among multiple tasks. A task is the most basic unit of work. An individual's work is composed of a series of task components clustered under a job name, and is completed by the individual. Therefore, task crafting is the primary form of job crafting. Relational crafting refers to when individuals change the form, time, and objects of communication during work. Cognitive crafting means that individuals change their perceptions of tasks and relationships in work, such as treating work as only discrete parts or as a whole.

However, the process path of "job characteristics–job crafting–occupational mental health" is still unclear. The preliminary theoretical model is shown in Figure 4.7. According to existing research experience, there may be two types: one is that the incoordination or mismatch of job demands/resources causes employees to craft their jobs and improve the status of job demands/resources with a view to producing positive results. The other is that positive work status gives rise to job crafting, which in turn improves the status of job demands/resources. In any case, this is a process of mutual influence, circulation, and gradual change.[106]

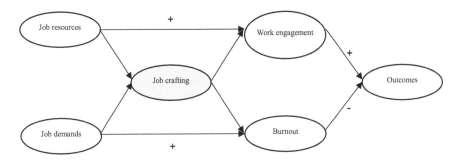

Figure 4.7 JD–R Model with New Dimensions of Personal Resources and Job Crafting.

Despite a lack of domestic research on job crafting among teachers, some researchers have still made preliminary explorations. For example, Qi Yajing and others made a six-month follow-up study of 332 primary and secondary school teachers with a job crafting scale and the Chinese version of the work engagement scale. They found that job crafting at the first point in time can significantly positively predict the work engagement at the second point in time, which indicates that job crafting is the "cause" while work engagement is the "effect."[107] According to a study by Yu Meifang of 465 primary and secondary school teachers in 2018, the mentor–apprentice guidance function (referring to the beneficial guidance role that the mentor provides comprehensive support to apprentices in the process of mentoring teachers), job crafting, and teaching competence are highly correlated, and job crafting plays a partially mediating role between the mentoring function and teaching competence.[108]

Job burnout is a direct constraint on teacher agency in their professional development,[109] and improving the competence of teachers is the fundamental way to overcome occupational stress and relieve job burnout. Therefore, in educational research, job burnout is usually regarded as an inverse indicator of teachers' professional development, and the JD–R model can also be used to guide the construction of the influencing mechanism of the competence of teachers in inclusive education. Specifically in our research context, job demands refer to when teachers need to invest emotions and implement behaviors to a certain extent and bear corresponding occupational stress from society; job resources means the school factors that can promote individuals to achieve work goals and realize personal development, that is, school climate for inclusive education; and job crafting points to teacher agency, which means that individual teachers actively move toward the realization of the professional development goals set by themselves, bring into play their inherent potential, and at the same time utilize external resources to improve their competence and change their professional development environment. According to the expanded JD–R model, job crafting may play an important mediating role in the path of job characteristics affecting teachers' professional development.

156 *Research into the Competence of Chinese Teachers*

This provides an important theoretical basis for us to take occupational stress, school climate for inclusive education, and teacher agency as three key factors that affect the improvement of teacher competence in inclusive education in our research.

However, how do these three factors act on the competence of teachers in inclusive education? No research is available to give systematical explanation of the specific internal developmental mechanism. Based on the above-mentioned theoretical models and available relevant research conclusions, our research aims to explore the mechanism of interaction between the competence of teachers and the three factors. We will test the following research hypotheses via empirical analysis:

Hypothesis 1: The school climate for inclusive education has a significant positive impact on teacher competence in inclusive education.

Hypothesis 2: Occupational stress has a significant negative impact on teacher competence in inclusive education.

Hypothesis 3: Teacher agency has a significant positive impact on teacher competence in inclusive education.

Hypothesis 4: Occupational stress can act as a significant mediator of the relationship between school climate for inclusive education and teacher competence in inclusive education.

Hypothesis 5: Teacher agency can act as a significant mediator of the relationship between school climate for inclusive education and teacher competence in inclusive education.

Hypothesis 6: Occupational stress and teacher agency can form a significant chain of mediators of the relationship between school climate for inclusive education and teacher competence in inclusive education.

Relationship between Main Influencing Factors and Models of their Mechanism of Action

So far, there is not much research into the factors that affect the competence of teachers in inclusive education, and most focuses only on internal or external factors. Little research has touched on the process by which both internal and external factors combined impose impacts on the competence of teachers in inclusive education. Therefore, our research, based on the above-mentioned theoretical models and research hypotheses, tries to determine the relations between teacher competence in inclusive education and the three influencing factors, and adopts a structural equation model to further explore the role of occupational stress and teacher agency in mediating the relations between school climate and teacher competence in the context of inclusive education.

With regard to data, SPSS 20.0, Amos 23.0, and R and other software were used for statistical processing and analysis, such as correlation analysis, regression analysis, intermediary test, structural equation model test, and so on.

Research into Relationship between Main Influencing Factors of Teacher Competence in Inclusive Education

In order to explore the impact of school climate for inclusive education, occupational stress, and teacher agency on teacher competence in inclusive education, we need to analyze the relations between the three factors and teacher competence by presenting their respective general scale.

Relationship between School Climate and Teacher Competence in Inclusive Education

A pairwise correlation analysis is made between school climate for inclusive education and its dimensions, and the competence of teachers in inclusive education and its dimensions, as shown in Table 4.4. The results show that the general scale of school climate for inclusive education and that of teacher competence in inclusive education have a significantly positive correlation ($r = 0.445$, $p < 0.01$), and the correlation is moderate ($0.40 \leqslant r \leqslant 0.70$).

The correlation coefficients of school climate for inclusive education and its two dimensions as well as teacher competence in inclusive education and its four dimensions are between 0.307 and 0.449. There is a significantly positive correlation between them ($p < 0.01$). The predictive effect on professional skills of teachers is stronger.

To give a clearer picture of the influence of school climate on teacher competence in inclusive education, a unary linear regression model was established to describe their relationship. The unary linear regression prediction model can be expressed as: $y = 1.884 + 0.395x + \varepsilon$.

Table 4.4 Correlation Analysis of School Climate, Competence of Teachers in Inclusive Education, and Their Dimensions (n=1,676)

	Professional attitude	Professional knowledge	Professional skills	Ability to get support	Teacher competence in inclusive education
Principal support	.323**	.307**	.417**	.358**	.408**
School-wide inclusive practices	.342**	.364**	.433**	.417**	.449**
School climate for inclusive education	.346**	.347**	.442**	.401**	.445**

Note: ** represents $p < 0.01$.

158   *Research into the Competence of Chinese Teachers*

Table 4.5 Correlation Analysis of Teachers' Occupational Stress, Competence in Inclusive Education, and Their Dimensions (n=1,676)

	Professional attitude	*Professional knowledge*	*Professional skills*	*Ability to get support*	*Teacher competence in inclusive education*
Workload	-.278**	-.271**	-.296**	-.281**	-.326**
Students' academic performance	-.249**	-.246**	-.229**	-.241**	-.279**
Social and school evaluation	-.203**	-.216**	-.176**	-.208**	-.232**
Professional development	-.181**	-.173**	-.246**	-.142**	-.217**
Students' problem behaviors	-.217**	-.185**	-.149**	-.176**	-.212**
Teachers' occupational stress	-.271**	-.263**	-.263**	-.253**	-.305**

Note: ** represents p < 0.01.

Relationship between Teachers' Occupational Stress and Competence in Inclusive Education

A pairwise correlation analysis is made between teachers' occupational stress and its dimensions, and their competence in inclusive education and its dimensions, as shown in Table 4.5. The results show that the general scale of teachers' occupational stress and that of teacher competence in inclusive education have a significantly negative correlation ($r = -0.305$, $p < 0.01$), and the correlation is low ($r < 0.40$).

The correlation coefficients of teachers' occupational stress and its five dimensions as well as teacher competence in inclusive education and its four dimensions are between -0.326 and -0.142. There is a significantly negative correlation between them ($p < 0.01$).

To give a clearer picture of the influence of occupational stress on teacher competence in inclusive education, a unary linear regression model was established to describe their relationship. The unary linear regression prediction model can be expressed as: $y = 4.514 - 0.296x + \varepsilon$.

Relationship between Teacher Agency and Their Competence in Inclusive Education

A pairwise correlation analysis is made between teacher agency and its dimensions, and the competence of teachers in inclusive education and its dimensions, as shown in Table 4.6. The results show that the general scale of teacher agency and that of teacher competence in inclusive education have a significantly positive correlation ($r = 0.611$, $p < 0.01$), and the correlation is moderate ($0.40 \leqslant r \leqslant 0.70$).

Table 4.6 Correlation Analysis of Teacher Agency, Teacher Competence in Inclusive Education, and Their Dimensions (n = 1,676)

	Professional attitude	*Professional knowledge*	*Professional skills*	*Ability to get support*	*Teacher competence in inclusive education*
Constructive participation	.372**	.395**	.573**	.412**	.508**
Self-efficacy in teaching	.501**	.535**	.650**	.532**	.642**
Teacher agency	.462**	.493**	.653**	.501**	.611**

Note: ** represents p < 0.01.

The correlation coefficients of teacher agency and its two dimensions as well as teacher competence in inclusive education and its four dimensions are between 0.372 and 0.653. There is a significantly positive correlation between them ($p < 0.01$). The predictive effect on professional skills of teachers is stronger.

In order to give a clearer picture of the influence of teacher agency on their competence in inclusive education, a unary linear regression model was established to describe their relationship. The unary linear regression prediction model can be expressed as: $y = 0.758 + 0.717x + \varepsilon$.

Multiple Regression Analysis

In order to further explore the direction of the relationship between school climate for inclusive education, teachers' occupational stress, teacher agency, and the competence of teachers in inclusive education, a multiple linear regression and forced entry method is adopted to analyze it. First, after testing, it is found that there is no multi-collinearity relationship between the variables. Then demographic variables such as school sector, gender, age, teaching experience, and experience of teaching LRC students are taken as control variables for multiple regression analysis, and set as virtual variables. On this basis, we analyze the predictive effect of the three influencing factors on teachers' overall competence in inclusive education.

As shown in Table 4.7, after controlling for demographic variables, the multivariate correlation coefficient of the three independent variables—"school climate for inclusive education," "occupational stress," and "teacher agency"—and the criterion variable—"the competence of teachers in inclusive education"—is 0.652, and its square is 0.426, indicating that the three independent variables can explain 42.6 percent of the variation of the variable of "the competence of teachers in inclusive education." The standardized regression coefficients of the two independent variables of "teacher agency" and "school climate for

160   *Research into the Competence of Chinese Teachers*

Table 4.7 Abstract of Multiple Regression Analysis of Influence of the Three Factors on Teacher Competence in Inclusive Education

Predictor	B	SE	Beta(β)	t
Intercept	1.256	0.149		8.414
School climate for inclusive education	0.152	0.019	0.171	7.778[***]
Occupational stress	–0.160	0.019	–0.165	–8.550[***]
Teacher agency	0.567	0.026	0.483	21.694[***]
Control variable	Joined	Joined	Joined	Joined
R = 0.652 R^2 = 0.426 Adjusted R^2 = 0.421 F = 87.949[***]				

Note: [***] represents $p < 0.01$.

inclusive education" are both positive, indicating that these two independent variables have a positive influence on the standard variables of "the competence of teachers in inclusive education." The standardized regression coefficient of the "occupational stress" variable is negative, which means that the "occupational stress" variable has a negative influence on the "teacher competence in inclusive education." In the regression model, the three predictors of "school climate for inclusive education," "occupational stress," and "teacher agency" all have significant effects on "teacher competence in inclusive education." From the perspective of standardized regression coefficients, among the independent variables of the three significant regression coefficients, the absolute value of the β coefficient of "teacher agency" is larger, indicating that the predictor of "teacher agency" has a higher explanatory power for "the competence of teachers in inclusive education" and can explain 48.3 percent of the variation of "teacher competence in inclusive education."

Models of Mechanism that Affects Teacher Competence in Inclusive Education

To understand the mediating role of occupational stress and teacher agency in the relationship between school climate and the competence of teachers in inclusive education, a rigorous attempt was made using a structural equation model. Having established the validity of the measurement model, the structural model was tested. Results revealed an adequate model fit, as shown in Table 4.8.

Figure 4.8 presents the standardized path coefficients among the four constructs, namely school climate for inclusive education, occupational stress, teacher agency, and teacher competence in inclusive education.

Bias-corrected bootstrap analysis (bootstrap = 5000) was applied to test the indirect effects of school climate on teacher competence in inclusive education via occupational stress and teacher agency. Confidence intervals (CIs) were also calculated in this analysis. When 0 does not fall within the range between the lower CI and the upper CI, the mediation effect is significant. The testing of indirect effects revealed that the mediating effects of occupational stress

Table 4.8 Assessment of Model Fit

Fit index	χ^2	df	p	χ^2/df	GFI	AGFI	NFI	IFI	TLI	CFI	RMSEA	SRMR(RMR)
Value	293.080	22	0.000	13.322	0.961	0.919	0.967	0.970	0.950	0.970	0.086	0.017
Criterion				<5.0	>0.90	>0.90	>0.90	>0.90	>0.90	>0.90	<0.10	<0.05

162 *Research into the Competence of Chinese Teachers*

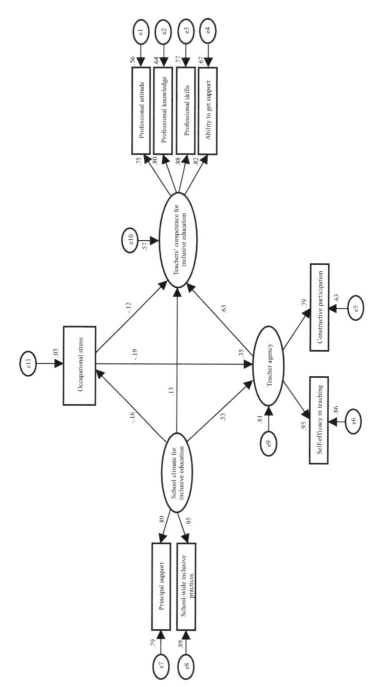

Figure 4.8 Model of Intermediary Effects of School Climate on Competence of Teachers in Inclusive Education via Occupational Stress and Teacher Agency.

Table 4.9 Direct and Mediating Effects of School Climate on Competence of Teachers in Inclusive Education via Occupational Stress and Teacher Agency

Effect	Path	Effect size	95% CI Lower	Upper
Direct effect	SCIE→TCIE	0.103	0.057	0.149
Mediating effect	SCIE→TOS→TCIE	0.016	0.009	0.025
	SCIE→TA→TCIE	0.258	0.212	0.307
	SCIE→TOS→TA→TCIE	0.015	0.009	0.022

Notes: SCIE = school climate for inclusive education; TOS = teachers' occupational stress; TA = teacher agency; TCIE = teacher competence in inclusive education; CI = confidence intervals.

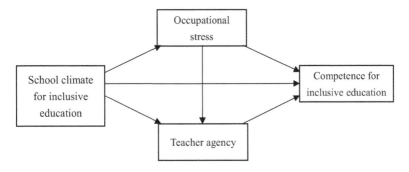

Figure 4.9 Model of Intermediary Factors for the Competence of Teachers in Inclusive Education.

and teacher agency on the relationship between school climate and teacher competence in inclusive education were both significant ($p \leq 0.001$), and the chain-style mediating effect of occupational stress and teacher agency was also significant ($p \leq 0.001$). Table 4.9 displays detailed statistical information and corresponding CIs at the 95% level.

Explanation of Main Influencing Factors and Their Mechanism of Action on Teacher Competence in Inclusive Education

Analysis of Main Influencing Factors and Their Mechanism of Action on Teacher Competence in Inclusive Education

Our research combines the school climate for inclusive education, teachers' occupational stress, and teacher agency to investigate the influence of teachers' own internal and external environments on the improvement of their competence in inclusive education, as shown in Figure 4.9. The main research conclusions are as follows.

164 *Research into the Competence of Chinese Teachers*

First, school climate for inclusive education has a significantly positive impact on the competence of teachers in inclusive education, which supports Hypothesis 1. As far as school administrators are concerned, the initiative to create a sound school climate for inclusive education is helpful to improve the competence of teachers in inclusive education. This is basically consistent with existing research results, indicating that school climate is an important external factor for the competence of teachers in inclusive education.

Second, teachers' occupational stress has a significantly negative impact on the competence of teachers in inclusive education, which supports Hypothesis 2. To be specific, high occupational pressure will affect the enthusiasm of teachers to carry out inclusive education, hinder the improvement of their competence in inclusive education, and is not conducive to their own professional development.

Third, teacher agency has a significantly positive impact on the competence of teachers in inclusive education, which supports Hypothesis 3. Compared with the school climate for inclusive education and teachers' occupational pressure, the predictive variable of teacher agency has a higher explanatory power to the competence of teachers in inclusive education; that is, among the three influencing factors, teacher agency has the greatest influence on their competence in inclusive education.

Fourth, teachers' occupational pressure plays a partially mediating role in the influence of school climate on their competence in inclusive education, that is, school climate for inclusive education influences teachers' occupational stress, which then impacts their competence in inclusive education. This supports Hypothesis 4. In other words, school climate for inclusive education has both direct and indirect impacts on the competence of teachers in inclusive education.

Fifth, teacher agency plays a partially mediating role in the process of school climate for inclusive education, influencing their competence in inclusive education. That is, school climate for inclusive education impacts the competence of teachers in inclusive education through influencing teacher agency, which supports Hypothesis 5. Moreover, the mediating effect size of this path is higher than that of others, that is, compared with the mediator of teachers' occupational stress, school climate for inclusive education is more likely to have an impact on the competence of teachers in inclusive education through the mediator of teacher agency.

Sixth, by constructing a structural equation model, we have verified that teachers' occupational stress and teacher agency have a chain-style mediating effect between the independent variable—school climate for inclusive education—and the dependent variable—the competence of teachers in inclusive education. A positive school climate reduces the occupational pressure of teachers, and thus strengthens teacher agency, and further promotes the competence of teachers in inclusive education. This supports Hypothesis 6.

According to these research conclusions, teacher agency is an important internal factor, having the greatest impact on the competence of teachers in inclusive education. This result is consistent with existing research results on the relationship between teacher agency and their professional development.[110,111] We hold that teachers' active constructive participation in educational practice is the fundamental driving force for their professional development. Teachers must actively base their practice paradigm on the development of special needs children, and take the initiative to meet the "beautiful risk of education." When they find that inclusive education is effective in improving classroom teaching, they will quickly break down the habitual barriers, reconstruct the teaching space,[112] throw themselves into the reform and practice of inclusive education, and be good at using the thinking of inclusive education to solve educational problems. In this process, they will increase their experience and accumulate strength, so that the conditions for improving their own agency will become increasingly abundant. On this basis, teachers will gradually establish their belief and confidence that they can help all students improve their learning ability and make progress. At the same time, they can actively cooperate with parents, leaders, colleagues, and professionals, and manage their classes in appropriate ways, gaining a variety of teaching efficacy such as inclusive teaching efficacy, cooperative support efficacy, classroom behavior management efficacy, and finally realizing improvement of their competence in inclusive education, professional development, and self-growth. Compared with school climate for inclusive education and teachers' occupational pressure, teacher agency has a greater influence on their competence in inclusive education, a result consistent with the conclusion of existing research into teachers' professional development.[113] It is also a confirmation that no matter how good the external environmental conditions placed before an indifferent individual are, his or her professional development will not be affected.[114]

School climate for inclusive education and teachers' occupational pressure are the important external factors. It has been proved that there is an inverse relationship between teachers' occupational stress and their competence in inclusive education, that is, the greater the teachers' occupational stress, the lower their competence in inclusive education, thus affecting their professional development, which is consistent with existing research conclusions.[115,116] Having certain special education knowledge and skills is the basic requirement for teachers to effectively implement inclusive education.[117] However, heavy inclusive education work, diverse and flexible cultivation goals, students' problem behaviors, multivariate evaluation of the society and school, and many factors beyond control cause greater psychological pressure on teachers, influence their enthusiasm to carry out inclusive education, and even give rise to job burnout that encourages them to avoid the practice of inclusive education. As a result, they may lose important opportunities to improve their competence in inclusive education.

A sound school climate for inclusive education, including the principal's efforts to give genuine care and support to teachers, build platforms, provide

166 *Research into the Competence of Chinese Teachers*

multi-channel opportunities to encourage teachers to participate in relevant activities, is beneficial to teachers' professional development, and encourages them to carry out inclusive education and improve their competence in this regard, which is consistent with existing research conclusions.[118,119,120] This further proves that school climate for inclusive education is an important protective factor for the improvement of the competence of teachers in inclusive education and an indispensable external condition for teachers' professional development. School climate featuring ideological style, values, and behavioral attitude shared by all school members, is a relatively enduring attribute of the school environment. It is a result of the interaction between the principal's behaviors and teachers' behaviors, having an extremely important impact on each teacher's professional attitude, knowledge, skills, and ability to get support. Nowadays, a school climate for inclusive education must contain certain spiritual factors, such as value orientation, ideological belief, and teaching methods of inclusive education, reflecting the unique style or personality of the school. Teachers immersed in a school climate featuring openness, acceptance, and sense of belonging will be guided to keep learning, make innovations with courage, and consciously improve their competence in inclusive education, so as to better provide high-quality education and related services for special needs children.

In our structural equation model, we find that teacher agency and teachers' occupational stress are mediating variables in the path of school climate for inclusive education influencing the competence of teachers in inclusive education, which form three groups of remarkable mediating effects. Two groups include independent mediating effects of these two variables, which are consistent with previous similar studies.[121,122] According to the mediating effect model, the effect size of teacher agency (β =0.258) is larger than that of teachers' occupational pressure (β =0.016), indicating that the independent mediating effect of teacher agency on the relationship between school climate and the competence of teachers in inclusive education is greater than that of teachers' occupational pressure. The results show that the school climate for inclusive education indirectly and significantly affects the competence of teachers in inclusive education through their agency. It can be seen that there is a path to improve the competence of teachers in inclusive education. To promote constant improvement of their competence through school climate, teachers need to transform their external influence into internal initiative. If we give enough attention to the factors with positive effects on teacher agency, and better meet the needs of teachers' professional development and stimulate their enthusiasm by creating a school culture atmosphere featuring openness, acceptance, and sense of belonging, encouraging teachers to air their different demands in the process of implementing inclusive education, and fostering an environment with mutual trust and cooperation for teaching and research, teachers will have greater agency and remarkably improve their competence.

Meanwhile, school administrators should also take effective measures to reduce teachers' occupational pressure, such as promoting service and sports activities with social and healthcare benefits to build a high-quality teaching contingent. It is important to fully realize the significance of inspiring teacher agency, so as to improve the competence of teachers in inclusive education and speed up their professional development.

In addition, we have found another group of significant mediating effects, that is, the chain-style mediating effects of "teachers' occupational stress → teacher agency." That is to say, in a good climate for inclusive education, we can take various measures to reduce teachers' occupational pressure, and encourage them to give full play to their agency in education and teaching, so as to improve their competence in inclusive education. This indicates that teachers' occupational pressure and agency have a synergistic effect. The chain-style mediating effect of "teacher's occupational pressure → teacher agency" has never been involved in previous studies. In this sense, one contribution of our research lies in taking teacher agency, occupational stress, and their chain-style effects as variables mediating the relationship between school climate and the competence of teachers in inclusive education, providing an empirical basis for the paths of school climate influencing the competence of teachers.

It is worth noting that between the two mediating variables of teacher agency and occupational pressure, teacher agency plays a central role. On the one hand, it acts as an independent mediator with a larger effect size. On the other hand, teacher agency also forms a chain of mediators with occupational pressure.

Theoretical Explanation of Main Influencing Factors and Their Mechanism of Action on Teacher Competence in Inclusive Education

In combination with the ecological approach for teachers' professional development, dynamic field theory, and the JD–R model, our research attempts to explain the mechanism of action on teacher competence in inclusive education. Mechanism refers to the mutual relationship between various parts of a system and their operation mode. Thus, the mechanism of action on teacher competence in inclusive education determines the improvement of the competence.

APPLICATION OF ECOLOGICAL APPROACH FOR TEACHERS' PROFESSIONAL DEVELOPMENT IN THE MECHANISM OF ACTION ON TEACHER COMPETENCE IN INCLUSIVE EDUCATION

Every creature in the world is conceived, grows, and matures in a certain ecological environment. Even if given sufficient nutrients and care, it will lose its spirituality and survival instinct and will be unable to survive in separation from the ecological environment. From the perspective of the ecological approach for teachers' professional development, the multiple relationships between teachers and school, special needs children and their parents, parents of typically developing children, and resource teachers make up a more complex ecological environment for the professional growth of teachers in the context

168 *Research into the Competence of Chinese Teachers*

of inclusive education.[123] Therefore, to improve the competence of teachers in inclusive education and the quality of inclusive education, we need to create a sound school climate for inclusive education featuring openness, acceptance, and sense of belonging, and take various effective measures to reduce teachers' occupational stress.

APPLICATION OF DYNAMIC FIELD THEORY IN MECHANISM OF ACTION ON
TEACHER COMPETENCE IN INCLUSIVE EDUCATION

According to dynamic field theory, the improvement of the competence of teachers in inclusive education is a systematic process, which not only arises from the dynamic generated by the contradictory movement of each subsystem itself, but also results from the resultant force formed by the mutual opposition and unified movement of each subsystem. There is no doubt that school climate for inclusive education and occupational stress, as important dynamic factors of the school field, have great impacts on teacher competence. On the one hand, a fair and democratic school culture and a harmonious and mutually helpful interpersonal atmosphere make it possible for teachers to improve their competence in inclusive education. On the other hand, occupational stress from children with special needs, parents, and school will also hinder teachers from taking the initiative to carry out inclusive education, thus losing important opportunities to improve their professional development. At the same time, teacher agency, which represents a teacher's subjective dynamic system, directly determines the improvement of their competence in inclusive education. In short, improvement of the competence of teachers in inclusive education is a process in which teachers' subjective dynamic and school field dynamic combine to act on it.

In fact, the mechanism of action on the competence of teachers in inclusive education is a contradictory movement between the teacher's subjective dynamic system and the critical fields of the teacher's school and society. Some research findings show that generation of individual dynamics lies in the pursuit of a "steady state," that is, to achieve a state of equilibrium, which includes the balance of the individual's body and mind and the balance between the individual and the outside world. The purpose of pursuing a "steady state" is to dissolve the "imbalance" and achieve a "balance." It can be seen that the origin of the improvement of the competence of teachers in inclusive education is the "imbalance" of teachers in a specific field, and it is just in this dynamic and complex process of dissolving the "imbalance" and achieving a "balance" that the competence of teachers in inclusive education is improved.[124] Dynamic field theory particularly emphasizes the subjective dynamic of teachers, holding that teachers play a decisive role in the process of their own professional development. Therefore, teachers should not passively respond to the external field, but should actively seek support and exert their own subjective initiative to acquire professional knowledge and abilities, and change professional attitudes. In this struggle with the external field, teachers actively deal with various difficulties, gradually free themselves from the "imbalanced" state, re-establish self-confidence, and form a new "balance" as soon as possible, thus promoting the improvement of their competence in inclusive education.

As demonstrated above, teacher agency is at the core position in the path of effects on their competence in inclusive education, which once again echoes their subjective dynamic system underlined by dynamic field theory on teachers' professional development.

APPLICATION OF JD–R MODEL IN MECHANISM OF ACTION ON TEACHER
COMPETENCE IN INCLUSIVE EDUCATION

In addition to the ecological approach and dynamic field theory of teachers' professional development, the JD–R model theory is also adopted in our research to explain the research results of teacher agency as a mediating variable in the mechanism of action on teacher competence in inclusive education.

According to our research findings, job crafting (teacher agency) plays an extremely important mediating role in the exertion of influence of job demands (occupational stress) and job resources (school climate for inclusive education) on job performance (the competence of teachers in inclusive education). Job crafting emphasizes the individual's agency in work, and pays attention to how individuals perceive and carry out the work. It can play a key role in both the energy excitation path and the energy loss path that affect teachers' job performance. In the energy excitation path, a sound school climate for inclusive education stimulates teacher agency, and then promotes the improvement of their competence in inclusive education. In the path of energy loss, excessive occupational stress may cause teachers to excessively consume psychological resources, lose motivation for professional development, and suffer job burnout and health problems. Facing the increasingly complex educational ecological environment, if teachers can spontaneously adjust and shape their educational and teaching situation according to their own characteristics, they will improve their competence in inclusive education and quickly adapt themselves to the environmental changes in inclusive education.

Strategies to Improve Teacher Competence in Inclusive Education

"From the perspective of any education policy or any problem, list all influential factors. These factors may be related to the solution of the problem, and are required for effective change."[125] How to improve the competence of teachers in inclusive education? The decision making of its promotion strategy needs to be evidence-based, that is, through evidence-based research we discover the factors that affect the competence of teachers in inclusive education and reveal their mechanism of action on teacher competence in inclusive education, and construct an improvement model on this basis in order to put forward strategies to effectively improve the competence of teachers in inclusive education.

170 *Research into the Competence of Chinese Teachers*

Based on our research findings and the above approach, we construct a model to improve the competence of teachers in inclusive education, shown in Figure 4.10, and put forward strategies for improvement in this regard.

Teacher Agency Is the Inner Foundation for Improving Their Competence in Inclusive Education

Chinese educationist Ye Lan stressed that there is no inevitable relationship between environment and teacher.[126] On the one hand, no matter how good the eco-environment is, it will not automatically be transformed into teacher development. On the other hand, even environments with many problems show examples of aspirational teachers who can always find space for possible development, hard-working teachers who will always explore a larger space for possible development, and pragmatic teachers who will always achieve their own real development.[127] According to Alyson Simpson, the teacher agency in an eco-environment provides dynamics for the professional development of teachers, and it shows an epistemological standpoint on which the work of teachers can be constructed. It is of great value to explore and bring into play teacher agency.[128] The most long-lasting motivation for the change in teachers' teaching behavior and improvement of professional competence comes from their inner active pursuit.[129] Teachers with strong agency can give full play to their initiative in their professional learning, actively set development goals, and use external resources and support to improve their competence as much as possible, so as to better promote their own professional development.[130] Previous empirical studies have shown that teacher agency is an internal core mediating factor between social and cultural environments,[131] and also a positive force for teachers to change their own work and working environment.[132] Our research results show that teacher agency not only has a significantly positive impact on the competence of teachers in inclusive education but also plays an important mediating role in the process of school climate imposing influence on the competence of teachers in inclusive education, which coincides with the conclusions of existing studies. It can be seen that giving full play to teacher agency is one of the important strategies to improve their competence in inclusive education.

Teacher agency in the context of inclusive education involves self-efficacy in teaching and constructive participation. So, we can start from the following two aspects to stimulate teacher agency.

ENHANCING SELF-EFFICACY IN TEACHING

First of all, teachers must establish a firm belief in inclusive education, and actively follow the principles of fairness and excellence, acceptance and tolerance, diversity and sense of belonging. Faced with a series of problems caused by LRC students, teachers must build up the confidence to be competent and unyielding in inclusive education. Secondly, teachers are encouraged to step out of the "comfort zone" of previous teaching, actively seeking support and

Research into the Competence of Chinese Teachers 171

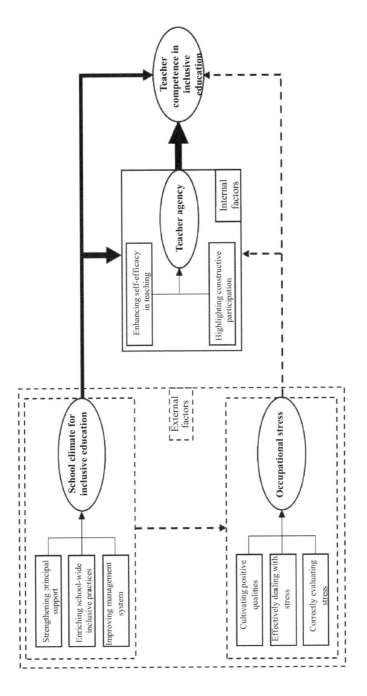

Figure 4.10 Model to Improve Competence of Teachers in Inclusive Education.

172 *Research into the Competence of Chinese Teachers*

facing the challenges of classrooms that accommodate increasingly diverse student bodies, students with special needs included. Thirdly, teachers should use a variety of approaches to tap every possible resource from every possible source, actively acquire the knowledge and skills related to instructing students with special educational needs, and formulate education and teaching goals reasonably in advance according to each child's needs, to provide them with fair and quality education.

Moreover, it is advisable for teachers to get positive feedback from children through regular assessment of and communication with children, which can enhance their sense of accomplishment and satisfaction in teaching, and stimulate their initiative to improve competence in inclusive education.

Finally, teachers should actively seek school support and assistance to solve difficulties in inclusive education, and maintain long-term close contact with special needs children's parents.

HIGHLIGHTING CONSTRUCTIVE PARTICIPATION

Constructive participation is of great importance. In terms of system construction, teachers must not only establish an effective inclusive education management system in the class, but also give suggestions for the formulation of school rules and regulations on inclusive education. With regard to professional development, in addition to participating in various teacher training and teachers' professional development activities, they must also fully tap their own potential, enhance the awareness of self-reflection, and actively follow the professional development process of "self-direction–self-motivation–self-monitoring–self-evaluation–self-reflection," gradually exploring a path geared to their own characteristics.

These two points also inspire us to focus on teacher agency in future teacher training activities. In addition to imparting theoretical knowledge and operational skills related to inclusive education, it is necessary to create rich courses that effectively meet teacher needs, and adopt innovative training methods, such as launching group learning to build a platform for exchanges among teachers and encouraging them to actively participate in it, fully stimulating their initiative in learning, in order to achieve best training effect. This requires trainers to change their role, from the traditional "teacher," "expert," "information publisher," or "standard answer verifier" to "inspirator," "facilitator," "server," or "collaborator" for teacher learning. In addition, we should not label teachers with "yes or no," but try to avoid negative evaluations to help teachers overcome learning obstacles and give them opportunities to achieve success and gain a strong sense of self-efficacy.

School Environment Is External Guarantee for Improving Teacher Competence in Inclusive Education

According to our research findings, the school climate for inclusive education is sufficiently predictive of teacher competence in inclusive education, and

Research into the Competence of Chinese Teachers 173

impacts competence by acting on teacher agency, while occupational stress forges an inverse relationship with competence. Therefore, to improve the external factors that affect teacher competence, we can take the following two measures.

ACTIVELY CREATE A SOUND SCHOOL CLIMATE FOR INCLUSIVE EDUCATION

School climate demonstrates the personality of a school, reflecting to a degree the overall quality and level of the school.[133] It has a positive effect on improving the professionalism of teachers. In combination with our research findings, we suggest that school administrators create a sound school climate for inclusive education from three aspects—principal support, school-wide inclusive practices, and management systems.

Strengthening Principal Support In the context of inclusive education, principals must first enrich their own inclusive education knowledge. While updating their own thinking on inclusive education, they also need to clearly convey the thinking to every staff member. Moreover, they should provide equal and all-round support to every inclusive education teacher, vigorously promote cooperation between regular class teachers and resource teachers, introduce resources from inside and outside the school to realize common education and teaching goals, and guarantee all children can truly participate in classroom study and receive high-quality education.

Enriching School-wide Inclusive Practices School administrators should pay attention to teachers' preparations for accepting special needs children, organize class teachers to actively communicate with parents to win the understanding of children and parents, and do everything possible to ensure sound home-school cooperation so as to lay a solid foundation for children with special needs to learn in regular classrooms smoothly.

School administrators should also carry out activities for teachers' professional development, such as training and school-based research into inclusive education, and teaching and research activities in the form of class observation to meet the demand of special needs children for teachers' help.

Improving the Management System School administrators must continuously improve the school management system and form an organized and orderly institutional culture. Schools can try to build a work network for inclusive education and, under the guidance of special education experts in each district, establish a hierarchical management work order with the principal taking overall responsibility and all teachers' participation. A standardized management and operation system must be established for the development planning of school's inclusive education, the reward mechanism for teachers implementing inclusive education, and the construction and use of resource rooms to build a self-supported school ecosystem, which is boon for improving the competence of teachers in inclusive education.

174 *Research into the Competence of Chinese Teachers*

MAKE GREAT EFFORTS TO REDUCE OCCUPATIONAL STRESS OF TEACHERS

Since greater occupational stress may result in a lower level of competence in inclusive education, reducing the occupational stress of teachers can be another strategy to improve their competence. To this end, teachers and school administrators are advised to take the following steps.

Correctly Evaluating Stress Teachers and school administrators should correctly evaluate the sources of occupational stress and explore positive pressures. Seligman and Csikszentmihalyi suggested that to reduce occupational stress, it is necessary to pay attention to research into human positive psychology, and recognize and understand the positive pressure and the way in which it is generated.[134] Therefore, teachers should have a correct understanding of the pressure to be faced, tap the positive pressure, and promote their own professional growth and development under the effect of positive pressure.

Cultivating Positive Qualities It is advisable to improve teacher competence by cultivating positive qualities. Michael Rutter pointed out that cultivating and developing good personality can help individuals relieve stress.[135] Teachers can do so by enhancing their positive experience to resist the negative emotions caused by occupational stress.

Dealing with Stress Effectively By carrying out various forms of activities, school administrators can help teachers master and use various strategies to deal with the difficulties and challenges that may arise in future work. This also requires teacher trainers to actively explore more effective teacher-training methods. Whether it is school-based training or participatory training, the purpose is to truly help teachers solve their practical problems in inclusive education.

In short, in the model to improve the competence of teachers in inclusive education, teacher agency serves as the internal motivation and the main channel for the improvement, while school climate and teachers' occupational stress act as external factors for their competence. These external factors mainly play a role through teacher agency. Therefore, if not bringing teacher agency into play, any path to improve teacher competence seems ineffective in the lack of dynamics.

Notes

1 Ma, Hongying 马红英, and Tan, Heping 谭和平. "Shanghai shi suiban jiudu jiaoshi xianzhuang diaocha" 上海市随班就读教师现状调查. *Chinese Journal of Special Education* 中国特殊教育 no. 1 (2010): 60–64.

2 Savolainen, H. "Responding to Diversity and Striving for Excellence: The Case of Finland." *Prospects Quarterly Review of Comparative Education* 39, no. 3 (2009): 256–269.

Research into the Competence of Chinese Teachers   175

3 Johnstone, C., and Chapman, D. "Contributions and Constraints to the Implementation of Inclusive Education in Lesotho." *International Journal of Disability, Development and Education* 56 (2009): 131–148.

4 Blecker, N., and Boakes, N. "Creating a Learning Environment for All Children: Are Teachers Able and Willing?" *International Journal of Inclusive Education* 14 (2010): 435–447.

5 Wang, Yan 王雁, Wang, Zhiqiang 王志强, and Feng, Yajing 冯雅静, et al. "Suiban jiudu jiaoshi zhuanye suyang xianzhuang ji yingxiang yinsu yanjiu" 随班就读教师专业素养现状及影响因素研究. *Teacher Education Research* 教师教育研究 27, no. 4 (2015): 46–52, 60.

6 Zhou, Dan 周丹. *Suiban jiudu jiaoshi nengdong xing jiegou ji xiangguan yinsu de zuoyong jizhi yanjiu* 随班就读教师能动性结构及相关因素的作用机制研究. Beijing: Beijing Normal University, 2019.

7 Li, Qiong 李琼, Zhang, Guoli 张国礼, and Zhou, Jun 周钧. "Zhongxiaoxue jiaoshi de zhiye yaliyuan yanjiu" 中小学教师的职业压力源研究. *Psychological Development and Education* 心理发展与教育 27, no. 1 (2011): 97–104.

8 Schaefer, J. *Impact of Teacher Efficacy on Teacher Attitudes Toward Classroom Inclusion.* Minneapolis: Capella University, 2010.

9 Liu, Chunling 刘春玲, Du, Xiaoxin 杜晓新, and Yao, Jian 姚健. "Putong xiaoxue jiaoshi dui teshu ertong jiena taidu de yanjiu" 普通小学教师对特殊儿童接纳态度的研究. *Chinese Journal of Special Education* 中国特殊教育 no. 3 (2000): 34–36.

10 Wei, Xiaoman 韦小满, and Yuan, Wende 袁文得. "Guanyu puxiao jiaoshi yu tejiao jiaoshi dui you teshu jiaoyu xuyao xuesheng suiban jiudu taidu de diaocha" 关于普小教师与特教教师对有特殊教育需要学生随班就读态度的调查. *Chinese Journal of Special Education* 中国特殊教育 no. 3 (2000): 31–33.

11 Deng, Meng 邓猛. "Putong xiaoxue suiban jiudu jiaoshi dui quanna jiaoyu taidu de chengxiang bijiao yanjiu" 普通小学随班就读教师对全纳教育态度的城乡比较研究. *Educational Research and Experiment* 教育研究与实验 no. 1 (2004): 61–66.

12 Zeng, Yaru 曾雅茹. "Putong xiaoxue jiaoshi dui suiban jiudu de taidu jiaoxue celüe yu suoxu zhichi de yanjiu" 普通小学教师对随班就读的态度、教学策略与所需支持的研究. *Chinese Journal of Special Education* 中国特殊教育 no. 12 (2007): 3–7.

13 Ma, Hongying 马红英, and Tan, Heping 谭和平. "Shanghai shi suiban jiudu jiaoshi xianzhuang diaocha" 上海市随班就读教师现状调查. *Chinese Journal of Special Education* 中国特殊教育 no. 1 (2010): 60–63.

14 Wang, Hongxia 王红霞, Peng, Xin 彭欣, and Wang, Yanjie 王艳杰. "Beijing shi haidian qu xiaoxue ronghe jiaoyu xianzhuang diaocha yanjiu baogao" 北京市海淀区小学融合教育现状调查研究报告. *Chinese Journal of Special Education* 中国特殊教育 no. 4 (2011): 37–41.

15 Zhang, Yuhong 张玉红, and Gao, Yuxiang 高宇翔. "Xinjiang putong xuexiao shisheng he jiazhang dui quanna jiaoyu jiena taidu de diaocha yanjiu" 新疆普通学校师生和家长对全纳教育接纳态度的调查研究. *Chinese Journal of Special Education* 中国特殊教育 no. 8 (2014): 14–20.

16 Zhao, Hong 赵红, and Xu, Li 徐莉. "Ronghe jiaoyu beijing xia youjiao gongzuozhe dui teshu ertong taidu de diaocha" 融合教育背景下幼教工作者对特殊儿童态度的调查. *Journal of Teacher Education* 教师教育学报 5, no. 1 (2018): 32–40.

17 Xiong, Qi 熊琪, Terry Cumming, and Li, Zehui 李泽慧. "Suiban jiudu jiaoshi ronghe jiaoyu jiaoxue xiaonenggan yanjiu" 随班就读教师融合教育教学效能感研究. *Chinese Journal of Special Education* 中国特殊教育 no. 2 (2019): 50–57.

18 Gao, Li 高利. "Zhongguo dalu diqu ronghe jiaoyu taidu yanjiu jinzhan ji qishi" 中国大陆地区融合教育态度研究进展及启示. *Journal of Suihua University* 绥化学院学报 39, no. 7 (2019): 19–23.

19 Wei, Xiaoman 韦小满, and Yuan, Wende 袁文得. "Guanyu puxiao jiaoshi yu tejiao jiaoshi dui you teshu jiaoyu xuyao xuesheng suiban jiudu taidu de diaocha" 关于普小教师与特教教师对有特殊教育需要学生随班就读态度的调查. *Chinese Journal of Special Education* 中国特殊教育 no. 3 (2000): 31–33.

20 Zhang, Ningsheng 张宁生, and Chen, Guanghua 陈光华. "Zailun ronghe jiaoyu puxiao jiaoshi yanzhong de 'suiban jiudu'" 再论融合教育：普小教师眼中的"随班就读." *Chinese Journal of Special Education* 中国特殊教育 no. 2 (2002): 1–6.

21 Zeng, Yaru 曾雅茹. "Putong xiaoxue jiaoshi dui suiban jiudu de taidu jiaoxue celüe yu suoxu zhichi de yanjiu" 普通小学教师对随班就读的态度、教学策略与所需支持的研究. *Chinese Journal of Special Education* 中国特殊教育 no. 12 (2007): 3–7.

22 Ma, Hongying 马红英, and Tan, Heping 谭和平. "Shanghai shi suiban jiudu jiaoshi xianzhuang diaocha" 上海市随班就读教师现状调查. *Chinese Journal of Special Education* 中国特殊教育 no. 1 (2010): 60–63.

23 Xu, Meijuan 徐梅娟. "Suiban jiudu banji shuxue jiaoshi tejiao zhishi yu jineng zhangwo qingkuang diaocha yanjiu" 随班就读班级数学教师特教知识与技能掌握情况调查研究. *Journal of Nanjing Special Education Institute* 南京特教学院学报 no. 4 (2011): 9–13.

24 Tan, Heping 谭和平, and Ma, Hongying 马红英. "Shanghai shi suiban jiudu jiaoshi zhuanyehua fazhan xuqiu de diaocha yanjiu" 上海市随班就读教师专业化发展需求的调查研究. *Journal of Schooling Studies* 基础教育 9, no. 2 (2012): 63–70.

25 Zhang, Yuhong 张玉红, and Gao, Yuxiang 高宇翔. "Xinjiang putong xuexiao shisheng he jiazhang dui quanna jiaoyu jiena taidu de diaocha yanjiu" 新疆普通学校师生和家长对全纳教育接纳态度的调查研究. *Chinese Journal of Special Education* 中国特殊教育 no. 8 (2014): 14–20.

26 Du, Lingyu 杜灵宇. *Yunnan shaoshu minzu nongcun diqu suiban jiudu jiaoshi zhihou peixun neirong xuqiu yanjiu—yi longchuan xian wei ge'an* 云南少数民族农村地区随班就读教师职后培训内容需求研究——以陇川县为个案. Kunming: Yunnan Normal University, 2018.

27 Wei, Shouhong 魏寿洪, Liao, Jin 廖进, and Cheng, Minfen 程敏芬. "Chengyu liangdi puxiao jiaoshi ronghe jiaoyu kecheng yu jiaoxue tiaozheng shishi xianzhuang yanjiu" 成渝两地普小教师融合教育课程与教学调整实施现状研究. *Chinese Journal of Special Education* 中国特殊教育 216, no. 6 (2018): 16–24.

28 Yan, Tingrui 颜廷睿, Guan, Wenjun 关文军, and Deng, Meng 邓猛. "Beijing shi zhongxiaoxue ronghe jiaoyu shishi qingkuang de diaocha yanjiu" 北京市中小学融合教育实施情况的调查研究. *Disability Research* 残疾人研究 no. 2 (2017): 90–96.

29 Wang, Yue 王悦. *Suiban jiudu jiaoshi ketang zhichi dui qi kecheng tiaozheng de yingxiang—ziwo xiaonenggan de zhongjie zuoyong* 随班就读教师课堂支持对其课程调整的影响——自我效能感的中介作用. Beijing: Beijing Normal University, 2018.

30 Wang, Yan 王雁, Wang, Zhiqiang 王志强, Feng, Yajing 冯雅静, et al. "Suiban jiudu jiaoshi zhuanye suyang xianzhuang ji yingxiang yinsu yanjiu" 随班就读教师专业素养现状及影响因素研究. *Teacher Education Research* 教师教育研究 27, no. 4 (2015): 46–52.

31 Wu, Yang 吴扬. "You'eryuan jiaoshi ronghe jiaoyu suyang de diaocha yanjiu" 幼儿园教师融合教育素养的调查研究. *Chinese Journal of Special Education* 中国特殊教育 no. 11 (2017): 8–13.

Research into the Competence of Chinese Teachers   177

32 Li, Jing 李静. "You'eryuan jiaoshi ronghe jiaoyu suyang yu peixun xuqiu fenxi—yi beijing diqu weili" 幼儿园教师融合教育素养与培训需求分析——以北京地区为例. *Teacher Development Research* 教师发展研究 no. 4 (2017): 62–68.

33 Yang, Xijie 杨希洁. "Suiban jiudu xuexiao canji xuesheng fazhan zhuangkuang yanjiu" 随班就读学校残疾学生发展状况研究. *Chinese Journal of Special Education* 中国特殊教育 no. 7 (2010): 3–10.

34 Boer, A. D. "Inclusive Education in Developing Countries: A Closer Look at Its Implementation in the Last 10 Years." *Educational Review* 67, no. 2 (2015): 179–195.

35 *Guojia zhongchangqi jiaoyu gaige he fazhan guihua gangyao zhongqi pinggu teshu jiaoyu zhuanti pinggu baogao (zhaiyao)* 《国家中长期教育改革和发展规划纲要》中期评估特殊教育专题评估报告（摘要）. Jiaoyubu guanwang 教育部官网, 2015. www.moe.gov.cn/jyb_xwfb/xw_fbh/moe_2069/xwfbh_2015n/xwfb_151130/151130_sfcl/201511/t20151130_221728.html.

36 Feng, Yajing 冯雅静, Li, Aifen 李爱芬, and Wang, Yan 王雁. "Woguo putong shifan zhuanye ronghe jiaoyu kecheng xianzhuang de diaocha yanjiu" 我国普通师范专业融合教育课程现状的调查研究. *Chinese Journal of Special Education* 中国特殊教育 no. 1 (2016): 9–15.

37 Yan, Tingrui 颜廷睿, Guan, Wenjun 关文军, and Deng, Meng 邓猛. "Beijing shi zhongxiaoxue ronghe jiaoyu shishi qingkuang de diaocha yanjiu" 北京市中小学融合教育实施情况的调查研究. *Disability Research* 残疾人研究 no. 2 (2017): 90–96.

38 Li, Xiu 李秀. "Puxiao jiaoshi dui suiban jiudu taidu de diaocha yanjiu—yi fujian sheng weili" 普小教师对随班就读态度的调查研究——以福建省为例. *Journal of Suihua University* 绥化学院学报 no. 4 (2016): 20–25.

39 Shi, Mengliang 石梦良, and Chen, Minyi 陈敏怡. "Guangdong sheng putong jiaoshi dui ronghe jiaoyu taidu de diaocha yanjiu" 广东省普通教师对融合教育态度的调查研究. *Journal of Changchun University* (Social Science Edition) 长春大学学报（社会科学版）no. 4 (2017): 106–111.

40 Zhang, Xiaodong 张晓东. *Xiaoxue suiban jiudu jiaoshi gongzuo yali xianzhuang diaocha yanjiu* 小学随班就读教师工作压力现状调查研究. Huangshi: Hubei Normal University, 2019.

41 Schon, Donald A. *The Reflective Practitioner: How Professionals Think In Action* 反映的实践者——专业工作者如何在行动中思考, translated by Linqing Xia 夏林清, 35. Beijing: Educational Science Press, 2007.

42 Qi, Juan 亓娟. *Wanbei diqu you'er jiaoshi ronghe jiaoyu suyang de diaocha yanjiu* 皖北地区幼儿教师融合教育素养的调查研究. Huaibei: Huaibei Normal University, 2017.

43 Huang, Ying 黄英. "Xiaozhang—xin jiaoshi zhuanye chengzhang de yinlingzhe" 校长——新教师专业成长的引领者. *Journal of Educational Development* 教育导刊 no. 4 (2007): 51–52.

44 Berry, Ruth A. W. "Novice Teachers' Conceptions of Fairness in Inclusion Classrooms." *Teaching and Teacher Education* 24, no. 5 (2008): 1149–1159.

45 Jiang, Xiaoying 江小英, Niu, Shuangshuang 牛爽爽, and Deng, Meng 邓猛. "Beijing shi putong zhongxiaoxue ronghe jiaoyu jiben qingkuang diaocha baogao" 北京市普通中小学融合教育基本情况调查报告. *Modern Special Education* 现代特殊教育 no. 14 (2016): 22–27.

46 Wang, Hongxia 王红霞, Peng, Xin 彭欣, and Wang, Yanjie 王艳杰. "Beijing shi haidian qu xiaoxue ronghe jiaoyu xianzhuang diaocha yanjiu baogao" 北京市海淀区小学融合教育现状调查研究报告. *Chinese Journal of Special Education* 中国特殊教育 no. 4 (2011): 37–42.

47 Xiong, Qi 熊琪, Terry Cumming, and Li, Zehui 李泽慧. "Suiban jiudu jiaoshi ronghe jiaoyu jiaoxue xiaoneng gan yanjiu" 随班就读教师融合教育教学效能感研究. *Chinese Journal of Special Education* 中国特殊教育 no. 2 (2019): 50–57.

48 Zhao, Fujiang 赵福江, and Liu, Jingcui 刘京翠. "Woguo zhongxiaoxue banzhuren gongzuo xianzhuang wenjuan diaocha yu fenxi" 我国中小学班主任工作现状问卷调查与分析. *Educational Science Research* 教育科学研究 no. 11 (2018): 38–43.

49 Geng, Shen 耿申. "Woguo zhongxiaoxue banzhuren gongzuo xianzhuang ji duice" 我国中小学班主任工作现状及对策. *Educational Science Research* 教育科学研究 no. 11 (2018): 44–50.

50 Hwang, Y. S., and Evans, D. "Attitudes Towards Inclusion: Gaps between Belief and Practice." *International Journal of Special Education* 26, no. 1 (2011): 136–145.

51 Zhang, Xiaodong 张晓东. *Xiaoxue suiban jiudu jiaoshi gongzuo yali xianzhuang diaocha yanjiu* 小学随班就读教师工作压力现状调查研究. Huangshi: Hubei Normal University, 2019.

52 Chen, Xi 陈奚. *Xin jiaoshi ruzhi shiyingxing yanjiu—jiyu shifan yu fei shifansheng de duibi* 新教师入职适应性研究——基于师范与非师范生的对比. Shanghai: Shanghai Normal University, 2019.

53 Campbell, E. "Teacher Agency in Curriculum Contexts." *Curriculum Inquiry* 42, no. 2 (2012): 183–190.

54 Emirbayer, M., and Mische, A. "What Is Agency?" *American Journal of Sociology* 103, no.4 (1998): 962–1023.

55 Guan, Wenjun 关文军, and Deng, Meng 邓猛. "Woguo gaodeng shifan yuanxiao zhong kaishe ronghe jiaoyu zhuanye (benke cengci) de sikao yu jianyi" 我国高等师范院校中开设融合教育专业（本科层次）的思考与建议. *Heilongjiang Researches on Higher Education* 黑龙江高教研究 no. 7 (2017): 105–109.

56 Wu, Yang 吴扬. "You'eryuan jiaoshi ronghe jiaoyu suyang de diaocha yanjiu" 幼儿园教师融合教育素养的调查研究. *Chinese Journal of Special Education* 中国特殊教育 no. 11 (2017): 8–13.

57 Qi, Juan 亓娟. *Wanbei diqu you'er jiaoshi ronghe jiaoyu suyang de diaocha yanjiu* 皖北地区幼儿教师融合教育素养的调查研究. Huaibei: Huaibei Normal University, 2017.

58 Liu, Jie 刘洁. "Shixi yingxiang jiaoshi zhuanye fazhan de jiben yinsu" 试析影响教师专业发展的基本因素. *Journal of Northeast Normal University* 东北师大学报 no. 6 (2004): 15–22.

59 Han, Shuping 韩淑萍. "Woguo jiaoshi zhuanye fazhan yingxiang yinsu yanjiu shuping" 我国教师专业发展影响因素研究述评. *Modern Educational Science* 现代教育科学 no. 9 (2009): 76–79, 90.

60 Sannino, A. "Teachers' Talk of Experiencing: Conflict, Resistance and Agency." *Teaching and Teacher Education* 26, no. 4 (2010): 838–844.

61 Sutherland, L., Howard, S., and Markauskaite, L. "Professional Identity Creation: Examining the Development of Beginning Preservice Teachers' Understanding of Their Work as Teachers." *Teaching and Teacher Education* 26, no. 3 (2010): 455–465.

62 Bandura, A. "Human Agency: The Rhetoric and the Reality." *American Psychologist* 46 (1991): 157–162.

63 Biesta, G., Priestley, M., and Robinson, S. "The Role of Beliefs in Teacher Agency." *Teachers and Teaching* 21, no. 6 (2015): 624–640.

64 Biesta, G., and Tedder, M. "Agency and Learning in the Lifecourse: Towards an Ecological Perspective." *Studies in the Education of Adults* 39, no. 2 (2007): 132–149.

65 Zhang, Na 张娜, and Shen, Jiliang 申继亮. "Jiaoshi zhuanye fazhan: nengdongxing de shijiao" 教师专业发展：能动性的视角. *Theory and Practice of Education* 教育理论与实践 32, no. 19 (2012): 35–38.

66 Eteläpelto, A., Vähäsantanen, K., Hökkä, P., et al. "What Is Agency? Conceptualizing Professional Agency at Work." *Educational Research Review* no. 10 (2013): 45–65.

67 Dai, Shuangxiang 戴双翔, and Jiang, Yong 姜勇. "Lun jiaoshi de ziyou" 论教师的自由. *Research on Educational Development* no. 1 (2008): 7–10.

68 Zhou, Dan 周丹. *Suiban jiudu jiaoshi nengdongxing jiegou ji xiangguan yinsu de zuoyong jizhi yanjiu* 随班就读教师能动性结构及相关因素的作用机制研究. Beijing: Beijing Normal University, 2019.

69 Mu, G. M., Wang, Y., Wang, Z., et al. "An Enquiry into the Professional Competence of Inclusive Education Teachers in Beijing: Attitudes, Knowledge, Skills, and Agency." *International Journal of Disability Development and Education* 62, no. 6 (2015): 571–589.

70 Wang, Yan 王雁, Wang, Zhiqiang 王志强, Feng, Yajing 冯雅静, et al. "Suiban jiudu jiaoshi zhuanye suyang xianzhuang ji yingxiang yinsu yanjiu" 随班就读教师专业素养现状及影响因素研究. *Teacher Education Research* 教师教育研究 27, no. 4 (2015): 46–52, 60.

71 Chen, Xiangming 陈向明. "Jiaoshi zui xuyao shenme suyang" 教师最需要什么素养. *Journal of the Chinese Society of Education* 中国教育学刊 no. 8 (2018): 3.

72 Zheng, Yuanwen 郑媛文, and Ren, Lihua 任丽华. "Taoyuan xian guoxiao ziyuan ban jiaoshi gongzuo yali yu gongzuo manyidu xiangguan zhi yanjiu" 桃园县国小资源班教师工作压力与工作满意度相关之研究. *Bulletin of National Education Research* 国民教育研究集刊 no. 14 (2006): 205–233.

73 Wallen, M., and Tormey, R. "Developing Teacher Agency through Dialogue." *Teaching and Teacher Education* 82 (2019): 129–139.

74 Cohen, J., McCabe, E. M., Michelli, N. M., et al. "School Climate: Research, Policy, Practice, and Teacher Education." *Teachers College Record* 111, no. 1 (2009): 180–213.

75 Schaefer, J. *Impact of Teacher Efficacy on Teacher Attitudes Toward Classroom Inclusion*. Minneapolis: Capella University, 2010.

76 Zhou, Dan 周丹. *Suiban jiudu jiaoshi nengdongxing jiegou ji xiangguan yinsu de zuoyong jizhi yanjiu* 随班就读教师能动性结构及相关因素的作用机制研究. Beijing: Beijing Normal University, 2019.

77 Zhang, Lili 张丽莉. *Suiban jiudu jiaoshi zhuanye suyang ketang zhichi xianzhuang ji guanxi yanjiu—yi ha'erbin shi weili* 随班就读教师专业素养、课堂支持现状及关系研究——以哈尔滨市为例. Beijing: Beijing Normal University, 2016.

78 Taylor, D. *A Case Study of Principal Leadership and School-wide Inclusion Practices in a Low-SES Elementary School*. Nacogdoches: Stephen F. Austin State University, 2005.

79 Mcleskey, J., Billingsley, B., and Waldron, N. L. "Principal Leadership for Effective Inclusive Schools." In Bakken, J. P., and Obiakor, F. E. *General and Special Education Inclusion in an Age of Change: Roles of Professionals Involved*, 55–74. Bingley: Emerald Group Publishing Limited, 2016.

80 Wang, Y., and Zhang, W. "The Effects of Principal Support on Teachers' Professional Skills: The Mediating Role of School-wide Inclusive Practices and Teacher Agency." *International Journal of Disability, Development and Education* 68, no. 6 (2021): 773–787.

81 Churchill, G. A., Ford, N. M., and Walker, O. C. "Organizational Climate and Job Satisfaction in the Salesforce." *Journal of Marketing Research* 13, no. 4 (1976): 323–332.

82 Pomirleanu, N., and Mariadoss B. John. "The Influence of Organizational and Functional Support on the Development of Salesperson Job Satisfaction." *Journal of Personal Selling & Sales Management* 35, no. 1 (2015): 33–50.

83 Robbins, Stephen P. *Zuzhi xingwei xue* 组织行为学, 340. Beijing: China Renmin University Press, 1996.

84 Zhan, Wenhui 詹文慧, Gao, Jinjin 高金金, and Chen, Yiwen 陈毅文. "Zuzhi qifen dui gongzuo juandai de yingxiang: gongzuo yali de zhongjie zuoyong" 组织气氛对工作倦怠的影响：工作压力的中介作用. *Journal of Zhejiang University* (Sciences Edition) 浙江大学学报(理学版) 40, no. 1 (2013): 112–118.

85 Huang, Yiyuan 黄益远. "Guanyu zhongxiaoxue jiaoshi zhiye yali de yanjiu" 关于中小学教师职业压力的研究. *Teaching and Management* 教学与管理 33 (2002): 9–10.

86 Kyriacou, C. "Teacher Stress and Burnout: An International Review." *Educational Research* 29, no. 2 (1987): 146–152.

87 Dixon, F. A., Yssel, N., McConnell, J. M., et al. "Differentiated Instruction, Professional Development, and Teacher Efficacy." *Journal for the Education of the Gifted* 37, no. 2 (2014): 111–127.

88 Mao, Jinping 毛晋平. "Zhongxue jiaoshi gongzuo yali yu jiaoxue xiaonenggan de guanxi" 中学教师工作压力与教学效能感的关系. *Chinese Journal of Clinical Psychology* 中国临床心理学杂志 no. 4 (2005): 83–84.

89 Schwarzer, R., and Hallum, S. "Perceived Teacher Self-efficacy as a Predictor of Job Stress and Burnout: Mediation Analyses." *Applied Psychology* 57 (2008): 152–171.

90 Kalliath, T. J., O'Driscoll, M. P., and Gillespie, D. F. "A Test of the Maslach Burnout Inventory in Three Samples of Healthcare Professionals." *Work and Stress* 14, no. 1 (2000): 35–50.

91 Wang, Fang 王芳, and Xu, Yan 许燕. "Zhongxiaoxue jiaoshi zhiye kujie zhuangkuang jiqi yu shehui zhichi de guanxi" 中小学教师职业枯竭状况及其与社会支持的关系. *Acta Psychologica Sinica* no. 5 (2004): 568–574.

92 Wu, Linfu 吴林富. *Jiaoyu shengtai guanli* 教育生态管理, 13. Tianjin: Tianjin Education Press, 2006.

93 Liu, Yanli 刘艳丽. "Zhiqian jiaoshi jiaoyu jishu nengli peiyang de shengtai queshi ji duice yanjiu" 职前教师教育技术能力培养的生态缺失及对策研究. *The Chinese Journal of ICT in Education* 中国教育信息化 no. 4 (2017): 14–15.

94 Song, Gaimin 宋改敏, and Chen, Xiangming 陈向明. "Jiaoshi zhuanye chengzhang yanjiu de shengtaixue zhuanxiang" 教师专业成长研究的生态学转向. *Modern Education Management* 现代教育管理 no. 7 (2009): 49–52.

95 Li, Sen 李森, and Cui, Youxing崔友兴. "Lun jiaoshi zhuanye fazhan dongli de xitong goujian he jizhi tanxi—jiyu lewenchang dongli lilun de shijiao" 论教师专业发展动力的系统构建和机制探析——基于勒温场动力理论的视角. *Theory and Practice of Education* 教育理论与实践 33, no. 4 (2013): 33–36.

96 Demerouti, E., Bakker, A. B., Nachreiner, F. et al. "The Job Demands–resources Model of Burnout." *Journal of Applied Psychology* 86, no. 3 (2001): 499.

97 Bakker, A., Demerouti, E., and Schaufeli, W. "Dual Processes at Work in a Call Centre: An Application of the Job Demands–resources Model." *European Journal of Work and Organizational Psychology* 12, no. 4 (2003): 393–417.

98 Liang, Wenyan 梁文艳. "Gongzuo yaoqiu gongzuo ziyuan yu jiaoshi de gongzuo manyidu—jiyu shanghai jiaoshi jiaoxue guoji diaocha shuju de shizheng yanjiu" 工作要求、工作资源与教师的工作满意度——基于上海教师教学国际调查数据的实证研究. *Educational Research* 教育研究 41, no. 10 (2020): 102–115.

99 Xanthopoulou, D., Bakker, A. B., Demerouti, E. et al. "Work Engagement and Financial Returns: A Diary Study on the Role of Job and Personal Resources." *Journal of Occupational and Organizational Psychology* 82, no. 1 (2009): 183–200.

100 Bakker, A., Demerouti, E., and Schaufeli, W. "Dual Processes at Work in a Call Centre: An Application of the Job Demands–resources Model." *European Journal of Work and Organizational Psychology* 12, no. 4 (2003): 393–417.

101 Fernet, C., Austin, S., and Vallerand, R. "The Effects of Work Motivation on Employee Exhaustion and Commitment: An Extension of the JD–R Model." *Work & Stress* 26, no. 3 (2012): 213–229.

102 Wrzesniewski, A., and Dutton, J. E. "Crafting a Job: Revisioning Employees as Active Crafters of Their Work." *Academy of Management Review* 26, no. 2 (2001): 179–201.

103 Tims, M., Bakker, A. B., and Derks, D. "Development and Validation of the Job Crafting Scale." *Journal of Vocational Behavior* 80, no. 1 (2012): 73–186.

104 Zhang, Chunyu 张春雨, Wei, Jia 韦嘉, Chen, Xieping 陈谢平, et al. "Gongzuo sheji de xin shijiao: yuangong de gongzuo chongsu" 工作设计的新视角：员工的工作重塑. *Advances in Psychological Science* 心理科学进展 20, no. 8 (2012): 1305–1313.

105 Wrzesniewski, A., and Dutton, J. E. "Crafting a Job: Revisioning Employees as Active Crafters of Their Work." *Academy of Management Review* 26, no. 2 (2001): 179–201.

106 Qi, Yajing 齐亚静, and Wu, Xinchun 伍新春. "Gongzuo yaoqiu–ziyuan moxing: lilun he shizheng yanjiu de tuozhan mailuo" 工作要求–资源模型：理论和实证研究的拓展脉络. *Journal of Beijing Normal University* (Social Science Edition) 北京师范大学学报（社会科学版）270, no. 6 (2018): 30–38.

107 Qi, Yajing 齐亚静, Wu, Xinchun 伍新春, and Wang, Xiaoli 王晓丽. "Zhongxiaoxue jiaoshi gongzuo chongsu yu gongzuo touru de jiaocha zhihou fenxi" 中小学教师工作重塑与工作投入的交叉滞后分析. *Chinese Journal of Clinical Psychology* 中国临床心理学杂志 24, no. 5 (2016): 935–938, 942.

108 Yu, Meifang 于梅芳. *Zhongxiaoxue jiaoshi de shitu zhidao gongneng jiqi duochong zhiye xiaoneng yanjiu* 中小学教师的师徒指导功能及其多重职业效能研究. Wuxi: Jiangnan University, 2018.

109 Qi, Yajing 齐亚静, Wang, Xiaoli 王晓丽, and Wu, Xinchun 伍新春. "Jiaoshi zhuanye fazhan nengdongxing ji yingxiang yinsu: jiyu gongzuo tezheng de tantao" 教师专业发展能动性及影响因素：基于工作特征的探讨. *Chinese Journal of Clinical Psychology* 中国临床心理学杂志 28, no. 4 (2020): 779–782, 778.

110 Wang, Zhenhong 王振宏, Wang, Kejing 王克静, You, Xuqun 游旭群, et al. "Jiaoshi xiaoneng gongzuo dongji yu xinjing dui jiaoxue chuangxin de yingxiang" 教师效能、工作动机与心境对教学创新的影响. *Psychological Science* 心理科学 33, no. 5 (2010): 1254–1257.

111 Wang, Shuanglong 王双龙. "Jiaoshi ziwo yishi yu xuexiao zhichi fenwei dui jiaoshi zhuanye fazhan de yingxiang yanjiu" 教师自我意识与学校支持氛围对教师专业发展的影响研究. *Educational Science Research* 教育科学研究 no. 11 (2017): 74–78.

182 *Research into the Competence of Chinese Teachers*

112 Cao, Taisheng 操太圣, and Qiao, Xuefeng 乔雪峰. "Nengdongxing yu jiaoshi bentixing anquan" 能动性与教师本体性安全. *Global Education* 全球教育展望 40, no. 5 (2011): 45–49.

113 Li, Sen 李森, and Cui, Youxing 崔友兴. "Lun jiaoshi zhuanye fazhan dongli de xitong goujian he jizhi tanxi—jiyu lewenchang dongli lilun de shijiao" 论教师专业发展动力的系统构建和机制探析——基于勒温场动力理论的视角. *Theory and Practice of Education* 教育理论与实践 33, no. 4 (2013): 33–36.

114 Ye, Lan 叶澜. "Gaishan fazhan 'shengjing' tisheng jiaoshi zijue 改善发展"生境"提升教师自觉." *Zhongguo Jiaoyu Bao* 中国教育报, Sep. 15, 2007.

115 Zhang, Guoli 张国礼, Bian, Yufang 边玉芳, and Dong, Qi 董奇. "Zhongxiaoxue jiaoshi jiaoxue suyang gongzuo yali zhuguan xingfugan de guanxi" 中小学教师教学素养、工作压力、主观幸福感的关系. *Chinese Journal of Special Education* 中国特殊教育 no. 4 (2012): 89–92.

116 Huang, Yilin 黄依林, and Liu, Haiyan 刘海燕. "Jiaoshi zhiye yali yanjiu zongshu" 教师职业压力研究综述. *Education Exploration* 教育探索 no. 6 (2006): 111–113.

117 Zhu, Nan 朱楠, and Wang, Yan 王雁. "'Fuhexing' teshu jiaoyu jiaoshi de peiyang—jiyu fuhexing de neihan fenxi" "复合型"特殊教育教师的培养——基于复合型的内涵分析. *Teacher Education Research* 教师教育研究 27, no. 6 (2015): 39–44.

118 Zhao, Changmu 赵昌木, and Xu, Jicun 徐继存. "Jiaoshi chengzhang de huanjing yinsu kaocha—jiyu bufen zhongxiaoxue shidi diaocha he fangtan de sikao" 教师成长的环境因素考察——基于部分中小学实地调查和访谈的思考. *Journal of Educational Science of Hunan Normal University* 湖南师范大学教育科学学报 no. 3 (2005): 16–22.

119 Guo, Hongxia 郭红霞. "Xinxi suyang cujin jiaoshi zhuanye nengli fazhan de neizai jizhi jiqi yangcheng" 信息素养促进教师专业能力发展的内在机制及其养成. *China Educational Technology* 中国电化教育 no. 5 (2012): 58–61.

120 Wang, Shuanglong 王双龙. "Xuexiao de zuzhi fenwei ziwo daoxiang xuexi dui jiaoshi zhuanye fazhan de yingxiang yanjiu" 学校的组织氛围、自我导向学习对教师专业发展的影响研究. *Journal of Teaching and Management* 教学与管理 no. 6 (2016): 55–59.

121 He, Wenjie 贺文洁, Li, Qiong 李琼, and Mu, Honghua 穆洪华. "Xuexiao wenhua fenwei dui xiangcun jiaoshi gongzuo manyidu de yingxiang: jiaoshi nengdongxing de zhongjie zuoyong" 学校文化氛围对乡村教师工作满意度的影响：教师能动性的中介作用. *Teacher Education Research* 教师教育研究 30, no. 3 (2018): 39–45, 128.

122 Zhan, Wenhui 詹文慧, Gao, Jinjin 高金金, and Chen, Yiwen 陈毅文. "Zuzhi fenwei dui gongzuo juandai de yingxiang: gongzuo yali de zhongjie zuoyong" 组织气氛对工作倦怠的影响：工作压力的中介作用. *Journal of Zhejiang University* (Sciences Edition) 浙江大学学报（理学版）40, no. 1 (2013): 112–118.

123 Yin, Shidong 殷世东. "Shengtai quxiang jiaoshi zhuanye fazhan de zuge yu yunzuo" 生态取向教师专业发展的阻隔与运作. *Teacher Education Research* 教师教育研究 26, no. 5 (2014): 36–41.

124 Li, Sen 李森, and Cui, Youxing 崔友兴. "Lun jiaoshi zhuanye fazhan dongli de xitong goujian he jizhi tanxi—jiyu lewenchang dongli lilun de shijiao" 论教师专业发展动力的系统构建和机制探析——基于勒温场动力理论的视角. *Theory and Practice of Education* 教育理论与实践 33, no. 4 (2013): 33–36.

125 Fullan, Michael. *Change Forces: Probing the Depths of Educational Reform* 变革的力量——透视教育改革, translated by National Institute of Education

Sciences International College, Toronto, Canada, 27. Beijing: Educational Science Publishing, 2004.

126 Ye, Lan 叶澜, Bai, Yimin 白益民, Wang, Zhan 王枬, et al. *Jiaoshi juese yu jiaoshi fazhan xintan* 教师角色与教师发展新探, 3. Beijing: Educational Science Publishing, 2001.

127 Ye, Lan 叶澜. "Gaishan fazhan 'shengjing' tisheng jiaoshi zijue 改善发展"生境"提升教师自觉." *Zhongguo Jiaoyu Bao* 中国教育报, Sep. 15, 2007.

128 Alyson, S., Guoyuan S., Julian W., et al. "A Dialogue about Teacher Agency: Australian and Chinese Perspectives." *Teaching and Teacher Education* 75 (2018): 316–326.

129 Jiang, Shanshan 姜珊珊. *You'eryuan jiaoshi shengrenli jiqi yingxiang yinsu yanjiu* 幼儿园教师胜任力及其影响因素研究. Beijing: Beijing Normal University, 2013.

130 Liu, Shengnan 刘胜男. *Jiaoshi zhuanye xuexi yingxiang yinsu jiqi zuoyong jizhi yanjiu* 教师专业学习影响因素及其作用机制研究. Shanghai: East China Normal University, 2016.

131 McNay, L. "Agency and Experience: Gender as a Lived Relation." *The Sociological Review* 52, no. 2 (2004): 175–190.

132 Sannino, A. "Teachers' Talk of Experiencing: Conflict, Resistance and Agency." *Teaching and Teacher Education* 26, no. 4 (2010): 838–844.

133 Zhang, Pingping 张平平, Li, Lingyan 李凌艳, and Xin, Tao 辛涛. "Xuexiao fenwei dui xuesheng shuxue chengji yingxiang de kuawenhua bijiao: jiyu duoshuiping fenxi de jieguo" 学校氛围对学生数学成绩影响的跨文化比较：基于多水平分析的结果. *Psychological Development and Education* 心理发展与教育 27, no. 6 (2011): 625–632.

134 Seligman, M. E. P., and Csikszentmihalyi, M. "Positive Psychology: An Introduction." *American Psychologist* 55, no. 2 (2000): 5–14.

135 Rutter, M. "Resilience in the Face of Adversity: Protective Factors and Resistance to Psychiatric Disorder." *British Journal of Psychiatry* 147, no. 6 (1985): 598–611.

References

Alyson, S., Guoyuan S., Julian W., et al. "A Dialogue about Teacher Agency: Australian and Chinese Perspectives." *Teaching and Teacher Education* 75 (2018): 316–326.

Bakker, A., Demerouti, E., and Schaufeli, W. "Dual Processes at Work in a Call Centre: An Application of the Job Demands–resources Model." *European Journal of Work and Organizational Psychology* 12, no. 4 (2003): 393–417.

Bandura, A. "Human Agency: The Rhetoric and the Reality." *American Psychologist* 46 (1991): 157–162.

Berry, Ruth A. W. "Novice Teachers' Conceptions of Fairness in Inclusion Classrooms." *Teaching and Teacher Education* 24, no. 5 (2008): 1149–1159.

Biesta, G., and Tedder, M. "Agency and Learning in the Lifecourse: Towards an Ecological Perspective." *Studies in the Education of Adults* 39, no. 2 (2007): 132–149.

Biesta, G., Priestley, M., and Robinson, S. "The Role of Beliefs in Teacher Agency." *Teachers and Teaching* 21, no. 6 (2015): 624–640.

Blecker, N., and Boakes, N. "Creating a Learning Environment for All Children: Are Teachers Able and Willing?" *International Journal of Inclusive Education* 14 (2010): 435–447.

184 *Research into the Competence of Chinese Teachers*

Boer, A. D. "Inclusive Education in Developing Countries: A Closer Look at Its Implementation in the Last 10 Years." *Educational Review* 67, no. 2 (2015): 179–195.

Campbell, E. "Teacher Agency in Curriculum Contexts." *Curriculum Inquiry* 42, no. 2 (2012): 183–190.

Cao, Taisheng 操太圣, and Qiao, Xuefeng 乔雪峰. "Nengdongxing yu jiaoshi bentixing anquan" 能动性与教师本体性安全. *Global Education* 全球教育展望 40, no. 5 (2011): 45–49.

Chen, Xi 陈奚. *Xin jiaoshi ruzhi shiyingxing yanjiu—jiyu shifan yu fei shifansheng de duibi* 新教师入职适应性研究——基于师范与非师范生的对比. Shanghai: Shanghai Normal University, 2019.

Chen, Xiangming 陈向明. "Jiaoshi zui xuyao shenme suyang" 教师最需要什么素养. *Journal of the Chinese Society of Education* 中国教育学刊 no. 8 (2018): 3.

Churchill, G. A., Ford, N. M., and Walker, O. C. "Organizational Climate and Job Satisfaction in the Salesforce." *Journal of Marketing Research* 13, no. 4 (1976): 323–332.

Cohen, J., McCabe, E. M., Michelli, N. M., et al. "School Climate: Research, Policy, Practice, and Teacher Education." *Teachers College Record* 111, no. 1 (2009): 180–213.

Dai, Shuangxiang 戴双翔, and Jiang, Yong 姜勇. "Lun jiaoshi de ziyou" 论教师的自由. *Research on Educational Development* 教育发展研究 no. 1 (2008): 7–10.

Demerouti, E., Bakker, A. B., Nachreiner, F. et al. "The Job Demands–resources Model of Burnout." *Journal of Applied Psychology* 86, no. 3 (2001): 499.

Deng, Meng 邓猛. "Putong xiaoxue suiban jiudu jiaoshi dui quanna jiaoyu taidu de chengxiang bijiao yanjiu" 普通小学随班就读教师对全纳教育态度的城乡比较研究. Educational Research and Experiment 教育研究与实验 no. 1 (2004): 61–66

Dixon, F. A., Yssel, N., McConnell, J. M., et al. "Differentiated Instruction, Professional Development, and Teacher Efficacy." *Journal for the Education of the Gifted* 37, no. 2 (2014): 111–127.

Du, Lingyu 杜灵宇. *Yunnan shaoshu minzu nongcun diqu suiban jiudu jiaoshi zhihou peixun neirong xuqiu yanjiu—yi longchuan xian wei ge'an* 云南少数民族农村地区随班就读教师职后培训内容需求研究——以陇川县为个案. Kunming: Yunnan Normal University, 2018.

Emirbayer, M., and Mische, A. "What Is Agency?" *American Journal of Sociology* 103, no.4 (1998): 962–1023.

Eteläpelto, A., Vähäsantanen, K., Hökkä, P., et al. "What Is Agency? Conceptualizing Professional Agency at Work." *Educational Research Review* no. 10 (2013): 45–65.

Feng, Yajing 冯雅静, Li, Aifen 李爱芬, and Wang, Yan 王雁. "Woguo putong shifan zhuanye ronghe jiaoyu kecheng xianzhuang de diaocha yanjiu" 我国普通师范专业融合教育课程现状的调查研究. *Chinese Journal of Special Education* 中国特殊教育 no. 1 (2016): 9–15.

Fernet, C., Austin, S., and Vallerand, R. "The Effects of Work Motivation on Employee Exhaustion and Commitment: An Extension of the JD–R Model." *Work & Stress* 26, no. 3 (2012): 213–229.

Fullan, Michael. *Change Forces: Probing the Depths of Educational Reform* 变革的力量——透视教育改革, translated by National Institute of Education Sciences International College, Toronto, Canada, 27. Beijing: Educational Science Publishing, 2004.

Gao, Li 高利. "Zhongguo dalu diqu ronghe jiaoyu taidu yanjiu jinzhan ji qishi" 中国大陆地区融合教育态度研究进展及启示. *Journal of Suihua University* 绥化学院学报 39, no. 7 (2019): 19–23.

Geng, Shen 耿申. "Woguo zhongxiaoxue banzhuren gongzuo xianzhuang ji duice" 我国中小学班主任工作现状及对策. *Educational Science Research* 教育科学研究 no. 11 (2018): 44–50.

Guan, Wenjun 关文军, and Deng, Meng 邓猛. "Woguo gaodeng shifan yuanxiao zhong kaishe ronghe jiaoyu zhuanye (benke cengci) de sikao yu jianyi" 我国高等师范院校中开设融合教育专业（本科层次）的思考与建议. *Heilongjiang Researches on Higher Education* 黑龙江高教研究 no. 7 (2017): 105–109.

Guo, Hongxia 郭红霞. "Xinxi suyang cujin jiaoshi zhuanye nengli fazhan de neizai jizhi jiqi yangcheng" 信息素养促进教师专业能力发展的内在机制及其养成. *China Educational Technology* 中国电化教育 no. 5 (2012): 58–61.

Guojia zhongchangqi jiaoyu gaige he fazhan guihua gangyao zhongqi pinggu teshu jiaoyu zhuanti pinggu baogao (zhaiyao) 《国家中长期教育改革和发展规划纲要》中期评估特殊教育专题评估报告（摘要）. Jiaoyubu guanwang 教育部官网, 2015. www.moe.gov.cn/jyb_xwfb/xw_fbh/moe_2069/xwfbh_2015n/xwfb_151130/151130_sfcl/201511/t20151130_221728.html.

Han, Shuping 韩淑萍. "Woguo jiaoshi zhuanye fazhan yingxiang yinsu yanjiu shuping" 我国教师专业发展影响因素研究述评. *Modern Educational Science* 现代教育科学 no. 9 (2009): 76–79, 90.

He, Wenjie 贺文洁, Li, Qiong 李琼, and Mu, Honghua 穆洪华. "Xuexiao wenhua fenwei dui xiangcun jiaoshi gongzuo manyidu de yingxiang: jiaoshi nengdongxing de zhongjie zuoyong" 学校文化氛围对乡村教师工作满意度的影响：教师能动性的中介作用. *Teacher Education Research* 教师教育研究 30, no. 3 (2018): 39–45, 128.

Huang, Yilin 黄依林, and Liu, Haiyan 刘海燕. "Jiaoshi zhiye yali yanjiu zongshu" 教师职业压力研究综述. *Education Exploration* 教育探索 no. 6 (2006): 111–113.

Huang, Ying 黄英. "Xiaozhang—xin jiaoshi zhuanye chengzhang de yinlingzhe" 校长——新教师专业成长的引领者. *Journal of Educational Development* 教育导刊 no. 4 (2007): 51–52.

Huang, Yiyuan 黄益远. "Guanyu zhongxiaoxue jiaoshi zhiye yali de yanjiu" 关于中小学教师职业压力的研究. *Teaching and Management* 教学与管理 33 (2002): 9–10.

Hwang, Y. S., and Evans, D. "Attitudes Towards Inclusion: Gaps between Belief and Practice." *International Journal of Special Education* 26, no. 1 (2011): 136–145.

Jiang, Shanshan 姜珊珊. *You'eryuan jiaoshi shengrenli jiqi yingxiang yinsu yanjiu* 幼儿园教师胜任力及其影响因素研究. Beijing: Beijing Normal University, 2013.

Jiang, Xiaoying 江小英, Niu, Shuangshuang 牛爽爽, and Deng, Meng 邓猛. "Beijing shi putong zhongxiaoxue ronghe jiaoyu jiben qingkuang diaocha baogao" 北京市普通中小学融合教育基本情况调查报告. *Modern Special Education* 现代特殊教育 no. 14 (2016): 22–27.

Johnstone, C., and Chapman, D. "Contributions and Constraints to the Implementation of Inclusive Education in Lesotho." *International Journal of Disability, Development and Education* 56 (2009): 131–148.

Kalliath, T. J., O'Driscoll, M. P., and Gillespie, D. F. "A Test of the Maslach Burnout Inventory in Three Samples of Healthcare Professionals." *Work and Stress* 14, no. 1 (2000): 35–50.

Kyriacou, C. "Teacher Stress and Burnout: An International Review." *Educational Research* 29, no. 2 (1987): 146–152.

Li, Jing 李静. "You'eryuan jiaoshi ronghe jiaoyu suyang yu peixun xuqiu fenxi—yi beijing diqu weili" 幼儿园教师融合教育素养与培训需求分析——以北京地区为例. *Teacher Development Research* 教师发展研究 no. 4 (2017): 62–68.

186 *Research into the Competence of Chinese Teachers*

Li, Qiong 李琼, Zhang, Guoli 张国礼, and Zhou, Jun 周钧. "Zhongxiaoxue jiaoshi de zhiye yaliyuan yanjiu"中小学教师的职业压力源研究. *Psychological Development and Education* 心理发展与教育 27, no. 1 (2011): 97–104.

Li, Sen 李森, and Cui, Youxing 崔友兴. "Lun jiaoshi zhuanye fazhan dongli de xitong goujian he jizhi tanxi—jiyu lewenchang dongli lilun de shijiao" 论教师专业发展动力的系统构建和机制探析——基于勒温场动力理论的视角. *Theory and Practice of Education* 教育理论与实践 33, no. 4 (2013): 33–36.

Li, Xiu 李秀. "Puxiao jiaoshi dui suiban jiudu taidu de diaocha yanjiu—yi fujian sheng weili" 普小教师对随班就读态度的调查研究——以福建省为例. *Journal of Suihua University* 绥化学院学报 no. 4 (2016): 20–25.

Liang, Wenyan 梁文艳. "Gongzuo yaoqiu gongzuo ziyuan yu jiaoshi de gongzuo manyidu—jiyu shanghai jiaoshi jiaoxue guoji diaocha shuju de shizheng yanjiu" 工作要求、工作资源与教师的工作满意度——基于上海教师教学国际调查数据的实证研究. *Educational Research* 教育研究 41, no. 10 (2020): 102–115.

Liu, Chunling 刘春玲, Du, Xiaoxin 杜晓新, and Yao, Jian 姚健. "Putong xiaoxue jiaoshi dui teshu ertong jiena taidu de yanjiu" 普通小学教师对特殊儿童接纳态度的研究. *Chinese Journal of Special Education* 中国特殊教育 no. 3 (2000): 34–36.

Liu, Jie 刘洁. "Shixi yingxiang jiaoshi zhuanye fazhan de jiben yinsu" 试析影响教师专业发展的基本因素. *Journal of Northeast Normal University* 东北师大学报 no. 6 (2004): 15–22.

Liu, Shengnan 刘胜男. *Jiaoshi zhuanye xuexi yingxiang yinsu jiqi zuoyong jizhi yanjiu* 教师专业学习影响因素及其作用机制研究. Shanghai: East China Normal University, 2016.

Liu, Yanli 刘艳丽. "Zhiqian jiaoshi jiaoyu jishu nengli peiyang de shengtai queshi ji duice yanjiu" 职前教师教育技术能力培养的生态缺失及对策研究. *The Chinese Journal of ICT in Education* 中国教育信息化 no. 4 (2017): 14–15.

Ma, Hongying 马红英, and Tan, Heping 谭和平. "Shanghai shi suiban jiudu jiaoshi xianzhuang diaocha" 上海市随班就读教师现状调查. *Chinese Journal of Special Education* 中国特殊教育 no. 1 (2010).

Mao, Jinping 毛晋平. "Zhongxue jiaoshi gongzuo yali yu jiaoxue xiaonenggan de guanxi" 中学教师工作压力与教学效能感的关系. *Chinese Journal of Clinical Psychology* 中国临床心理学杂志 no. 4 (2005): 83–84.

Mcleskey, J., Billingsley, B., and Waldron, N. L. "Principal Leadership for Effective Inclusive Schools." In Bakken, J. P., and Obiakor, F. E. *General and Special Education Inclusion in an Age of Change: Roles of Professionals Involved.* Bingley: Emerald Group Publishing Limited, 2016: 55–74.

McNay, L. "Agency and Experience: Gender as a Lived Relation." *The Sociological Review* 52, no. 2 (2004): 175–190.

Mu, G. M., Wang, Y., Wang, Z., et al. "An Enquiry into the Professional Competence of Inclusive Education Teachers in Beijing: Attitudes, Knowledge, Skills, and Agency." *International Journal of Disability Development and Education* 62, no. 6 (2015): 571–589.

Pomirleanu, N., and Mariadoss B. John. "The Influence of Organizational and Functional Support on the Development of Salesperson Job Satisfaction." *Journal of Personal Selling & Sales Management* 35, no. 1 (2015): 33–50.

Qi, Juan 亓娟. *Wanbei diqu you'er jiaoshi ronghe jiaoyu suyang de diaocha yanjiu* 皖北地区幼儿教师融合教育素养的调查研究. Huaibei: Huaibei Normal University, 2017.

Qi, Yajing 齐亚静, and Wu, Xinchun 伍新春. "Gongzuo yaoqiu–ziyuan moxing: lilun he shizheng yanjiu de tuozhan mailuo" 工作要求-资源模型：理论和实证研究的拓

展脉络. *Journal of Beijing Normal University* (Social Science Edition) 北京师范大学学报（社会科学版） 270, no. 6 (2018): 30–38.

Qi, Yajing 齐亚静, Wang, Xiaoli 王晓丽, and Wu, Xinchun 伍新春. "Jiaoshi zhuanye fazhan nengdongxing ji yingxiang yinsu: jiyu gongzuo tezheng de tantao" 教师专业发展能动性及影响因素：基于工作特征的探讨. *Chinese Journal of Clinical Psychology* 中国临床心理学杂志 28, no. 4 (2020): 779–782, 778.

Qi, Yajing 齐亚静, Wu, Xinchun 伍新春, and Wang, Xiaoli 王晓丽. "Zhongxiaoxue jiaoshi gongzuo chongsu yu gongzuo touru de jiaocha zhihou fenxi" 中小学教师工作重塑与工作投入的交叉滞后分析. *Chinese Journal of Clinical Psychology* 中国临床心理学杂志 24, no. 5 (2016): 935–938, 942.

Robbins, Stephen P. *Zuzhi xingwei xue* 组织行为学, 340. Beijing: China Renmin University Press, 1996.

Rutter, M. "Resilience in the Face of Adversity: Protective Factors and Resistance to Psychiatric Disorder." *British Journal of Psychiatry* 147, no. 6 (1985): 598–611.

Sannino, A. "Teachers' Talk of Experiencing: Conflict, Resistance and Agency." *Teaching and Teacher Education* 26, no. 4 (2010): 838–844.

Savolainen, H. "Responding to Diversity and Striving for Excellence: The Case of Finland." *Prospects Quarterly Review of Comparative Education* 39, no. 3 (2009): 256–269.

Schaefer, J. *Impact of Teacher Efficacy on Teacher Attitudes toward Classroom Inclusion.* Minneapolis: Capella University, 2010.

Schon, Donald A. *The Reflective Practitioner: How Professionals Think In Action* 反映的实践者——专业工作者如何在行动中思考, translated by Linqing Xia 夏林清, 35. Beijing: Educational Science Press, 2007.

Schwarzer, R., and Hallum, S. "Perceived Teacher Self-efficacy as a Predictor of Job Stress and Burnout: Mediation Analyses." *Applied Psychology* 57 (2008): 152–171.

Seligman, M. E. P., and Csikszentmihalyi, M. "Positive Psychology: An Introduction." *American Psychologist* 55, no. 2 (2000): 5–14.

Shi, Mengliang 石梦良, and Chen, Minyi 陈敏怡. "Guangdong sheng putong jiaoshi dui ronghe jiaoyu taidu de diaocha yanjiu" 广东省普通教师对融合教育态度的调查研究. *Journal of Changchun University* (Social Science Edition) 长春大学学报（社会科学版）no. 4 (2017): 106–111.

Song, Gaimin 宋改敏, and Chen, Xiangming 陈向明. "Jiaoshi zhuanye chengzhang yanjiu de shengtaixue zhuanxiang" 教师专业成长研究的生态学转向. *Modern Education Management* 现代教育管理 no. 7 (2009): 49–52.

Sutherland, L., Howard, S., and Markauskaite, L. "Professional Identity Creation: Examining the Development of Beginning Preservice Teachers' Understanding of Their Work as Teachers." *Teaching and Teacher Education* 26, no. 3 (2010): 455–465.

Tan, Heping 谭和平, and Ma, Hongying 马红英. "Shanghai shi suiban jiudu jiaoshi zhuanyehua fazhan xuqiu de diaocha yanjiu" 上海市随班就读教师专业化发展需求的调查研究. *Journal of Schooling Studies* 基础教育 9, no. 2 (2012): 63–70.

Taylor, D. *A Case Study of Principal Leadership and School-wide Inclusion Practices in a Low-SES Elementary School.* Nacogdoches: Stephen F. Austin State University, 2005.

Tims, M., Bakker, A. B., and Derks, D. "Development and Validation of the Job Crafting Scale." *Journal of Vocational Behavior* 80, no. 1 (2012): 73–186.

Wallen, M., and Tormey, R. "Developing Teacher Agency through Dialogue." *Teaching and Teacher Education* 82 (2019): 129–139.

Wang, Fang 王芳, and Xu, Yan 许燕. "Zhongxiaoxue jiaoshi zhiye kujie zhuangkuang jiqi yu shehui zhichi de guanxi" 中小学教师职业枯竭状况及其与社会支持的关系. *Acta Psychologica Sinica* no. 5 (2004): 568–574.

Wang, Hongxia 王红霞, Peng, Xin 彭欣, and Wang, Yanjie 王艳杰. "Beijing shi haidian qu xiaoxue ronghe jiaoyu xianzhuang diaocha yanjiu baogao" 北京市海淀区小学融合教育现状调查研究报告. *Chinese Journal of Special Education* 中国特殊教育 no. 4 (2011): 37–42.

Wang, Shuanglong 王双龙. "Xuexiao de zuzhi fenwei ziwo daoxiang xuexi dui jiaoshi zhuanye fazhan de yingxiang yanjiu" 学校的组织氛围、自我导向学习对教师专业发展的影响研究. *Journal of Teaching and Management* 教学与管理 no. 6 (2016): 55–59.

Wang, Shuanglong 王双龙. "Jiaoshi ziwo yishi yu xuexiao zhichi fenwei dui jiaoshi zhuanye fazhan de yingxiang yanjiu" 教师自我意识与学校支持氛围对教师专业发展的影响研究. *Educational Science Research* 教育科学研究 no. 11 (2017): 74–78.

Wang, Y., and Zhang, W. "The Effects of Principal Support on Teachers' Professional Skills: The Mediating Role of School-wide Inclusive Practices and Teacher Agency." *International Journal of Disability, Development and Education* 68, no. 6 (2021): 773–787.

Wang, Yan 王雁, Wang, Zhiqiang 王志强, Feng, Yajing 冯雅静, et al. "Suiban jiudu jiaoshi zhuanye suyang xianzhuang ji yingxiang yinsu yanjiu" 随班就读教师专业素养现状及影响因素研究. *Teacher Education Research* 教师教育研究 27, no. 4 (2015): 46–52, 60.

Wang, Yue 王悦. *Suiban jiudu jiaoshi ketang zhichi dui qi kecheng tiaozheng de yingxiang—ziwo xiaonenggan de zhongjie zuoyong* 随班就读教师课堂支持对其课程调整的影响——自我效能感的中介作用. Beijing: Beijing Normal University, 2018.

Wang, Zhenhong 王振宏, Wang, Kejing 王克静, You, Xuqun 游旭群, et al. "Jiaoshi xiaoneng gongzuo dongji yu xinjing dui jiaoxue chuangxin de yingxiang" 教师效能、工作动机与心境对教学创新的影响. *Psychological Science* 心理科学 33, no. 5 (2010): 1254–1257.

Wei, Shouhong 魏寿洪, Liao, Jin 廖进, and Cheng, Minfen 程敏芬. "Chengyu liangdi puxiao jiaoshi ronghe jiaoyu kecheng yu jiaoxue tiaozheng shishi xianzhuang yanjiu" 成渝两地普小教师融合教育课程与教学调整实施现状研究. *Chinese Journal of Special Education* 中国特殊教育 216, no. 6 (2018): 16–24.

Wei, Xiaoman 韦小满, and Yuan, Wende 袁文得. "Guanyu puxiao jiaoshi yu tejiao jiaoshi dui you teshu jiaoyu xuyao xuesheng suiban jiudu taidu de diaocha" 关于普小教师与特教教师对有特殊教育需要学生随班就读态度的调查. *Chinese Journal of Special Education* 中国特殊教育 no. 3 (2000): 31–33.

Wrzesniewski, A., and Dutton, J. E. "Crafting a Job: Revisioning Employees as Active Crafters of Their Work." *Academy of Management Review* 26, no. 2 (2001): 179–201.

Wu, Linfu 吴林富. *Jiaoyu shengtai guanli* 教育生态管理, 13. Tianjin: Tianjin Education Press, 2006.

Wu, Yang 吴扬. "You'eryuan jiaoshi ronghe jiaoyu suyang de diaocha yanjiu" 幼儿园教师融合教育素养的调查研究. *Chinese Journal of Special Education* 中国特殊教育 no. 11 (2017): 8–13.

Xanthopoulou, D., Bakker, A. B., Demerouti, E. et al. "Work Engagement and Financial Returns: A Diary Study on the Role of Job and Personal Resources." *Journal of Occupational and Organizational Psychology* 82, no. 1 (2009): 183–200.

Xiong, Qi 熊琪, Terry Cumming, and Li, Zehui 李泽慧. "Suiban jiudu jiaoshi ronghe jiaoyu jiaoxue xiaonenggan yanjiu" 随班就读教师融合教育教学效能感研究. *Chinese Journal of Special Education* 中国特殊教育 no. 2 (2019): 50–57.

Xu, Meijuan 徐梅娟. "Suiban jiudu banji shuxue jiaoshi tejiao zhishi yu jineng zhangwo qingkuang diaocha yanjiu" 随班就读班级数学教师特教知识与技能掌握情况调查研究. *Journal of Nanjing Special Education Institute* 南京特教学院学报 no. 4 (2011): 9–13.

Yan, Tingrui 颜廷睿, Guan, Wenjun 关文军, and Deng, Meng 邓猛. "Beijing shi zhongxiaoxue ronghe jiaoyu shishi qingkuang de diaocha yanjiu" 北京市中小学融合教育实施情况的调查研究. *Disability Research* 残疾人研究 no. 2 (2017): 90–96.

Yang, Xijie 杨希洁. "Suiban jiudu xuexiao canji xuesheng fazhan zhuangkuang yanjiu" 随班就读学校残疾学生发展状况研究. *Chinese Journal of Special Education* 中国特殊教育 no. 7 (2010): 3–10.

Ye, Lan 叶澜. "Gaishan fazhan 'shengjing' tisheng jiaoshi zijue 改善发展"生境"提升教师自觉." *Zhongguo Jiaoyu Bao* 中国教育报, Sep. 15, 2007.

Ye, Lan 叶澜, Bai, Yimin 白益民, Wang, Zhan 王枬, et al. *Jiaoshi juese yu jiaoshi fazhan xintan* 教师角色与教师发展新探, 3. Beijing: Educational Science Publishing, 2001.

Yin, Shidong 殷世东. "Shengtai quxiang jiaoshi zhuanye fazhan de zuge yu yunzuo" 生态取向教师专业发展的阻隔与运作. *Teacher Education Research* 教师教育研究 26, no. 5 (2014): 36–41.

Yu, Meifang 于梅芳. *Zhongxiaoxue jiaoshi de shitu zhidao gongneng jiqi duochong zhiye xiaoneng yanjiu* 中小学教师的师徒指导功能及其多重职业效能研究. Wuxi: Jiangnan University, 2018.

Zeng, Yaru 曾雅茹. "Putong xiaoxue jiaoshi dui suiban jiudu de taidu jiaoxue celüe yu suoxu zhichi de yanjiu" 普通小学教师对随班就读的态度、教学策略与所需支持的研究. *Chinese Journal of Special Education* 中国特殊教育 no. 12 (2007): 3–7.

Zhan, Wenhui 詹文慧, Gao, Jinjin 高金金, and Chen, Yiwen 陈毅文. "Zuzhi qifen dui gongzuo juandai de yingxiang: gongzuo yali de zhongjie zuoyong" 组织气氛对工作倦怠的影响：工作压力的中介作用. *Journal of Zhejiang University* (Sciences Edition) 浙江大学学报(理学版) 40, no. 1 (2013): 112–118.

Zhang, Chunyu 张春雨, Wei, Jia 韦嘉, Chen, Xieping 陈谢平, et al. "Gongzuo sheji de xin shijiao: yuangong de gongzuo chongsu" 工作设计的新视角：员工的工作重塑. *Advances in Psychological Science* 心理科学进展 20, no. 8 (2012): 1305–1313.

Zhang, Guoli 张国礼, Bian, Yufang 边玉芳, and Dong, Qi 董奇. "Zhongxiaoxue jiaoshi jiaoxue suyang gongzuo yali zhuguan xingfugan de guanxi" 中小学教师教学素养、工作压力、主观幸福感的关系. *Chinese Journal of Special Education* 中国特殊教育 no. 4 (2012): 89–92.

Zhang, Lili 张丽莉. *Suiban jiudu jiaoshi zhuanye suyang ketang zhichi xianzhuang ji guanxi yanjiu—yi ha'erbin shi weili* 随班就读教师专业素养、课堂支持现状及关系研究—以哈尔滨市为例. Beijing: Beijing Normal University, 2016.

Zhang, Na 张娜, and Shen, Jiliang 申继亮. "Jiaoshi zhuanye fazhan: nengdongxing de shijiao" 教师专业发展：能动性的视角. *Educational Theory and Practice of Education* 教育理论与实践 32, no. 19 (2012): 35–38.

Zhang, Ningsheng 张宁生, and Chen, Guanghua 陈光华. "Zailun ronghe jiaoyu puxiao jiaoshi yanzhong de 'suiban jiudu'" 再论融合教育：普小教师眼中的"随班就读." *Chinese Journal of Special Education* 中国特殊教育 no. 2 (2002): 1–6.

Zhang, Pingping 张平平, Li, Lingyan 李凌艳, and Xin, Tao 辛涛. "Xuexiao fenwei dui xuesheng shuxue chengji yingxiang de kuawenhua bijiao: jiyu duoshuiping fenxi de jieguo" 学校氛围对学生数学成绩影响的跨文化比较：基于多水平分析的结果. *Psychological Development and Education* 心理发展与教育 27, no. 6 (2011): 625–632.

Zhang, Xiaodong 张晓东. *Xiaoxue suiban jiudu jiaoshi gongzuo yali xianzhuang diaocha yanjiu* 小学随班就读教师工作压力现状调查研究. Huangshi: Hubei Normal University, 2019.

Zhang, Yuhong 张玉红, and Gao, Yuxiang 高宇翔. "Xinjiang putong xuexiao shisheng he jiazhang dui quanna jiaoyu jiena taidu de diaocha yanjiu" 新疆普通学校师生和家长对全纳教育接纳态度的调查研究. *Chinese Journal of Special Education* 中国特殊教育 no. 8 (2014): 14–20.

Zhao, Changmu 赵昌木, and Xu, Jicun 徐继存. "Jiaoshi chengzhang de huanjing yinsu kaocha—jiyu bufen zhongxiaoxue shidi diaocha he fangtan de sikao" 教师成长的环境因素考察——基于部分中小学实地调查和访谈的思考. *Journal of Educational Science of Hunan Normal University* 湖南师范大学教育科学学报 no. 3 (2005): 16–22.

Zhao, Fujiang 赵福江, and Liu, Jingcui 刘京翠. "Woguo zhongxiaoxue banzhuren gongzuo xianzhuang wenjuan diaocha yu fenxi" 我国中小学班主任工作现状问卷调查与分析. *Educational Science Research* 教育科学研究 no. 11 (2018): 38–43.

Zhao, Hong 赵红, and Xu, Li 徐莉. "Ronghe jiaoyu beijing xia youjiao gongzuozhe dui teshu ertong taidu de diaocha" 融合教育背景下幼教工作者对特殊儿童态度的调查. *Journal of Teacher Education* 教师教育学报 5, no. 1 (2018): 32–40.

Zheng, Yuanwen 郑媛文, and Ren, Lihua 任丽华. "Taoyuan xian guoxiao ziyuan ban jiaoshi gongzuo yali yu gongzuo manyidu xiangguan zhi yanjiu" 桃园县国小资源班教师工作压力与工作满意度相关之研究. *Bulletin of National Education Research* 国民教育研究集刊 no. 14 (2006): 205–233.

Zhou, Dan 周丹. *Suiban jiudu jiaoshi nengdong xing jiegou ji xiangguan yinsu de zuoyong jizhi yanjiu* 随班就读教师能动性结构及相关因素的作用机制研究. Beijing: Beijing Normal University, 2019.

Zhu, Nan 朱楠, and Wang, Yan 王雁. "'Fuhexing' teshu jiaoyu jiaoshi de peiyang—jiyu fuhexing de neihan fenxi" "复合型"特殊教育教师的培养——基于复合型的内涵分析. *Teacher Education Research* 教师教育研究 27, no. 6 (2015): 39–44.

5 International Experience in Cultivation of the Competence of Teachers in Inclusive Education

Teacher education covers pre-service cultivation, induction training, and in-service training, which form a sustainable lifelong education process. The pre-service cultivation of the competence of teachers in inclusive education is highly conducive for them to embrace the concept of inclusive education, develop a firm belief in the implementation of inclusive education, accept and support diversity, treat every student in inclusive classes fairly, make flexible use of teaching methods and textbooks, and improve the ability to meet diverse learning needs and respond to the resulting challenges.

In relevant policy documents issued in China, it has been advocated to cultivate teacher candidates to have certain competence in inclusive education, basically through special education courses. However, due to insufficient policy rigidity and poor implementation, the special education courses of normal and comprehensive universities are not satisfactory. Although the number of inclusive education and special education-related courses offered to normal university students has increased in recent years, these courses are elective, meaning that they have strong flexibility and greater freedom in the aspects of content and evaluation. These courses are organized by professional course teachers in colleges and universities according to their own understanding of special education, inclusive education, and the LRC program, without really considering the actual needs of ordinary teachers in inclusive settings and the status and role of the courses in the pre-service cultivation of teachers.[1] Moreover, the concept of inclusive education has not been embodied in the teacher cultivation system, and the concept, knowledge, and skills of inclusive education have not been included in the teacher cultivation curriculum.

In some Western countries that began to implement inclusive education earlier, teacher education institutions have continuously carried out reform and made explorations to cultivate teacher candidates to have certain competence in inclusive education, well responding to the challenges and demands brought by the admission of disabled children and the increasing differences in educatees. Therefore, it is necessary to tap into the international experience in cultivating the competence of teachers in inclusive education so as to provide some reference and inspiration for the cultivation of the competence of

DOI: 10.4324/9781003432982-6

192 *International Experience in Cultivation of the Competence*

Chinese teachers in inclusive education. This chapter revolves around the pre-service cultivation of the competence of teachers in inclusive education.

Cultivation Model of the Competence of Teachers in Inclusive Education

As an initial phase of professional development and lifelong learning, pre-service cultivation may be the key to improving the competence of teachers in inclusive education.[2] Firstly, pre-service cultivation can help shape their attitude toward inclusive education and form the belief in implementing inclusive education. If teachers are exposed to inclusive education at the beginning of their teacher education, and nourished in an inclusive environment, they will not only be able to accept diversity and regard the inclusive class as normal, but also provide quality teaching in the inclusive class and smoothly address various challenges in their respective classrooms and schools. Secondly, pre-service cultivation of the competence of teachers in inclusive education can improve their knowledge and ability to meet the diverse needs of students with different cultural backgrounds, which will have a certain impact on their subsequent education and teaching work. Thirdly, it is more efficient and impressive to cultivate the competence of teachers in inclusive education before their induction than to change their attitude and behavior after.[3] Moreover, being allowed to learn, experience, and practice inclusive teaching methods from the very first day of their professional development, all teachers are encouraged to continuously improve inclusive education. Therefore, pre-service cultivation of the competence of teachers in inclusive education is an important aspect to promote inclusive education.

Development Process of the Cultivation of the Competence of Teachers in Inclusive Education

Developed countries and regions including the US, the UK, Germany, New Zealand and Norway have taken the lead in making changes in the field of teacher education since the initiation of inclusive education, requiring the cultivation of the competence of teachers in inclusive education. Special education or inclusive education courses with a certain number of credit hours are included in the pre-service cultivation of teachers in the form of compulsory or elective courses.[4,5,6] In 2008, the South Korean Ministry of Education required 30 hours of inclusive education or special education-related courses be offered to pre-service teachers. In 2009, the "Introduction to Special Education" was introduced as a compulsory course for all teacher education programs and one of the requirements for teacher qualification.[7] In developing countries such as Mexico, the pre-service teacher education curriculum for pre-school and primary education majors was modified in 1997 and 1999 respectively, and a one-semester special education course was introduced to provide pre-service teachers with some basic knowledge of the philosophy of school inclusion, cultivate positive attitudes of pre-service teachers toward special needs

International Experience in Cultivation of the Competence 193

children, and improve their skills in identifying and supporting special needs children.[8] All colleges of education in West African countries such as Ghana offer pre-service teachers two-credit special or inclusive education courses in the second year.[9]

Next, let us take the US as an example to detail the development process of the cultivation of the competence of teachers in inclusive education.

Period of 'Independent Curriculum' (1970s–late 20th Century)

The *Education for All Handicapped Children Act* (EAHCA or *Public Law 94–142*) enacted by the US Congress in 1975 proposed to provide free and appropriate public education for special needs students in the least restrictive environment, and required development of individualized education plans for special needs students; but most teachers at that time did not have the corresponding competence in inclusive education. In response to this law, all the states in the country took various steps, including setting state professional standards for teachers, specifying the number of credit hours of special education course in teacher education programs, and providing common guidelines for state accreditation of universities or colleges to launch teacher education programs. Some states formulated and implemented rules for teacher cultivation as well as guidelines for teacher education programs based on their own development needs, while some states adopted professional standards for teachers formulated by various professional teacher education organizations, requiring teachers to have certain competence in inclusive education to adapt to the changes brought about by special needs students studying in regular schools. The National Association of State Directors of Teacher Education and Certification (NASDTEC) formulated *The Standards for State Approval of Teacher Education* in 1981, with the purpose of providing states with detailed rules for implementation of the procedures and standards related to the accreditation of teacher education programs. It required pre-service teachers to have the skills for diagnosing students' abilities, to design teaching plans for all students in the least restrictive environment, and to develop special education knowledge.[10] In the same year, the federal Dean's Grant Program was launched to support teacher education institutions to cooperate in cultivating ordinary teachers and special education teachers, achieving to a certain extent the integration of the two.[11] This period was dominated by the technical rational view of teacher education, and the "competence-based" teacher education model, that is, the ability that pre-service teachers should acquire and the standards that they should achieve were clearly defined, and they were guided to meet these requirements.[12]

However, in the early days, only some states required pre-service teachers to have the attitude, knowledge, and ability to teach students with special needs, and mandated teacher education institutions to offer special education courses so that pre-service teachers could understand the characteristics and needs of special needs children and adolescents.[13,14] For examples, the Maryland

194 *International Experience in Cultivation of the Competence*

required that, as of July 1, 1985, all applicants for teacher certification must take a three-credit special education course, teacher education programs must meet the interstate teacher education standards, and teachers should know the basic principles and legal basis of inclusive education for students with special needs, their characteristics, and the impact on the education plan, understand how to identify and evaluate students with special needs, have the ability to formulate and implement teaching strategies to meet the individual needs of students with special needs, and comprehend the functions and responsibilities of each participant in the communication process as well as the attitudes of other teachers and typically developing students toward special needs students and its influence. Alabama required pre-service teachers to take a three-credit special education course, and that teacher education programs should be subject to state certification requirements and interstate teacher education standards.[15]

With the comprehensive implementation of *Public Law 94–142* and inclusive education, "setting up independent courses" became the main way of cultivating the competence of teachers in inclusive education in the US from the 1970s to the end of the 20th century. It meant that one or two special courses in inclusive education or special education were added to the pre-service teacher cultivation program, so as to provide opportunities for pre-service teachers of general education majors to learn special education or inclusive education courses. After completing certain credits, pre-service teachers could apply for professional certification. It was an operable and convenient way to cultivate the competence of teachers in inclusive education. In this period, the orientation of "knowledge supplement" of inclusive education or special education courses was very obvious. The main content of the courses offered was the introduction of basic knowledge of special education and special needs children, and the proportion of purely knowledge content is much higher than that of skill content.[16,17] Although only one or two courses on inclusive education theory were offered, relevant studies showed that these courses still had a positive impact on pre-service teachers' attitudes toward inclusive education.[18]

Even though it was simple and operable to cultivate pre-service teachers' competence in inclusive education through "independent courses," this practice also faced great challenges: First, if only one or two inclusive education or special education courses were offered, it was hard to ensure that pre-service teachers could obtain certain competence in inclusive education to meet the educational needs of all students. A study found that some teachers felt unprepared to deal with an inclusive environment, felt unable to teach effectively in inclusive classrooms,[19] which may be due to the inadequacy in the number and types of special education or inclusive education courses offered by pre-service teacher education institutions.[20] Second, the content of the courses and its application were limited, which widened the gap with changing school and classroom practice. The courses focused on legislation, disability categories, and characteristics, and aimed to enrich pre-service teachers' understanding of special education, with little attention to the practical application of inclusive education knowledge and skills.[21,22] Some states required pre-service teachers to take a course that introduces special education and disability categories.[23] Would such courses increase pre-service teachers' stereotypes toward special needs students? Finally, the teacher education curriculum lacked an overall design, focusing more on incorporating special education content and experience into the curriculum of pre-service teachers, rather than redesigning the entire pre-service curriculum. Moreover, it did not take the diverse needs of students as the premise of teaching and teacher cultivation, so that pre-service teachers could not be fully prepared for inclusive education.

Period of 'Setting up Independent Courses' Coexisting with 'Program-level Inclusion' (21st Century–Today)

In the early 1990s, independent courses set up to supplement teachers' knowledge of inclusive education increasingly appeared in teacher cultivation programs. However, it was still difficult for teachers who had taken such courses in the pre-service phase to implement inclusive education.[24,25] This practical dilemma also prompted researchers to rethink the effect of setting up independent courses, what competencies for inclusive education that pre-service teachers should have, and how to cultivate pre-service teachers' competence in inclusive education. Based on reflection on the effects of the "knowledge supplement" type of inclusive education courses and the rethinking of the demand for inclusive education competence, teacher education institutions tried to shift the orientation of the courses from "knowledge supplement" to "skill improvement." The content was no longer confined to the discipline logic and knowledge system of special education itself, but turned to focus on skills as needed. Meanwhile, implementation of the courses paid more attention to the direct interaction between pre-service teachers and inclusive education practice, emphasizing that teachers should construct their own personalized knowledge via independent exploration, experience, and perception in the interaction with real teaching situations to finally realize the practice.[26,27] Guided by the view of teacher education that advocates reflective practice, the goal of pre-service teacher cultivation was to cultivate reflective professionals who can make sound judgments in their own classrooms, and conduct debugging-mode teaching according to different cultural backgrounds and students' learning needs at various academic levels.[28,29] Based on this, inclusive education courses gradually increased the practices of long-term participation in inclusive practice, a large number of team cooperation projects, action research and independent exploration in teaching practice, and the design and evaluation of inclusive education courses with the team as the unit to enhance pre-service teachers' understanding of the theory and practice of inclusive education.[30]

With the further development of the concept and practice of inclusive education, the individuality and differences of all children were respected and valued. At the same time, more and more children with special educational needs entered regular schools for education. If teachers wanted to be

196 *International Experience in Cultivation of the Competence*

truly competent for inclusive education practice, what they needed was more than simple superimposition of "general education knowledge" and "special education knowledge." Even when field work for special needs students was added into the courses, it was still difficult to really improve pre-service teachers' competence in inclusive education and prepare them for inclusive classrooms.[31,32] With the advent of the 21st century, the InTASC interpreted professional standards for teachers, promulgated the *No Child Left Behind Act* in 2001, and reauthorized the *Individuals with Disabilities Education Act* in 2004, focusing on the need for teachers to be equipped with competence in inclusive education to educate all students well. With the development of inclusive education and the reform of teacher education, the reform of cultivation of the competence of teachers in inclusive education directly pointed to the barriers between ordinary teacher cultivation and special education teacher cultivation. Teacher education institutions and teacher educators tried to merge the original programs and named it the "inclusive teacher cultivation program," embodying the integration of ordinary teacher cultivation and special education teacher cultivation.[33] The "inclusive teacher cultivation program" integrated inclusive education concepts, knowledge, and skills into all courses, rather than providing students with a separate inclusive education course. At the same time, it provided a large number of practice opportunities, such as teaching in special education schools and inclusive classes as interns, and held various seminars to promote students' practical teaching skills and reflective ability. After meeting graduation requirements, students could obtain both general education teacher and special education teacher qualifications to serve as an ordinary teacher or special education teacher in regular schools according to the actual needs of school work and personal wishes.[34] In this way, there were no longer "ordinary" and "special" teachers in regular schools, and a teacher could switch between the two roles. It directly reflects the fundamental requirement of teacher cultivation for inclusive education.[35]

The inclusive teacher cultivation program broke the model of separate cultivation of ordinary teachers and special education teachers, and formed a dual-credential teacher cultivation model of "general teacher certification + special education teacher certification." A typical example is the Elementary Inclusive Education Program launched by Teachers College, Columbia University. Students in this program will earn an M.A. degree and pursue New York State certification in both childhood education and teaching students with disabilities.[36] Compared to setting up independent courses, the program-level inclusion becomes a more ideal way to prepare pre-service teachers for inclusive education.[37] However, the program-level inclusion also faces a series of challenges, such as the need to invest more manpower, material resources and financial resources, the need for general education and special education majors to overcome difficulties for sincere cooperation, and the guidance of advanced ideas of teacher education institutions. And it is greatly influenced by the system and culture of teacher education institutions themselves.[38] Therefore, general courses for inclusive education are still prevalent in the cultivation of inclusive education teachers in the US.

By reviewing the development process of the cultivation of the competence of teachers in inclusive education in the US, we find that inclusive education brings an opportunity for teacher education reform, and the "inclusive teacher cultivation program" will become one of the important trends of teacher cultivation programs.

Cultivation Models of the Competence of Teachers in Inclusive Education

Ever more teacher education institutions have incorporated inclusive education knowledge and skills into teacher education programs in different ways to cultivate pre-service teachers' competence in inclusive education. After long-term exploration, these teacher education institutions have, based on the two approaches of "setting up independent courses" and "program-level inclusion," developed three models to cultivate pre-service teachers' competence in inclusive education: the discrete model, the integrated model, and the merged model.[39]

Discrete Model

The discrete model corresponds to "setting up independent courses" in the development process of the cultivation of the competence of teachers in inclusive education, that is, pre-service teachers of general education majors can obtain the initial teacher qualification of general education by taking one or two independent additional courses of inclusive education. In the cultivation programs of the discrete model, one or more inclusive education courses are embedded into the existing curriculum system, which lacks cross-course and practical cooperation. The teacher cultivation programs of special education and general education are basically independent of each other, and the cooperation between general education colleges and special education colleges and between their teacher educators is the least. In this case, pre-service teachers who apply for an initial license in special education must also complete all the additional courses and field practice in the special education teacher cultivation programs. This model is extremely popular in teacher cultivation programs for its simplicity and operability. Meanwhile, the current discrete model has also overcome the defect in the past of neglecting the practice of inclusive education, and some teacher cultivation programs add the practice content of inclusive education courses. For example, the University of Wisconsin-Madison has the "Elementary Education: Early Childhood/English as a Second Language" program, adopting the discrete model. It sets up an independent three-credit compulsory course of "Inclusive School Strategy," and increases the content of inclusive education in teaching practice to help pre-service teachers respond to children with special educational needs in regular classes.[40]

198 *International Experience in Cultivation of the Competence*

This part looks at a teacher cultivation program in Australia that adopts the discrete model to cultivate the competence of teachers in inclusive education, and gives a brief introduction to the independent inclusive education courses in the program as well as its impact on pre-service teachers.[41] This nine-week (18 hours) inclusive education course is aimed at pre-service teachers of primary or secondary education to help them understand that only by truly understanding special needs students, rather than just knowing their characteristics, can they successfully teach students. It also provides pre-service teachers with a range of inclusive education strategies to deal with special needs students in their classes. Its content includes understanding the structure of inclusive education, local policies, and regulations that support inclusive education, and the arguments for and against inclusive education, recognizing how educators' attitudes affect the teaching environment, and learning about four effective research-based teaching strategies in inclusive classrooms, namely cooperative learning, peer tutoring, differentiated teaching, and cooperative teaching. A presentation by a parent of a severely disabled student will also be given during the course to enable pre-service teachers to understand the perspectives of families of special needs children in inclusive education. This course is implemented through teaching, seminars, lectures, and other ways. Pre-service teachers are required to actively participate in class discussion, give class presentations, and read the texts of inclusive education.

Course evaluation is carried out in two ways. First, pre-service teachers give a class presentation with the theme of "how to use an effective inclusive teaching strategy in class." Second, an examination is carried out to determine their understanding of the key concepts covered by the course (25 percent of the scores), as well as analysis and application of the knowledge and skills learned through cases (75 percent of the scores). After completing the inclusive education courses, the inclusive education competence of pre-service teachers has been effectively improved. Firstly, the positive attitude of pre-service teachers toward inclusive education has been enhanced and, at the same time, they realize that correct implementation of inclusive education will not increase the workload or bring negative influence to classroom management. Secondly, pre-service teachers' concerns about the implementation of inclusive education are reduced, including concerns about whether other students in the class will accept the special needs students, and concerns about the impact of admitting special needs students on the academic achievement of other students in the class. Finally, pre-service teachers have improved their skills in inclusive education, including the use of inclusive teaching strategies and collaboration with other professionals.

Integrated Model

The integrated model corresponds to the "program-level inclusion" in the development process of the cultivation of the competence of teachers in inclusive education. It means teacher educators of both general education colleges and special education colleges cooperate to redesign some pre-service courses in a planned and systematic way, so as to realize to a certain extent the mutual complementarity of the general education and special education courses, and integrate and coordinate the course learning and practical experience to prepare all pre-service teachers to educate all students. In the cultivation programs of the integrated model, teacher educators in both general education colleges and special education colleges recognize each other's expertise and have a deep understanding of their respective roles and contributions in their respective program. Under this cultivation model, pre-service teachers can obtain one or two initial teacher qualifications. Usually, they will first obtain the initial teacher qualification for general education, and then choose whether to obtain the initial teacher qualification for special education.

This part gives a brief introduction to the inclusive-model teacher cultivation program of the University of North Carolina at Charlotte. As increasing numbers of special needs students enter regular classrooms, the traditional segregated cultivation of general education teachers and special education teachers leads both types of teachers to believe that they are ill-prepared for inclusive education. Therefore, the Department of Special Education and Child Development and the Department of Reading and Elementary Education under the University of North Carolina at Charlotte launched the "B.A. in Special Education–General Curriculum and Elementary Education K-6 Dual Program."[42] It is a four-year undergraduate program that allows student teachers to earn a bachelor's degree and dual qualifications for special education–general curriculum and elementary education prior to graduation, and graduates can teach in inclusive settings from preschool to grade 6.

Based on extensive collaboration between teacher educators of elementary education and special education majors, this program was developed according to the North Carolina Professional Teaching Standards and the 10 InTASC Standards for new teachers. With an annual enrollment of only 30 students, it selects pre-service teachers with a strong interest and passion for both special and elementary education and a desire to acquire knowledge and skills to effectively teach a diverse student body. Students in this program are required to complete at least 120 credit hours in four years. As a whole, all courses and required credits can be divided into the following categories: General Education Courses (31–35 credit hours), Foundation Courses (6–7 credits), Major Courses (78 credits), Licensure Courses (3 credits), and Unrestricted Elective Courses (credits required for graduation as needed). The foundation and major courses with a total of 84 credits cover both the general education and special education fields, and recognize that the general education courses and inclusive education courses complement each other.[43] The two foundation courses—"Foundations of Education and Diversity in Schools" and "Introduction to Students with Special Needs"—must be completed in the first year with a grade of C or better to be eligible for the program. The general education courses and "Introduction to Special Education and Dual Credential Program" should be completed in the third semester. The major courses include

200 *International Experience in Cultivation of the Competence*

many inclusive education courses such as "Assessment in Special Education," "Teaching Mathematics to Learners with Special Needs," "Teaching Reading to Elementary Learners with Special Needs," "Instructional Planning in Special Education," "Classroom Management," and so on. At the same time, in order to improve the practical ability of pre-service teachers, there are clear requirements for internship in each semester, which includes both experience in regular classroom and practice in resource rooms. The fourth academic year is a one-year internship, which provides long-term observation, interaction, and teaching opportunities for pre-service teachers.

During the four-year cultivation process, this program collects data in every semester through various methods such as practicum logs, feedback of the intern tutor to pre-service teacher, organizing class discussions, and program questionnaires to evaluate whether the pre-service teachers effectively apply the knowledge and skills of general and special education to teaching prac-tice. Informal discussions with pre-service teachers and focus groups are also arranged to provide personalized support.

Graduates of this program are prepared to consistently implement inclu-sive education, differentiated teaching, and cooperative teaching, use a var-iety of ways to guide students' learning, establish standards for students and provide assessment feedback, develop curriculum plans consistent with state and district plans, monitor and adjust curriculum plans, collaborate with other professionals, demonstrate leadership in professional situations, communicate and collaborate with families, and obtain the initial teacher qualification in general education and special education.

Merged Model

The merged model corresponds to the "program-level inclusion" in the develop-ment process of the cultivation of the competence of teachers in inclusive edu-cation. It means that on the basis of integrating multi-major resources, teacher educators in the fields of general education and special education cooperate closely to redesign and integrate all pre-service courses and practices based on a set of common values, and fully incorporate cultivation of competence in inclusive education into the whole curriculum system. The merged model requires consistent collaboration between various departments of general education and special education as well as a high degree of interdependence. Graduates from the program can earn initial teacher qualifications in both general education and special education to work as both ordinary and special education teachers. However, the initial teacher qualifications are limited to teach students with mild and moderate disabilities instead of those with severe and extremely severe disabilities.

This part gives a brief introduction to the program of the University of Edinburgh in Scotland, the Professional Graduate Diploma in Education Primary, which adopts the merged model. To remove barriers to participa-tion, meet the needs of different students, and promote educational equity,

Scotland has enacted several pieces of legislation, including the *Curriculum for Excellence* (2004), the *Additional Support for Learning Act* (2004), and *Getting it Right for Every Child* (2006), replacing special educational needs with "additional support needs," showing a richer connotation of inclusion for students who need support for any reason. At the same time, teacher education in Scotland has undergone many reforms. In order to guarantee the quality of teacher education programs, Scotland has promulgated *The Standards for Registration: Mandatory Requirements for Registration with the General Teaching Council for Scotland* (2012),[44] the *Guidelines for ITE Programmes in Scotland* (2013)[45] and other documents to give guidance and impose requirements for the professional standards for teachers, pre-service cultivation programs, and preparation of their courses.

The 36-week Professional Graduate Diploma in Education Primary program is designed to produce successful, reflective teachers, sensitive to the demands of pupils, responsive to changes within the education system, and committed to their own continuing professional development.[46] Students of this program must take and pass six compulsory courses, spending 18 weeks on professional placement in schools and around 18 weeks learning on campus. Each of the courses covers elements of early years, middle primary years, and upper primary years.

With a focus on cultivation of the competence of student teachers for inclusive education, this program deepens the students' understanding of the extra needs and diversity of children in the practice of inclusive education.[47] It is mainly implemented by teacher educators of the University of Edinburgh and tutors of the internship institutions, with different courses for teaching preparation and teaching practice. Teaching preparation takes the form of lectures, workshops, online learning, mentoring or independent learning, enabling student teachers to learn in depth and discuss how to meet the needs of all students. Moreover, a variety of evaluation methods are used to evaluate the quality of the pre-service cultivation of the competence of teachers in inclusive education. The teaching preparation courses use written assessment, reports, student files, and papers/research projects to assess pre-service teachers' learning results while the practicum adopts practice-based assessment, oral reports, and presentations to evaluate the results of the pre-service teachers' practice.

The success of this program depends on its design, in which objectives, courses, and assessment are interconnected. In order to meet the cultivation objectives and the assessment of the General Teaching Council for Scotland, this program adopts the merged model to make pre-service teachers competent to meet the needs of all pupils, and continually improves itself by adjusting the cultivation objectives and courses, forming a circulating, efficient cultivation model. However, since it is hard to ensure that every teacher masters and values the knowledge of inclusive education, cultivation quality may be unsatisfactory.

At present, the discrete model, the integrated model, and the merged model are all adopted to cultivate the pre-service teachers' competence in inclusive

202 *International Experience in Cultivation of the Competence*

education. The discrete model is simple and operable while the latter two outperform it with close cooperation between teacher education institutions and other institutions such as regular schools, effective integration of high-quality teacher cultivation programs, sufficient inclusive education courses, and numerous inclusive education practices.

Research into Implementation of Teachers' Inclusive Education Competence Cultivation Programs

How to cultivate the competence of teachers in inclusive education to prepare them for all children in the classroom? Teacher education institutions and teacher educators have explored this topic for decades, summarizing diversified cultivation models. It has also been proven that inclusive education courses have a significant positive impact on pre-service teachers' attitudes toward inclusive education and their confidence and efficacy in implementing inclusive teaching.[48,49,50] However, no consensus has yet been reached on how to make the inclusive education curriculum and the cultivation of the competence of teachers in inclusive education more effective.[51]

Therefore, this part mainly adopts a literature research method and uses key words such as "pre-service (teacher)," "initial teacher," "student teacher," "teacher preparation," "teacher education," and "inclusion" or "inclusive" to search 2010–2019 empirical studies on the cultivation of the competence of teachers in inclusive education in the ProQuest database, to explore the current implementation status of international teachers' inclusive education cultivation programs. The selection criteria were as follows: (1) the subjects were pre-service teachers (preschool education, primary education, and secondary education majors), excluding pre-service teachers of special education majors, professional assistants, and in-service teachers; (2) the research content covers specific implementation of inclusive education courses; (3) there is evaluation of cultivation programs, that is, there are scales or questionnaires to assess the attitude, knowledge or ability of pre-service teachers. As a result, a total of 16 studies were obtained.

According to a statistical analysis of the 16 studies, 14 focused on the discrete model, namely setting up one or two independent courses in inclusive education or special education, and only two talked about long-term cultivation programs—a dual-credential inclusive teacher cultivation program that adopts the integrated model (four years) and the "Scottish Teachers for a New Era" program that adopts the merged model (four years). It can be seen that the discrete model is the most popular choice worldwide for the cultivation of teachers' inclusive education competence. Since most studies focused on one or two independent courses, and some covered two groups of participants, it is difficult to analyze the implementation process and effect of the cultivation of competence in inclusive education from the perspective of the teacher cultivation program. Therefore, this part reviews, from the perspective of course implementation, the current situation of the implementation of foreign

International Experience in Cultivation of the Competence 203

teachers' inclusive education competence cultivation programs, with a focus on analyzing how to implement inclusive education courses and exploring the cultivation effect. The nature, duration, content, teaching methods, and evaluation of the inclusive education courses are listed to provide reference for the cultivation of the competence of teachers in inclusive education in China.

Implementation Status of Teachers' Inclusive Education Competence Cultivation Programs

As shown in Table 5.1, a total of 2,168 pre-service teachers participated in the 20 courses mentioned in the 16 studies. The number of participants in each course ranged from 20 to 777. Most of the participants are pre-service teachers majoring in primary, secondary, and preschool education, and most of them are undergraduate.

Name and Duration of Inclusive Education Courses

By duration, the 20 courses are divided into three types: short course (one), semester course (17), and long-term program (two).[52] The short course, namely the "Inclusive Physical Education Training Workshop," lasts about six hours,[53] while the duration of the long-term programs is four years. The duration of semester courses generally ranges from 13 to 62 hours, with an average (excluding practice hours) of 33.2 hours. With regard to course name or theme, the short course is to provide inclusive physical education in the form of workshop; most of the semester courses are named or themed by inclusive education (five), introduction to special education (three), and special and inclusive education (three); and other courses are themed by physical education course adjustment (two), inclusive teaching strategies (one), special education and teaching (one), challenging behavior course focusing on behavioral problems (one), and study of diversity (one). With regard to the two long-term programs, the dual-credential inclusive teacher cultivation program focuses on the diversity of schools so that pre-service teachers can teach ordinary and special needs children in today's multicultural schools and classrooms. Its curriculum includes not only special education courses, but also probation and internship in inclusive environments and special schools. The "Scottish Teachers for a New Era" program focuses on inclusive education and social justice, emphasizing the need for the curriculum to prepare teachers who will promote equal opportunities for all children and provide learning opportunities for students with emotional and behavioral disabilities.

With respect to the semester courses, some researchers also pointed out that it was not enough for an introduction to inclusive education or special education to provide a general overview of disability and law, and several compulsory courses should also be offered to pre-service teachers to provide them with teaching strategies and opportunities to apply them in the classroom.[54] In general, both semester courses and long-term programs have a positive impact

Table 5.1 Basic Information of International Teachers' Inclusive Education Competence Cultivation Programs (2010–2019)

Serial number	Literature information	Participants	Course name, nature and duration	Course content	Course evaluation	Course evaluation results
1	Lancaster, J., and Bain, A. "The Design of Pre-service Inclusive Education Courses and Their Effects on Self-efficacy: A Comparative Study."	36 Australian pre-service primary school teachers.	Group A: Inclusive Education, compulsory course, 39 hours (13 weeks).	Theory: Communication, reading and math difficulties, social and emotional difficulties, assistive technologies, and inclusive teaching methods.	Coursework and exam.	The pre-service teachers' self-efficacy of future interaction with disabled people has been significantly improved.
			Group B: Inclusive Education, compulsory course, 39 hours.	Theory: The same as above. Practice: Participate in two community-based after-school programs for 11 hours.	Coursework, practice assignments, and exam.	The pre-service teachers' self-efficacy of future interaction with disabled people has been significantly improved.
2	Sosu, E. M., Mtika, P., and Colucci-Gray, L. "Does Initial Teacher Education Make a Difference? The Impact of Teacher Preparation on Student Teachers' Attitudes toward Educational Inclusion."	196 Scottish pre-service primary school teachers.	"Scottish Teachers for a New Era" program, four years.	First and second years Theory: Learning theory and teaching methods; Practice: 21 consecutive days of probation in a school. Third and fourth years Theory: Professional knowledge, skills and values of pre-service teachers, curriculum	Practice assignments.	The pre-service teachers have developed a positive attitude toward educational justice, their attitude toward inclusive education has been improved

				and teaching knowledge, inclusive teaching methods, legislation on children's rights, ethics of care, and knowledge of autism and dyslexia; Practice: Internship (10 weeks in the third year, 14 weeks in the fourth year).		significantly, and they have a high expectation for the study of all children. Their concept of inclusion focuses on creating a sense of belonging, fairness, and sensitivity, and providing a supportive environment for all children to be participants in the classroom.
3	Forlin, C., and Chambers, D. "Teacher Preparation for Inclusive Education: Increasing Knowledge but Raising Concerns."	67 Australian pre-service preschool and primary school teachers.	Study of Diversity, elective, 39 hours (13 weeks).	Theory: Inclusive education policy, and topics on disability, gender, and culture. Practice: 10 hours' contact with one or more persons with disabilities, or find and comment on a local community plan on inclusive education.	Practice assignments.	The pre-service teachers' attitude toward inclusive education has becomes more positive, their concern about the implementation of inclusive education has slightly increased, their confidence in

(*Continued*)

Table 5.1 (Continued)

Serial number	Literature information	Participants	Course name, nature and duration	Course content	Course evaluation	Course evaluation results
						teaching disabled children has been significantly enhanced, and their awareness of special education legislation has been significantly improved.
4	Gao, W., and Mager, G. "Enhancing Pre-service Teachers' Sense of Efficacy and Attitudes toward School Diversity through Preparation: A Case of One US Inclusive Teacher Program."	168 American dual-credential pre-service primary school and preschool teachers.	Dual Credential Inclusive Teacher Cultivation Program, four years.	Theory: Introduction to Education. Practice: 20 hours' probation in an inclusive environment. Theory: Introduction to Special Education. Practice: 20 hours' probation in a regular classroom.	Coursework, practice assignments, and portfolio assessment.	The pre-service teachers' sense of personal teaching and general teaching efficacy has been significantly improved, their positive attitude toward inclusive education has been remarkably enhanced, and their professional belief in diversity has been notably strengthened.

| 5 | Male, D. B. "The Impact of a Professional Development Programme on Teachers' Attitudes toward Inclusion." | 48 UK postgraduate pre-service teachers. | Concepts and Contexts of Special and Inclusive Education, 62 hours (10 weeks). | Theory: Understanding the problems and dilemmas in special and inclusive education. | Not provided. | The pre-service teachers' positive attitude toward inclusive education has been significantly improved. |
| 6 | Sharma, U. "Changing Pre-service Teachers' Beliefs to Teach in Inclusive Classrooms in Victoria, Australia." | 27 Australian pre-service primary school teachers and secondary school teachers. | Special and Inclusive Education, elective, 20 hours, 10 weeks. | Theory: International and local policies on inclusive education, arguments for and against inclusive education, inclusive teaching strategies, and case studies of teachers with high inclusive education competence. Practice: Visit an inclusive school. | Classroom work, and exam. | The pre-service teachers' positive attitude toward inclusive education has been significantly enhanced, their emotion toward special needs students has been notably improved, and their concern about the implementation of inclusive education has been greatly reduced. |

(*Continued*)

Table 5.1 (Continued)

Serial number	Literature information	Participants	Course name, nature and duration	Course content	Course evaluation	Course evaluation results
7	Swain, K. D., Nordness, P. D., and Leader-Janssen, E. "Changes in Pre-service Teacher Attitudes toward Inclusion."	777 American pre-service primary and secondary school teachers and teachers of lalopathology.	Introduction to Special Education, one semester.	Theory: Special education law and litigation, disability categories supported by the *Individuals with Disabilities Education Act*, curriculum adjustments, and behavior management. Practice: 20 hours of live experience, observing and teaching in special and inclusive environments.	Practice assignments.	The pre-service teachers' positive attitude toward inclusive education has been significantly enhanced.
8	Zundans-Fraser, L., and Lancaster, J. "Enhancing the Inclusive Self-efficacy of Pre-service Teachers through Embedded Course Design."	38 Australian pre-service preschool teachers and primary school teachers.	Embedded inclusive education course, 14 weeks.	Theory: Inclusive education legislation and policy, inclusive practice, family-centred practice, individualized curriculum, early intervention, social interaction, communication, and transition service.	Coursework, and exam (weekly).	The pre-service teachers' self-efficacy of future interaction with disabled people has been significantly improved.

9	Killoran, I., Woronko, D., and Zaretsky, H. "Exploring Pre-service Teachers' Attitudes toward Inclusion."	81 Canadian pre-service primary and secondary school teachers.	Inclusive Education, elective, 36 hours (eight days or 12 weeks).	Theory: Social prejudices and stereotypes about the disabled, social construction of disability, and the concept of inclusive education as a human right.	Not provided.	The pre-service teachers' positive attitude toward inclusive education has been significantly enhanced.
10	Pedersen, S. J., Cooley, P. D., and Hernandez, K. "Are Australian Pre-service Physical Education Teachers Prepared to Teach Inclusive Physical Education?"	31 pre-service teachers of physical education at the University of Tasmania.	Physical Education Adjustment Course, elective, 13 hours.	Theory: Lectures on sports, pedagogical knowledge, and experiential activities for the disabled (13 hours). Practice: five hours of practice in a special school.	Coursework, practice assignments, and exam.	The pre-service teachers' positive attitude toward teaching of disabled students with attention deficit hyperactivity disorder and autism has been improved.
		25 pre-service physical education teachers at the Bendigo Campus, La Trobe University.	Physical Education Adjustment Course, elective, 13 hours.	Theory: Labelling theory, development of the individualized program, program support group strategy, and medical and safety considerations (13 hours). Practice: 40 hours of probation in physical education class in segregated and inclusive schools.	Coursework.	The pre-service teachers' positive attitude toward teaching of disabled students with attention deficit hyperactivity disorder and autism has been significantly improved.

(Continued)

Table 5.1 (Continued)

Serial number	Literature information	Participants	Course name, nature and duration	Course content	Course evaluation	Course evaluation results
11	Peebles, J. L., and Mendaglio, S. "The Impact of Direct Experience on Pre-service Teachers' Self-efficacy for Teaching in Inclusive Classrooms."	141 Canadian pre-service primary and secondary school teachers.	Inclusive Education, compulsory course, 39 hours (10 weeks).	Theory: Students' diversified educational needs, educational significance, and teaching strategies. Practice: three-week internship, organizing individualized and group teaching and making plans.	Coursework, and practice assignments.	The pre-service teachers' self-efficacy of inclusive teaching has been significantly improved.
12	Sharma, U., and Sokal, L. "The Impact of a Teacher Education Course on Pre-service Teachers' Beliefs about Inclusion:AnInternational Comparison."	25 Australian pre-service primary and secondary school teachers.	Special and Inclusive Education, 18 hours (nine weeks).	Theory: International policy on inclusive education, arguments for and against inclusive education, teaching strategies, and case studies of teachers with high inclusive education competence. Practice: Visit an inclusive primary school.	Classroom work and exam.	The pre-service teachers' positive attitude toward inclusive education has been significantly improved, their concern about the implementation of inclusive education has been remarkably reduced, and their self-efficacy of inclusive teaching has been greatly improved.

		60 Canadian pre-service teachers.	Introduction to Special Education, compulsory course, 30 hours (15 weeks).	Theory: Knowledge of special education. Practice: Field visits to the living and learning places of disabled children, interview with resource teachers, and putting forward suggestions on learning plans for disabled children.	Exam.	The pre-service teachers' positive attitude toward inclusive education has been significantly weakened, their concern about the implementation of inclusive education has been remarkably reduced, and their self-efficacy of inclusive teaching has been greatly improved.
13	O'Neill, S. C. "Preparing Pre-service Teachers for Inclusive Classrooms: Does CompletingCoursework on Managing Challenging Behaviours Increase Their Classroom Management Sense of Efficacy?"	20 Australian pre-service primary school teachers.	Challenging Behavior, elective, 20 hours (10 weeks).	Theory: Functional behavior analysis and behavior support plan for the first seven weeks; strategies for managing excessive behaviors, Colvin's cycle of escalation, the main characteristics of the students with autism and oppositional defiant disorder, and intervention strategies. Practice: three-week professional experience probation.	Practice assignments.	The pre-service teachers' efficacy of classroom management has been significantly improved.

(*Continued*)

Table 5.1 (Continued)

Serial number	Literature information	Participants	Course name, nature and duration	Course content	Course evaluation	Course evaluation results
14	Sharma, U., and Nuttal, A. "The Impact of Training on Pre-service Teacher Attitudes, Concerns, and Efficacy toward Inclusion."	30 Australian pre-service primary and secondary school teachers.	Inclusive Education Teaching Strategy, elective, 18 hours (nine weeks).	Theory: The structure of inclusive education, local policies and regulations, opinions for and against inclusive education, and four effective inclusive teaching strategies.	Classroom work and exam.	The pre-service teachers' positive attitude toward inclusive education has been significantly enhanced, their concern about the implementation of inclusive education has been remarkably reduced, and their self-efficacy of inclusive teaching has been greatly improved.
15	Rakap, S., Cig, O., and Parlak-Rakap, A. "Preparing Preschool Teacher Candidates for Inclusion: Impact of Two Special Education Courses on Their Perspectives."	29 American pre-service preschool teachers.	Introduction to Special Education, compulsory course, 56 hours (14 weeks).	Theory: A general overview of disability and related laws, special education purposes, planning and provision of special education services.	Coursework.	The pre-service teachers' positive attitude toward inclusive education has been improved to some extent, and their discomfort

No.	Reference	Sample			Results
			Special Education Curriculum and Instruction, compulsory course, 56 hours (14 weeks).	Theory: Inclusive teaching strategies, behavioral intervention plans, curriculum design and teaching. Practice: 14-week probation in a kindergarten.	Practice assignments and thesis. ... in interaction with disabled children decreased. The pre-service teachers' positive attitude toward inclusive education has been improved to some extent, and they feel much more comfortable in interaction with disabled children.
16	Neville, R. D., Makopoulou, K., and Hopkins, W. G. "Effect of an Inclusive Physical Education (IPE) Training Workshop on Trainee Teachers' Self-Efficacy."	366 pre-service primary and secondary school physical education teachers in England.	Inclusive Physical Education Training Workshop, about 6 hours.	Design of inclusive learning environments through four different types of activities: open activities; adjustment activities; parallel activities; and independent activities.	Design teaching activities and share the results. The pre-service teachers' self-efficacy of inclusive teaching has been significantly improved.

214 *International Experience in Cultivation of the Competence*

on pre-service teachers' attitudes toward inclusive education and their knowledge and skills in this regard. This is consistent with most previous research findings.[55,56] However, this is not always the case. Some researchers found a downward trend in the attitudes of secondary pre-service teachers who, thus, gradually develop more negative attitudes during the four years of undergraduate study.[57] This means that although the inclusive education curriculum can generate positive attitudes among pre-service teachers, such changes may be difficult to develop and sustain in the long run. In future researchers should give consideration to the following aspects. On the one hand, they should continue to study the impact of the discrete model on the inclusive education competence of pre-service teachers. A longitudinal study of the integrated model and merged model should be carried out to explore the development and change in pre-service teachers' attitude, knowledge, skills, and efficacy during the program, and to find out the key factors for the change in their attitude. On the other hand, the method of horizontal comparison can also be used to explore the influence of different inclusive education courses and inclusive teacher cultivation programs on the inclusive education competence of pre-service teachers.

Content and Evaluation of Inclusive Education Curriculum

In the semester courses, most of the courses related to inclusive education are selective courses (seven) and compulsory courses (six), while the nature of the other four courses has not been reported. The curriculum is generally divided into two parts: theoretical and practical. The practical courses are usually attached to the theoretical courses, or embedded in the integrated or merged model of the teacher cultivation program as a separate practice. This part will analyze and summarize the teaching contents of the 17 courses from the theoretical and practical aspects. The content of the inclusive education theoretical courses is mainly set based on the logic of "what" and "how," that is declarative knowledge and procedural knowledge.[58,59] Declarative knowledge covers categories and characteristics of students with special needs (10 courses), connotation and development of inclusive education and special education (eight courses), and laws, regulations, and policies of inclusive education and special education (seven courses). Procedural knowledge involves teaching strategies associated with successful inclusion, including cooperative learning (six courses), peer assistance (five courses), course evaluation (four courses), course design and adjustment (three courses), differentiated teaching (four courses), behavior management (four courses), individualized education plan and curriculum (three courses), working with families and professionals (two courses), cognitive strategies (two courses), collaborative teaching (one course), general learning design (one course), and so on. For example, the nine-week elective course of inclusive education teaching strategy in the study by Sharma and Nuttal includes not only declarative knowledge, such as the structure of

International Experience in Cultivation of the Competence   215

inclusive education, local policies, and regulations regarding inclusive education, but also procedural knowledge such as cooperative learning, peer assistance, differentiated teaching, and collaborative teaching strategies.[60] It can be seen that teacher education institutions have incorporated inclusive education courses into their cultivation plans as selective or compulsory courses, and taken inclusive education in a broad sense as the core content of the curriculum, emphasizing the provision of educational support for all students. Although some teacher education institutions still regard special education, special and inclusive education as the course name, their course content focuses on the knowledge and skills more adapted to inclusive settings. For example, the "Introduction to Special Education" course in the study of Swain and his partners covers special education law and litigation, the disability category, course adjustment strategies, and behavior management strategies, and requires pre-service teachers to observe and teach for 20 hours in special and inclusive environments.[61] At present, there is no consensus on what theoretical knowledge should be included in teacher competence cultivation programs. The curriculum content involved in the studies is consistent with previous studies.[62,63] In future, it is still necessary to continue to explore whether compulsory and selective inclusive education courses have significantly different effects in the cultivation of teachers' inclusive education competence, so as to further determine the status and role of inclusive education courses. Research into the content of the inclusive education courses should also be furthered to explore what knowledge and skills will influence teachers to carry out inclusive education so as to support pre-service teachers in getting prepared to teach all children.

Only 11 semester courses and two long-term programs for inclusive education contain additional or separate practical courses for pre-service teachers, mainly including probation (5–40 hours in 3–14 weeks) and internship in inclusive kindergartens, primary schools or special schools (10 courses). The practicum includes visiting schools, learning about and researching all children and inclusive education, observing, developing, and implementing teaching plans for children with disabilities in inclusive schools, special schools, or communities, directly communicating with disabled children, and assessing inclusive education community programs. For example, the 10-week elective course of challenging behavior has professional probation in the last three weeks. During the probation, pre-service teachers need to apply the knowledge of behavior management they have learned in the early stage to the intervention in problematic behaviors of students in the inclusive education environment.[64] Long-term programs that offer individual internship require longer practice of teaching in inclusive or special schools, and communicating and cooperating with other professionals. Take the "Scottish Teachers for a New Era" program as an example. In the first two years of cultivation, pre-service teachers are required to undergo probation for 21 consecutive days in schools to study different factors affecting children's growth and learning. In the third and fourth years, they will practice in an inclusive environment for 10 weeks and

216 *International Experience in Cultivation of the Competence*

14 weeks respectively, required to collaborate with professionals to support all students.[65] Overall, the majority of semester courses and long-term programs offer practical courses, and only seven courses have no field work. Compared with the theoretical courses, the practical courses of semester courses are generally shorter, some of the hands-on content is limited to school visit.[66] As Loreman pointed out, practical experience is an indispensable part of the cultivation of the pre-service teachers' competence in inclusive education. An inclusive environment has enough resources to give pre-service teachers an opportunity to challenge existing attitudes, and provide support for them to examine and reflect on existing attitudes.[67] In contrast to separate inclusive education theoretical courses, the courses that incorporate inclusive environmental practices will have better results.[68,69] At the same time, the duration of internship may also lead to differences in pre-service teachers' attitudes,[70] and those with an internship of more than 30 days have higher teaching efficacy in inclusive classrooms.[71] Although many studies support the positive effects of practice on pre-service teachers, the study by Lancaster and Bain found no significant difference in the effects of the two types of curriculum design conditions—mere course learning and a combination of course learning and hands-on experience—on pre-service teachers; that is, participation in field practice has no significant effect on pre-service teachers' beliefs.[72] Future research needs to continue to investigate and explore the relationship between theoretical courses and practical experience, what length of practical experience will cause significant changes in the attitude of pre-service teachers, and how to design and implement practical courses in the inclusive education curriculum for pre-service teachers, so as to achieve an optimal inclusive education curriculum.

From the perspective of current short-term and semester courses or long-term programs in the field of inclusive education, the course evaluation mostly adopts the combination of formative evaluation and summative evaluation, which usually includes coursework, internship assignments, and examination, and takes probation and internship as important elements of course evaluation. Coursework includes class presentations, reading relevant literature, participating in class discussions, and so on. For example, in his study, Umesh Sharma[73] asked three pre-service teachers to work together in a group to present a class presentation on the topic of breaking down barriers to the implementation of inclusive education in the classroom. Participants were required to use a sociological model of disability and a reflective practice model to identify and address barriers to the implementation of inclusive education. For long-term program evaluation, in addition to course evaluation, the dual-credential inclusive teacher cultivation program also adopts portfolio evaluation based on four criteria: planning and teaching with clear goals, planning and delivering instruction to involve all students meaningfully, effectively using technical strategies in the planning and implementation of the curriculum, and maintaining a respectful, cooperative, challenging, and culturally responsive learning environment.[74]

Implementation Effect of Teachers' Inclusive Education Competence Cultivation Programs

Teachers' inclusive education competence cultivation programs not only find out the pre-service teachers' mastery of the curriculum through course evaluation, but also take their attitude, sense of efficacy, knowledge, and concerns about inclusive education as the evaluation indices, so as to test the effectiveness of the curriculum or program. The 20 courses were evaluated mainly from the aspects of attitudes toward inclusive education, teachers' sense of efficacy, concerns about implementation of inclusive education, and mastery of inclusive education knowledge and strategies. Most of the studies confirmed the positive influence of inclusive education courses or inclusive education competence cultivation programs on pre-service teachers. In 14 courses, the attitude of pre-service teachers toward inclusive education was measured and, on the whole, their attitude became more positive. Among them, reports of 11 courses reveal a significantly enhanced positive attitude of pre-service teachers toward inclusive education, while reports of the other three courses show certain positive influence but not at a statistically significant level, and the report of one course reveals a significant decline in the positive attitude of pre-service teachers toward inclusive education. In 12 courses/programs, pre-service teachers' efficacy was measured, including the efficacy of inclusive teaching (six courses), the efficacy of future interactions with disabled persons (five courses), and the efficacy of classroom management (one course), all showing significant improvements. For example, through a 14-week inclusive education course, researchers found that the efficacy of future interactions between pre-service teachers and persons with disabilities was significantly improved after the course learning.[75] In five courses, the pre-service teachers' concerns about the implementation of inclusive education were measured, including concerns about the lack of resources, the decline of academic performance, and the increase of workload, and the results showed that their concerns decreased after they had undertaken inclusive education courses. Reports of four courses revealed a significant decline in pre-service teachers' concerns, and that of one course showed that the pre-service teachers' mastery of special education-related legal knowledge was significantly improved.

In general, most of the studies confirmed the positive influence of the short-term courses, semester courses, and long-term programs of inclusive education competence cultivation through pre- and post-test, that is, the neutral or negative attitude of pre-service teachers toward inclusive education changed into a more positive attitude after undertaking the inclusive education courses, their sense of teaching efficacy was greatly improved, their mastery of inclusive education knowledge and strategies was significantly increased, and their concerns about implementation of inclusive education dropped dramatically. The results are consistent with the findings of previous studies.[76,77] Only one study found that, in contrast to the positive attitude of Australian pre-service teachers toward inclusive education, the attitude of Canadian pre-service teachers toward inclusive education weakened significantly. This may be due to the diversified curriculum implementation in Canada, the differences in instructors or the negative experience of pre-service teachers in getting along with the disabled.[78] It should be noted that while most of the pre-service teachers in the studies expressed positive attitudes, we need to consider the effect of social expectations, that is, pre-service teachers may be inclined to give socially acceptable statements.[79] Holding a positive attitude toward inclusion is a satisfactory response, but attitude does not necessarily indicate behavior. Some study has shown that although pre-service teachers have a more positive attitude toward the inclusion of children with disabilities after undertaking the courses, when asked whether they believe that most children with disabilities can be included in regular classrooms, 30.4 percent of pre-service teachers said they disagreed or were unsure.[80] As for future research, it is advisable to consider investigating the types of positive and negative experiences that pre-service teachers have when they come into contact with disabled children during their internship to determine how they affect pre-service teachers' attitudes toward and confidence in implementing inclusive education. Qualitative research methods should also be considered to find out the real attitudes of pre-service teachers and the factors for their attitude changes by observing and interviewing them.

In addition, there may be a close relationship between the four evaluation indicators—attitude toward inclusive education, teacher's sense of efficacy, inclusive education-related knowledge level, and concerns about implementation of inclusive education. Some researchers found that a teacher's sense of efficacy and inclusive education-related knowledge level are positively correlated with his or her attitude toward inclusive education, and negatively correlated with his or her concerns about the implementation of inclusive education. That is, the higher the teacher's sense of efficacy and knowledge level are, the more positive the attitude of pre-service teachers will be, and there will be fewer concerns about the implementation of inclusive education.[81,82,83] However, it should be noted that merely improving the knowledge level and sense of efficacy of pre-service teachers is not enough to improve their attitudes toward inclusive education and dispel their concerns. Some study has shown that pre-service teachers were worried about their ability to teach in an inclusive classroom at the beginning of the course, while the majority of them felt ready for inclusive education at the end of the course, but they still worried about whether they would gain due support to teach all children.[84] Therefore, it is necessary to provide teachers with continuous and appropriate inclusive education training and corresponding resource guarantee. Future research should use a large number of samples from different teacher education institutions to further investigate the influence of inclusive education courses on pre-service teachers' attitude toward inclusive education, their sense of efficacy, inclusive education-related knowledge level, and concerns about implementation of inclusive education, so as to provide a basis for the design and evaluation of the cultivation of pre-service teachers' inclusive education competence.

International Experience in Cultivation of the Competence   219

Moreover, it is necessary to further explore the effective implementation of the inclusive education curriculum and inclusive education competence cultivation models. As the European Agency for Development in Special Needs and Inclusive Education pointed out, it is important to further explore the evidence for the effectiveness of teachers' inclusive education competence cultivation, evaluate the effectiveness of different cultivation models and curricula, course content, and teaching methods, so as to fulfil the cultivation of qualified teachers to meet the diverse needs of all children.[85]

Characteristics of and Prospects for the Cultivation of the Competence of Teachers in Inclusive Education

Nowadays, the cultivation of the competence of teachers in inclusive education shows a trend of diversification, and effective cultivation of the pre-service teachers' competence in inclusive education has become an international challenge. Ever more researchers and teacher educators are exploring the factors for success in the cultivation. Through analyzing the current international teachers' inclusive education competence cultivation programs, we have found that these programs have many common characteristics in terms of cultivation basis, model, objectives, process, and evaluation. This part aims at summarizing these characteristics, experience and challenges, and then putting forward some suggestions for the cultivation of the competence of Chinese teachers in inclusive education.

Characteristics of the Cultivation of the Competence of Teachers in Inclusive Education

Basis for the Cultivation of the Competence of Teachers in Inclusive Education: Professional Standards for Teachers

Professional standards for teachers that stipulate the basic professional requirements for qualified teachers are the basic guidelines for the professional development of teachers, and also an important basis for teacher cultivation, qualification, training, and evaluation. In the US, Canada, Australia and other countries and regions, teachers' professional standards have been formulated and revised, clearly reflecting the role and status of teachers in inclusive education as well as requirements for their competence. These standards provide norms and directions for teacher education institutions to cultivate pre-service teachers.[86,87,88]

The *InTASC Model Core Teaching Standards: A Resource for State Dialogue*[89] released in 2011 expounds in detail the responsibilities of teachers in inclusive education. The eight standards of learner development, learning differences, learning environments, assessment, planning for instruction, instructional strategies, professional learning and ethical practice, and leadership and collaboration in three general categories of the learner and learning, instructional practice, and professional responsibility are permeated with the concept and practical requirements of inclusive education. Some teacher education institutions, such as the University of North Carolina at Charlotte and the University of Northern Colorado, cultivate pre-service teachers according to these standards.

In addition, the US teacher education institution accreditation standards and pre-service teacher cultivation standards also cover competence in inclusive education. The standards published by the Council for the Accreditation of Educator Preparation (CAEP) in 2013 were designed to cultivate high-quality teachers. Teacher education institutions are required to cultivate qualified teachers from the aspects of pre-service teacher selection, curriculum setting, result evaluation, and quality assurance and improvement. Competence in inclusive education, as one of the objectives of pre-service teacher cultivation, is also involved. For example, in Standard 1 "Content and Pedagogical Knowledge," it is emphasized that teacher education institutions should ensure pre-service teachers develop a deep understanding of the critical concepts and principles of their discipline and, by completion, are able to use discipline-specific practices flexibly to advance the learning of all students, and demonstrate an understanding of the 10 InTASC standards at the appropriate progression level(s) in the following categories: the learner and learning, content, instructional practice, and professional responsibility.[90] In 2018, CAEP worked out the *K–6 Elementary Teacher Preparation Standards*.[91] It shows the concept of inclusive education in all aspects, approved as one of pre-service teacher cultivation standards in various states. The four standards—understanding and addressing each child's developmental and learning needs, assessing, planning, and designing contexts for learning, supporting each child's learning using effective instruction, and developing as a professional—highlight the concept, knowledge, and skills of inclusive education. For example, the standard of assessing, planning, and designing contexts for learning requires pre-service teachers to differentiate instructional plans to meet the needs of diverse students in the classroom, and to organize and manage effective small group instruction to differentiate teaching so as to meet the learning needs of each student, as well as individual instruction to provide targeted, focused, intensive instruction that improves or enhances each student's learning.

Both the cultivation standards for in-service and pre-service teachers, and the accreditation standards of teacher education institutions set clear expectations for the professional practice and behaviors of teachers, and provide a solid basis and direction for teacher cultivation. These standards contain specific provisions for and clear expressions of teachers' inclusive education competence, so that pre-service teachers can have a clear understanding of their responsibility for inclusive education and their important position in the implementation of inclusive education and, on this basis, strive for continuous professional development and growth. At the same time, following these standards, teacher education institutions have formed a virtuous circle in development of teacher cultivation programs, enrollment, curriculum setting,

International Experience in Cultivation of the Competence 221

achievement evaluation, quality assurance and improvement, effectively promoting the cultivation of the competence of teachers in inclusive education.

Cultivation Models of the Competence of Teachers in Inclusive Education:
Diversified Cultivation Models

Through theoretical and practical exploration, two methods have been developed to cultivate the competence of teachers in inclusive education, setting up independent courses and launching programs, and diversified cultivation models have taken shape, including the discrete model, the integrated model, and the merged model. Therefore, teacher cultivation programs are developed on the basis of a unified conceptual framework. By adjusting the existing curriculum, cooperating with other colleges to design courses or integrate resources to reset all pre-service courses, teacher education institutions incorporate the cultivation of pre-service teachers' inclusive education competence into the pre-service cultivation programs to ensure that pre-service teachers acquire the basic attitude, knowledge, and skills for inclusive education.

Some teacher cultivation programs have also made positive innovations to the existing models, such as the development of a discrete model of online teaching, that is, offering a separate online course of inclusive education to cultivate the pre-service teachers' competence in inclusive education. A case in point is the "Inclusive Practices in Education Settings" offered by the University of Tasmania in Australia, which adopts the model of online teaching, using online video-recorded interviews to connect the theory and practice of inclusive education in a course for student teachers. It has been found that such online interview courses improve pre-service teachers' engagement and learning, as well as the consistency in understanding the theory and practice of inclusive education.[92]

What is more, the teacher cultivation programs also actively seek in-depth cooperation with schools to cultivate the pre-service teachers' competence in inclusive education. For example, the "Immersion Program for Special Education," which aims to promote the learning and development of pre-service teachers in inclusive education, has engaged in deep collaboration with primary schools and forged close cooperation between university and school guidance teams. Some undergraduate seniors are selected and provided with an opportunity of one-year inclusive practice.[93] In addition to teaching the "Diversity and Inclusive Education" course, university tutors also need to work closely with other tutors in teacher cultivation programs, coordinators of the primary schools for internship, and schools for internship, and in-service teachers to ensure that the pre-service teachers are immersed in inclusive teaching practices. School tutors will provide the pre-service teachers with professional guidance, including timely feedback, and demonstrate a range of strategies that respond to the diverse special educational needs of students. It is found that in-depth cooperation between the double-tutor teacher cultivation program and the internship school can greatly reduce the

222   *International Experience in Cultivation of the Competence*

anxiety of pre-service teachers and enhance their inclusive education competence, ensuring their high-quality inclusive practice in future, and promoting them to observe, discuss, experiment, and reflect on the theory and practice of inclusive education.

Core of the Cultivation of the Competence of Teachers in Inclusive Education: Establishing Belief in Inclusive Education

The concept of inclusive education lays stress on the equal access to education for all children as well as teachers' respect for the diversity of children to meet their different educational needs. This undoubtedly requires teachers to re-understand and review their roles and responsibilities in the implementation of inclusive education. At the same time, they must have the attitude, knowledge, and ability of inclusive education in order to provide high-quality instruction for all children to the greatest extent. Children with special educational needs need more support than typically developing children, and whether they are able to get support often depends on the beliefs of the teachers.[94] Given that teachers' positive belief in inclusive education is a key factor for successful implementation of inclusive education,[95,96,97] most teachers' inclusive education competence cultivation programs focus on the teachers' belief in and attitude toward inclusive education.

For example, the Inclusive Practice Project (IPP) launched by the School of Education, University of Aberdeen in Scotland, centers on three cultivation goals: preparing teachers for development of all students in an inclusive school, cultivating effective teachers of the courses, and helping them achieve high-level professional practice. With the concept of inclusive education running through the whole process of cultivation, this project stresses teachers' responsibility to support all students' learning, and the need to promote an understanding of engagement in inclusive education.[98,99] The courses help pre-service teachers realize that all students are different, human differences should not be ignored or denied, and teachers must believe they have the ability to teach all children. It put forward that teacher education must consider differences as the central concept of human development from the very beginning to promote the transformation of teachers' beliefs. For example, teachers need to adopt a "sociocultural" theoretical perspective to understand and cope with the complexity of teaching different types of students, and must constantly develop innovative ways of working with others to support the learning of all children. A 12-week special education elective course offered by a city university in Australia to Grade 3 or 4 pre-service teachers for preschools, primary, and secondary schools advocates that "inclusive education is quality education." Pre-service teachers are cultivated to understand the concept and practice of teaching in an inclusive environment. After course learning, pre-service teachers all showed a more positive attitude toward inclusive education.[100] The teacher cultivation program of a university in New York embraces the belief that "excellent teachers value diversity, and know how to meet the needs of diverse students." Pre-service teachers are expected to establish the value of respecting and valuing differences in the classroom and the school community, and adjust their goals and strategies to support the learning of students with special needs, and use information about students' life backgrounds, such as culture and language, to develop a richer inclusive learning environment for individuals and the class.[101]

In short, most teachers' inclusive education competence cultivation programs emphasize the establishment of a belief in inclusive education, and make pre-service teachers realize the significance and value of inclusive education and fully accept inclusive education through offering inclusive education courses and sufficient practice, laying a solid foundation for the learning of inclusive education knowledge and skills. In this process, pre-service teachers no longer regard teaching children with special educational needs as the responsibility of special education teachers, but as their own responsibility, and work effectively with special education teachers to make thoughtful decisions that take into account the needs of different students and flexibly choose teaching methods to provide high quality instruction.[102,103]

Approach to Cultivation of the Competence of Teachers in Inclusive Education: Providing Sufficient Inclusive Education Practice

Practice has long been regarded as a key element of pre-service teacher cultivation programs.[104] It is also one of the central links of teacher cultivation programs. By integrating courses with pre-service teachers' field practice, the teacher cultivation programs promote pre-service teachers' mastery of teaching concepts, knowledge, and skills. By providing field practice of inclusive education, the teacher cultivation programs enable pre-service teachers to face different types of disadvantaged students that they have never encountered before, including children with special educational needs, and to actively modify and construct inclusive education knowledge and skills based on their previous experience. In particular, high-quality practical courses and cooperation between special education and general education pre-service teachers in practice will have a positive impact on their attitudes toward inclusive education.[105]

For example, a researcher designed an eight-week probation in an inclusive school, during which pre-service teachers had the opportunity to observe and implement inclusive teaching practice. After the probation, their attitudes toward inclusive education became more optimistic, and the most significant change was that they became less worried or anxious about inclusive classroom teaching, and their belief in and attitude toward inclusive education turned more positive.[106] A teacher cultivation program titled "Early Childhood/Early Childhood Special Education (EC/ECSE)" at a Midwestern city university in the US underlines inclusion as a real classroom practice that integrates field experience with courses. It provides 753 hours of observation, probation, and teaching practice in inclusive settings for pre-service teachers.[107] For example, the "Early Childhood Curriculum I" involves the content of inclusive education, including adjustment of the teaching plan, inclusive teaching with university teacher educators, teamwork in an inclusive environment, environmental adjustment, curriculum adjustment, and so on, requiring 16 hours of on-site probation as well as structured observation and reflection in an inclusive environment. Pre-service teachers should have at least 152 hours of observation and probation prior to the internship, 200 hours of teaching practice in an inclusive environment for the first time, and 400 hours of teaching practice for the second time. The courses and inclusive practice provided in the program have not only enhanced the positive attitude, confidence, and teaching skills of pre-service teachers, but also further promoted their understanding and reflection on inclusive education. As one pre-service teachers noted, "I have learned that teaching students with special needs is very challenging, but if we have enough patience and adjust the curriculum plans and strategies to meet their needs, they are likely to develop and learn at their own pace." Another observed that "my experience with students in partner schools has been the most useful part of my inclusive classroom strategies, which are not valuable until I actually use them in my teaching."

So, it is necessary to improve the inclusive education belief, attitudes, knowledge, and skills of pre-service teachers through sufficient inclusive practices.[108,109] Most teachers' inclusive education competence cultivation programs regard inclusive education practice as an indispensable and important link, either integrating it into the curriculum probation or infiltrating it into the educational practice of the whole program, so that pre-service teachers can establish a positive belief in inclusive education that will "take root" in future inclusive practice. They can also try to observe, assess, plan, teach, reflect, communicate, and collaborate in an inclusive environment to support the educational needs of all children and improve their inclusive teaching practice and quality of teaching.

Guarantee for Cultivation of the Competence of Teachers in Inclusive Education: Attaching Importance to Program Evaluation

Program evaluation is a necessary link in the operation of teacher cultivation programs. The cultivation programs of teachers' inclusive education competence that adopt the discrete model evaluate their inclusive education curriculum mainly through coursework, practical work, and examination, sometimes supplemented by questionnaires or interviews to further evaluate the inclusive education competence of pre-service teachers. Cultivation programs that adopt the integrated or merged model conduct dynamic monitoring and evaluation of the whole cultivation process, and include the pre-service teachers' competence in inclusive education in each evaluation link as a part of teachers' professional competence.

The primary school pre-service teacher cultivation program of the University of Northern Colorado measures the professional concept, knowledge, and skills of pre-service teachers from various aspects including admission selection, major selection, course learning performance, pre-internship evaluation, and internship evaluation. It also organizes the self-evaluation of its implementation process and the evaluation of the organizational cultivation results, so as to guarantee cultivation quality.[110] Before the internship, pre-service teachers should complete all required courses, and their GPA should not be lower than 3.0. They can only enter internship after comprehensive inspection of their past performance and scores by university teachers. Pre-service teachers can only complete the 16-week field practice under the supervision and coordination of university tutors and internship tutors after passing through pre-internship evaluation and meeting internship standards. Upon completion of the internship, pre-service teachers must meet the following standards: Achieve an 80 percent proficiency assessment in the "Capstone Unit of Instruction"; gain at least qualified scores on all items of "Professional Disposition Qualities"; score "proficient," "mature," or "exemplary" in all categories of the university tutor's final on-site evaluation form; pass the final online evaluation of both university tutor and internship tutor; attend seminars organized by university advisors; and meet professional teacher standards of InTASC and other agencies.[111] In view of the evaluation of cultivation results, the satisfaction level of graduates evaluated by the program and the primary and secondary schools for internship are used as the basis for testing the quality of the program. On the one hand, the role and effect of pre-service cultivation accepted by graduates on their own teaching can be checked, and the performance of graduates in work can be understood. On the other hand, feedback on the quality and problems of teacher cultivation can also be obtained from third-party employers. The results of the 2013–2014 academic year found that the overall satisfaction level of graduates was high, and a majority of them (68.86 percent) had a high level of satisfaction with the preparation to teach special needs students.[112] According to a survey of the satisfaction of principals of the primary and secondary schools where the graduates teach, it was found that the graduates met or even exceeded the principals' expectations in setting appropriate teaching objectives for students with special needs.[113]

Effective and scientific program evaluation is not only the quality guarantee for the cultivation of the competence of teachers in inclusive education, but also an important driving force for the continuous improvement of the programs. By collecting and using a variety of data, the progress and achievements of pre-service teachers' cultivation can be effectively monitored, and the progress and efficiency of program implementation can be regularly evaluated and tracked, so that the cultivation of the competence of teachers in inclusive education can be fully implemented and have a basis to follow. Objective, diversified, scientific, and sustainable comprehensive evaluation is used to improve teaching and learning, make evidence-based decisions, and ultimately guarantee the quality of pre-service teacher cultivation, and promote the continuous improvement and progress of teacher cultivation programs.

226 *International Experience in Cultivation of the Competence*

Challenges Facing Cultivation of the Competence of Teachers in Inclusive Education

In order to equip pre-service teachers with competence in inclusive education, a series of questions must be clarified. What does competence in inclusive education include? What is the common inclusive knowledge base required of pre-service teachers in order to promote curriculum coherence? What level of inclusive education knowledge preparation is required? Which cultivation model can more effectively shape pre-service teachers' competence in inclusive education? How best to integrate inclusive education curricula and practices? How to construct inclusive education practices to promote pre-service teachers' understanding and acceptance of special needs students?[114] How should teacher educators prepare for inclusive pre-service teacher education? How should teacher education institutions collaborate with other institutions? Most importantly, are pre-service teachers who have taken the cultivation programs effectively teaching all students in the classroom? By examining the current situation of the international cultivation of the competence of teachers in inclusive education, we find that the inclusive education curriculum, teacher educators, and cooperation between teacher education institutions and other institutions are facing a series of interwoven and interactive challenges.

Defects of Inclusive Education Curriculum

Existing inclusive education or special education courses are mostly set up as elective courses or module courses, which are not organically combined with teacher education courses. The curriculum system lacks the integration of diversified and different themes, and the curriculum content is not enough to enable pre-service teachers to meet the needs of children with special educational needs in regular classes. In addition, the teaching methods of the courses are mainly theoretical and lack a practical basis.[115,116,117] At the same time, because the cultivation content determines pre-service teachers' understanding of inclusive education, there are still some teacher cultivation programs that follow the tradition of special education, and their education objects are more targeted at special needs children, which are not suitable for the current inclusive education situation. Therefore, teacher education institutions must review the curriculum of inclusive education, complete the transformation from traditional special education to inclusive education, integrate inclusive education into the core curriculum of teacher education, and ensure that pre-service teachers are ready for inclusive education.

Disconnect between Inclusive Education Theory and Practice

The disconnect between the theory and practice of inclusive education and between teacher education institutions and local schools have a profound impact on the cultivation quality of the competence of teachers in inclusive education. The current inclusive education curriculum is usually based on one or two courses. Although pre-service teachers have an understanding and positive attitude toward inclusive education after learning it, studies have found that pre-service teachers are not adequately prepared to implement inclusive education.[118,119,120] The reasons are as follows. First, the current inclusive education courses offered are few and focus on theoretical learning, which fail to cultivate pre-service teachers' ability to solve practical inclusive teaching problems and reflect on teaching practice. Second, teacher educators lack support and supervision for pre-service teachers. This is because some teacher educators themselves lack the competence in inclusive education, which makes it difficult to help pre-service teachers link theory with practice; thus they cannot effectively support pre-service teachers to solve practical problems. At the same time, teacher educators are too busy to supervise the practical courses. In addition, pre-service teachers face practical struggles during internship in the schools that do not support an inclusive education philosophy. Internship schools and tutors that emphasize competition and test scores may neglect special needs students in their classes, so pre-service teachers shake their belief in inclusive education.[121]

Teacher Educators Lack Professional Competence in Inclusive Education

One of the key issues preventing teacher education institutions from cultivating the pre-service teachers' competence in inclusive education is that teacher educators often lack the ability to promote inclusive education.[122] As professionals involved in the development, design, and implementation of teachers' inclusive education competence cultivation programs, teacher educators may lack experience in the theory and practice of inclusive education. This is due to the following reasons. First, teacher educators may be more familiar with the theory and practice of special education, and lack experience in the theory and practice of inclusive education. Second, although teacher educators have rich theories of inclusive education, they often lack first-hand experience in the practice of inclusive education. Third, teacher educators in subject areas are often not qualified to guide and evaluate pre-service teachers' ability to plan and implement inclusive teaching.[123] Finally, the cultivation of the competence of teachers in inclusive education is still a relatively new research field, and a systematic and complete knowledge base has not been established. As a result, few guidelines are provided to teacher educators for the development and design of inclusive education curricula.[124]

Lack of Cooperation within Teacher Education Institutions

Teacher education institutions consist of different departments. Teacher educators hold that there are barriers between departments, and their development is discrete, led and separated by departments, resulting in a lot of duplication of work. They work in teams yet without cooperation.[125] Each department has its own professional development program, and focuses on issues related to inclusive education to varying degrees. In addition, teacher educators in the special education field collaborate less with those in subject areas and other fields such as speech pathology, psychology, and so on.[126] Generally, teacher educators in the field of special education are not experts in the subject area, and teachers in the same subject area rarely have the opportunity to acquire competence in inclusive education, so they cannot provide knowledge and personalized guidance in curriculum adjustment and other aspects for pre-service teachers. Therefore, teacher education institutions must make efforts to cooperate with different departments or colleges to promote the cultivation of the pre-service teachers' competence in inclusive education.

Enlightenment and Suggestions on Cultivation of the Competence of Chinese Teachers in Inclusive Education

Setting Inclusive Education Courses as Compulsory Courses and Incorporating Them into Pre-service Cultivation Programs

At present, in its various policies China only encourages and advocates that teacher education institutions set up courses related to inclusive education. Although the *National Standard for Assessing the Quality of Teaching in Undergraduate Programs Offered by Regular Higher Education Institutions* released by the Ministry of Education in 2018 ruled that an "Introduction to Special Education" is required in the basic courses of all pedagogic programs, and "Preschool Education for Special Needs Children" should be set up in the specialized courses of preschool education programs, teacher education institutions still have great autonomy to decide whether to offer inclusive education courses, and most of them have not done so. Some study shows that long-term programs and follow-up courses (additional courses) can ensure the continued development of the competence of teachers in inclusive education.[127] Compared with long-term programs and setting of multiple inclusive education courses, a semester course may be more in line with the reality of teacher education institutions, and according to the existing research, semester courses can effectively change teachers' attitude toward inclusive education. Therefore, in order to equip pre-service teachers with certain competence in inclusive education, inclusive education courses should be incorporated into the core curriculum of pre-service education programs as soon as possible, and inclusive education courses should be set as compulsory courses with a duration of at least one semester and no less than 32 class hours. The content of inclusive education courses can cover the categories and characteristics of disability, the connotation and development of inclusive and special education, the regulations and policies concerning inclusive and special education, inclusive curriculum and teaching knowledge, effective inclusive teaching strategies, and the practical experience of an inclusive environment. Meanwhile, the inclusive education courses must reflect the concepts of equality, inclusion, and human rights.

International Experience in Cultivation of the Competence   229

Inclusive Education Curriculum Should Highlight Practice and Cultivate the
Pre-service Teachers' Competence in Inclusion

The importance of field experience in inclusive settings should be emphasized in teachers' inclusive education competence cultivation programs, and practice should be highlighted in the curriculum of inclusive education, so as to bridge the gap between the theory and practice of inclusive education for pre-service teachers. Theoretical courses on inclusive education alone are not enough to cultivate teachers' ability to deal with the big differences in classrooms, which will make teachers unable to meet the diversified educational needs of students. Some researchers have found that interaction and experience with students (including special needs children and typically developing children) in an inclusive education environment play a crucial role in the whole pre-service teachers' cultivation process. Practical experience has greatly improved the attitude of pre-service teachers toward inclusive education and their ability in cooperation, observation, reflection and feedback.[128] To prepare pre-service teachers well to teach today's children with special educational needs, we must engage pre-service teachers in the cycle of curriculum and practice, and adopt methods that profoundly influence the learning experience, such as cooperative learning, to repeatedly expose pre-service teachers to inclusive educational practices.[129] Therefore, it is suggested that the practical experience of pre-service teachers in inclusive settings should be increased in the inclusive education curriculum. First of all, we should increase the proportion of class hours for practice in the curriculum plan, and adopt cooperative learning and other inclusive teaching methods in the course organization. Secondly, field experience in the special and inclusive environment should be provided in the same semester as inclusive education courses, so that pre-service teachers can have a preliminary understanding of the implementation of inclusive education and get feedback from various aspects of teaching practice. Finally, during the pre-service teachers' practice, they should be arranged in classes and internship schools that have disabled children and embrace the concept of inclusive education as far as possible, so as to provide them with the opportunity to observe, teach, evaluate and reflect, and develop their practical ability of inclusive teaching and shape their positive attitude toward inclusive education.

Stressing Evaluation of Pre-service Teachers' Attitude Toward Inclusive Education to
Ensure Effectiveness of the Cultivation of Their Competence in Inclusive Education

Pre-service teachers' attitude toward inclusive education, sense of efficacy, knowledge of inclusive education, and concerns about the implementation of inclusive education are taken as important indicators in the evaluation of teachers' inclusive education competence cultivation programs. A review of previous studies shows that attitude toward inclusive education is used as an indicator to measure the learning results of pre-service teachers in semester courses or long-term programs. This is because teachers' attitude toward and

230 *International Experience in Cultivation of the Competence*

belief in inclusive education are key factors that affect the successful implementation of inclusive education. Therefore, it is suggested that teachers' inclusive education competence cultivation programs should pay attention to pre-service teachers' attitude, sense of efficacy, knowledge level, concerns, and other indicators at the very beginning, and make adjustments according to the changes of these indicators, so as to equip pre-service teachers with necessary inclusive education competence, improve their attitude, sense of efficacy, and knowledge of inclusive education, and reduce their concerns about the implementation of inclusive education. The cultivation of attitude and sense of efficacy should be included into every link of the cultivation of the competence of teachers in inclusive education, and pre-service teachers should be encouraged to support the concept of inclusive education through various ways. Teacher education institutions are also required to use interviews, observations, reflective logs, examinations, and other methods to check pre-service teachers' concept, knowledge, and skills of inclusive education, to effectively monitor and regularly evaluate the progress and effect of pre-service teacher cultivation from the aspects of admission selection, major selection, course learning performance, pre-internship evaluation, and internship evaluation, so as to ensure the effectiveness of teachers' inclusive education competence cultivation.

Improving Teacher Educators' Competence in Inclusive Education and Promoting Full Cooperation between Teacher Education Institutions and Other Institutions

It is a systematic project to fulfil the cultivation of the competence of teachers in inclusive education. Teacher education institutions play a key role in cultivating the pre-service teachers' competence in inclusive education,[130,131] so they must be "sensitive" and "respond" positively to this task. Accordingly, this requires a change in the entire teacher education system to actively cope with the challenges brought by implementation of inclusive education to teacher education.[132] Teacher education institutions and teacher educators should actively change their roles and responsibilities. Principals of teacher education institutions need to play the role of leaders of inclusive education to promote teacher educators to understand and recognize the concept of inclusive education. The professional development of teacher educators in inclusive education is also a key element in the cultivation of pre-service teachers' inclusive education competence. Therefore, teacher education institutions need to provide more opportunities for teacher educators to cooperate in inclusive education, and reflect on, discuss, and promote inclusive education course teaching as participants and collaborators. The purpose is to ensure curriculum developers' and implementers' understanding of special needs and inclusive education, and promote pre-service teachers' understanding of the link between inclusive education theory and teaching practice.[133,134,135] In addition, teacher education institutions should promote the establishment of inclusive education teams, integrate teacher educators

International Experience in Cultivation of the Competence   231

in the fields of inclusive education and subject teaching with resources from other schools of teacher education institutions, such as schools of psychology and schools of information technology, as well as regular primary and secondary schools, kindergartens, and special education schools, to adjust and integrate subject courses and inclusive education courses, and form a complementary curriculum system. The knowledge and skills related to inclusive education should be included in teacher education and subject curriculum. For example, differentiated teaching knowledge can be interspersed into pedagogy, psychology, and other subject courses. Finally, teacher education institutions should speed up the exploration of the cultivation models suitable for the development of local LRC programs, study semester courses, multiple inclusive education courses, and long-term cultivation programs, and probe the effects of different cultivation models. It is also advisable for them to cooperate with other institutions, such as information technology schools in universities, to develop MOOCs (massive open online courses) for cultivation of the competence of teachers in inclusive education, explore diversified cultivation methods, and finally find out the best practice model to improve the pre-service teachers' competence in inclusive education.

Notes

1 Feng, Yajing 冯雅静, Li, Aifen 李爱芬, and Wang, Yan 王雁. "Woguo putong shifan zhuanye ronghe jiaoyu kecheng xianzhuang de diaocha yanjiu" 我国普通师范专业融合教育课程现状的调查研究. *Chinese Journal of Special Education* 中国特殊教育 no. 1 (2016): 9–15, 29.

2 Stites, M. L., Rakes, C. R., Noggle, A. K., et al. "Pre-service Teacher Perceptions of Preparedness to Teach in Inclusive Settings as an Indicator of Teacher Preparation Program Effectiveness." *Discourse and Communication for Sustainable Education* 9, no. 2 (2018): 21–39.

3 Wang, Yan 王雁, Fan, Wenjing 范文静, and Feng, Yajing 冯雅静. "Woguo putong jiaoshi ronghe jiaoyu suyang zhiqian peiyang de sikao ji jianyi" 我国普通教师融合教育素养职前培养的思考及建议. *Journal of Educational Studies* 教育学报 14, no. 6 (2018): 81–87.

4 Booth, T., Nes, K., and Strømstad, M. *Developing Inclusive Teacher Education*, 9. London: Taylor & Francis e-Library, 2005.

5 Zhao, Wei 赵微. "Yingguo peiyang putong shizi juyou tejiao jineng" 英国培养普通师资具有特教技能. *Chinese Journal of Special Education* 中国特殊教育 no. 4 (1998): 35–38.

6 Cao, Jieqiong 曹婕琼, and Zan, Fei 昝飞. "Meiguo riben zhongguo dalu diqu ronghe jiaoyu de bijiao yu sikao" 美国、日本、中国大陆地区融合教育的比较与思考. *Chinese Journal of Special Education* 中国特殊教育 no. 4 (2003): 70–74.

7 Song, J., Sharma, U., and Choi, H. "Impact of Teacher Education on Pre-service Regular School Teachers' Attitudes, Intentions, Concerns and Self-efficacy about Inclusive Education in South Korea." *Teaching and Teacher Education* 86 (2019): 1–9.

8 Romero-Contreras, S., Garcia-Cedillo, I., Forlin, C., et al. "Preparing Teachers for Inclusion in Mexico: How Effective Is This Process?" *Journal of Education for Teaching* 39, no. 5 (2013): 509.

9 Nketsia, W., and Saloviita, T. "Pre-service Teachers' Views on Inclusive Education in Ghana." *Journal of Education for Teaching* 39, no. 4 (2013): 429–441.

10 Hartle, H. *Teaching Handicapped Students in the Regular Classroom: State Pre-service Certification Requirements and Program Approval Standards*, 2–5. Washington, DC: American Association of Colleges for Teacher Education, 1982. https://files.eric.ed.gov/fulltext/ED221513.pdf.

11 Kleinhammer-Tramill, J. "An Analysis of Federal Initiatives to Prepare Regular Education Students to Serve Students with Disabilities: Deans' Grants, REGI and Beyond." *Teacher Education and Special Education* 26, no. 3 (2003): 230–245.

12 He, Juling 何菊玲. *Jiaoshi jiaoyu fanshi yanjiu* 教师教育范式研究, 86. Beijing: Educational Science Publishing House, 2009.

13 Smith, J. E., and Schindler, W. J. "Certification Requirements of General Educators concerning Exceptional Pupils." *Exceptional Children* 46 (1980): 430–432.

14 Ganschow, L., Weber, D. B., and Davis, M. "Pre-service Teacher Preparation for Mainstreaming." *Exceptional Children* 51, no. 1 (1984): 74–76.

15 See note 11 above, 16–20.

16 Jones, S. D., and Messenheimer-Young, T. "Content of Special Education Courses for Pre-service Regular Education Teachers." *Teacher Education and Special Education* 12, no. 4 (1989): 154–159.

17 Feng, Yajing 冯雅静, and Wang, Yan 王雁. "Ronghe jiaoyu beijing xia meiguo putong jiaoshi zhiqian peiyang de biange licheng he tezheng." *Chinese Journal of Special Education* 中国特殊教育 no. 1 (2021): 3–9.

18 Zundans-Fraser, L., and Lancaster, J. "Enhancing the Inclusive Self-efficacy of Pre-service Teachers through Embedded Course Design." *Education Research International* 52 (2012): 1–8.

19 Fullerton, A., Ruben, B. J., and McBride, S., et al. "Evaluation of a Merged Secondary and Special Education Program." *Teacher Education Quarterly* 38, no. 2 (2011): 45–60.

20 He, Y., and Cooper, J. "Struggles and Strategies in Teaching: Voices of Five Novice Secondary Teachers." *Teacher Education Quarterly* 38, no. 2 (2011): 97–116.

21 Fender, M. J., and Fiedler, C. "Pre-service Preparation of Regular Educators: A National Survey of Curriculum Content in Introductory Exceptional Children and Youth Courses." *Teacher Education and Special Education* 13 (1990): 203–209.

22 Allady, R. A., Neilsen-Gatti, S., and Hudson, T. M. "Preparation for Inclusion in Teacher Education Pre-service Curricula." *Teacher Education and Special Education* 36, no. 4 (2013): 298–311.

23 Kozleski, E. B., and Waitoller, F. R. "Teacher Learning for Inclusive Education: Understanding Teaching as a Cultural and Political Practice." *International Journal of Inclusive Education* 14, no. 7 (2010): 655–666.

24 Askamit, D. L. "Practicing Teachers' Perceptions of Their Pre-service Preparation for Mainstreaming." *Teacher Education and Special Education* 13, no. 1(1990): 21–29.

25 Welch, M. "Teacher Education and the Neglected Diversity: Preparing Educators to Teach Students with Disabilities." *Journal of Teacher Education* 47, no. 5 (1996): 355–366.

26 Lombardi, T. P., and Hunka, N. J. "Preparing General Education Teachers for Inclusive Classrooms: Assessing the Process." *Teacher Education and Special Education* 24, no. 3 (2001), 183–197.

27 See note 18 above.

International Experience in Cultivation of the Competence 233

28 Zeichner, K. "Xin ziyou zhuyi sixiang he meiguo jiaoshi jiaoyu de biange" 新自由主义思想和美国教师教育的变革. In *"Gongping junheng xiaolü—duoyuan shehui beijing xia de jiaoyu zhengce" guoji xueshu yantaohui huiyi lunwenji* "公平、均衡、效率——多元社会背景下的教育政策"国际学术研讨会会议论文集, 20. Shanghai: The Institute of Schooling Reform and Development, East China Normal University, 2008.

29 Zhou, Jun 周钧. "Dangqian meiguo daxue jiaoyu xueyuan jiaoshi jiaoyu gaige" 当前美国大学教育学院教师教育改革. *Teacher Education Research* 教师教育研究 22, no. 1 (2010): 71–75.

30 Nowacek, E. J., and Blanton, L. P. "A Pilot Project Investigating the Influence of a Collaborative Methods Course on Pre-service Elementary Education Teachers." *Teacher Education and Special Education* 19, no. 4 (1996): 298–312.

31 Davern, L. "Parents' Perspectives on Personnel Attitudes and Characteristics in Inclusive School Settings: Implications for Teacher Preparation Programs." *Teacher Education and Special Education* 22 (1999): 165–182.

32 Gettinger, M., Stoiber, K. C., Goetz, D., et al. "Competencies and Training Needs for Early Childhood Inclusion Specialists." *Teacher Education and Special Education* 22 (1999): 41–54.

33 See note 3 above.

34 See note 18 above.

35 Florian, L. and Linklater, H. "Preparing Teachers for Inclusive Education: Using Inclusive Pedagogy to Enhance Teaching and Learning for All." *Cambridge Journal of Education* 40, no. 4 (2010): 369–386.

36 Ni, Pingping 倪萍萍, and Zan, Fei 昝飞. "Guowai zhiqian ronghe jiaoyu jiaoshi peiyang moshi jiqi dui woguo de qishi" 国外职前融合教育教师培养模式及其对我国的启示. *Journal of Schooling Studies* 基础教育 12, no. 1 (2015): 93–99.

37 Ladson-Billings, G. J. "Is the Team All Right? Diversity and Teacher Education." *Journal of Teacher Education* 56, no. 3 (2005): 229–234.

38 Miller, P. S., and Stayton, V. D. "Blended Interdisciplinary Teacher Preparation in Early Education and Intervention: A National Study." *Topics in Early Childhood Special Education* 18 (1998): 49–58.

39 Pugach, M., and Blanton, L. "A Framework for Conducting Research on Collaborative Teacher Education." *Teaching and Teacher Education* 25 (2009): 575–582.

40 *Elementary Education: Early Childhood/English as a Second Language.* Madison: University of Wisconsin-Madison, 2022. https://guide.wisc.edu/undergraduate/education/curriculum-instruction/elementary-education-bse/elementary-education-early-childhood-english-second-language-bse/.

41 Sharma, U., and Nuttal, A. "The Impact of Training on Pre-service Teacher Attitudes, Concerns, and Efficacy Towards Inclusion." *Asia-Pacific Journal of Teacher Education* 44, no. 2 (2015): 142–155.

42 *General Curriculum and Elementary Education K-6, B. A. Dual Program.* Charlotte: University of North Carolina at Charlotte. https://catalog.uncc.edu/preview_program.php?catoid=29&poid=7544.

43 *Special Education + Elementary Education Dual Undergraduate Program.* Charlotte: University of North Carolina at Charlotte https://spcd.uncc.edu/sites/spcd.uncc.edu/files/media/SPEL_Dual_Program_Clinical_and_Assessment_Map.pdf.

44 *Standards for Registration: Mandatory Requirements for Registration with the General Teaching Council for Scotland.* Edinburgh: The General Teaching Council

234 *International Experience in Cultivation of the Competence*

for Scotland, 2012. https://dera.ioe.ac.uk/16191/1/standards-for-registration-1212.pdf.

45 *Guidelines for Initial Teacher Education Programmes in Scotland*. Edinburgh: General Teaching Council for Scotland, 2018. https://dera.ioe.ac.uk/19281/.

46 *Professional Graduate Diploma in Education (PGDE) Primary*. Edinburgh: The University of Edinburgh. www.ed.ac.uk/education/graduate-school/taught-degrees/pgde/primary.

47 Liu, Bin 刘斌. *Yingguo quanna jiaoshi zhiqian peiyang de ge'an yanjiu—yi aidingbao daxue weili* 英国全纳教师职前培养的个案研究——以爱丁堡大学为例. Beijing: Beijing Normal University, 2018.

48 Kraska, J., and Boyle, C. "Attitudes of Preschool and Primary School Pre-service Teachers Towards Inclusive Education." *Asia-Pacific Journal of Teacher Education* 42, no. 3 (2014): 228–246.

49 Sharma, U., Shaukat, S., and Furlonger, B. "Attitudes and Self-efficacy of Pre-service Teachers Towards Inclusion in Pakistan." *Journal of Research in Special Educational Needs* 15, no. 2 (2014): 97–105.

50 Purdue, K., Gordon-Burns, D., and Gunn, A., et al. "Supporting Inclusion in Early Childhood Settings: Some Possibilities and Problems for Teacher Education." *International Journal of Inclusive Education* 13, no. 8 (2009): 805–815.

51 Kim, J. "Influence of Teacher Preparation Programmes on Pre-service Teachers' Attitudes Toward Inclusion." *International Journal of Inclusive Education* 15, no. 3 (2011): 355–377.

52 Chen, Guanghua 陈光华, and Li, Maofen 李茂粉. "Guoji ronghe jiaoshi jiaoyu moshi yanjiu de huigu—jiyu jin shinian wenxian de yuan fenxi" 国际融合教师教育模式研究的回顾——基于近10年文献的元分析. *Chinese Journal of Special Education* 中国特殊教育 no. 8 (2019): 21–27.

53 Neville, R. D., Makopoulou, K., and Hopkins, W. G. "Effect of an Inclusive Physical Education (IPE) Training Workshop on Trainee Teachers' Self-Efficacy." *Research Quarterly for Exercise and Sport* 91, no. 1 (2019): 1–13.

54 Rakap, S., Cig, O., and Parlak-Rakap, A. "Preparing Preschool Teacher Candidates for Inclusion: Impact of Two Special Education Courses on Their Perspectives." *Journal of Research in Special Educational Needs* 17, no. 2 (2017): 98–109.

55 Costello, S., and Boyle, C. "Pre-service Secondary Teachers' Attitudes Towards Inclusive Education." *Australian Journal of Teacher Education* 38, no. 4 (2013): 129–143.

56 Anderson, K., Smith, J., Olsen, J., et al. "Systematic Alignment of Dual Teacher Preparation." *Rural Special Education Quarterly* 34, no. 1 (2015): 30–36.

57 See note 57 above, 128–143.

58 Kurniawati, F., De Boer, A. A., Minnaert, A. E. M. G., et al. "Characteristics of Primary Teacher Cultivation Programmes on Inclusion: A Literature Focus." *Educational Research* 56, no. 3 (2014): 310–326.

59 Chen, Qi 陈琦, and Liu, Rude 刘儒德. *Dangdai Jiaoyu Xinlixue* 当代教育心理学, 251–252. Beijing: Beijing Normal University Publishing Group, 2007.

60 See note 43 above.

61 Swain, K. D., Nordness, P. D., and Leader-Janssen, E. "Changes in Pre-service Teacher Attitudes Toward Inclusion." *Preventing School Failure* 56, no. 2 (2012): 75–81.

62 Rouse, M. "Reforming Initial Teacher Education: A Necessary But Not Sufficient Condition for Developing Inclusive Practice." In C. Forlin (ed.), *Teacher*

Education for Inclusion: Changing Paradigms and Innovative Approaches, 47–55. Abingdon: Routledge, 2010.

63 Sharma, U., Forlin, C., and Loreman, T. "Impact of Training on Pre-service Teachers' Attitudes and Concerns about Inclusive Education and Sentiments about Persons with Disabilities." *Disability & Society* 23, no. 7 (2008): 773–785.

64 O'Neill, S. C. "Preparing Pre-service Teachers for Inclusive Classrooms: Does Completing Coursework on Managing Challenging Behaviours Increase Their Classroom Management Sense of Efficacy?" *The Australasian Journal of Special Education* 40, no. 2 (2016): 117–140.

65 Sosu, E. M., Mtika, P., and Colucci-Gray, L. "Does Initial Teacher Education Make a Difference? The Impact of Teacher Preparation on Student Teachers' Attitudes Towards Educational Inclusion." *Journal of Education for Teaching* 36, no. 4 (2010): 389–405.

66 Sharma, U. "Changing Pre-service Teachers' Beliefs to Teach in Inclusive Classrooms in Victoria, Australia." *Australian Journal of Teacher Education* 37, no. 10 (2012): 53–66.

67 Loreman, T., Sharma, U., Earle, C., et al. "The Development of an Instrument for Measuring Pre-service Teachers' Sentiments, Attitudes and Concerns about Inclusive Education." *International Journal of Special Education* 22, no. 2 (2007): 150–159.

68 Sokal, L., Woloshyn, D., and Funk-Unrau, S. "How Important Is Practicum to Pre-service Teacher Development for Inclusive Teaching? Effects on Classroom Management Efficacy." *Alberta Journal of Educational Research* 59, no. 2 (2013): 285–298.

69 Sokal, L., and Sharma, U. "Do I Really Need a Course to Learn to Teach Students with Disabilities? I've Been Doing It for Years." *Canadian Journal of Education* 40, no. 4 (2017): 739–760.

70 Pedersen, S. J., Cooley, P. D., and Hernandez, K. "Are Australian Pre-service Physical Education Teachers Prepared to Teach Inclusive Physical Education?" *Australian Journal of Teacher Education* 39, no. 8 (2014): 53–62.

71 Specht, J., McGhie-Richmond, D., Loreman, T., et al. "Teaching in Inclusive Classrooms: Efficacy and Beliefs of Canadian Pre-service Teachers." *International Journal of Inclusive Education* 20, no. 1 (2016): 1–15.

72 Lancaster, J., and Bain, A. "The Design of Pre-service Inclusive Education Courses and Their Effects on Self-efficacy: A Comparative Study." *Asia-Pacific Journal of Teacher Education* 38, no. 2 (2010): 117–128.

73 See note 68 above.

74 Gao, W., and Mager, G. "Enhancing Pre-service Teachers' Sense of Efficacy and Attitudes Toward School Diversity through Preparation: A Case of One US Inclusive Teacher Program." *International Journal of Special Education* 26, no. 2 (2011): 92–107.

75 See note 19 above.

76 See note 65 above.

77 Taylor, R. W., and Ravic, P. R. "Impacting Pre-service Teachers' Attitudes Toward Inclusion." *Higher Education Studies* 2, no. 3 (2012): 16–23.

78 Sharma, U., and Sokal, L. "The Impact of a Teacher Education Course on Pre-service Teachers' Beliefs about Inclusion: An International Comparison." *Journal of Research in Special Educational Needs* 15, no. 4 (2015): 276–284.

79 Male, D. B. "The Impact of a Professional Development Programme on Teachers' Attitudes Towards Inclusion." *Support for Learning* 26, no. 4 (2011): 182–186.

236 *International Experience in Cultivation of the Competence*

80 McCray, E. D., and McHatton, P. A. "Less Afraid to Have Them in My Classroom: Understanding Pre-service General Educators' Perceptions about Inclusion." *Teacher Education Quarterly* 38, no. 4 (2011): 135–155.

81 Forlin, C., and Chambers, D. "Teacher Preparation for Inclusive Education: Increasing Knowledge but Raising Concerns." *Asia-Pacific Journal of Teacher Education* 39, no. 1 (2011): 17–32.

82 See note 80 above.

83 See note 76 above.

84 See note 68 above.

85 European Agency for Development in Special Needs and Inclusive Education. *Teacher Education for Inclusion: Key Policy Messages*. Odense: European Agency for Development in Special Needs Education, 2011.

86 Feng, Yajing 冯雅静, Zhu, Nan 朱楠, and Wang, Yan 王雁. "Meiguo guojiaxing jiaoshi zhuanye biaozhun zhong ronghe jiaoyu xiangguan yaoqiu tanxi" 美国国家性教师专业标准中融合教育相关要求探析. *Teacher Education Research* 教师教育研究 28, no. 4 (2016): 121–128.

87 Yu, Tingjie 俞婷婕. "Zhuanye quxiang de jueze: aodaliya jiaoshi zhuanye biaozhun yingxiang xia de daxue jiaoshi jiaoyu kecheng shezhi" 专业取向的抉择：澳大利亚教师专业标准影响下的大学教师教育课程设置. *Tsinghua Journal of Education* 清华大学教育研究 37, no. 6 (2016): 46–52.

88 Wu, Na 巫娜. *Zhongguo–jianada zhongxiaoxue jiaoshi zhuanye biaozhun bijiao yanjiu* 中国—加拿大中小学教师专业标准比较研究. Chongqing: Southwest University, 2018.

89 Interstate Teacher Assessment and Support Consortium (InTASC). *InTASC Model Core Teaching Standards: A Resource for State Dialogue*, 11–19. Washington, DC: Council of Chief State School Officers, 2011. www.ccsso.org/sites/default/files/2017–11/InTASC_Model_Core_Teaching_Standards_2011.pdf.

90 Tao Deng 邓涛, "Meiguo jiaoshi jiaoyu renzheng gaige: jigou chongjian he biaozhun zaigou" 美国教师教育认证改革：机构重建和标准再构. *Teacher Education Research* 教师教育研究 28, no. 1 (2016): 110–115.

91 *CAEP 2018 K–6 Elementary Teacher Preparation Standards* [Initial Licensure Programs]. Washington, DC: Council for the Accreditation of Educator Preparation, 2021. http://caepnet.org/~/media/Files/caep/standards/2018-caep-k-6-elementary-teacher-prepara.pdf?la=en.

92 Rayner, C., and Allen, J. M. "Using Online Video-recorded Interviews to Connect the Theory and Practice of Inclusive Education in a Course for Student Teachers." *The Australasian Journal of Special Education* 37, no. 2 (2013): 107–124.

93 Grima-Farrell, C. "Mentoring Pathways to Enhancing the Personal and Professional Development of Pre-service Teachers." *International Journal of Mentoring and Coaching in Education* 4 (2015): 255–268.

94 Jordan, A., Glenn, C., and McGhie-Richmond, D. "The Supporting Effective Teaching (Set) Project: The Relationship of Inclusive Teaching Practices to Teachers' Beliefs about Disability and Ability, and about Their Roles as Teachers." *Teaching and Teacher Education* 26, no. 2 (2010): 259–266.

95 Tiwari, A., Das, A. K., and Sharma, M. "Inclusive Education a 'Rhetoric' or 'Reality'? Teachers' Perspectives and Beliefs." *Teaching and Teacher Education* 52, no. 12 (2015): 128–136.

96 Cameron, D. L. "Teacher Preparation for Inclusion in Norway: A Study of Beliefs, Skills, and Intended Practices." *International Journal of Inclusive Education* 21, no. 10 (2017): 1028–1044.

International Experience in Cultivation of the Competence 237

97 Boyle, C., Scriven, B., Durning, S., et al. "Facilitating the Learning of All Students: The 'Professional Positive' of Inclusive Practice in Australian Primary Schools." *Support for Learning* 26, no. 2 (2011): 72–78.

98 Florian, L., and Rouse, M. "The Inclusive Practice Project in Scotland: Teacher Education for Inclusive Education." *Teaching and Teacher Education* 25, no. 4 (2009): 594–601.

99 Spratt, J., and Florian, L. "Inclusive Pedagogy: From Learning to Action, Supporting Each Individual in the Context of 'Everybody.'" *Teaching and Teacher Education* 49 (2015): 89–96.

100 Varcoe, L., and Boyle, C. "Pre-service Primary Teachers' Attitudes Towards Inclusive Education." *Educational Psychology* 34, no. 3 (2014): 323–337.

101 Mueller, M., and Hindin, A. "An Analysis of the Factors That Influence Pre-service Elementary Teachers' Developing Dispositions about Teaching All Children." *Issues in Teacher Education* 20, no. 1 (2011): 17–34.

102 Pugach, M. C. "What Do We Know about Preparing Teachers to Work with Students with Disabilities?" In M. Cochran-Smith, and K. Zeichner (eds.), *Studying Teacher Education: The Report of the AERA Panel on Research and Teacher Education*, 549–590. Mahwah, NJ: Lawrence Erlbaum, 2005.

103 Kirby, M. "Implicit Assumptions in Special Education Policy: Promoting Full Inclusion for Students with Learning Disabilities." *Child & Youth Care Forum* 46, no. 2 (2016): 175–191.

104 Ferrier-Kerr, J. "Establishing Professional Relationships in Practicum Settings." *Teaching and Teacher Education* 25, no. 6 (2009): 790–797.

105 Kosnik, C., and Beck, C. *Priorities in Teacher Education: The 7 Key Elements of Pre-service Preparation*, 104. London and New York: Routledge, 2009.

106 Lambe, J., and Bones, R. "The Effect of School-based Practice on Student Teachers' Attitudes Towards Inclusive Education in Northern Ireland." *Journal of Education for Teaching* 33, no. 1 (2007): 99–113.

107 Voss, J. A., and Bufkin, L. J. "Teaching All Children: Preparing Early Childhood Pre-service Teachers in Inclusive Settings." *Journal of Early Childhood Teacher Education* 32, no. 4 (2011): 338–354.

108 Blair, C. "Classroom Teacher's Perceptions of Pre-service Education Related to Teaching the Handicapped." *Journal of Teacher Education* 34, no. 2 (1983): 52–54.

109 Lambe, J., and Bones, R. "Student Teachers' Attitudes to Inclusion: Implications for Initial Teacher Education in Northern Ireland." *International Journal of Inclusive Education* 10, no. 6 (2006): 511–527.

110 Fu, Shuqiong 付淑琼. *Meiguo zhongxiaoxue zhuoyue jiaoshi zhiqian peiyang de zhiliang baozhang jizhi yanjiu* 美国中小学卓越教师职前培养的质量保障机制研究, 88–123. Shanghai: East China Normal University, 2016.

111 *Fall 2021 Student Teaching Handbook* (EDEL 454). Greeley: University of Northern Colorado, 2021. www.unco.edu/cebs/teacher-education/pdf/edel-454-handbook-f-21c.pdf.

112 *Alumni Survey*. Greeley: University of Northern Colorado. www.unco.edu/education-behavioral-sciences/pdf/alumni-survey-b.pdf.

113 *Employer Survey: Spring 2014*. Greeley: University of Northern Colorado. www.unco.edu/education-behavioral-sciences/pdf/employer-survey-principal-c.pdf.

114 See note 20 above.

238 *International Experience in Cultivation of the Competence*

115 Ahsan, M. T., Sharma, U., and Deppeler, J. M. "Challenges to Prepare Pre-service Teachers for Inclusive Education in Bangladesh: Beliefs of Higher Educational Institutional Heads." *Asia-Pacific Journal of Education* 32, no. 2 (2012): 241–257.

116 Pijl, S. J. "Preparing Teachers for Inclusive Education: Some Reflections from the Netherlands." *Journal of Research in Special Educational Needs* 10, no. 1 (2010): 197–201.

117 Kaplan, I. Tuijin quanna jiaoshi jiaoyu: changdao zhinan 推进全纳教师教育：倡导指南, translated by Congman Rao 饶从满, et al., 65. Changchun: Northeast Normal University, 2015.

118 Majoko, T. "Mainstream Early Childhood Education Teacher Preparation for Inclusion in Zimbabwe." *Early Child Development and Care* 187, no. 11 (2017): 1649–1665.

119 Chireshe, R. "The State of Inclusive Education in Zimbabwe: Bachelor of Education (Special Needs Education) Students' Perceptions." *Journal of Social Science* 34, no. 3 (2013): 223–228.

120 Hornby, G. "Preparing Teachers to Work with Parents and Families of Learners with SEN in Inclusive Schools." In C. Forlin (ed.), *Teacher Education for Inclusion: Changing Paradigms and Innovative Approaches*, 93–101. London: Routledge, 2010.

121 Smith, E. R., and Avetisian, V. "Learning to Teach with Two Mentors: Revisiting the 'Two Worlds Pitfall' in Student Teaching." *The Teacher Educator* 46, no. 4 (2011): 335–354.

122 Forlin, C., and Nguyet, T. D. "A National Strategy for Supporting Teacher Educators to Prepare Teachers for Inclusion." In C. Forlin (ed.), *Teacher Education for Inclusion: Changing Paradigms and Innovative Approaches*, 34–44. London: Routledge, 2010.

123 Zhang, J., Wright, A. M., Kim, E., et al. "A Collaborative Journey Toward Inclusive Teacher Education Programs." *Curriculum and Teaching Dialogue* 21, no. 1 (2019): 37–51, 161, 164–165.

124 Walker, N., and Laing, S. "Development and Initial Validation of a Questionnaire to Improve Preparation of Pre-service Teachers for Contemporary Inclusive Teaching." *The e-Journal of Business Education & Scholarship of Teaching* 13, no. 2 (2019): 16–34.

125 Booth, T., Nes, K., and Stromstad, M. "Views from the Institution: Overcoming Barriers to Inclusive Teacher Education." In T. Booth, K. Nes, and M. Stromstad, *Developing Inclusive Teacher Education*, 33–57. London: Routledge Falmer, 2003.

126 Delano, M. E., Keefe, L., and Perner, D. "Personnel Preparation: Recurring Challenges and the Need for Action to Ensure Access to General Education." *Research and Practice for Persons with Severe Disabilities* 33, no. 4 (2008): 232–240.

127 See note 60 above.

128 Laura, M. G. *Preparing Pre-service Teachers for Inclusive Field-based Experience: A Case Study of Field-based Tutoring Experience*. New York: University at Buffalo, State University of New York, 2009.

129 Bain, A., Lancaster, J., Zundans, L., et al. "Embedding Evidence-based Practice in Pre-service Teacher Preparation." *Teacher Education and Special Education* 32, no. 3 (2009): 215–225.

130 Sharma, U., Forlin, C., Loreman, T., et al. "Pre-service Teachers' Attitudes, Concerns and Sentiments about Inclusive Education: An International Comparison

of the Novice Pre-service Teachers." *International Journal of Special Education* 21 (2006): 80–93.

131 Romi, S., and Leyser, Y. "Exploring Inclusion Pre-service Training Needs: A Study of Variables Associated with Attitudes and Self-efficacy Beliefs." *European Journal of Special Needs Education* 21, no. 1 (2006): 85–105.

132 See note 3 above.

133 Kaplan, I., and Lewis, I. *Promoting Inclusive Teacher Education: Curriculum.* UNESCO Office Bangkok and Regional Bureau for Education in Asia and the Pacific, 2013.

134 Florian, L. "Teacher Education for the Changing Demographics of Schooling: Inclusive Education for Each and Every Learner." In L. Florian and N. Pantić (eds.), *Teacher Education for the Changing Demographics of Schooling: Issues for Research and Practice* (*Inclusive Learning and Educational Equity*, Volume 2), 9–20. Cham: Springer, 2017.

135 Villegas, A. M., Ciotoli, F., and Lucas, T. "A Framework for Preparing Teachers for Classrooms That Are Inclusive of All Students." In L. Florian and N. Pantić (eds.), *Teacher Education for the Changing Demographics of Schooling: Issues for Research and Practice* (*Inclusive Learning and Educational Equity*, Volume 2), 133–148. Cham: Springer, 2017.

References

Ahsan, M. T., Sharma, U., and Deppeler, J. M. "Challenges to Prepare Pre-service Teachers for Inclusive Education in Bangladesh: Beliefs of Higher Educational Institutional Heads." *Asia-Pacific Journal of Education* 32, no. 2 (2012): 241–257.

Allady, R. A., Neilsen-Gatti, S., and Hudson, T. M. "Preparation for Inclusion in Teacher Education Pre-service Curricula." *Teacher Education and Special Education* 36, no. 4 (2013): 298–311.

Alumni Survey. Greeley: University of Northern Colorado. www.unco.edu/education-behavioral-sciences/pdf/alumni-survey-b.pdf.

Anderson, K., Smith, J., Olsen, J., et al. "Systematic Alignment of Dual Teacher Preparation." *Rural Special Education Quarterly* 34, no. 1 (2015): 30–36.

Askamit, D. L. "Practicing Teachers' Perceptions of Their Pre-service Preparation for Mainstreaming." *Teacher Education and Special Education* 13, no. 1(1990): 21–29.

Bain, A., Lancaster, J., Zundans, L., et al. "Embedding Evidence-based Practice in Pre-service Teacher Preparation." *Teacher Education and Special Education* 32, no. 3 (2009): 215–225.

Blair, C. "Classroom Teacher's Perceptions of Pre-service Education Related to Teaching the Handicapped." *Journal of Teacher Education* 34, no. 2 (1983): 52–54.

Booth, T., Nes, K., and Stromstad, M. "Views from the Institution: Overcoming Barriers to Inclusive Teacher Education." In T. Booth, K. Nes, and M. Stromstad, *Developing Inclusive Teacher Education*, 33–57. London: Routledge Falmer, 2003.

Booth, T., Nes, K., and Strømstad, M. *Developing Inclusive Teacher Education*, 9. London: Taylor & Francis e-Library, 2005.

Boyle, C., Scriven, B., Durning, S., et al. "Facilitating the Learning of All Students: The 'Professional Positive' of Inclusive Practice in Australian Primary Schools." *Support for Learning* 26, no. 2 (2011): 72–78.

240 *International Experience in Cultivation of the Competence*

CAEP 2018 K–6 Elementary Teacher Preparation Standards [Initial Licensure Programs]. Washington, DC: Council for the Accreditation of Educator Preparation, 2021. http://caepnet.org/~/media/Files/caep/standards/2018-caep-k-6-elementary-teacher-prepara.pdf?la=en.

Cameron, D. L. "Teacher Preparation for Inclusion in Norway: A Study of Beliefs, Skills, and Intended Practices." *International Journal of Inclusive Education* 21, no. 10 (2017): 1028–1044.

Cao, Jieqiong 曹婕琼, and Zan, Fei 昝飞. "Meiguo riben zhongguo dalu diqu ronghe jiaoyu de bijiao yu sikao" 美国、日本、中国大陆地区融合教育的比较与思考. *Chinese Journal of Special Education* 中国特殊教育 no. 4 (2003): 70–74.

Chen, Guanghua 陈光华, and Li, Maofen 李茂粉. "Guoji ronghe jiaoshi jiaoyu moshi yanjiu de huigu—jiyu jin shinian wenxian de yuan fenxi" 国际融合教师教育模式研究的回顾——基于近10年文献的元分析. *Chinese Journal of Special Education* 中国特殊教育 no. 8 (2019): 21–27.

Chen, Qi 陈琦, and Liu, Rude 刘儒德. *Dangdai Jiaoyu Xinlixue* 当代教育心理学, 251–252. Beijing: Beijing Normal University Publishing Group, 2007.

Chireshe, R. "The State of Inclusive Education in Zimbabwe: Bachelor of Education (Special Needs Education) Students' Perceptions." *Journal of Social Science* 34, no. 3 (2013): 223–228.

Costello, S., and Boyle, C. "Pre-service Secondary Teachers' Attitudes Towards Inclusive Education." *Australian Journal of Teacher Education* 38, no. 4 (2013): 129–143.

Davern, L. "Parents' Perspectives on Personnel Attitudes and Characteristics in Inclusive School Settings: Implications for Teacher Preparation Programs." *Teacher Education and Special Education* 22 (1999): 165–182.

Delano, M. E., Keefe, L., and Perner, D. "Personnel Preparation: Recurring Challenges and the Need for Action to Ensure Access to General Education." *Research and Practice for Persons with Severe Disabilities* 33, no. 4 (2008): 232–240.

Elementary Education: Early Childhood/English as a Second Language. Madison: University of Wisconsin-Madison, 2022. https://guide.wisc.edu/undergraduate/education/curriculum-instruction/elementary-education-bse/elementary-education-early-childhood-english-second-language-bse/.

Employer Survey: Spring 2014. Greeley: University of Northern Colorado. www.unco.edu/education-behavioral-sciences/pdf/employer-survey-principal-c.pdf.

European Agency for Development in Special Needs and Inclusive Education. *Teacher Education for Inclusion: Key Policy Messages*. Odense: European Agency for Development in Special Needs Education, 2011.

Fall 2021 Student Teaching Handbook (EDEL 454). Greeley: University of Northern Colorado, 2021. www.unco.edu/cebs/teacher-education/pdf/edel-454-handbook-f-21c.pdf.

Fender, M. J., and Fiedler, C. "Pre-service Preparation of Regular Educators: A National Survey of Curriculum Content in Introductory Exceptional Children and Youth Courses." *Teacher Education and Special Education* 13 (1990): 203–209.

Feng, Yajing 冯雅静. *Putong jiaoshi zhiqian peiyang zhong 'shijian daoxiang' de ronghe jiaoyu tongshi kecheng goujian yanjiu* 普通教师职前培养中"实践导向"的融合教育通识课程构建研究. Beijing: Beijing Normal University, 2015.

Feng, Yajing 冯雅静, and Wang, Yan 王雁. "Ronghe jiaoyu beijing xia meiguo putong jiaoshi zhiqian peiyang de biange licheng he tezheng." *Chinese Journal of Special Education* 中国特殊教育 no. 1 (2021): 3–9.

Feng, Yajing 冯雅静, Li, Aifen 李爱芬, and Wang, Yan 王雁. "Woguo putong shifan zhuanye ronghe jiaoyu kecheng xianzhuang de diaocha yanjiu" 我国普通师范专业融合教育课程现状的调查研究. *Chinese Journal of Special Education* 中国特殊教育 no. 1 (2016): 9–15, 29.

Feng, Yajing 冯雅静, Zhu, Nan 朱楠, and Wang, Yan 王雁. "Meiguo guojiaxing jiaoshi zhuanye biaozhun zhong ronghe jiaoyu xiangguan yaoqiu tanxi" 美国国家性教师专业标准中融合教育相关要求探析. *Teacher Education Research* 教师教育研究 28, no. 4 (2016): 121–128.

Ferrier-Kerr, J. "Establishing Professional Relationships in Practicum Settings." *Teaching and Teacher Education* 25, no. 6 (2009): 790–797.

Florian, L. "Teacher Education for the Changing Demographics of Schooling: Inclusive Education for Each and Every Learner." In L. Florian and N. Pantić (eds.), *Teacher Education for the Changing Demographics of Schooling: Issues for Research and Practice* (*Inclusive Learning and Educational Equity*, Volume 2), 9–20. Cham: Springer, 2017.

Florian, L. and Linklater, H. "Preparing Teachers for Inclusive Education: Using Inclusive Pedagogy to Enhance Teaching and Learning for All." *Cambridge Journal of Education* 40, no. 4 (2010): 369–386.

Florian, L., and Rouse, M. "The Inclusive Practice Project in Scotland: Teacher Education for Inclusive Education." *Teaching and Teacher Education* 25, no. 4 (2009): 594–601.

Forlin, C., and Chambers, D. "Teacher Preparation for Inclusive Education: Increasing Knowledge but Raising Concerns." *Asia-Pacific Journal of Teacher Education* 39, no. 1 (2011): 17–32.

Forlin, C., and Nguyet, T. D. "A National Strategy for Supporting Teacher Educators to Prepare Teachers for Inclusion." In C. Forlin (ed.), *Teacher Education for Inclusion: Changing Paradigms and Innovative Approaches*, 34–44. London: Routledge, 2010.

Fu, Shuqiong 付淑琼. *Meiguo zhongxiaoxue zhuoyue jiaoshi zhiqian peiyang de zhiliang baozhang jizhi yanjiu* 美国中小学卓越教师职前培养的质量保障机制研究, 88–123. Shanghai: East China Normal University, 2016.

Fullerton, A., Ruben, B. J., and McBride, S., et al. "Evaluation of a Merged Secondary and Special Education Program." *Teacher Education Quarterly* 38 (2011): 45–60.

Ganschow, L., Weber, D. B., and Davis, M. "Pre-service Teacher Preparation for Mainstreaming." *Exceptional Children* 51, no. 1 (1984): 74–76.

Gao, W., and Mager, G. "Enhancing Pre-service Teachers' Sense of Efficacy and Attitudes Toward School Diversity through Preparation: A Case of One US Inclusive Teacher Program." *International Journal of Special Education* 26, no. 2 (2011): 92–107.

General Curriculum and Elementary Education K-6, B. A. Dual Program. Charlotte: University of North Carolina at Charlotte. https://catalog.uncc.edu/prev iew_program.php?catoid=29&poid=7544.

Gettinger, M., Stoiber, K. C., Goetz, D., et al. "Competencies and Training Needs for Early Childhood Inclusion Specialists." *Teacher Education and Special Education* 22 (1999): 41–54.

Grima-Farrell, C. "Mentoring Pathways to Enhancing the Personal and Professional Development of Pre-service Teachers." *International Journal of Mentoring and Coaching in Education* 4 (2015): 255–268.

242 *International Experience in Cultivation of the Competence*

Guidelines for Initial Teacher Education Programmes in Scotland. Edinburgh: General Teaching Council for Scotland, 2018. https://dera.ioe.ac.uk/19281/.

Hartle, H. *Teaching Handicapped Students in the Regular Classroom: State Pre-service Certification Requirements and Program Approval Standards,* 2–5. Washington, DC: American Association of Colleges for Teacher Education, 1982. https://files.eric.ed.gov/fulltext/ED221513.pdf.

He, Juling 何菊玲. *Jiaoshi jiaoyu fanshi yanjiu* 教师教育范式研究, 86. Beijing: Educational Science Publishing House, 2009.

He, Y., and Cooper, J. "Struggles and Strategies in Teaching: Voices of Five Novice Secondary Teachers." *Teacher Education Quarterly* 38, no. 2 (2011): 97–116.

Hornby, G. "Preparing Teachers to Work with Parents and Families of Learners with SEN in Inclusive Schools." In C. Forlin (ed.), *Teacher Education for Inclusion: Changing Paradigms and Innovative Approaches,* 93–101. London: Routledge, 2010.

Interstate Teacher Assessment and Support Consortium (InTASC). *InTASC Model Core Teaching Standards: A Resource for State Dialogue,* 11–19. Washington, DC: Council of Chief State School Officers, 2011. www.ccsso.org/sites/default/files/2017–11/InTASC_Model_Core_Teaching_Standards_2011.pdf.

Jones, S. D., and Messenheimer-Young, T. "Content of Special Education Courses for Pre-service Regular Education Teachers." *Teacher Education and Special Education* 12, no. 4 (1989): 154–159.

Jordan, A., Glenn, C., and McGhie-Richmond, D. "The Supporting Effective Teaching (Set) Project: The Relationship of Inclusive Teaching Practices to Teachers' Beliefs about Disability and Ability, and about Their Roles as Teachers." *Teaching and Teacher Education* 26, no. 2 (2010): 259–266.

Kaplan, I. *Tuijin quanna jiaoshi jiaoyu: changdao zhinan* 推进全纳教师教育：倡导指南, translated by Congman Rao 饶从满, et al., 65. Changchun: Northeast Normal University, 2015.

Kaplan, I., and Lewis, I. *Promoting Inclusive Teacher Education: Curriculum.* UNESCO Office Bangkok and Regional Bureau for Education in Asia and the Pacific, 2013.

Kim, J. "Influence of Teacher Preparation Programmes on Pre-service Teachers' Attitudes Toward Inclusion." *International Journal of Inclusive Education* 15, no. 3 (2011): 355–377.

Kirby, M. "Implicit Assumptions in Special Education Policy: Promoting Full Inclusion for Students with Learning Disabilities." *Child & Youth Care Forum* 46, no. 2 (2016): 175–191.

Kleinhammer-Tramill, J. "An Analysis of Federal Initiatives to Prepare Regular Education Students to Serve Students with Disabilities: Deans' Grants, REGI and Beyond." *Teacher Education and Special Education* 26, no. 3 (2003): 230–245.

Kosnik, C., and Beck, C. *Priorities in Teacher Education: The 7 Key Elements of Pre-service Preparation,* 104. London and New York: Routledge, 2009.

Kozleski, E. B., and Waitoller, F. R. "Teacher Learning for Inclusive Education: Understanding Teaching as a Cultural and Political Practice." *International Journal of Inclusive Education* 14, no. 7 (2010): 655–666.

Kraska, J., and Boyle, C. "Attitudes of Preschool and Primary School Pre-service Teachers Towards Inclusive Education." *Asia-Pacific Journal of Teacher Education* 42, no. 3 (2014): 228–246.

Kurniawati, F., De Boer, A. A., Minnaert, A. E. M. G., et al. "Characteristics of Primary Teacher Cultivation Programmes on Inclusion: A Literature Focus." *Educational Research* 56, no. 3 (2014): 310–326.

Ladson-Billings, G. J. "Is the Team All Right? Diversity and Teacher Education." *Journal of Teacher Education* 56, no. 3 (2005): 229–234.

Lambe, J., and Bones, R. "Student Teachers' Attitudes to Inclusion: Implications for Initial Teacher Education in Northern Ireland." *International Journal of Inclusive Education* 10, no. 6 (2006): 511–527.

Lambe, J., and Bones, R. "The Effect of School-based Practice on Student Teachers' Attitudes Towards Inclusive Education in Northern Ireland." *Journal of Education for Teaching* 33, no. 1 (2007): 99–113.

Lancaster, J., and Bain, A. "The Design of Pre-service Inclusive Education Courses and Their Effects on Self-efficacy: A Comparative Study." *Asia-Pacific Journal of Teacher Education* 38, no. 2 (2010): 117–128.

Laura, M. G. *Preparing Pre-service Teachers for Inclusive Field-based Experience: A Case Study of Field-based Tutoring Experience*. New York: University at Buffalo, State University of New York, 2009.

Liu, Bin 刘斌. *Yingguo quanna jiaoshi zhiqian peiyang de ge'an yanjiu—yi aidingbao daxue weili* 英国全纳教师职前培养的个案研究——以爱丁堡大学为例. Beijing: Beijing Normal University, 2018.

Lombardi, T. P., and Hunka, N. J. "Preparing General Education Teachers for Inclusive Classrooms: Assessing the Process." *Teacher Education and Special Education* 24, no. 3 (2001), 183–197.

Loreman, T., Sharma, U., Earle, C., et al. "The Development of an Instrument for Measuring Pre-service Teachers' Sentiments, Attitudes and Concerns about Inclusive Education." *International Journal of Special Education* 22, no. 2 (2007): 150–159.

Majoko, T. "Mainstream Early Childhood Education Teacher Preparation for Inclusion in Zimbabwe." *Early Child Development and Care* 187, no. 11 (2017): 1649–1665.

Male, D. B. "The Impact of a Professional Development Programme on Teachers' Attitudes Towards Inclusion." *Support for Learning* 26, no. 4 (2011): 182–186.

McCray, E. D., and McHatton, P. A. "Less Afraid to Have Them in My Classroom: Understanding Pre-service General Educators' Perceptions about Inclusion." *Teacher Education Quarterly* 38, no. 4 (2011): 135–155.

Miller, P. S., and Stayton, V. D. "Blended Interdisciplinary Teacher Preparation in Early Education and Intervention: A National Study." *Topics in Early Childhood Special Education* 18 (1998): 49–58.

Mueller, M., and Hindin, A. "An Analysis of the Factors That Influence Pre-service Elementary Teachers' Developing Dispositions about Teaching All Children." *Issues in Teacher Education* 20, no. 1 (2011): 17–34.

Neville, R. D., Makopoulou, K., and Hopkins, W. G. "Effect of an Inclusive Physical Education (IPE) Training Workshop on Trainee Teachers' Self-Efficacy." *Research Quarterly for Exercise and Sport* 91, no. 1 (2019): 1–13.

Ni, Pingping 倪萍萍, and Zan, Fei 昝飞. "Guowai zhiqian ronghe jiaoyu jiaoshi peiyang moshi jiqi dui woguo de qishi" 国外职前融合教育教师培养模式及其对我国的启示. *Journal of Schooling Studies* 基础教育 12, no. 1 (2015): 93–99.

Nketsia, W., and Saloviita, T. "Pre-service Teachers' Views on Inclusive Education in Ghana." *Journal of Education for Teaching* 39, no. 4 (2013): 429–441.

Nowacek, E. J., and Blanton, L. P. "A Pilot Project Investigating the Influence of a Collaborative Methods Course on Pre-service Elementary Education Teachers." *Teacher Education and Special Education* 19, no. 4 (1996): 298–312.

O'Neill, S. C. "Preparing Pre-service Teachers for Inclusive Classrooms: Does Completing Coursework on Managing Challenging Behaviours Increase Their

244   *International Experience in Cultivation of the Competence*

Classroom Management Sense of Efficacy?" *The Australasian Journal of Special Education* 40, no. 2 (2016): 117–140.

Pedersen, S. J., Cooley, P. D., and Hernandez, K. "Are Australian Pre-service Physical Education Teachers Prepared to Teach Inclusive Physical Education?" *Australian Journal of Teacher Education* 39, no. 8 (2014): 53–62.

Pijl, S. J. "Preparing Teachers for Inclusive Education: Some Reflections from the Netherlands." *Journal of Research in Special Educational Needs* 10, no. 1 (2010): 197–201.

Professional Graduate Diploma in Education (PGDE) Primary. Edinburgh: The University of Edinburgh. www.ed.ac.uk/education/graduate-school/taught-degrees/pgde/primary.

Pugach, M., and Blanton, L. "A Framework for Conducting Research on Collaborative Teacher Education." *Teaching and Teacher Education* 25 (2009): 575–582.

Pugach, M. C. "What Do We Know about Preparing Teachers to Work with Students with Disabilities?" In M. Cochran-Smith, and K. Zeichner (eds.), *Studying Teacher Education: The Report of the AERA Panel on Research and Teacher Education*, 549–590. Mahwah, NJ: Lawrence Erlbaum, 2005.

Purdue, K., Gordon-Burns, D., and Gunn, A., et al. "Supporting Inclusion in Early Childhood Settings: Some Possibilities and Problems for Teacher Education." *International Journal of Inclusive Education* 13, no. 8 (2009): 805–815.

Rakap, S., Cig, O., and Parlak-Rakap, A. "Preparing Preschool Teacher Candidates for Inclusion: Impact of Two Special Education Courses on Their Perspectives." *Journal of Research in Special Educational Needs* 17, no. 2 (2017): 98–109.

Rayner, C., and Allen, J. M. "Using Online Video-recorded Interviews to Connect the Theory and Practice of Inclusive Education in a Course for Student Teachers." *The Australasian Journal of Special Education* 37, no. 2 (2013): 107–124.

Romero-Contreras, S., Garcia-Cedillo, I., Forlin, C., et al. "Preparing Teachers for Inclusion in Mexico: How Effective Is This Process?" *Journal of Education for Teaching* 39, no. 5 (2013): 509.

Romi, S., and Leyser, Y. "Exploring Inclusion Pre-service Training Needs: A Study of Variables Associated with Attitudes and Self-efficacy Beliefs." *European Journal of Special Needs Education* 21, no. 1 (2006): 85–105.

Rouse, M. "Reforming Initial Teacher Education: A Necessary But Not Sufficient Condition for Developing Inclusive Practice." In C. Forlin (ed.), *Teacher Education for Inclusion: Changing Paradigms and Innovative Approaches*, 47–55. Abingdon: Routledge, 2010.

Sharma, U. "Changing Pre-service Teachers' Beliefs to Teach in Inclusive Classrooms in Victoria, Australia." *Australian Journal of Teacher Education* 37, no. 10 (2012): 53–66.

Sharma, U., and Nuttal, A. "The Impact of Training on Pre-service Teacher Attitudes, Concerns, and Efficacy Towards Inclusion." *Asia-Pacific Journal of Teacher Education* 44, no. 2 (2015): 142–155.

Sharma, U., and Sokal, L. "The Impact of a Teacher Education Course on Pre-service Teachers' Beliefs about Inclusion: An International Comparison." *Journal of Research in Special Educational Needs* 15, no. 4 (2015): 276–284.

Sharma, U., Forlin, C., and Loreman, T. "Impact of Training on Pre-service Teachers' Attitudes and Concerns about Inclusive Education and Sentiments about Persons with Disabilities." *Disability & Society* 23, no. 7 (2008): 773–785.

Sharma, U., Forlin, C., Loreman, T., et al. "Pre-service Teachers' Attitudes, Concerns and Sentiments about Inclusive Education: An International Comparison of the Novice Pre-service Teachers." *International Journal of Special Education* 21 (2006): 80–93.

Sharma, U., Shaukat, S., and Furlonger, B. "Attitudes and Self-efficacy of Pre-service Teachers towards Inclusion in Pakistan." *Journal of Research in Special Educational Needs* 15, no. 2 (2014): 97–105.

Smith, E. R., and Avetisian, V. "Learning to Teach with Two Mentors: Revisiting the 'Two Worlds Pitfall' in Student Teaching." *The Teacher Educator* 46, no. 4 (2011): 335–354.

Smith, J. E., and Schindler, W. J. "Certification Requirements of General Educators concerning Exceptional Pupils." *Exceptional Children* 46 (1980): 430–432.

Sokal, L., and Sharma, U. "Do I Really Need a Course to Learn to Teach Students with Disabilities? I've Been Doing It for Years." *Canadian Journal of Education* 40, no. 4 (2017): 739–760.

Sokal, L., Woloshyn, D., and Funk-Unrau, S. "How Important Is Practicum to Pre-service Teacher Development for Inclusive Teaching? Effects on Classroom Management Efficacy." *Alberta Journal of Educational Research* 59, no. 2 (2013): 285–298.

Song, J., Sharma, U., and Choi, H. "Impact of Teacher Education on Pre-service Regular School Teachers' Attitudes, Intentions, Concerns and Self-efficacy about Inclusive Education in South Korea." *Teaching and Teacher Education* 86 (2019): 1–9.

Sosu, E. M., Mtika, P., and Colucci-Gray, L. "Does Initial Teacher Education Make a Difference? The Impact of Teacher Preparation on Student Teachers' Attitudes Towards Educational Inclusion." *Journal of Education for Teaching* 36, no. 4 (2010): 389–405.

Special Education + Elementary Education Dual Undergraduate Program. Charlotte: University of North Carolina at Charlotte. https://spcd.uncc.edu/sites/spcd.uncc.edu/files/media/SPEL_Dual_Program_Clinical_and_Assessment_Map.pdf.

Specht, J., McGhie-Richmond, D., Loreman, T., et al. "Teaching in Inclusive Classrooms: Efficacy and Beliefs of Canadian Pre-service Teachers." *International Journal of Inclusive Education* 20, no. 1 (2016): 1–15.

Spratt, J., and Florian, L. "Inclusive Pedagogy: From Learning to Action, Supporting Each Individual in the Context of 'Everybody.'" *Teaching and Teacher Education* 49 (2015): 89–96.

Standards for Registration: Mandatory Requirements for Registration with the General Teaching Council for Scotland. Edinburgh: The General Teaching Council for Scotland, 2012. https://dera.ioe.ac.uk/16191/1/standards-for-registration-1212.pdf.

Stites, M. L., Rakes, C. R., Noggle, A. K., et al. "Pre-service Teacher Perceptions of Preparedness to Teach in Inclusive Settings as an Indicator of Teacher Preparation Program Effectiveness." *Discourse and Communication for Sustainable Education* 9, no. 2 (2018): 21–39.

Swain, K. D., Nordness, P. D., and Leader-Janssen, E. "Changes in Pre-service Teacher Attitudes Toward Inclusion." *Preventing School Failure* 56, no. 2 (2012): 75–81.

Deng, Tao 邓涛, "Meiguo jiaoshi jiaoyu renzheng gaige: jigou chongjian he biaozhun zaigou" 美国教师教育认证改革：机构重建和标准再构. *Teacher Education Research* 教师教育研究 28, no. 1 (2016): 110–115.

Taylor, R. W., and Ravic, P. R. "Impacting Pre-service Teachers' Attitudes Toward Inclusion." *Higher Education Studies* 2, no. 3 (2012): 16–23.

246 *International Experience in Cultivation of the Competence*

Tiwari, A., Das, A. K., and Sharma, M. "Inclusive Education a 'Rhetoric' or 'Reality'? Teachers' Perspectives and Beliefs." *Teaching and Teacher Education* 52, no. 12 (2015): 128–136.

Varcoe, L., and Boyle, C. "Pre-service Primary Teachers' Attitudes Towards Inclusive Education." *Educational Psychology* 34, no. 3 (2014): 323–337.

Villegas, A. M., Ciotoli, F., and Lucas, T. "A Framework for Preparing Teachers for Classrooms That Are Inclusive of All Students." In L. Florian and N. Pantić (eds.), *Teacher Education for the Changing Demographics of Schooling: Issues for Research and Practice* (*Inclusive Learning and Educational Equity*, Volume 2), 133–148. Cham: Springer, 2017.

Voss, J. A., and Bufkin, L. J. "Teaching All Children: Preparing Early Childhood Pre-service Teachers in Inclusive Settings." *Journal of Early Childhood Teacher Education* 32, no. 4 (2011): 338–354.

Walker, N., and Laing, S. "Development and Initial Validation of a Questionnaire to Improve Preparation of Pre-service Teachers for Contemporary Inclusive Teaching." *The e-Journal of Business Education & Scholarship of Teaching* 13, no. 2 (2019): 16–34.

Wang, Yan 王雁, Fan, Wenjing 范文静, and Feng, Yajing 冯雅静. "Woguo putong jiaoshi ronghe jiaoyu suyang zhiqian peiyang de sikao ji jianyi" 我国普通教师融合教育素养职前培养的思考及建议. *Journal of Educational Studies* 教育学报 14, no. 6 (2018): 81–87.

Welch, M. "Teacher Education and the Neglected Diversity: Preparing Educators to Teach Students with Disabilities." *Journal of Teacher Education* 47, no. 5 (1996): 355–366.

Wu, Na 巫娜. *Zhongguo–jianada zhongxiaoxue jiaoshi zhuanye biaozhun bijiao yanjiu* 中国—加拿大中小学教师专业标准比较研究. Chongqing: Southwest University, 2018.

Yu, Tingjie 俞婷婕. "Zhuanye quxiang de jueze: aodaliya jiaoshi zhuanye biaozhun yingxiang xia de daxue jiaoshi jiaoyu kecheng shezhi" 专业取向的抉择：澳大利亚教师专业标准影响下的大学教师教育课程设置. *Tsinghua Journal of Education* 清华大学教育研究 37, no. 6 (2016): 46–52.

Zeichner, K. "Xin ziyou zhuyi sixiang he meiguo jiaoshi jiaoyu de biange" 新自由主义思想和美国教师教育的变革. In *"Gongping junheng xiaolü—duoyuan shehui beijing xia de jiaoyu zhengce" guoji xueshu yantaohui huiyi lunwenji* "公平、均衡、效率——多元社会背景下的教育政策"国际学术研讨会会议论文集, 20. Shanghai: The Institute of Schooling Reform and Development, East China Normal University, 2008.

Zhang, J., Wright, A. M., Kim, E., et al. "A Collaborative Journey Toward Inclusive Teacher Education Programs." *Curriculum and Teaching Dialogue* 21, no. 1 (2019): 37–51, 161, 164–165.

Zhao, Wei 赵微. "Yingguo peiyang putong shizi juyou tejiao jineng" 英国培养普通师资具有特教技能. *Chinese Journal of Special Education* 中国特殊教育 no. 4 (1998): 35–38.

Zhou, Jun 周钧. "Dangqian meiguo daxue jiaoyu xueyuan jiaoshi jiaoyu gaige" 当前美国大学教育学院教师教育改革. *Teacher Education Research* 教师教育研究 22, no. 1 (2010): 71–75.

Zundans-Fraser, L., and Lancaster, J. "Enhancing the Inclusive Self-efficacy of Pre-service Teachers through Embedded Course Design." *Education Research International* 52 (2012): 1–8.

6 Research into the Training of the Competence of Teachers in Inclusive Education

Systematic pre-service training, strict examinations and admission systems, and regular in-service training systems are considered indispensable for developing a professional teaching contingent for inclusive education.[1] However, the normal colleges and universities in China cultivate special and general education teachers separately, and there is no requirement of compulsory special education credits for regular normal students, so the majority of student teachers are unable to teach an inclusive class before they enter the teaching profession.[2] In view of this reality, in-service training is particularly important for improving Chinese teachers' inclusive education competence. Many policy documents in China make clear provisions for the in-service training of teachers' inclusive education competence. The *Action Plan for the Development and Improvement of Special Education during the 14th Five-Year Plan Period* requires efforts to promote the provision of special education courses in normal majors, list them as compulsory courses and increase their proportion, incorporate them into the indicator system of professional certification of normal majors, implement the requirement of special education-related content in teacher qualification examination, organize training for all principals and teachers in special education schools and regular schools in the LRC program, and make inclusive education a compulsory part of continuing education for teachers in regular schools.[3] These policy documents have also formed an important basis and institutional guarantee for carrying out in-service training of teachers' inclusive education competence. However, existing documents have not made clear stipulations on many details of the training, such as training objectives, duration, evaluation methods, and funding guarantee. Their operability is weak, and their coercive force needs to be improved. For this reason, the current in-service training that aims at improving teachers' inclusive education competence is not professional enough, and the training effect in practice is unsatisfactory.

To this day, we still cannot help asking: How do Chinese teachers understand and implement inclusive education? How is the training for the improvement of teachers' inclusive education competence carried out? What attempts and explorations have been made by various regions and schools to improve

DOI: 10.4324/9781003432982-7

248   *Research into the Training of the Competence of Teachers*

teachers' inclusive education competence? This chapter will explore these issues.

Listening to the Voice of Teachers: Teachers' Understanding and Practice of Inclusive Education

Phenomena and Problems

Thanks to its moral concept that "education is a basic human right" and its value judgment of "human rights, fairness, and mainstreaming," inclusive education has dominated discourse in the global education field, which has been confirmed and promoted in the form of educational policies or documents in many countries. Under the influence of this trend, a series of policies have been put forward to promote the development of inclusive education in China. In recent years, "inclusive education" has gradually replaced the "LRC program" in relevant national policies with great momentum. This provides strong institutional support for the implementation of inclusive education.

It is noteworthy that, "Inclusion is the policy framework. What is at issue is the interpretation and implementation of inclusion in practice."[4] Since teachers are the most important implementers of inclusive education, whether they can maintain a positive attitude toward the development of inclusive education, and whether they have appropriate professional knowledge and educational awareness to respond to students with special needs directly determine the success or failure of the implementation of inclusive education.[5] However, many studies show that in many countries, including China, most teachers still hold a negative attitude toward inclusive education, as evidenced by their conditional identification, neutral observation, and even caution and suspicion, and very few teachers expressed full recognition and acceptance.[6,7] Moreover, teachers' own "perceived behavioral control (knowledge, ability, and self-efficacy)" is low in inclusive education. As a result, teachers only make "symbolic changes" in teaching practice in inclusive classrooms rather than real innovation in education and teaching.[8] For example, although most teachers have the consciousness of providing support for the classroom learning of special needs students, the support content and measure are very simple.[9] They tend to choose teaching adjustment strategies that are convenient, easy to use, and affective, and that do not affect the majority of ordinary students.[10] However, it is rare to adjust the course content and teaching strategies that require more time and energy as well as strong professional ability.[11] All these lead to an unsatisfactory effect of inclusive education practice, and many special needs students in regular schools even return to special schools.[12]

Thus, it can be seen that inclusive education has not had a substantial impact on teachers' classroom teaching practice but falls into the category of "difficult implementation." Existing studies often directly ask teachers "what difficulties and challenges they encounter in the process of implementing inclusive education," and then make a brief summary to analyze the factors that make implementation difficult. These influencing factors mainly focus on the external environment and teachers themselves. The former involves the performance-based education evaluation system, large class sizes, inadequate teachers, and poor support systems, while the latter touches upon the limited time and energy of individual teachers, lack of professional knowledge and skills, medical views about disability, and so on.[13,14,15] What is more, existing studies to some extent regard teachers as passive implementers of inclusive education and pay insufficient attention to the process of inclusive education implementation. In fact, teachers endow certain meaning and interpretation to inclusive education, and carry out classroom teaching based on it, which affects the final effect of inclusive education. Therefore, our research centers on teachers, follows the qualitative research paradigm, and conducts in-depth interviews with teachers to make clear how they understand and practice the concept or policy of inclusive education. Moreover, we try to explore the reasons and mechanism behind it.

Theoretical Basis

Although the official policy texts form a strong institutional environment for the implementation of inclusive education, the actual effect of the operation in regular schools is not satisfactory. In other words, the institutionalization of inclusive education has not been realized within school organization. Institutional change is one of the core issues in the new institutionalism of sociology. It discusses how to institutionalize organizations.[16,17,18] In recent years, some scholars in China try to take this opportunity to analyze how institutional change occurs and develops in the education field, and provide a new way of thinking to explain the difficulties in inclusive education implementation from the organizational perspective.[19,20] But how the system affects the process of school-wide activities has not been fully revealed. Generally speaking, this is related to the theoretical deficiency of the new institutionalism of sociology.

In addition to institutional change, the new institutionalism of sociology also pays attention to the elements and types of institutions, the influence and mechanism of institutions on organizational structure, and the institutional environment that affects organization.[21] This school of institutionalism has expanded the connotation of institutional analysis and focused on the role of meaning and culture in institutional change, to some extent breaking the complete restriction of the structural elements of old institutionalism on individual behaviors. But it still sees "people" in organizations as passive carriers and recipients of meaning.[22,23] In fact, institutional change is not only influenced by the external environment since its actual operation depends on the meaning construction of the active individuals within the organization and their corresponding actions.[24] Therefore, it is necessary to explore the micro basis of institutional operation.[25,26] In view of this, this research tries to bring the "people" in the organization back into the field of institutional analysis, that is, regular school teachers are invited in the capacity of the subject of action to

250 *Research into the Training of the Competence of Teachers*

explain how they understand and practice inclusive education, thus presenting the individual meaning construction and coping strategies as well as the operational institution generated on this basis. This is expected to provide a new perspective for analysis of the difficult implementation of inclusive education.

Research Method

This research focuses on what kind of meaning and understanding teachers endow to the policy of inclusive education, then what kind of actions they take, and finally what kind of inclusive education form they construct in practice. This is a process in line with the qualitative research paradigm that lays emphasis on meaning, interpretation, and subjectivity. To explore and understand meaning is the fundamental way for qualitative research to probe into social phenomena, and also the focus and key of qualitative research.[27] Therefore, this research adopts the meaning–interpretation-oriented qualitative research method to answer the questions.

Participants

Qualitative research follows the optimal principle of "typical and rich connotation"[28] when selecting cases to condense the required information to the greatest extent. In this research, teachers were selected to participate in the research from the districts where inclusive education was performed well in Beijing and Shanghai through purposive sampling and convenience sampling. Specifically, with the assistance of the principals of the special education resource centers in Haidian District of Beijing and Changning District of Shanghai, the researchers got in touch with the administrators of the schools that had carried out inclusive education in the districts, and invited the teachers who were undertaking the LRC program. Finally, a total of 11 teachers were selected as participants, as shown in Table 6.1. Working at four different primary and secondary schools, they differed in age, teaching years, subject, and so on, but all of them had been working in inclusive settings for more than two years. They had basically formed a stable understanding of inclusive education with personal characteristics, and could provide rich and detailed information.

Data Collection and Analysis

The semi-structured in-depth interview method is used for data collection. On the premise of following the research theme closely, more abundant themed information is excavated. The questions mainly involve (1) What kind of obstacles do special needs students have? What characteristics and manifestations do they have? (2) How to solve the problems of special needs students? (3) How do you understand the policies related to inclusive education? (4) How do you view inclusive education? (5) What adjustments have been made for special needs students in the actual teaching process? How does it work? (6) How to

Table 6.1 Information on Participants

Participant (teacher)	Gender	Age	City and school	Number of years teaching	Number of years engaging in inclusive education and categories of their disabled students	Subject	Concurrent post
Lin	Male	>35	Shanghai XJ Secondary School	22	Three years Intellectual disability, autism.	Math	Class tutor
Ni	Female	>35	Shanghai XJ Secondary School	24	Two years ADHD.	English	Class tutor, grade team leader
Zhu	Female	>35	Shanghai XJ Secondary School	17	Three years Dyslexia.	Chinese	—
Yang	Male	>35	Shanghai XJ Secondary School	25	Two years Intellectual disability.	English	—
Xu	Female	>35	Shanghai HM Primary School	20	Four years Autism.	English	—
Jiang	Female	>35	Shanghai HM Primary School	22	Four years Autism.	Math	—
Zhao	Female	30	Beijing QH No. 1 Primary School	8	Four years Autism.	Math, Chinese	Class tutor
Niu	Female	34	BY Affiliated Primary School	12	Two years Autism.	Chinese, math	Class tutor
Zheng	Female	26	BY Affiliated Primary School	4	Four years Autism, ADHD.	Music	—
Wang	Female	34	BY Affiliated Primary School	12	Seven years Intellectual disability, autism, physical impairment.	Fine arts	—
Zhou	Female	>35	BY Affiliated Primary School	20	19 years Hearing impairment, intellectual disability, autism, physical disability.	English	—

252　*Research into the Training of the Competence of Teachers*

deal with the confusions and challenges encountered in the process of putting the concept of inclusive education into practice? The interviews with 11 teachers lasted from 40 to 65 minutes, and were recorded with the consent of the interviewees. The interviews were made in a spare conference room or psychological counseling room in a quiet and private environment.

After anonymous processing, all the interview data were analyzed by using the coding method of grounded theory and the MAXQDA18.0 software. The whole process was completed jointly by two researchers, and the credibility was improved through peer check. In the open coding stage, the interview text was carefully read and coded line by line, and a tentative coding scheme was preliminarily defined. Then axial coding was carried out to select the most representative or most frequent initial codes to classify, integrate and organize a large number of data, and thus develop analytic categories. The continuous comparison method was used through the whole process to make continuous comparison among data and categories, and constantly modify the analytic categories to improve the reliability of data analysis. Finally, we got seven core categories, and analyzed their attributes and dimensions. In the thematic coding phase, the possible relationships among various categories were identified and rewoven together to bring forth a new theme. The coding process is described in Table 6.2.

Research Findings: Sketch of Teachers' Understanding and Practice of Inclusive Education

Implementation of inclusive education depends on front-line teachers in regular schools.[29,30] How do they view inclusive education and do they agree that they play a decisive role in its implementation, or even decide the success or failure of inclusive education?[31] In the actual teaching process, teachers interpret inclusive education based on their own cognitive experience, and generate unique understanding and practice it accordingly.

Teachers' Understanding of Inclusive Education

It is found that although most teachers agree and affirm that inclusive education is to some extent beneficial to the social development of special needs students, when it comes to the implementation of inclusive education in the classroom, few teachers can really accept it, and they are more inclined to explain their views and understanding of inclusive education from the negative side, showing a cautious and reserved attitude.

"GOOD FOR PARENTS OF SPECIAL NEEDS STUDENTS": INCLUSIVE EDUCATION IS AN OPTION TO AVOID STIGMATIZATION

In the interviews, many teachers agreed that inclusive education did provide parents with more options for the placement of their children. But in the process

Table 6.2 Some Examples of Coding Process

Level 3: Thematic coding	Level 2: Axial coding	Level 1: Open Coding			Source materials (excerpts)
		Category	Attributes and dimensions	Labeling	
Inclusive practice	Formalized teaching adjustment	Pursuit of efficiency	Ensure normal teaching: primary – secondary.	Completing normal teaching assignments. Considering normal teaching time and schedule.	"If he spends a few more minutes, I will not be able to finish the heavy teaching task," said Niu. Q: "Have you made any teaching adjustments for this child in your class? What kind of methods do you use?" A: "Not much, because of time and schedule," said Zhou.
			Class average score: high – low.	Not affecting the class average score.	"As a LRC student, his score is excluded from the class average," Ni Hongmin said.
		Teaching adjustment	Knowledge objective: having – not having.	Having no requirements on knowledge and study.	"No requirement on knowledge and study is made for them," said Niu.
			Teaching requirements: high – low.	Answering simple questions.	"Some simple questions are set for him to answer," said Jiang.
		Formulation and implementation of individualized education plans (IEPs)	Collaboration in IEP formulation: having – not having.	Teachers make individualized educational plans.	Q: "Are the plans made by the English, math, and Chinese teachers together?" A: "No, separately," said Xu.
			IEP implementation: Substantial – formalistic.	Formalized documentation.	"This routine is being done, but the effect is still up for debate. It is more formalistic," said Yang.

254 *Research into the Training of the Competence of Teachers*

of communicating with parents, they found that some parents strongly denied their children's intellectual or developmental impairment. Ms Zhao said: "Our class has a student with mild intellectual disability, but he has no certificate because his parents deny his intellectual disability. Instead, they think he is very smart, able to learn everything, they insisted on sending their child to a regular school." On the one hand, these parents want their children to socialize with typically developing peers in the mainstream environment to improve their social adaptability and, at the same time, receive higher quality education in regular classes. On the other hand, this is done in order to avoid their children from being "labeled" in special schools. Mr Lin explained: "Parents of the special needs students may feel that inclusive education is more appropriate. Thus, they avoid sending their children to a special school because this might bring a label to their children, or there might be discrimination or something else that they couldn't accept."

Although teachers understand the parents' choice, they think it is not good for the development of special needs students. As Mr Yang said, "In the education system of regular schools, normal teaching, after all, is still the major task." Teachers have to give priority to the overall interests of the majority of students in the class, and it is difficult to provide special attention or individualized services for a very few special needs students.

"UNABLE TO LEARN MUCH IN CULTURAL COURSES, THEY'D BETTER GO TO A SPECIAL SCHOOL"

In actual teaching, teachers will always classify students based on their own judgment of their ability or learning potential, and carry out teaching practice acordingly. According to Hermina's study in 2014, teachers generally divide students into "normal students" and "not normal students." The former includes students with strong learning ability and those at average level. They can solve their own problems under the general guidance of teachers. In particular, as for those students at average level, because they are likely to improve their marks through hard work, teachers devote most time and energy to them. The latter refers to students who have weak ability in learning and often need additional support, time, teaching strategies, and course adjustment or learning materials, usually holding a diagnostic certificate.[32] These students are found unable to learn course content that requires higher order thinking. Some students' cognitive level could not even meet the requirements of daily communication. Therefore, teachers concluded that it was difficult for them to achieve academic success. Just as Ms Jiang said, "In the cultural courses of a regular school, he could not learn anything because his intellectual level is not up to standard." "So in terms of knowledge and learning, we may lodge no requirements on them," Ms Niu added, "we devote less time and energy to them." Since special schools have professional teachers and curriculum, teachers generally believe that special needs students can get more attention and more appropriate development opportunities if they attend special schools. Ms Zheng said:

> I still think it is more appropriate for them to go to special schools. Having received relevant training, teachers in special schools have a better understanding of the problems and emotional responses of special needs students, and can take corresponding countermeasures. The content they teach is more suitable for special needs students to survive in society.

THEY CAUSE NEGATIVE INTERFERENCE WITH CLASSROOM DISCIPLINE AND CLASS ATMOSPHERE

Given the large class size, teachers especially pursue "orderly" classroom discipline because this can reduce interference in the teaching process, and successfully achieve the teaching objectives. But the presence of special needs students seems to be a challenge to classroom order. Teachers hold that special needs students are subject to their own physical and mental development, so their self-control ability is relatively weak, and they are readily show emotional and behavioral problems in class, which will interfere with the learning of other students as well as teaching in the class. As Ms Zheng noted:

> In class, sometimes he suddenly starts to cry, but I don't know why. When the child is absent, the class is quiet, and the students are attentive. However, when the child lies on a stool or puts his feet in the air in the back of the classroom, his act would distract the normal children and affect their learning process.

Some special needs students with aggressive behaviors often have physical conflict with other students, affecting the harmony of the class atmosphere and even the personal safety of other students. As Ms Jiang said: "He has no idea how to play with others. He just finds it funny to hit someone and then be chased. When playing together, boys often tend to have physical conflict." It is a series of emotional and behavioral problems of special needs students that make them a potential "order threat" to the class. This is also one of the important reasons why teachers cannot really recognize and accept inclusive education.

"SOMETHING THAT HAS TO BE DONE" AND "EXTRA WORKLOAD"

From the individual point of view, teachers threw into doubt the significance and value of inclusive education. The heavy teaching workload has made them miserable and means they lack enough time and energy to learn the relevant content of inclusive education. Although they lack the necessary knowledge

256 *Research into the Training of the Competence of Teachers*

and skills to carry out inclusive education, they have to comply with this requirement under the pressure of the external institutional environment. A teacher argued in an interview that inclusive education is "something that has to be done." "There is no preparation or a lack of preparation. Just like the school that must accept these children, we must teach them," said Ms Zheng. Based on rational considerations, teachers think that implementation of inclusive education will not only greatly increases their workload, but also produces no continuous positive effect on their own education and teaching. Therefore, "it is not worth spending too much energy on it." Ms Zhu continued:

> In the face of such a special child, I find him different from other children in learning rhythm, learning content and other aspects, greatly increasing our workload and pressure. After all, I teach two classes but meet only one child of this kind. In a new class in future, I may not meet such a child since the probability is fairly small.

Usually, teaching and research is rarely designed specifically for special needs students. "Our teaching and research is aimed at typically developing students, because the special needs students are relatively few, and they belong to vulnerable groups, not receiving much attention from society. It is impossible to specially conduct research for one or two such children," Ms Zhao noted. Moreover, it is impossible for them to devote time to the training of inclusive education. Ms Jiang said:

> If we attend a training, it must be for most children, i.e. the training for general education. Since I teach math, I definitely will go to a professional training in math. I won't take any time to attend a training just for one or two special needs students in my class.

In the interviews, teachers repeatedly emphasized their identity as regular school teachers to distinguish themselves from special school teachers and inclusive education teachers. They regard promoting the growth and development of special needs students as the responsibility of the students' parents and special education personnel rather than their own. And, in practice, they not only expect the parents to actively seek professional support and provide effective information to deal with the problems of special needs students, but also insist that some parents should shoulder the responsibility of accompanying their children in school and improve weaknesses of their children in family life. When a special needs student has a problem in the class, teachers will at first turn to the resource teacher or the teacher in charge of special education in the school, believing that the special education personnel should take the main responsibility of educating the special needs students. "After all, we are not special education teachers, and it should be undertaken by professionals who can provide them with more professional guidance," Mr Lin expressed. In addition, the regional special education center will also assign itinerant tutors to the schools to provide one-on-one "pull-out" tutoring or rehabilitation training for special needs students in resource rooms on a weekly basis. This kind of "pull-out" service further strengthens teachers' understanding that "teaching special needs students is the responsibility of special education personnel."

Teachers' Practice of Inclusive Education

In practice, teachers have to make a series of "formalized" adjustments based on the above understanding to meet the requirements of the inclusive education policy, resulting in the fact that the real practice of inclusive education is different from that described in the concept and policy.

EDUCATIONAL GOAL: TO GUIDE THEM IN BEHAVIOR RATHER THAN KNOWLEDGE LEARNING

In the eyes of teachers, special needs students, limited by their cognitive level, cannot achieve the teaching objectives of regular schools. Thus, teachers generally have no expectations for their studies, just requiring them not to interfere with classroom discipline and teaching order. As Ms Xu said: "My goal is not high, and my requirement for them is to behave well in class. Even if they can't control their thoughts in class, they should at least sit there obediently." Only two teachers said they gave special consideration to special needs students when making teaching plans, but most teachers did not set clear goals for them in knowledge learning. On the one hand, the learning content for special needs students is mainly based on transcription and retelling and, on the other hand, they are only asked to participate in some simple explicit activities (such as group activities and collective reading) in class to have a pleasant experience. "As for him, it's OK to just feel the joy of English," Ms Zhou said.

Teachers hold that, rather than knowledge learning, it is more important to help special needs students learn normative behavior and develop basic living habits to adapt to school life. Mr Lin noted:

> We mainly train his normative habits … . For example, he can walk into the right classroom, go to the bathroom during break, and even walk to his seat as soon as the bell rings. There are few objectives in mastery of knowledge of them, and the main objective is to adapt them to school life.

TEACHING ACTIVITIES: FORMAL ADJUSTMENT RATHER THAN SUBSTANTIVE INNOVATION

The technical environment inside regular schools has imposed requirements on teaching efficiency, so that teachers regard the average score of the class, the students' promotion rate, and the high school entrance exam pass rate as the "lifeline" and "top priority" of the class. Teachers face the burden of teaching,

258   *Research into the Training of the Competence of Teachers*

class management, and school instruction, coupled with the frustration of investing time and energy in special needs students but not getting matched feedback. Therefore, after rational calculation based on profit and loss, inclusive education has to be carried out in a selective way.[33] First of all, teachers make simple and easy adjustments for special needs students, including designating seats for special needs students, specially setting simple questions for them, assigning less homework, reducing the difficulty of tasks, and providing opportunities for them to participate in classroom teaching as much as possible. Nevertheless, teachers' classroom teaching changes are all symbolic structural changes,[34] rather than pedagogical innovations in teaching methods and strategies. Secondly, in the process of making individualized education plans (IEPs), there is a lack of necessary communication and collaboration between teachers of different disciplines, and between teachers and professionals of special education guidance centers. Moreover, IEP mostly appears in various archival materials in the form of traceism. As Mr Yang said: "This routine is being done, but the effect is poor since it is more formalist. Everyone is very busy. For such a special student, one may get half or even no results with double the effort. So we just try to manage it."

ENERGY INPUT: "GIVING PRIORITY TO TYPICALLY DEVELOPING CHILDREN"

Almost all the teachers repeatedly mentioned in our interviews that their primary task was to complete normal teaching, so they would focus their energy on typically developing students, and fail to take into account the needs of special needs students in the teaching process. "Since my time and energy are limited, I must first take care of the typically developing children, and then pay attention to [the special needs student] as much as possible," Ms Zhu noted. The following teachers gave clear expression to their intensive teaching arrangement.

Ms Niu said:

We already have a heavy teaching task. Our Chinese course adopts the textbooks published by Beijing Normal University. In a semester of 20 weeks, we have only 18 weeks to teach after deducting two weeks of break. We have a total of 16 units to teach, containing very much content. So it is impossible for me to make special adjustments for him in class.

"Our class has 37 members. In a 40-minute lesson, if each student is taken care of for one minute, the 37 minutes will soon be over. So if he needs to be given a few more minutes, I won't be able to finish the teaching task," said Ms Wang.

Due to limited time and energy, teachers only provide discrete guidance to special needs students when other students do not need guidance during self-study in the classroom. "During group activities, sometimes I would go to their group and talk to him individually," said Ms Xu. It can be seen that extra

Research into the Training of the Competence of Teachers 259

attention and individual counseling are given to special needs students on the premise of not affecting typically developing students and normal teaching progress.

Analysis and Discussion

Generally speaking, the concept of inclusive education and policy initiatives have not been taken for granted by teachers in regular schools, nor have they formed a powerful effect. From the perspective of understanding, teachers still hold a negative attitude and view of inclusive education. The vast majority of teachers adhere to a practical "partial inclusion" orientation, and regard formalized adjustment as the biggest change in the teaching process. In the end, teachers construct a "symbolic" inclusive education in practice which is far from the ideal implementation. So why do teachers have such an understanding? What is the mechanism of action behind this? This research thinks that the sociological theory of new institutionalism can provide an "effective prescription" to explain this phenomena.

Behind the Understanding: Cultural–Cognitive Schema Shared by Teachers

According to the theory of new institutionalism, people's understanding process is shaped by the cultural framework in which they reside, and some categories, schemas, and beliefs in people's minds influence their choice of behavior. An individual is not even aware that he or she has made a choice, but only that what he or she has done is "taken for granted." When actors have a shared understanding of a particular situation, it means that they will give their behavior a deeper cultural legitimacy than an institutional interpretation of rules and norms. In this research, a set of shared cognitive schema owned by the teacher group enables the teachers to make the above explanation and understanding, which further affects their implementation behavior and makes them take it for granted, even beyond the influence of inclusive education policy. This shared cognitive schema is highlighted in the following three aspects.

AN IDENTITY SCHEMA: "I AM A REGULAR SCHOOL TEACHER, NOT A SPECIAL EDUCATION TEACHER"

In the interviews, teachers repeatedly emphasized their identity as a regular school teacher rather than a special education teacher. With such an identity schema, it is natural for them to identify what is their duty, what they should do, and what is an externally imposed task. For teachers in regular schools, the inclusive education promoted by administrative power is such an externally imposed task, and teaching special needs students is regarded as non-regular work. As a result, even regional special education centers that provide teachers with training opportunities and support resources are often turned away

260   *Research into the Training of the Competence of Teachers*

because teachers are already overwhelmed by the burden of teaching, class management, and various assignments. This understanding directly affects the implementation of inclusive education by teachers. In the process of classroom teaching, they will try to pay attention to special needs students only after taking care of the majority of students.

EXAM-ORIENTED EDUCATION SCHEMA: "PRAGMATISM OF ATTENDING A HIGHER SCHOOL" AND "PUTTING SCORES FIRST"

The pursuit of high scores and promotion rate are undoubtedly the most common value choice for teachers in the "world of selection by exam."[35] In this research, this schema is embodied in teachers' special attention to teaching time and their emphasis on and control of teaching order and classroom discipline. Under the pressure of exam-oriented education, teachers compete for time and resources to teach academic knowledge, complete teaching progress, and strive to improve students' results. In addition, facing the reality of a large class size, teachers' emphasis on orderly classroom discipline is also an essential element to ensure the progress and quality of teaching.[36] The exam-oriented schema makes teachers automatically and resolutely set implementation of inclusive education against the teaching quality and average score of the class. Teachers mentioned many times in our interviews that the implementation of inclusive education would inevitably involve a lot of time and energy, which would affect teaching progress. A series of emotional and behavioral problems exhibited by special needs students have a negative impact on other students' listening, which further affects the quality of classroom teaching and lowers the average score of the class. This echoes the findings of many previous studies, that is, teachers encounter many difficulties in the implementation of inclusive education, such as the frequently mentioned "lack of time," "large class size," and "existing education evaluation system," which reflects the influence of exam-oriented schema rooted in teachers' minds. As a result, teachers spend less time and energy on special needs students but focus on improving scores and promotion rates for the majority of typically developing students.

VIEW OF SEEING SPECIAL NEEDS STUDENTS AS DEFECTIVE

It is not difficult to find that most teachers still hold a view of seeing special needs students as defective. With this view, teachers believe that special needs students have poor cognitive ability and can hardly achieve good academic results. Therefore, they have no expectations for the study of special needs students and any other teaching-related activities for them, but just try their best to make them participate and feel happy. It is even rarer to design personalized courses or make special adjustments in teaching content and strategies according to the characteristics and needs of special needs students. Instead, teachers think that developing the adaptability of special needs students should be given top priority, so they will be more involved in taking care of those students, managing and controlling their behaviors. In their eyes, special school is a more appropriate form of placement for special needs students.

Behind the Cultural–Cognitive Schema: The Game between Two Sets of Institutional Logic

The above cognitive assumption and behavioral habit that teachers themselves take for granted actually reflect the power of institutional logic behind.[37] "Institutional logic" refers to a set of belief systems that control behaviors in a specific organizational domain, which provides guidance for the participants of the organization on how to carry out actions.[38] All organizations in an organizational domain have their formal and informal values, rules, customs, and interests, which structure and model various organizational behaviors with different mechanisms of action.[39] In the complex organizational domain of society, schools have gradually formed a self-interested institutional logic of pursuing promotion rate to survive and develop,[40] emphasizing competition, examination, selection, and comparison. At the same time, as the government advocates inclusive education, schools and teachers are also faced with another set of inclusive education institutional logic that emphasizes "respect for human rights, striving for fairness, tolerating differences, and appreciating diversity." These two sets of institutional logic have different value orientations and even contradict each other, but they coexist in schools.

However, as Lu Naigui said,[41] the institutional logic of these two dissonant value orientations differs in status. As a dependent policy, the existence of inclusive education depends on whether it can avoid serious contradiction with the requirements of "expressionism" in schools. In other words, the new institutional logic of inclusive education has not shaken the original institutional logic of schools. This is because, in the view of new institutionalism, the formation of institutions needs to rely on the three pillars—regulation, norm, and culture-cognition—at the same time.[42] A new institution must conform to the corresponding institutional environment and organizational culture, and accord with the social rules recognized and internalized by the organization and its members.[43] Without the support of the cultural-cognitive model, the formation of a new institution will be fairly difficult if it only changes the policy provisions and ethical and moral norms. Therefore, although our government and education administration vigorously advocate inclusive education, and its importance and value concept have been unanimously recognized by schools and their teachers, teachers only regard it as an administrative order, so it has not been internalized in the minds of school teachers to integrate into the cognitive schema that guides their teaching behavior and understanding of educational phenomena. The value orientation of inclusive education, which pays attention to individual differences, emphasizes diversified teaching, and pursues popularization of education, is rejected by the original institution logic of schools. The selection function of school education deeply rooted in

262   *Research into the Training of the Competence of Teachers*

the people's heart and the traditional talent cultivation view[44] have combined to throw the inclusive education system into a crisis of "legitimacy" to be recognized by the public. As a result, the institutional logic of pursuing promotion rate firmly occupies a dominant position in the school organization, and is internalized into a shared understanding framework by teachers in the school organization, which has gained solid legitimacy and become the basis for teachers' practice.

Coping Strategy of School Organizations and Teachers: "Policy–Practice Loose Coupling"

Although the concept of inclusive education has not been internalized into the cognitive schema of teachers, inclusive education required by policy is still exerting influence on teachers. Inclusive education has been developing for nearly 40 years and gradually becoming an official expression in China. It has been advocated and carried out within the framework of educational policies, affecting teachers' perception and belief. Many studies have shown that teachers are more supportive of inclusive education policies ethically. However, in the face of the actual difficulties in the implementation process, they show a cautious and unacceptable attitude toward inclusive education, but are forced by global trends and growing administrative pressures to implement it.[45] The requirements of the external institutional environment and the internal technical environment of the organization are often inconsistent. If the legitimacy-related pressure and efficiency are contradictory, what are the organizational countermeasures? According to John W. Meyer, an important strategy for organizations is to separate internal operation from organizational structure,[46] that is, organizations are more inclined to comply with the requirements of institutional logic on the surface, but consciously adopt the "policy–practice" loose coupling strategy in daily operation to meet their internal demands for efficiency.[47] The "formalized" adjustment made by teachers in practice in this research is such a strategy, and its purpose is to ensure that teaching performance and promotion rate are not "disturbed." The inclusive education system has brought symbolic changes rather than substantial significance to the internal operation of schools. This phenomenon has also been fully verified in many foreign studies. For example, Ashwini Tiwari and his partners found that the inclusive official discourse had little effect on the classroom teaching practice of ordinary Indian teachers. Teachers only accept the inclusive education policy theoretically and show "ritual compliance," but it is not necessarily translated into practice. According to the study by Keith Young,[48] primary school teachers in Ireland generally support the value concept of inclusive education, but their practice does not show the initiative to implement inclusive education due to the limitations of external factors. They think that the implementation of inclusive education is a distant "utopia." While interviewing teachers in American inclusive classes, some researchers found that although most teachers believed that curriculum adjustment for special needs students was reasonable and effective, they encountered many difficulties in the preparation of alternative materials, assessment, classroom management, and classroom environment construction in the actual multi-level teaching, only adopting those adjustment strategies that do not require a lot of time and effort.[49,50]

In short, inclusive education has become a widely accepted "good" institution due to the strong power of its own values, and has been adopted by different countries under the initiative of international organizations. But so far no country has achieved high-quality and effective inclusive education.[51] It is obvious that inclusive education has become a "rationalized myth."

Conclusion and Suggestions

Within the school organization is a technical environment characterized by the pursuit of promotion rate and the emphasis on competition, examination, and selection. Teachers who have worked therein for a long time have developed a set of shared cultural–cognitive schema under the influence of this institutional cultural framework, and, based on this, they can understand and implement inclusive education policy. This set of cognitive schema is so deeply rooted in the minds of teachers that it deconstructs the legitimate basis of the inclusive education system from the cultural–cognitive perspective. In practice, teachers comply with the requirements of inclusive education policy and recognize the benefits of inclusive education for the social development of special needs students. However, in daily teaching, they consciously adopt the "policy–practice" loose coupling strategy, as evidenced by the low expectations for special needs students, formalized adjustment, and devotion of most of their time and energy to the majority of students to ensure student achievement and promotion rate. As a result, a symbolic inclusive education system that is completely different from that in the policy discourse has taken shape in schools.

But this does not mean that inclusive education will never "land." Based on existing research findings, we believe that the development of inclusive education can be further promoted from the following angles. First, in the process of pre-service education, it is advisable to pay close attention to the cultivation of the competence of teachers in inclusive education, help them correctly understand the concept of inclusive education, shape a positive attitude toward inclusive education, and enable them to be competent for future teaching in an inclusive classroom. Efforts should be made to break the long-established binary system of training teachers in special education and general education separately in China, spread the inclusive education concept of "diversity, heterogeneity, and equality" into various aspects of teacher education, encourage teachers to take responsibility for teaching all students, including those with special needs, and form the corresponding identity. In this way, the legitimacy-related crisis of inclusive education can be resolved at the cultural and cognitive level.

264 *Research into the Training of the Competence of Teachers*

Secondly, we should firmly advocate the evaluation concept of "whole-person development," weaken the simple exam-oriented tendency, reduce the conflict between the inclusive education system and the technical environment inside schools, so as to strengthen the coupling degree between inclusive education policy and practice, and replace the formalized adjustment with real innovation in education and teaching. At the same time, it is necessary to speed up the reform for improving the inclusive education-related supporting system, such as course evaluation, the teacher development system, and the development of the professional support system. Teachers who undertake inclusive education should be given practical material rewards, such as extra allowances and subsidies, as stipulated in policy, and also preference in the evaluation of performance and professional titles.

Finally, a supervision, inspection, and accountability mechanism for the implementation of inclusive education should be gradually established and improved, which should be included into school evaluation indicators to dissolve the loose coupling between the policy and practice of inclusive education.

Related Research into Training of the Competence of Teachers in Inclusive Education

Theoretical Research into Teacher Training: Elements and Models of Effective Teacher Training

Teacher training is a critical way to promote the professional development of teachers, and it is also a need of teachers' lifelong learning. Therefore, the Chinese government has attached great importance to teacher training and invested a lot into it. For a long time, the effectiveness of teacher training has been a major concern of all sectors of society, and many scholars are committed to exploring the key links or core elements of effective teacher training. These core elements mainly include "analysis of training needs," "analysis of trainees," "training objectives," "training theme," "training content," "training methods," "training teachers," and "training effect evaluation." Then, what is the role of each of these seven core elements? How are they related to each other? In recent years, some researchers have tried to construct models of effective teacher training to clarify the relationship between the elements. In these models, at the core is the analysis of training needs; in the inner layer is training design, covering training objectives, training courses, and training forms; in the middle layer is the implementation of training, mainly including the analysis of trainees and training teachers; and in the outermost layer is the training effect evaluation, including formative evaluation and summative evaluation.

Among all the elements, analysis of training needs is the core and the starting point of teacher training. It is not only the premise for determining training objectives and designing training courses, but also the basis for

Research into the Training of the Competence of Teachers 265

evaluating training effects.[52] According to the stratification of needs, the in-service training needs can be divided into four categories: social needs, organizational needs, occupational needs, and individual needs. Analysis of social needs is mainly based on the social background of the training program, to answer questions such as what is the social value of the training, and what role it can play in the process of educational reform and development? Analysis of organizational needs centers on the expectations of trainees' working units for the training. Analysis of occupational needs aims to explore the needs of trainees' professional development. Individual needs refer to teachers actively feeling the need for training when they encounter difficulties in teaching.[53] Researchers or training organizers should pay most attention to occupational needs and individual needs to determine the gap between the current situation and the ideal state of teachers' professional competence, so as to effectively narrow the gap between the competence of teachers and post standards.

Next, the training manager should formulate the training objective according to the results of the analysis. Training objective is a description of the expected training results, which aims to answer questions such as what is the training trying to achieve, what changes, improvements, and development are teachers expected to have in the training, and what results will the training program achieve? It is mainly reflected in the three dimensions of knowledge, ability, and understanding and experience, aiming to narrow the gap between the status quo of teachers' own professional competence and the job requirements. In addition, it is important to accurately articulate the objective. The objective statement should be specific and evaluable, usually written with the ABCD (audience, behavior, condition, and degree) method.[54]

In terms of training content, the training manager should set targeted and systematic training courses according to the results of needs analysis and training objective. There is an internal logical relationship between the training course and the training objective. In preparation for the courses, it is advised to organize it from three dimensions: course content, course type, and course logic. The selection of course content should meet the need to arouse students' learning motivation. Course type refers to the course area, covering subject knowledge, conditional knowledge, practical knowledge, and operational skills. Course logic mainly means that the course should be constructed on the basis of students' existing experience, and the organization of course content should encourage trainees to ponder the problems that have bothered them in teaching practice and then find a solution.[55]

With regard to training form, the role of trainees as participants should be given full play. An effective way of training should be based on the grasp of learners' learning rules. It is based on their own experience that teachers understand and accept trainers' views.[56] In view of this characteristic, the training should be more interactive, and provide opportunities for dialogue and cooperation. During current teacher training process, there are rich forms

266 *Research into the Training of the Competence of Teachers*

of interactive participation, including discussion, participation, interaction, case study, group cooperation and so on. Of course, the training form should be selected in accordance with the training content.

In the middle layer of training implementation, it is necessary to analyze the characteristics of the trainees and trainers. For an effective teacher training program, an in-depth analysis of trainees' individual needs should be made.[57] In addition to some background variables (such as the subject, school sector, post, educational background, age, gender, and so on), the most important thing is to analyze the level and stage of the trainees' professional ability and their knowledge structure. The professional development of teachers varies in different stages. Since each stage has its particularity, the training purpose and content change with the stage. Therefore, the teacher training program should take full account of teachers' job requirements and professional development level. Excellent trainers are an important guarantee for effective training, so training managers should strictly select trainers, optimize training resources, and build a multi-subject teacher training contingent. It is of great importance to absorb theoretical experts, practical experts, outstanding front-line teachers, and scientific research experts into the contingent to provide continuous guidance for trainees even after training.[58]

Finally, in the outermost layer of training evaluation, the training manager should pay close attention to the "training effect" and monitor and control training quality throughout the whole process. An evaluation system that comprises formative evaluation, summative evaluation, and post-program evaluation should be constructed to evaluate trainees. Formative evaluation is directed at trainees' classroom performance and in-class work. Summative evaluation includes quantitative evaluation and qualitative evaluation, usually made in the form of analysis of the assignments completed by trainees, demonstration of the skills acquired by them, and reporting of the training results. Post-program evaluation centers on whether trainees can apply what they have learned from the training to classroom teaching, and ultimately improve the performance of their respective school, class, and students.[59]

These elements constitute a training model with close internal links, but in addition to them, external institutional policies and resources should also be included into the training model.[60] Based on these core elements and the training model, this research reviews relevant training studies aimed at improving teachers' inclusive education competence.

Research into Teachers' Needs of Inclusive Education Competence Training

In the process of investigating teachers' needs of in-service training, it is particularly important to select a scientific needs analysis method for data analysis. The two most classic and influential training needs analysis models in the field of management are the OTP model and the performance analysis model. The OTP model emphasizes that training needs can be accurately, systematically, and objectively analyzed only by making an overall analysis of persons, tasks, and organization. Although the performance analysis model is not as influential as the former in literature research, it has a higher status in practical application. It focuses on the gap between expected performance and actual performance, and analyzes the reasons for the gap, so as to specifically analyze training needs. However, originating from the field of commercial training, these two analytical models do not reflect the characteristics of the teaching profession and are not highly applicable to the field of teacher training. Some scholars have realized this problem and put forward specific analysis models for teacher training needs. For example, Yu Xin created the "iceberg model" and the "bow and arrow model."[61] Based on the OTP model and the performance analysis model, Shen Junhong and her partners constructed a "behavior-oriented advanced model of teacher training needs analysis" with new class teachers of primary and secondary schools in Haidian District as examples. This model includes three stages. The task of the first stage is to construct the ideal behavior of teachers in the same position; that of the second stage is to analyze the behavioral gap, investigate the actual behavior of the target group of teachers, and then compare the ideal behavior with the actual behavior; and that of the third stage is to analyze the causes of the behavioral gap and determine whether it can be solved through training, so as to identify training needs. Only when the behavioral gap is caused by the lack of teachers' knowledge and skills, and can be bridged through training at the present stage, can the behavioral gap be transformed into training needs. Finally, training courses are designed according to needs, including course module, module theme, content under the theme, and appropriate training form.[62]

In existing studies of training for the improvement of teachers' inclusive education competence, researchers mostly adopt a simple percentage-based statistical method to conduct a questionnaire survey of the respondents and then make statistical analysis of the data according to the corresponding dimensions, and finally determine the content and form of the teacher training needed by proportion from high to low.[63,64,65] This kind of study simply equates training needs analysis with "training desire" analysis. Training should respond to teachers' desire, a premise to mobilize teachers' enthusiasm to participate in training. However, if the satisfaction of training desire is taken as the value and the only reliance of needs analysis, such analysis may lose its subjectivity and lead to narrow positioning. It will also obscure the leading role of trainers in guiding the professional development of teachers.[66] This is because some teachers may be restricted by their theoretical level, consciousness of professional development, ability in critical reflection, and their own position, unable to effectively identify some of their own objective needs, or ignore the "non-individual" needs.[67] However, in recent years, some researchers who have realized these problems have started to adopt or draw lessons from classic needs analysis models, and comprehensively use a variety of methods to conduct triangulation research, in an attempt to overcome these drawbacks, and dig out the objective and real training needs, and design training courses on this basis.

268   *Research into the Training of the Competence of Teachers*

For example, Du Lingyu investigated the in-service training needs of teachers in an ethnic minority area in Yunnan Province according to the "behavior-oriented advanced model of teacher training needs analysis," and developed a framework for the training courses accordingly. She first determined the ideal inclusive education competence that teachers should have, and then defined the standards for "ideal behaviors" from three dimensions—the knowledge and skills of, and attitude toward, inclusive education. Among them, the dimension of knowledge involves five items: "physical and mental characteristics, development rules and educational needs of children with various types of disabilities," "educational policies, laws and regulations concerning LRC program," "frontier of teaching management and reform and development of inclusive education," "basic introduction to special education and inclusive education," and "special education research methods." The dimension of skills covers nine items, including "specific teaching strategies of inclusive education," "development and adjustment strategies of inclusive education courses and teaching materials," "formulation and implementation of individualized education plans," and "differentiated teaching ability." The dimension of attitude involves two items: "positive inclusive education concept" and "integrated view about education for special needs children." Secondly, the self-designed *Questionnaire on LRC Program Teachers' Needs for In-service Training* was issued to respondents to find out the current situation of LRC program teachers' professional competence and their needs for in-service training in the area. The higher the score of each item in each dimension, the poorer the competence, thus the more training was needed. At the same time, interviews were conducted with teachers and school administrators to gain an in-depth understanding of the development status of teachers' inclusive education competence as well as the development of inclusive education in the area. Thirdly, according to the score of each item in each dimension of the questionnaire, the result was compared with the ideal behavior to find out the behavioral gap. Fourthly, based on in-depth interviews with the teachers, the causes of the behavioral gap were analyzed and then prioritized to see whether they could be solved through training so as to determine the training needs. After that, the training courses were designed according to the needs, specific class hours were set, and the corresponding training methods were given according to the classification and integration of the content that need to be supplemented and those that were given top priority in each dimension.[68]

Research into Teachers' Inclusive Education Competence Training Content, Approach, and Model

Existing research into inclusive education teachers training models mostly introduce foreign training programs or models, and summarize and refine the experience, while research into indigenized training models is not yet mature. For example, Feng Yajing's research in 2012 summarized the common practices and experiences of some foreign inclusive education teacher training programs in training personnel, content and form, mainly including the following five aspects: diversifying training subjects, focusing on the cultivation of teachers' belief, providing teachers with sufficient and extensive opportunities to participate in inclusive education practice, taking teachers' cooperative and sharing ability as the core competence to be cultivated and trained, and stressing the effect evaluation after implementation of the program.[69] In their study in 2019, Du Yuan and Sun Ying adopted the literature analysis method to compare and analyze the typical methods of improving teachers' professional competence in inclusive education in regular schools in the US, the EU, the UK, and Hong Kong. They summarized multiple paths for improvement: guiding the teachers with professional standards for inclusive education teachers; guiding them to develop a belief in inclusive education; guiding them through cooperative community for professional development of inclusive education teachers; and guiding their independent professional development via school reform for inclusive education. On this basis, some specific suggestions were put forward for improving the competence of teachers in inclusive education on the Chinese mainland.[70] In addition, some researchers also made a careful analysis of the practice in Hong Kong. In order to vigorously promote inclusive education in Hong Kong, a three-stage professional development program to improve the competence of teachers in inclusive education was launched in 2007 under the tripartite cooperation of the Education Bureau, the Education University of Hong Kong, and primary and secondary schools. In the first stage, corresponding training is to be provided for all the teachers involved. The Hong Kong Education Bureau deployed special funds and designated the Education University of Hong Kong to design a five-year "teacher professional development framework" for inclusive education according to the response-to-intervention model. It provides in-service teachers with systematic basic training, advanced training, and special training courses that "cater for different learning needs." Principals of primary and secondary schools can select teachers to participate in appropriate training. The primary training consists of 30 credit hours, which mainly guides teachers to master the essential knowledge and skills, teaching strategies, course adjustment strategies, assessment techniques, and other primary interventions for children with special needs. Advanced training with 90 credit hours instructs teachers on how to provide secondary intervention for high-risk students. Special training with 90–120 credit hours guides teachers to provide more targeted tertiary interventions for students according to different disability categories.[71,72] In the second stage, experts go into the schools to provide continuous and effective on-site support. A professional team composed of members from the Education University of Hong Kong, front-line teachers and volunteers enters the school to provide on-site consultation for special needs children and their parents, and also give on-site training for teachers. And school-based training is adopted to explain professional knowledge and help solve problems concerning differentiated teaching, behavior management of special needs students, and whole-school promotion of inclusive education. In the third stage, each school organizes

270   *Research into the Training of the Competence of Teachers*

teachers to learn from each other through cooperative lesson preparation, classroom observation, and after-class discussion, and constantly reflect and deepen their understanding in the process of participation, so as to realize their own professional growth.[73] The efforts of the above scholars provide a valuable reference and inspiration for China to improve the training of teachers' inclusive education competence.

In addition, according to the relevant literature retrieved, some domestic researchers have also begun to explore indigenized training models to improve teachers' inclusive education competence. Basically, they can start from the core elements of effective training to clarify training ideas and design training programs. Their research is rich in exploration of training content, training approach or form, but have not formed an overall, systematic training model. For example, Huang Meixian took C District of Shanghai as a case study to investigate the current situation of professional training of LRC program teachers through interviews in 2010.[74] The research divided the training in C District into several stages: (1) Determine the training objective from three aspects, that is professional affection, professional knowledge, and professional skills after reviewing the studies concerning the connotation of the professional competence of LRC program teachers. (2) Make clear the status quo of the competence of teachers in inclusive education and training needs through questionnaire survey and interview, including their educational background, teaching experience, years of experience in teaching LRC students, professional attitude, professional knowledge and skills, and training effects. Results showed that the professional level of the teachers in C district was still relatively low, so it was necessary to provide professional training for them. (3) Design the training program and define the training subject and methods. The training subject was mainly the Special Education and Rehabilitation Guidance Center of C District (hereinafter referred to as the Special Education Center), which is specifically responsible for the development of inclusive education in the district. It has gradually explored and formed professional training approaches for teachers' inclusive education competence at the district level, school level, and teacher level respectively. The training content was determined according to the training purpose. There were usually several ways to choose the training content: referring to the special teaching materials for LRC program teachers; searching relevant research literature; and summarizing some strategies and methods according to existing experience. At the same time, a variety of training methods were adopted to meet the training needs of teachers, including the organization of expert lectures, lesson observation and evaluation, visit and study, or exchange of views and discussion. Itinerant tutors provided "one-on-one, face-to-face" guidance. Some active schools organized school-based research in the form of literature study and case discussion, where teachers get together to discuss the performance of special needs students in their respective classes.

Existing Problems

According to existing research, the in-service training of inclusive education has made a certain amount of progress. Effective training models, especially diversified training methods, have been explored in various areas and schools. However, it is still necessary to understand that there are many problems to be solved in training.

Needs Analysis Is "Vague" and Lacks Diagnosis of Personalized and Hierarchical Needs

On the one hand, many researchers and trainers have a biased understanding of training needs analysis, resulting in a "vague" needs analysis. Existing training programs and processes show that understanding of and attention paid to training needs are still far from adequate. Except for the clear guidance on training needs analysis model in Du Lingyu's study in 2018, it finds no expression in the other studies. Most researchers simply equate training needs analysis with training desire analysis, asking participants to "say" their "desired training content" and "favorite training form" through questionnaires or interviews. But this kind of expression is "individual, subjective, and conscious," thus hiding real needs. Such superficial understanding makes it difficult to bring into play the real role of needs analysis. Training needs analysis is the most important basis for determining the training theme and selecting the training content. If understanding of the needs analysis is biased, the selected training theme and content may not be what teachers really need. On the other hand, many needs analyses also lack diagnosis of personalized and hierarchical needs. Existing research only points out the reality of "teachers' poor competence in inclusive education" and takes it as the basis for training necessity, without combining it with needs analysis. It is easy for researchers and trainers to ignore the differences in training needs of teachers caused by their own teaching experience, professional title, educational background, stage of professional development, years of participation in inclusive education, disability types of their special needs students, and other factors; so they treat the training needs of all teachers equally and focus on the needs of most teachers or the most important needs, but ignore the individual needs of teachers. This also makes it impossible for trainers to carry out targeted teacher training, and the training effect is unsatisfactory.

Training Features Discrete Elements

Although existing research also contains several core elements of effective training, these elements are discrete, resulting in a stagnant, immature training system. For example, the selection of training content is relatively casual, and there is a lack of internal logic to the contents. This also makes it difficult for

272   *Research into the Training of the Competence of Teachers*

many teachers in charge of training to choose the content. This is because there is no scientific analysis of training needs, and the orientation and expression of training objectives are not clear and specific. Unclear training objectives further lead to the lack of targeted training evaluation.

Improvement Measures

Based on analysis of these problems, efforts should be made in the following aspects to improve the effectiveness of teachers' inclusive education competence training. First of all, scientific training needs analysis should be given top priority to improve the effectiveness and accuracy of the training. Researchers or training organizers should correctly understand the connotation and essence of training needs analysis and orientate training needs by stages under the guidance of the "teacher training needs analysis model." It is advisable to analyze the behavioral gap according to the ideal behavior standards set based on the dimensions of teachers' core competence described in existing studies, and then find out the causes and determine the training needs. Training objectives and courses should be designed according to the results of needs analysis. Secondly, the training program should be designed based on the overall effective training system. According to the results of needs analysis and training objectives, targeted content can be selected to overcome the drawbacks of the casual selection of training content in the past. At the same time, it is of great importance to ensure that training content is logical and systematic, and choose the appropriate training form according to the characteristics of the training content itself. Finally, it is encouraged to make full use of relevant policies, institutions, resource support, and other external forces, and incorporate them into the training system to help and adjust the "dynamic cycle" within the teacher training system.

Training Model for Improvement of Teachers' Inclusive Education Competence—Experience from C District of S City

This section mainly takes as a case study the Special Education Guidance Center of C District in S City (hereinafter referred to as the Special Education Center), which provides training for the improvement of the competence of teachers in inclusive education. Through interviews, we learned about what explorations it had made into the training. Then, we summarized the experience and problems, and sought countermeasures to improve the training.

Research Method

This research adopts the case study method of qualitative research, as well as a mix of purposive sampling and convenience sampling. The selection of C District of S City as the case was mainly made based on the following considerations.

C District began to carry out the LRC program in regular primary schools in 1994, two years earlier than the rest of the city. In 2006, as the *Several Opinions of S City Education Commission on Strengthening the Management of the LRC program* was issued, C District officially launched the LRC program in regular junior high schools. In recent years, under the guidance of the Education Bureau of S City, C District has comprehensively improved the quality of the LRC program through project-oriented guidance and tripartite cooperation among the administrative department for education, special schools, and regular schools with the LRC program. Specifically, the Special Education Center has established cooperative partnerships with institutions of higher learning, kindergartens, vocational and technical colleges, research institutes, and so on to apply for and undertake a number of national-level and municipal education commission's projects or experimental projects to explore effective ways to improve teachers' inclusive education competence, achieving obvious results. It has aroused a good response in the fields of special education and general education, and accumulated a certain amount of experience.

Selection and Introduction of Respondents

In order to have a thorough and detailed understanding of the useful practices of the Special Education Center in improving the training of teachers' inclusive education competence, members of our research team conducted one-to-one semi-structured interviews with 10 teachers. They include four teachers from the Special Education Center, two from the Special Education Primary Vocational School (hereinafter referred to as the Primary Vocational School), three from HG Kindergarten, and one from HM Primary School in C District. Basic information about the 10 teachers is shown in Table 6.3.

Table 6.3 Basic Information on Respondents

Respondent (teacher)	Type/post	Number of working years	Interview duration	Remarks
Xia	Special Education Center of C District in S City Head	15	70 mins	——
Huang	Special Education Center of C District in S City Itinerant tutor	12	54 mins	Master
Wang 1	Special Education Center of C District in S City Itinerant tutor	7	58 mins	Master

(Continued)

274 *Research into the Training of the Competence of Teachers*

Table 6.3 (Continued)

Respondent (teacher)	Type/post	Number of working years	Interview duration	Remarks
Liu	Special Education Center of C District in S City Itinerant tutor	1	54 mins	Master
Wang 2	Special Education Primary Vocational School of C District in S City Teacher	29	45 mins	Having provided itinerant guidance for five years.
Yu	Special Education Primary Vocational School of C District in S City Teacher	22	43 mins	Having provided itinerant guidance for 11 years.
Yao	HG Kindergarten of C District in S City	3	51 mins	Having taught special needs students for one year. Bachelor.
Hu	HG Kindergarten of C District in S City	5	51 mins	Having taught special needs students for one year. Bachelor.
Zhu	HG Kindergarten of C District in S City	9	51 mins	Having taught special needs students for two years. Bachelor.
Jiang	HG Primary School of C District in S City	14	39 mins	Having taught special needs students for two years. Bachelor.

Data Collection Method

The semi-structured interview method was used for data collection by making a recording with the consent of interviewees. In the interview with teachers from the Special Education Center of C District, the questions were mainly about various aspects of the specific guidance work undertaken by itinerant tutors, such as its form, frequency, effect, and existing problems. The interviews with teachers from HG Kindergarten and HM Primary School played an auxiliary role, aiming to understand the actual development of the training from the perspective of teachers who had received inclusive education training.

Research into the Training of the Competence of Teachers 275

They were mutually verified with interviews with teachers from the Special Education Center. Interview questions mainly focused on the current difficulties in teaching the LRC program, and training approaches, forms, and effects.

In addition, we also collected relevant textual data, such as the work records of the Special Education Center, and the master's thesis of a teacher called Huang from the Special Education Center on the topic of the training of LRC program teachers in C District. These data provide strong support for a comprehensive understanding of the training of inclusive education teachers in C District.

Methods of Data Collation and Analysis

All interview data were transcribed and imported into MAXQDA18.0 software for analysis. The analysis of the interview data was carried out by referring to the three-level coding method. Firstly, open coding was carried out and the native discourse used by the respondents was labeled. Secondly, the axial coding method was used to classify these codes meaningfully, and the relationship between them was made clear in the process of repeated comparison. Finally, the selected core categories were linked to other support categories and then integrated into a higher-level coding. Taking the core category of "multi-level training approach" as an example, the coding process of this research is briefly shown in Table 6.4.

Table 6.4 Some Examples of Coding Process

Third-level coding	*Second-level coding*	*First-level coding*	*Source materials (excerpts)*
Multi-level training approach	Municipal level	Developing three municipal-level online quality courses for teachers to fulfil the requirement of completing 360 credit hours of training per academic year.	"Three municipal-level online quality courses for teachers have been developed," said Huang.
	District level	Establishing diversified teaching and research groups of the LRC program.	"For the in-service training, we have set up some specialized teaching and research groups…" said Director Xia of the Special Education Center.
		Regular itinerant guidance.	"Four resource teachers provide itinerant guidance and resource teaching for 17 secondary schools in the district," said Huang. "I provide itinerant guidance for five half days every week," said Wang.

(*Continued*)

276　Research into the Training of the Competence of Teachers

Table 6.4 (Continued)

Third-level coding	Second-level coding	First-level coding	Source materials (excerpts)
	School level	LRC Program BBS.	"BBS LRC Program was launched in 2007..." said Huang, "We gradually moved from BBS to mobile apps such as 'Meipian' or Wechat group."
		Teachers' professional development projects and themed school-based teaching research.	"The teachers are encouraged to apply to the center for a project, which can be an individual case of a student, or even a universal instructional plan..." said Yu. "In fact, starting from 2017, this program is designated themed school-based teaching and research activity. It calls for each school to set up a small project..." Huang said.
		Inclusive education knowledge included into the school-based training.	"Another project was launched and promoted comprehensively last year, i.e. including inclusive education knowledge into the school-based training..." Xia said.
	Teacher level	Self-study, writing educational stories.	"I pay attention to the special needs children, and write some learning stories from time to time..." said Zhu.

Status Quo of Training in C District of S City

Training Concept

The Special Education Center of C District advocates the concept of comprehensive inclusive education in terms of training value, that is, full acceptance. It proposes the concept of "potential, support, inclusion, and career," and believes that all students, regardless of their gender, age, learning ability, learning style, cultural background, and family economic status, should receive appropriate education in the mainstream education system, not limited to students with disabilities. Under the concept of comprehensive inclusive education, the Special Education Center has created a "gifted project," which is highly sought after by parents and teachers. That is to say, it issues an enrollment notice to primary and middle schools in the district and welcomes students who are interested in it to sign up. After registration, the center will conduct screening, and finally form a small class of fewer than 20 students for characteristic thinking training. In addition, when providing assistance, the Special Education Center will also give consideration to the most urgent needs of teachers, and include "underachievers," "marginal students," and "students with problems," who are of greatest concern to teachers, into the category of inclusive education, because they are more likely to be troubled by these students in normal teaching. As a result, itinerant tutors are more likely to be accepted by the schools.

Professional and Diversified Trainers

The Special Education Center of C District, established in 1994, is responsible for developing inclusive education, and managing, organizing, and supervising the professional training of the competence of teachers in inclusive education in the district. In recent years, it has attracted experts from universities and research institutes, backbone teachers, advanced workers engaged in inclusive education, parents of special needs students, and so on, to develop a diversified, professional contingent of training teachers. With the Special Education Center as the base camp, they provide itinerant guidance for grassroots schools, identify disabled children and adolescents, offer psychological education consultation, and give guidance to teaching and scientific research work.

Multi-level Training Approach

Due to the lack of human resources and discrete assignments in the initial stage, the Special Education Center of C District at first provided no substantial itinerant guidance and training. In September 2006, it moved into the Primary Vocational School of C District. With the help of teachers and scientific researchers in special education, the number of its itinerant tutors was increased. After years of exploration, it initiated a multi-level professional training approach to improve teachers' inclusive education competence, covering "city-district-school-teachers." It first cultivated a group of local resource teachers in the schools that had carried out the LRC program in the whole district, and then let them guide the subject teachers and class teachers in the schools that undertook the LRC program, and finally involved all the teachers in the schools.

MUNICIPAL LEVEL

Under the organization and requirements of the Education Commission of S City, the Special Education Center of C District developed three municipal-level online quality courses for teachers to fulfil the requirement of completing 360 credit hours of training per academic year. The three courses are "Training Course for LRC program teachers in Secondary and Primary Schools," "Professional Courses for Kindergarten Teachers' Improvement in Preschool Inclusive Education," and "General History of Inclusive Education for Beginning Teachers." The first course, taught by teachers of Changning Special Education Center, mainly focuses on the analysis and explanation of the problems encountered by primary and secondary school teachers in the

278   *Research into the Training of the Competence of Teachers*

process of teaching LRC students. The other two are taught by professors in special education from H Normal University. In particular, the "General History of Inclusive Education for Beginning Teachers" is designed to cultivate teachers' awareness of inclusive education to accept students with special needs from the beginning of their service. "We provide training for beginning teachers in the whole S City. They need such training. We think the training on general history of inclusive education is very helpful for their future teaching career. This will also be conducive to the students," said teacher Huang from the Special Education Center.

DISTRICT LEVEL

Establishing Diversified Teaching and Research Groups of the LRC Program   Organized by the Special Education Center of C District, training on various matters and professional knowledge and skills are conducted for backbone teachers engaged in inclusive education in all schools in the district. At the beginning, the classification of the teaching and research groups was not clear, and the assignments were discrete and random. But with the development and exploration of the work, experience was gradually accumulated, and a clear working idea figured out. At present, the training of the district-level teaching and research groups is directed at backbone teachers in charge of teaching guidance and the LRC program in each school to drive the overall development of inclusive education. The Special Education Center has established diversified teaching and research groups according to different classification criteria such as professional field, type of special needs students, and age group. They include the Teaching and Research Group of the Preschool Inclusive Education Center, the Teaching and Research Group of the Teaching and Instruction Center, the Teaching and Research Group of the Resource Teacher Center, the Teaching and Research Group of the Universal Instructional Design Center, the Teaching and Research Group of the Curriculum Development Center, and the Teaching and Research Group of the ADHD Students Center, each holding a teaching and research seminar at least once a month. Different groups have different members, specific tasks, and forms of work. For example, members of the Teaching and Research Group of the Teaching and Instruction Center are the teaching directors in charge of the LRC program in each school, also responsible for the reception of various special inspections, and the handling of sudden and difficult cases. In contrast, the teaching and research groups in other professional fields will analyze and discuss the puzzles encountered in practice through "learning by doing." After the training, teachers will practice it while teaching. If they encounter any problem again, they will continue to analyze and discuss it. Such a cyclic operation has promoted the continuous development of teachers' inclusive education knowledge and skills. "In fact, we advocate learning by doing. We keep improving our practice through constant training, not just at specific times," Huang added.

Next, let us take the Teaching and Research Group of the Preschool Inclusive Education Center, the Teaching and Research Group of the Resource Teacher Center, and the Teaching and Research Group of the Universal Instructional Design Center as examples to introduce their main work content and forms.

The Teaching and Research Group of the Preschool Inclusive Education Center was established in 2014, with Professor Zhou from H Normal University as the tutor. "The establishment of the Teaching and Research Group of the Preschool Inclusive Education Center means a shift from discrete explorations in preschool inclusive education to systematic itinerant guidance," teacher Wang from the Special Education Center noted. In order to build a mature teaching and research contingent, this group went to an inclusive kindergarten to give itinerant guidance at least once a month. From school years 2014 to 2018, five rounds of itinerant guidance were given. So far, it has absorbed a total of 35 inclusive teachers from seven inclusive kindergartens in the district. Together with the research team of Professor Zhou from H Normal University and itinerant tutors from the center, they have formed a relatively mature and stable teaching and research team. In addition, this group also plans to jointly build an Early Inclusive Education Alliance in C District with the seven inclusive kindergartens to provide inclusive education support service for all kindergartens in the district.

The Early Inclusive Education Alliance is responsible for integrating multiple resources to provide higher quality inclusive education for special needs children. First, it serves as a departmental information communication platform. It has a working group composed of preschool special education experts, doctors, and itinerant tutors to ensure smooth communication and operation. Second, it is a resource-sharing platform that provides the inclusive education experience of core kindergartens, and educational resources such as expert reports, featured courses, teaching examples, achievement manuals, books and materials, and so on. Third, it acts as a platform for teachers' professional improvement. It helps teachers strengthen their responsibility for inclusive education and develop a good attitude toward it. At the same time, teachers can improve their ability to assess, intervene, and develop individualized education plans for children with the help of the alliance. Fourth, it is a home-kindergarten resource-sharing platform. In the alliance, parents can obtain relevant special education knowledge and resources according to their own needs, such as school resources, expert teams, volunteer organizations, and internet resources. Fifth, it functions as a service extension and development platform. On the one hand, it promotes the improvement of inclusive courses and activities, and on the other hand, it shares the inclusive education experience and organizes online and offline exchange activities. The following is a brief introduction to the daily work of the Teaching and Research Group of the Preschool Inclusive Education Center based on interviews with its itinerant tutors.

280 *Research into the Training of the Competence of Teachers*

First of all, in the preparation stage before entering a kindergarten, this group is mainly responsible for coordinating the schedule of the kindergarten and the expert. Teacher Wang from the Special Education Center explained:

> We need to talk to the kindergarten principal first to find out what information and support he needs. If we can give him the information he wants, he's willing to accept it. If we just criticize him for doing something wrong, our relationship will be very difficult to maintain. After making an appointment with the kindergarten principal to carry out our activity, we contact the expert to determine the time to enter the kindergarten for observation.

After entering the kindergarten, the expert and teachers of this group attend class, observe the performance of special needs children in play activities, interview teachers, and collect the diagnosis and evaluation information about these children in the past to fully understand their characteristics. On this basis, a seminar will be held. During the discussion, teachers of this group will repeatedly emphasize that ordinary teachers should not only focus on the problems of special needs children, but should pay more attention to tapping the potential of the children and seeing their "shining points," needs, and interests. Participants in the seminar include experts, itinerant tutors of the group, front-line kindergarten teachers and the parents of the special needs children. They will express their opinions concerning the problems of the special needs children, and work out solutions and suggestions to solve the problems through discussion. In this process, everyone is equal, sharing their own rich experience and wisdom. This group also encourages kindergarten teachers to take the special needs children as cases to conduct action research, write learning stories or papers, and have them compiled into books by the Special Education Center, so as to provide a greater platform for them to share their experiences or puzzles. Wang said:

> An annual meeting of preschool education is held in S City. Professor Zhou proposed to hold a special forum on preschool inclusive education. Invitations were sent to four districts to make a report. As for our district, a teacher of the preschool special education center went to deliver a report on a case of learning story to introduce the development of preschool inclusive education in our district.

In addition, this group also provides parents with some support services at weekends, such as inviting their children to the Special Education Center for rehabilitation training, inviting distinguished doctors there to see special needs children, and providing psychological counseling for parents.

With regard to the Teaching and Research Group of the Resource Teacher Center, its establishment can be traced back to the "double resource teachers system," which had been explored since the implementation of the LRC program in junior high schools in C District in 2006. At that time, only three pilot schools were selected to enroll students with special needs in the district. However, because the junior high school curriculum was difficult and required high cognitive ability of students, and the schools and teachers were also facing the pressure of high school entrance examinations, it was more difficult to carry out the LRC program in junior high schools. Most special needs students just idled in the classrooms, so many teachers showed confusion and even refused to accept them. Based on this background, the Special Education Center of C District decided to station three backbone teachers with a special education background from the Primary Vocational School in the three pilot junior high schools as itinerant resource teachers respectively. At the same time, one backbone teacher in each pilot school was selected to act as a resource teacher, thus forming a "double resource teachers" system in each pilot school. Both teachers provided one-on-one guidance for special needs students in the resource room. The itinerant resource teacher was mainly responsible for rehabilitation courses, while the resource teacher in the school for subject-oriented remedial teaching. A curriculum schedule posted on the door of the resource room clearly showed which students attend what classes in what time period. "The double resource teachers system actually helped the Special Education Center to cultivate its own resource teachers in regular schools," Huang noted.

This continued until 2015, when the LRC program was widely implemented in junior high schools in C District. Many schools set up resource rooms since there were not enough teachers to support the double resource teachers system. Thus, the Special Education Center set up the specialized Teaching and Research Group of the Resource Teacher Center with the original six resource teachers from the first three pilot schools as the backbone and other teachers selected from the resource teachers of junior high schools that had carried out the LRC program. It was designed to share and spread the experience in the double resource teachers system.

The Teaching and Research Group of the Universal Instructional Design Center was designed to address the challenge for teachers in inclusive schools.[75] Curriculum design is the key to the success of inclusive education. This group is committed to guiding ordinary teachers to meet the needs of every student, including special needs students. "With regard to universal instructional design, we usually invite the experts from H Normal University to do lesson studies to help inclusive teachers gain some better teaching strategies, so that they can take care of the whole class including the special needs students," Huang said. Teacher Yu from the Primary Vocational School added:

Due to great work pressure, our teachers had an antipathy toward the individualized education plans in the beginning. The school is very big, with a student body of more than 1,000, but it only has one special needs student. The teachers were unwilling to devote even 50 percent of their energy to the one in a thousand children. It's really unfair to the teachers. However, the universal instructional design is different. It can help teachers

282 *Research into the Training of the Competence of Teachers*

better educate the underachievers and those with learning difficulties, such as dysaudia and dyslexia. This not only relieves teachers' burden, but also helps them in teaching.

Many primary school teachers also mentioned "universal instructional design" applied to their lesson preparation and teaching. According to several teachers' instructional plans that follow the principles of universal instructional design, they made specific analysis for special needs students, and recorded in detail their learning needs, the universal instructional strategies used, the results and the subsequent improvement. Teacher Jiang from HM Primary School noted:

After repeated lesson studies, we changed the instructional design based on teaching materials to a new student-oriented instructional mode featuring diversified presentation and heterogeneous grouping through various forms of cooperation to realize that every student can have an opportunity to show ... After three lesson studies, we discovered students' confusion. Following the theory of universal instructional design, our instructional design is directed at all the students at different levels in the class, giving them sufficient time and space for independent thinking and communication, and encouraging them to adopt different strategies to solve problems. Thus, every student can experience the joy of success.

Since universal instructional design takes into account the needs of all students, including special needs students, teachers in regular schools speak highly of it. Jiang noted:

In our district, there are teaching researches and open classes for special needs students. Last year, we gave open classes on inclusive education. As for my own inclusive lesson, it was studied three times. In the process, experts from H Normal University and teachers from the Special Education Center told me of its deficiencies. Then, I went back to revise my lesson plan. It was not until the third time that I finalized the lesson plan. At first, I found it exhausting and stressful. But after three lesson studies, I found myself having gotten started in inclusive education. It is practical for any class and all students, so I feel I have improved a lot in my teaching.

Itinerant Guidance   After 2015, special needs students were enrolled in all 17 junior high schools in the district, so all the four itinerant resource teachers from the Primary Vocational School had five half days a week to give itinerant guidance, and each of them was responsible for four or five schools on average. If some school was in greater need, the teacher in charge would go there once or even twice a week; if not, the teacher in charge might visit the school once a month. Their assignments include helping teachers identify and evaluate students with abnormal academic or behavioral performance; guiding school teachers to develop individualized education plans for special needs students; communicating with the class teacher and parents to understand the emotional behavior problems of the special needs students and find targeted solutions; and providing individual counseling and rehabilitation training for students in need. Due to the deficiency of resource teachers, individualized guidance for LRC students is mainly provided by the resource teachers of regular schools with the assistance of itinerant resource teachers.

SCHOOL LEVEL

Training activities at the school level are mainly carried out by the Special Education Center of C District and those backbone teachers together to continuously improve the professional competence of LRC program teachers for inclusive education. Each school organizes relevant subject teachers of the LRC program to form a teaching and research group to discuss the problems occurring in the daily education and teaching of the inclusive class, and then find a solution.

Bulletin Board System (BBS) LRC Program   Since 2007, the "BBS LRC Program" of C District has been operated to enhance teachers' attention to and knowledge and skills for the LRC program by means of full discussion and everyone's participation. Huang reported:

> The BBS content mainly includes the most vivid stories and cases of the LRC program written by the teachers of special needs students. Containing confusion and conflicts, these stories aroused resonance or collective thinking in the whole group. For those particularly confusing stories, we had a format for BBS posts: introduce a case; raise a question on the focus of the case; and interpret the case and determine a topic for everyone to discuss.

With the rapid development of electronic science and technology, such online discussions have gradually evolved into more convenient forms of communication using mobile apps. "Later, we gradually moved from BBS to mobile apps such as "Meipian" or Wechat groups. We can discuss and learn all the time," Huang said.

Teachers' Professional Development Projects and Themed School-based Teaching Research   Due to limited human and material resources, the Special Education Center encouraged each school to carry out its own teaching and research activities according to its actual situation. A program titled "For the Development of Every Child" was launched to attract research reports made by LRC program teachers on their own problems in practice under the guidance of experts from the center. This way of action research can effectively

284   *Research into the Training of the Competence of Teachers*

improve teachers' professional ability and research skills. Teacher Yu from the Primary Vocational School noted:

> Teachers are encouraged to apply to the center for a project, which can be an individual case of a student, or even a universal instructional plan that we are implementing in the school, such as the instructional plan with three cycles and two reflections. In the progress of the project, some experts will provide them guidance, and we will also attend the class to give evaluation, and then help them make some changes.

Teacher Yao from HG Kindergarten reported:

> In the past two years, I made a case study of a child in my class. Some experts of the Special Education Center helped me complete the paper. They told me about research methods, interventions, and how to record and take photos and videos. This child really made some progress in a few months. I often informed them of the project progress. Finally, my research project was smoothly concluded.

Later, it gradually evolved into themed school-based teaching and research activity, which mainly promoted teachers in regular schools to carry out teaching and research activities together with itinerant resource teachers. The Special Education Center allocated 1,000 yuan as the starting fund to the teaching and research group of each school, expecting teachers to improve their competence in inclusive education through action research. Huang noted:

> In fact, starting from 2017, this program is designated themed school-based teaching and research activity. It calls for each school to set up a small project, and then organizes a teaching and research activity of LRC program teachers every month according to this small project. The itinerant tutor and resource teacher from the Special Education Center also come to join the activity. A report on this project shall be completed every year.

In the school-based teaching and research activity, teachers in regular schools or kindergartens will also discuss the problems encountered in implementation of the LRC program. Sometimes they will discuss problems according to a preset theme, and sometimes they talk about new problems. For example, when a teacher encounters a sudden behavioral problem of a special needs student, they will discuss it together. "The teaching and research activity focuses on a preset theme or some random topic. For example, if a teacher has no idea how to guide a special needs student to deal with his problem, others will discuss it and help find a solution," said teacher Hu from HG Kindergarten.

Inclusive Education Knowledge Included in School-based Training   To help teachers develop awareness of inclusive education, the Special Education

Center of C District cooperates with schools to promote the spread of inclusive education knowledge. As the schools hold regular staff meetings and rich school-based training every Friday afternoon, the Special Education Center provides relevant inclusive education courses it has developed for school-based training. These courses are delivered by designated experts to every LRC program teacher in the district by stages. They are developed according to the needs of teachers and constantly adjusted in accordance with their feedback. At present, the Special Education Center and the backbone resource teachers of the schools are committed to developing a "curriculum menu" that spreads inclusive education knowledge into the schools, trying to meet the common and personalized needs of teachers as much as possible. Huang noted:

> In the beginning, the training themes of various schools were collected to find the most popular, like the most ordered dish in a menu. Moreover, the theme can also be customized according to one's own needs. In my opinion, after a certain period of accumulation, an inclusive education curriculum menu can be formed. This task is being done.

TEACHER LEVEL

Independent research and training activities of teachers refer to the fact that they spontaneously study and do research to solve problems in the actual work, and improve their professional knowledge and skills in special education.

Prescribing the Participants of Each Training Approach

C District has tried to explore various training approaches at the municipal, district, school, and teacher levels, so that every teacher can get suitable training and guidance, and the participants of each training approach are clearly prescribed.

The participants in the teaching and research groups are those in charge of teaching and learning and the backbone teachers in regular schools. If a teacher who is undertaking the LRC program has problems or confusion in the actual work, he can consult and accept guidance from the itinerant resource teacher. The teaching and research training of the schools is provided for subject teachers, usually Chinese, math, and English teachers. Of course, if school leaders and teachers are willing, the target of the training can be expanded to all subject teachers. A typical example is the school-based training on inclusive education provided at the staff meeting held every Friday afternoon. It is for all the teachers in the school.

Taking Every Opportunity to Provide Teachers with "Implicit Training"

In addition to this "explicit" training, the Special Education Center of C District attaches great importance to "implicit training or research" in daily

286 *Research into the Training of the Competence of Teachers*

work, seizing every opportunity to improve teachers' inclusive education competence. In interviews, many teachers repeatedly mentioned "implicit training." It includes the "identification and evaluation meeting," "seminar on transition service," "instructional supervision," and so on, regularly organized by the Education Bureau and the Special Education Center of C District. These activities help enrich teachers' knowledge and experience.

IDENTIFICATION AND EVALUATION MEETING

After a student with special needs enters a regular school, he or she may face the problem of identification and evaluation. How then to identify a student as a "LRC student?" In this respect, the Special Education Center of C District is fairly professional and cautious. First of all, it strives to collect related data as much as possible. After preliminary observation and relevant medical data collection, it will assist the school to hold an expert appraisal meeting to officially and scientifically recognize the "suspected" student with special needs. Members of the appraisal committee include special education experts, doctors, experienced backbone teachers of the LRC program, parents with successful experience, the parents and class teacher of the student with special needs, and the school's director of teaching and learning. They discuss whether a student is eligible to apply for the LRC program. Then, experienced backbone teachers share their experience in how to take good care of the special needs student and how to create a favorable class atmosphere, and so on to help teachers prepare for future challenges.

SEMINAR ON TRANSITION SERVICES

The US *Individuals with Disabilities Education Act* made new provisions for transition services in 2004: "Transition Services means a coordinated set of activities for a child with a disability that is designed to be within a results-oriented process, that is focused on improving the academic and functional achievement of the child with a disability to facilitate the child's movement from school to post-school activities."[76] However, the "transition services" mentioned by the teachers in this section covers a wider scope, involving the transition between different school sectors of special needs students, such as the transition from kindergarten to primary school, primary school to junior high school or vocational school. The exchange and sharing between various parties at the seminar also help the class teacher and subject teachers to have a more specific understanding of the characteristics, abilities, interests, and needs of the LRC students. Wang stated:

> What does the transition service mean? It means that we first make an appraisal, and then collect data to make clear the next school the special needs student should attend. We will bring together the teachers of the next school sector with his or her present teachers, and then invite doctors and

Research into the Training of the Competence of Teachers 287

special education experts to discuss his or her case. This is actually a very good opportunity for the teachers in the next school sector to get to know the child. In the meeting, his or her present teachers mainly introduce his or her situation, how they dealt with it, and some effective experience, whether it is successful, or still regrettable. It is a process of self-improvement. It is also a learning process for the teachers in the next school sector. Every student's case requires a discussion for half an hour or one hour.

INSTRUCTIONAL SUPERVISION

Instructional supervision is carried out by the Education Bureau of C District in order to promote inclusive education via evaluation. Huang noted:

> In 2008, the Education Bureau of C District issued a red header document which tells in great detail what is instructional supervision, and in particular provides an evaluation form. This evaluation form covers education management, educational research, and education and teaching with sub-items. The grading rules are very detailed. For each school, they can look at the rules to see what they have to do.

Every year, a "1+1+1+X" team will be set up for itinerant instructional supervision. The three "1s" respectively represent the special education experts from colleges and universities, doctors, and itinerant tutors from the Special Education Center, and the "X" represents the parents of special needs students. The supervision team members will go to a regular school to listen to lessons as well as the reports on the summary, reflection, and self-rating of the school's director of teaching and learning and LRC program teachers in the past year, and discuss the difficulties and doubts of ordinary teachers to help them develop or improve the individualized education plans and universal instructional design for special needs students. A teacher also named Wang from the Primary Vocational School noted:

> As for instructional supervision, we will invite special education experts and medical experts according to the different cases of each school. If the student is deaf, we will invite a doctor from ENT department; if it's a behavioral problem, we will invite a doctor from the mental health center; and if it is developmental delay, we will invite a doctor from the child care department of a children's hospital, etc … We not only inspect their work, but also discuss how to make a better individualized education plan for the child, and then listen to a lesson which also requires them to apply the universal instructional concept. This factually triggers a district-wide universal instructional competition.

While teacher Zhu from HG Kindergarten reported: "We formulate an individualized education plan for every special needs student with joint efforts

288 *Research into the Training of the Competence of Teachers*

due to our limited professional knowledge in special education. Parents and experts also join us to make the plan more valuable."

Although it is an inspection, it allows for face-to-face exchanges with teachers to develop better individualized education plans for special needs students and improve the inclusive education competence of ordinary teachers. Huang stated:

> In the process of face-to-face discussion, teachers can also voice their own confusions and problems in the process of education and teaching so that the experts present can give them advice. Perhaps some problems that have puzzled teachers for a long time will suddenly become clear. So instructional supervision can also be used as a way to improve teachers' concept and skills.

In addition to instructional supervision, there are also special inspections of resource rooms, individualized education, transition services, and follow-up services for inclusive education in C District. The inspection results are integrated with the annual evaluation of the school. Therefore, these special inspections have indeed played a role in promoting the implementation of evaluation. Strict supervision and the inspection mechanism ensures solid implementation of the LRC program in the schools. In the actual inspection, the Special Education Center makes more use of this opportunity to communicate with LRC program teachers to understand their confusion, and seize every opportunity to improve the inclusive education competence of ordinary teachers. Yu said:

> Of course, we do it not purely for inspection. In fact, it is mainly positive encouragement. But in the process of inspection, we'll say what's going well in your resource room and what can be improved. We have specific inspection on their individualized education plans to see their strengths and weak points for improvement. Through various means, we try to help them perform better in implementation of the LRC program.

Taking Various Training Methods According to Training Needs

The C District can adopt various training methods according to actual training needs during the professional training of inclusive education teachers. In the process of organizing the training of the teaching and research groups, the teaching and research counselors will organize expert lectures, lesson observation and evaluation, visit and study, or exchange and discussion according to the training objective and focus of each stage. The itinerant tutors will provide one-to-one and face-to-face guidance. LRC program teachers can directly communicate with the itinerant tutors about the problems and confusions encountered in the actual teaching process and seek solutions. Some schools that actively carry out school-based teaching research into the LRC program have adopted

Research into the Training of the Competence of Teachers   289

literature study, case discussion, action research, and other means. Literature study is mainly conducted by the teacher in charge of teaching and research, who searches various relevant articles according to the topic and organizes other teachers to study together. As for case discussion, the teachers get together to talk about the performance of special needs students and probe solutions. Action research means that teachers in the teaching and research group design action plans based on the problems and confusions encountered in the teaching practice of the LRC program, to solve the problems and finally present the research report. In this process, it not only develops teachers' awareness of research, but also improves their competence in inclusive education.

Training Effect

First of all, most teachers' attitude has gradually changed from initial rejection to moral acceptance of the inclusive education concept. They are now able to view the impact of inclusive education on students in a more prudent and rational way. As a teacher at the Special Education Center put it, "We have waged through the hardest stage." Huang reported:

> In the beginning, many teachers complained about their lack of expertise … . But now such complaint is rarely heard … . They used to argue that special needs children should go to special school. When we gave itinerant guidance, we were directly criticized. I really felt very embarrassed and humble. But now they at least agree that these students should be included in regular class. Some teachers have realized that these special needs students don't just mean trouble but can be seen as an educational resource to create a better educational environment and resources for all students.

Zhu added:

> When a special needs child first sat in my classroom, I thought it inclusive. I just hoped him to stay there and not make any trouble. He was excluded from our activities, and given no questions. I wouldn't ask him to repeat my words or to identify something. But now, my thinking has changed. The special needs students should indeed learn something in my class. I also set some goals for them. I pay attention to them, but don't give up on the ordinary children.

While teacher Jiang from HM Primary School said:

> I think there are both advantages and disadvantages of inclusive education for a special needs student. In the academic courses, he still lags behind other students due to his low intelligence level, which I think is a disadvantage for him. But what's good for him, I think, is that studying with typically developing kids, he can learn a lot of normal interaction, and work with others.

290   *Research into the Training of the Competence of Teachers*

Secondly, in daily teaching practice, most teachers can consciously pay special attention to and promote the classroom participation of special needs students, and make judgments on their behavioral problems from the functional perspective of applied behavior analysis. The most commonly used teaching adjustment is the easy "simplification and reduction," such as assigning special student seats, setting simple questions specifically for them, assigning less homework, reducing the difficulty of tasks, and providing opportunities for them to participate in classroom teaching as much as possible. There are also a few teachers who can consciously try stratified teaching after the lesson study of "universal instructional design." Huang explained:

> After receiving itinerant guidance for a certain period of time, teachers have actually changed their mindset and developed a proper understanding of the behaviors of these children, and know how to properly deal with their misbehaviors. For example, when a special needs child left the classroom, a teacher spotted that he didn't go to the bathroom but used the excuse to escape. Finally, I gradually realized I need to make some adjustments for different students in their studies, and reduce the degree of difficulty for them to fit their cognitive ability. But in terms of character and behavior, they should be treated equally.

Jiang added: "When the students are doing group activities, I go to his (the special needs student's) group and check on them. Because sometimes he is not very clear, I will tell him more... My requirements on him are much lower... ." While Hu reported:

> The teaching objectives will also be stratified, and the requirements on him [the special needs student] will be lowered. Take hand washing for example. We ask the children to wash their hands according to the seven-step washing method, but for him, because his small muscle development is poor, he can't rub or knead, he is just required to pull up the sleeves, and take the soap.

What is more, the training effect is also reflected in the teachers' stronger awareness of actively seeking professional support. Some teachers said in an early interview that they had no way to seek professional support and help. Now, the Special Education Center of C District provides teachers with a stable and specific consultation channel and professional support centers, which is of great benefit to teachers to solve their daily teaching problems.

Analysis and Summary

As mentioned above, the head of the Special Education Center of C District analyzed the three development models of special education, concluding that the implementation of inclusive education would ultimately depend on the mesoscopic organizational model. The inclusive education with Chinese

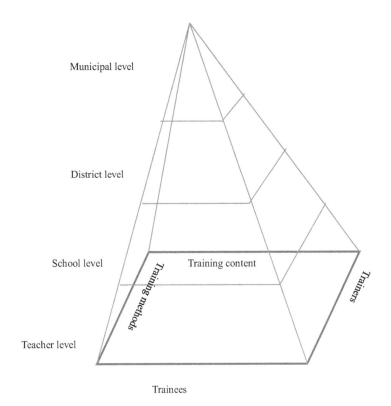

Figure 6.1 Multi-level and Multi-dimensional Full-coverage Training Network.

characteristics should be based on the functional transformation of special schools, the establishment of special education guidance centers, as well as a collaborative operation mechanism between the center and regular schools. With regard to the in-service training designed to improve the competence of teachers in inclusive education, the Special Education Center has established a professional support system with the help of the professional teachers in special schools, and initially explored a multi-level training approach, involving "city-district-school-teachers." At each level, there are corresponding trainers, trainees, guidance content, and guidance/training methods. As a result, a multi-level and multi-dimensional training network with full coverage is formed, as shown in Figure 6.1.

Inclusive Education Support and Promotion by Special Education Center

The Special Education Center plays an important role in administrative management and supporting services, and is considered irreplaceable in promoting regional inclusive education and improving the inclusive education competence of teachers. For teachers in regular schools, the implementation of inclusive education will inevitably consume a lot of time and energy, which will affect their teaching progress. The negative sentiments and disapproval of teachers were the common problems encountered by the LRC program at the beginning. How should this barrier be broken down to align the professional support of the Special Education Center with the needs of regular schools, and gain their trust? This was the main problem to be solved to improve the competence of teachers in inclusive education in C district. To this end, the Special Education Center of C District, based on the actual needs of teachers in regular schools, tried to provide teachers with professional support not limited to students with disabilities, changing "giving" and "implantation" into professional support for needs, and obtaining the "access card" to give inclusive education guidance. However, the practice of inclusive education guidance in C District showed that instrumental support and assistance made teachers dependent on itinerant tutors, which could not revitalize the internal vitality of the schools in the implementation of inclusive education. As the subject of the implementation of inclusive education, general education schools were always in a passive state and still held negative attitudes toward the concept and implementation of inclusive education. Therefore, a mechanism for coordinated implementation of inclusive education between the Special Education Center and general education schools was put forward, so as to provide professional support for the LRC program of regular schools, and improve the general education schools' awareness of their responsibility in the implementation of inclusive education, and enhance the initiative of their teachers to carry out LRC program.

First, the Special Education Center has nurtured backbone teachers to make sure that "a single spark can start a prairie fire." On the one hand, the "double resource teacher system" was initiated to improve the practical participation of teachers in the LRC program, enhance backbone teachers' ability in inclusive education, and widely cultivate resource teachers in general education schools. On the other hand, diversified professional teaching and research groups have been formed with backbone teachers, and rich and effective courses were developed in response to teachers' needs. It also innovated training methods by carrying out group learning to build a platform for exchanges among teachers, fully stimulating their learning initiative, and achieving the best training effect through "learning by doing."

Second, it has made unremitting efforts to change the concept of school administrators and give them guidance on the management of the LRC program. Specifically, it guides school administrators to update their concept of inclusive education and clearly convey the new concept to everyone working in the school. Administrators are encouraged to provide equal and all-round support for every teacher that undertakes inclusive education, introduce resources inside and outside the school, reduce the pressure on teachers, and create an inclusive, positive, and open school climate for inclusive education.

Research into the Training of the Competence of Teachers 293

Third, it has built a platform of communication with experts to provide professional support for teachers. It launched online quality courses to be shared by teachers. Experts from colleges and universities, research institutes, backbone teachers, and advanced workers engaged in inclusive education, parents of special needs students, and other forces were brought together to form a professional and diversified training contingent that was tasked to provide online training for grassroots schools. On the one hand, such training can greatly improve the professional competence of teachers with the help of external resources and support. On the other hand, in the form of online study with credit hours, the training promotes teachers' professional growth by improving their inclusive education competence, and solve the contradiction between their work and study, relieve their work pressure, and awaken their motivation for independent learning.

Building a Learning Community and Giving Play to the Leading Role of Backbone Teachers

Teacher agency is an internal core mediating factor between social and cultural environments,[77] and also a positive force for teachers to change their work and their working environment.[78] How can teachers in general education schools be made to change their existing cognitive schema, jump out of the "comfort zone" of previous teaching, actively face the big differences in the classroom, embrace the new educational and teaching environment, and adopt an optimistic, positive attitude to face the possible problems in education and teaching? It was the key problem to be solved in C District to improve teachers' inclusive education competence. Therefore, C District called for backbone teachers and school administrators to build a school-wide learning community for independent research and training.

First, the Special Education Center has launched teachers' professional development projects and themed school-based teaching research projects to encourage teachers to conduct independent research. Front-line teachers who are engaged in the LRC program and preschool inclusive education are encouraged to apply for a research project each based on the problems they have encountered in practice. They do the project in the form of action research through literature study and case discussion. In the process, they can realize cyclic professional development featuring "self-guidance, self-motivation, self-monitoring, self-evaluation, and self-reflection," and gradually find a path geared to their own characteristics.

Second, it has operated the BBS LRC program to stimulate all teachers to participate in discussion by solving practical problems. Containing confusion and conflicts, teachers' stories arouse resonance or collective thinking. Thus, teachers can spontaneously do study and research to solve problems in the iractual workplace, and improve their professional knowledge and skills in inclusive education.

294 *Research into the Training of the Competence of Teachers*

Taking Various Measures to Create an Inclusive School Atmosphere

Whether a school has formed an inclusive atmosphere directly affects the improvement of its teachers' inclusive education competence. The Special Education Center joins hands with regular schools to create an inclusive atmosphere through spreading inclusive education knowledge into the schools as well as implicit training.

First, the Special Education Center provides external learning resources for schools to create an atmosphere for all staff members to learn inclusive education knowledge and skills. Teachers are encouraged to understand the needs of each child, and set educational and teaching objectives accordingly, so as to provide fair and quality education for each child. Such whole-staff training can also help teachers build a firm belief in inclusive education, and make the principles of fairness and excellence, acceptance and inclusiveness, diversity and sense of belonging rooted in their hearts, and more importantly, become a kind of culture and habit in their daily lives.

Second, it has vigorously promoted "implicit training" based on practical activities to give teachers a sense of participation and achievement. Through the "implicit training" of "identification and evaluation meeting," "seminar on transition service," "instructional supervision," and so on, teachers constantly enrich their knowledge and experience through communication with experts and experienced teachers. What is more, regular evaluation and communication with special needs children enables teachers to obtain positive feedback from the children, thus enhancing their own sense of achievement and satisfaction in teaching and stimulating their initiative to improve their inclusive education competence.

In general, although the Special Education Center of C District has initially explored a multi-level training network covering all teachers, and achieved some success and accumulated valuable experience, there is still a long way to go for the training designed to improve the teachers' inclusive education competence in the district. For example, some teachers are still not active in participating in the teaching and research training and receiving itinerant guidance, and the relationship between the Special Education Center and regular schools has not completely changed from the state of "giving" and "receiving." It is difficult to carry out school-based teaching research and teachers' independent research on a regular basis. Under the pressure of "expressionist" culture, teachers in regular schools with limited time and energy are "forced" to pay more attention to inclusive education. The teaching and research activities and training they attend still revolve around typically developing students. Most of the discussions about special needs students are "generated" rather than "preset," and few teaching and research activities are specially arranged to discuss the problems arising from special needs students. The selection of training content is still relatively arbitrary, but systematic and targeted content is really needed. All these problems will have a negative impact on the training effect and hinder the promotion of inclusive education. However, the defects do not obscure its merits. On the one hand, the experience provided by the district can provide a useful reference for the training of teachers' inclusive education competence. On the other hand, it also shows that it is critical to continuously conduct context-based action research and explore more models, approaches, and strategies of training, so as to improve the effectiveness of future training, and then truly enhance teachers' inclusive education competence to ensure the stable and long-term development of inclusive education.

Notes

1 Xie, Zhengli 谢正立, and Deng, Meng 邓猛. "Lun ronghe jiaoyu jiaoshi juese ji xingcheng lujing" 论融合教育教师角色及形成路径. *Teacher Education Research* 教师教育研究 30, no. 6 (2018): 25–30.

2 Tian, Boqiong 田波琼, Shen, Renhong 申仁洪, and Liao, Lili 廖丽莉. "Sugelan zhongxiaoxue ronghe jiaoyu jiaoshi zhiqian peiyang de beijing, tedian ji qishi—yi IPP xiangmu weili" 苏格兰中小学融合教育教师职前培养的背景、特点及启示——以IPP项目为例. *Primary & Secondary Schooling Abroad*外国中小学教育 no. 10 (2017): 39–46.

3 *Guowuyuan bangongting guanyu zhuanfa jiaoyubu deng bumen "Shisiwu" teshu jiaoyu fazhan tisheng xingdong jihua de tongzhi* 国务院办公厅关于转发教育部等部门"十四五"特殊教育发展提升行动计划的通知. Jiaoyubu wangzhan 教育部网站, 2021. www.moe.gov.cn/jyb_xxgk/moe_1777/moe_1778/202201/t20220125_596312.html.

4 Lindsay, G. "Inclusive Education: A Critical Perspective." *British Journal of Special Education* 30, no. 1 (2003): 3–12.

5 Lu, Naigui 卢乃桂. "Ronghe jiaoyu zai xianggang de chixu fazhan—jianlun teshu xuexiao de juese zhuanbian" 融合教育在香港的持续发展——兼论特殊学校的角色转变. *Chinese Journal of Special Education* 中国特殊教育 no. 11 (2004): 82–91.

6 Zhang, Yuexin 张悦歆. "Puxiao jiaoshi dui canji ertong suiban jiudu de taidu yanjiu" 普校教师对残疾儿童随班就读的态度研究. *Journal of Educational Studies* 教育学报 12, no. 3 (2016): 104–113.

7 De Boer, A., Pijl, S. J., and Minnaert, A. "Regular Primary Schoolteachers' Attitudes Towards Inclusive Education: A Review of the Literature." *International Journal of Inclusive Education* 15, no. 3 (2011): 331–353.

8 Tiwari, A., Das, A. K., and Sharma, M. "Inclusive Education a 'Rhetoric' or 'Reality'? Teachers' Perspectives and Beliefs." *Teaching and Teacher Education* 52, no. 12 (2015): 128–136.

9 Guan, Wenjun 关文军. "Ronghe jiaoyu xuexiao canji xuesheng ketang canyu de tedian ji jiaoshi tigong de zhichi yanjiu" 融合教育学校残疾学生课堂参与的特点及教师提供的支持研究. *Chinese Journal of Special Education* 中国特殊教育 no. 12 (2017): 3–10.

10 Zeng, Yaru 曾雅茹. "Putong xiaoxue jiaoshi dui suiban jiudu de taidu jiaoxue celüe yu suoxu zhichi de yanjiu" 普通小学教师对随班就读的态度、教学策略与所需支持的研究. *Chinese Journal of Special Education* 中国特殊教育 no. 12 (2007): 5–9.

11 Westwood, P. "'Differentiation' as a Strategy for Inclusive Classroom Practice: Some Difficulties Identified." *Australian Journal of Learning Disabilities* 6, no. 1 (2001): 5–11.

12 Fu, Wangqian 傅王倩, and Xiao, Fei 肖非. "Suiban jiudu ertong huiliu xianxiang de zhixing yanjiu" 随班就读儿童回流现象的质性研究. *Chinese Journal of Special Education* 中国特殊教育 no. 3 (2016): 5–11.

296 *Research into the Training of the Competence of Teachers*

13 Young, K., Mannix-McNamara, P., and Coughlan, B. "Authentic Inclusion–Utopian Thinking? Irish Post-primary Teachers' Perspectives of Inclusive Education." *Teaching and Teacher Education* 68, no. 11 (2017): 1–11.
14 See note 8 above.
15 See note 6 above.
16 Meyer, J. W., and Rowan, B. "Institutionalized Organizations: Formal Structure as Myth and Ceremony." *American Journal of Sociology* 83, no. 2 (1997): 340–363.
17 Zucker, L. G. "Institutional Theories of Organization." *Review of Sociology* 13, no. 1 (1987), 443–464.
18 Dimaggio, P., and Powell, W. W. "The Iron Cage Revisited: Institutional Isomorphism and Collective Rationality in Organizational Fields." *American Sociological Review* 48, no. 2 (1983), 143–166.
19 Yin, Hongbiao 尹弘飚. "Lun kecheng biange de zhiduhua—jiyu xin zhidu zhuyi de fenxi" 论课程变革的制度化——基于新制度主义的分析. *Journal of Higher Education* 高等教育研究 30, no. 4 (2009): 75–81.
20 Ke, Zheng 柯政. "Xuexiao biange kunnan de xin zhidu zhuyi jieshi" 学校变革困难的新制度主义解释. *Peking University Education Review* 北京大学教育评论 no. 1 (2007): 42–54.
21 Guo, Jianru 郭建如. "Shehuixue zuzhi fenxi zhong de xinlao zhidu zhuyi yu jiaoyu yanjiu" 社会学组织分析中的新老制度主义与教育研究. *Peking University Education Review* 北京大学教育评论 no. 3 (2008): 136–151, 192.
22 Zucker, L. G. "The Role of Institutionalization in Cultural Persistence." *American Sociological Review* 42, no. 5 (1977): 726–743.
23 Dimaggio, P. "Interest and Agency in Institutional Theory." In L. Zucker (ed.), *Institutional Patterns and Organizations: Culture and Environment*, 3–21. Cambridge, Massachusetts: Ballinger Publishing Company, 1988.
24 Hallett, T., and Meanwell, E. "Accountability as an Inhabited Institution: Contested Meanings and the Symbolic Politics of Reform." *Symbolic Interaction* 39, no. 3 (2016): 374–396.
25 Hallett, T. "Symbolic Power and Organizational Culture." *Sociological Theory* 21, no. 2 (2003): 128–149.
26 Hallett, T. "Between Deference and Distinction: Interaction Ritual through Symbolic Power in an Educational Institution." *Social Psychology Quarterly* 70, no. 2 (2007): 148–171.
27 Bazeley, P. *Qualitative Data Analysis: Practical Strategies*, 156. London: Sage, 2013.
28 Ying, Xing 应星. "Zhixing yanjiu de fangfalun zai fansi" 质性研究的方法论再反思. *Journal of Guangxi University for Nationalities* (Philosophical and Social Science Edition), no. 4 (2016): 59–63.
29 Gunnthorsdottir, H., and Bjarnason, D. S. "Conflicts in Teachers' Professional Practices and Perspectives about Inclusion in Icelandic Compulsory Schools." *European Journal of Special Needs Education* no. 4 (2014): 491–504.
30 See note 7 above.
31 Hodkinson, A. "Inclusive and Special Education in the English Educational System: Historical Perspectives, Recent Developments and Future Challenges." *British Journal of Special Education* 37, no. 2 (2010): 61–67.
32 See note 29 above.
33 March, J. G. *A Primer on Decision Making*, 37. New York: The Free Press, 1994.
34 Singal, N. "Working Towards Inclusion: Reflections from the Classroom." *Teaching and Teacher Education* 24, no. 6 (2008): 1516–1529.

35 Zhou, Xu 周序, and Liu, Qinglong 刘庆龙. "Jiaoshi yu yingshi jiaoyu: cong chongtu zouxiang hejie" 教师与应试教育：从冲突走向和解. *Journal of Educational Science of Hunan Normal University* 湖南师范大学教育科学学报 16, no. 5 (2017): 92–97.

36 See note 34 above.

37 See note 20 above, 42–54, 189.

38 Wei, Xiaomei 魏小梅, and Li, Baoqing 李宝庆. "Xin gaokao jincheng zhong xuexiao biange de kunjing yu yingdui celue: xin zhidu zhuyi de shijiao" 新高考进程中学校变革的困境与应对策略：新制度主义的视角. *Research on Educational Development* 教育发展研究 37, no. 22 (2017): 16–24.

39 Ke, Zheng 柯政. "Jiaoshi de wenhua renzhi shi ruhe yingxiang kecheng zhengce shishi de: yi 'yanjiuxing xuexi' zhengce weili" 教师的文化认知是如何影响课程政策实施的：以"研究性学习"政策为例. *Global Education* 全球教育展望 no. 3 (2011): 41–50.

40 See note 38 above.

41 See note 5 above.

42 See note 19 above.

43 Zhang, Mengmeng 张猛猛. "Daxue zhangcheng shishi de dangxia kunjing yu pojie zhice—jiyu xin zhidu zhuyi de shijiao" 大学章程实施的当下困境与破解之策——基于新制度主义的视角. *Jiangsu Higher Education* 江苏高教 no. 3 (2019): 37–43.

44 See note 38 above.

45 See note 8 above.

46 Zhou, Xueguang 周雪光. *Zuzhi shehuixue shijiang* 组织社会学十讲, 77. Beijing: Social Sciences Academic Press, 2003.

47 Chen, Yang 陈扬. "Zuzhi duoyuan yingdui celue qianyan yanjiu pingshu: cong 'zhidu luoji' dao 'zuzhi shenfen'" 组织多元应对策略前沿研究评述：从"制度逻辑"到"组织身份." *East China Economic Management* 华东经济管理 29, no. 10 (2015): 146–151.

48 See note 13 above.

49 See note 11 above.

50 Gaitas, S., and Martins, M. A. "Teacher Perceived Difficulty in Implementing Differentiated Instructional Strategies in Primary School." *International Journal of Inclusive Education* 21, no. 5 (2016): 1–13.

51 Deng, Meng 邓猛, and Su, Hui 苏慧. "Ronghe jiaoyu zai zhongguo de jiajie yu zai shengcheng: jiyu shehui wenhua shijiao de fenxi" 融合教育在中国的嫁接与再生成：基于社会文化视角的分析. *Journal of Educational Studies* 教育学报 8, no. 1 (2012): 85–91.

52 Cai, Yingqi 蔡迎旗, and Zheng, Jie 郑洁. "You'eryuan jiaoshi peixun xuqiu de shizheng yanjiu" 幼儿园教师培训需求的实证研究. *Educational Research and Experiment* 教育研究与实验 no. 1 (2008): 66–70.

53 Du, Lingyu 杜灵宇. *Yunnan shaoshu minzu nongcun diqu suiban jiudu jiaoshi zhihou peixun neirong xuqiu yanjiu* 云南少数民族农村地区随班就读教师职后培训内容需求研究, 23. Kunming: Yunnan Normal University, 2018.

54 Yu, Xin 余新. "Youxiao jiaoshi peixun de qige guanjian huanjie—yi 'guopei jihua—peixunzhe yanxiu xiangmu' peixun guanlizhe yanxiuban weili" 有效教师培训的七个关键环节——以"国培计划——培训者研修项目"培训管理者研修班为例. *Educational Research* 教育研究 31, no. 2 (2010): 77–83.

55 Wang, Xiuying 王秀英. "Youxiao jiaoshi peixun de yaosu yu moxing jiangou" 有效教师培训的要素与模型建构. *The Inservice Education and Training of School Teachers* 中小学教师培训 no. 4 (2015): 18–21.

56 Zhu, Xudong 朱旭东, and Song, Huan 宋萑. "Lun jiaoshi peixun de hexin yaosu" 论教师培训的核心要素. *Teacher Education Research* 教师教育研究 25, no. 3 (2013): 1–8.

57 See note 54 above.

58 See note 56 above.

59 See note 56 above.

60 Li, Huanhuan 李欢欢, and Huang, Jin 黄瑾. "'Gao suzhi shan baojiao' you'er jiaoshi peixun moxing zhi goujian" "高素质善保教"幼儿教师培训模型之构建. *Journal of the Chinese Society of Education* 中国教育学刊 no. 2 (2019): 11–17.

61 Yu, Xin 余新. *Jiaoshi peixunshi zhuanye xiulian* 教师培训师专业修炼, 90–110. Beijing: Educational Science Publishing House, 2014.

62 Shen, Junhong 申军红, Wang, Yongxiang 王永祥, and Hao, Guoqiang 郝国强. "Jiaoshi peixun xuqiu fenxi moxing jiangou yanjiu—yi haidian qu zhongxiaoxue xinren banzhuren weili" 教师培训需求分析模型建构研究——以海淀区中小学新任班主任为例. *Teacher Education Research* 教师教育研究, no. 6 (2016): 75–82.

63 Xu, Shuai 徐帅, and Zhao, Bin 赵斌. "Teshu jiaoyu jiaoshi zhuanye fazhan yuqi peixun xuqiu de guanxi yanjiu" 特殊教育教师专业发展与其培训需求的关系研究. *Journal of Educational Development* 教育导刊 no. 10 (2015): 79–82.

64 Li, Jing 李静. "You'eryuan jiaoshi ronghe jiaoyu suyang yu peixun xuqiu fenxi—yi beijing diqu weili" 幼儿园教师融合教育素养与培训需求分析——以北京地区为例. *Teacher Development Research* 教师发展研究 no. 4 (2017): 67–73.

65 Wang, Hongxia 王红霞, Peng, Xin 彭欣, and Wang, Yanjie 王艳杰. "Beijing shi haidian qu xiaoxue ronghe jiaoyu xianzhuang diaocha yanjiu baogao" 北京市海淀区小学融合教育现状调查研究报告. *Chinese Journal of Special Education* 中国特殊教育 no. 4 (2011): 37–41.

66 Yan, Jiaping 严加平. "Jiaoshi 'xiangyao de' jiushi 'xuqiu' le ma—OTP moshi jiqi zai jiaoshi xuexi xuqiu fenxi zhong de yunyong" 教师"想要的"就是"需求"了吗——OTP模式及其在教师学习需求分析中的运用. *Shanghai Research on Education* 上海教育科研 no. 12 (2013): 35–38.

67 Zhao, Decheng 赵德成, and Liang, Yongzheng 梁永正. "Peixun xuqiu fenxi: neihan moshi yu tuijin" 培训需求分析：内涵、模式与推进. *Teacher Education Research* 教师教育研究 no. 6 (2010): 11–16.

68 See note 53 above.

69 Feng, Yajing 冯雅静. "Guowai ronghe jiaoyu shizi peixun de bufen jingyan he qishi" 国外融合教育师资培训的部分经验和启示. *Chinese Journal of Special Education* 中国特殊教育 no. 12 (2012): 5–9.

70 Du, Yuan 杜媛, and Sun, Ying 孙颖. "Putong xuexiao jiaoshi ronghe jiaoyu zhuanye suyang tisheng lujing de fenxi ji qishi" 普通学校教师融合教育专业素养提升路径的分析及启示. *Disability Research* 残疾人研究 no. 9 (2019): 71–79.

71 Ibid.

72 Yu, Yuzhen 余玉珍, and Yin, Hongbiao 尹弘飚. "Xianggang ronghe jiaoyu zhengce xia de jiaoshi zhuanye fazhan" 香港融合教育政策下的教师专业发展. *Journal of South China Normal University* (Social Science Edition) no. 6 (2014): 44–49.

73 See note 70 above.

74 Huang, Meixian 黄美贤. *"Suiban jiudu" jiaoshi de zhuanye peixun wenti yu duice yanjiu—yi shanghai shi C qu wei ge'an* "随班就读"教师的专业培训问题与对策研究——以上海市C区为个案. Shanghai: East China Normal University, 2010.

75 Zhou, Jiaxian 周加仙. "Weile meiwei xuesheng de fazhan: jiyu nao yu renzhi kexue de tongyong jiaoxue sheji" 为了每位学生的发展：基于脑与认知科学的通用教学设计. *Global Education* 全球教育展望 39, no. 1 (2010): 15–20.

Research into the Training of the Competence of Teachers 299

76 Lin, Xiaoxiao 林潇潇, and Deng, Meng 邓猛. "Meiguo xuexi zhang'ai xuesheng de zhuanxian ji dui woguo teshu jiaoyu de qishi" 美国学习障碍学生的转衔及对我国特殊教育的启示. *Chinese Journal of Special Education* 中国特殊教育 no. 3 (2014): 42–47.

77 McNay, L. "Agency and Experience: Gender as a Lived Relation." *The Sociological Review* 52, no. 2 (2004): 175–190.

78 Sannino, A. "Teachers' Talk of Experiencing: Conflict, Resistance and Agency." *Teaching and Teacher Education* 26, no. 4 (2010): 838–844.

References

Bazeley, P. *Qualitative Data Analysis: Practical Strategies*, 156. London: Sage, 2013.

Cai, Yingqi 蔡迎旗, and Zheng, Jie 郑洁. "You'eryuan jiaoshi peixun xuqiu de shizheng yanjiu" 幼儿园教师培训需求的实证研究. *Educational Research and Experiment* 教育研究与实验 no. 1 (2008): 66–70.

Chen, Yang 陈扬. "Zuzhi duoyuan yingdui celüe qianyan yanjiu pingshu: cong 'zhidu luoji' dao 'zuzhi shenfen'" 组织多元应对策略前沿研究评述：从"制度逻辑"到"组织身份," *East China Economic Management* 华东经济管理 29, no. 10 (2015): 146–151.

De Boer, A., Pijl, S. J., and Minnaert, A. "Regular Primary Schoolteachers' Attitudes Towards Inclusive Education: A Review of the Literature." *International Journal of Inclusive Education* 15, no. 3 (2011): 331–353.

Deng, Meng 邓猛, and Su, Hui 苏慧. "Ronghe jiaoyu zai zhongguo de jiajie yu zai shengcheng: jiyu shehui wenhua shijiao de fenxi" 融合教育在中国的嫁接与再生成：基于社会文化视角的分析. *Journal of Educational Studies* 教育学报 8, no. 1 (2012): 85–91.

Dimaggio, P. "Interest and Agency in Institutional Theory." In L. Zucker (ed.), *Institutional Patterns and Organizations: Culture and Environment*, 3–21. Cambridge, Massachusetts: Ballinger Publishing Company, 1988.

Dimaggio, P., and Powell, W. W. "The Iron Cage Revisited: Institutional Isomorphism and Collective Rationality in Organizational Fields." *American Sociological Review* 48, no. 2 (1983), 143–166.

Du, Lingyu 杜灵宇. *Yunnan shaoshu minzu nongcun diqu suiban jiudu jiaoshi zhihou peixun neirong xuqiu yanjiu* 云南少数民族农村地区随班就读教师职后培训内容需求研究, 23. Kunming: Yunnan Normal University, 2018.

Du, Yuan 杜媛, and Sun, Ying 孙颖. "Putong xuexiao jiaoshi ronghe jiaoyu zhuanye suyang tisheng lujing de fenxi ji qishi" 普通学校教师融合教育专业素养提升路径的分析及启示. *Disability Research* 残疾人研究 no. 9 (2019): 71–79.

Feng, Yajing 冯雅静. "Guowai ronghe jiaoyu shizi peixun de bufen jingyan he qishi" 国外融合教育师资培训的部分经验和启示. *Chinese Journal of Special Education* 中国特殊教育 no. 12 (2012): 5–9.

Fu, Wangqian 傅王倩, and Xiao, Fei 肖非. "Suiban jiudu ertong huiliu xianxiang de zhixing yanjiu" 随班就读儿童回流现象的质性研究. *Chinese Journal of Special Education* 中国特殊教育 no. 3 (2016): 5–11.

Gaitas, S., and Martins, M. A. "Teacher Perceived Difficulty in Implementing Differentiated Instructional Strategies in Primary School." *International Journal of Inclusive Education* 21, no. 5 (2016): 1–13.

Guan, Wenjun 关文军. "Ronghe jiaoyu xuexiao canji xuesheng ketang canyu de tedian ji jiaoshi tigong de zhichi yanjiu" 融合教育学校残疾学生课堂参与的特点及教师提供的支持研究. *Chinese Journal of Special Education* 中国特殊教育 no. 12 (2017): 3–10.

300 *Research into the Training of the Competence of Teachers*

Gunnthorsdottir, H., and Bjarnason, D. S. "Conflicts in Teachers' Professional Practices and Perspectives about Inclusion in Icelandic Compulsory Schools." *European Journal of Special Needs Education* no. 4 (2014): 491–504.

Guo, Jianru 郭建如. "Shehuixue zuzhi fenxi zhong de xinlao zhidu zhuyi yu jiaoyu yanjiu" 社会学组织分析中的新老制度主义与教育研究. *Peking University Education Review* 北京大学教育评论 no. 3 (2008): 136–151, 192.

Guowuyuan bangongting guanyu zhuanfa jiaoyubu deng bumen "Shisiwu" teshu jiaoyu fazhan tisheng xingdong jihua de tongzhi 国务院办公厅关于转发教育部等部门"十四五"特殊教育发展提升行动计划的通知. Jiaoyubu wangzhan 教育部网站, 2021. www.moe.gov.cn/jyb_xxgk/moe_1777/moe_1778/202201/t20220125_596312.html.

Hallett, T. "Symbolic Power and Organizational Culture." *Sociological Theory* 21, no. 2 (2003): 128–149.

Hallett, T. "Between Deference and Distinction: Interaction Ritual through Symbolic Power in an Educational Institution." *Social Psychology Quarterly* 70, no. 2 (2007): 148–171.

Hallett, T., and Meanwell, E. "Accountability as an Inhabited Institution: Contested Meanings and the Symbolic Politics of Reform." *Symbolic Interaction* 39, no. 3 (2016): 374–396.

Hodkinson, A. "Inclusive and Special Education in the English Educational System: Historical Perspectives, Recent Developments and Future Challenges." *British Journal of Special Education* 37, no. 2 (2010): 61–67.

Huang, Meixian 黄美贤. *"Suiban jiudu" jiaoshi de zhuanye peixun wenti yu duice yanjiu—yi shanghai shi C qu wei ge'an* "随班就读"教师的专业培训问题与对策研究——以上海市C区为个案. Shanghai: East China Normal University, 2010.

Ke, Zheng 柯政. "Xuexiao biange kunnan de xin zhidu zhuyi jieshi" 学校变革困难的新制度主义解释. *Peking University Education Review* 北京大学教育评论 no. 1 (2007): 42–54.

Ke, Zheng 柯政. "Jiaoshi de wenhua renzhi shi ruhe yingxiang kecheng zhengce shishi de: yi 'yanjiuxing xuexi' zhengce weili" 教师的文化认知是如何影响课程政策实施的：以"研究性学习"政策为例. *Global Education* 全球教育展望 no. 3 (2011): 41–50.

Li, Huanhuan 李欢欢, and Huang, Jin 黄瑾. "'Gao suzhi shan baojiao' you'er jiaoshi peixun moxing zhi goujian" "高素质善保教"幼儿教师培训模型之构建. *Journal of the Chinese Society of Education* 中国教育学刊 no. 2 (2019): 11–17.

Li, Jing 李静. "You'eryuan jiaoshi ronghe jiaoyu suyang yu peixun xuqiu fenxi—yi beijing diqu weili" 幼儿园教师融合教育素养与培训需求分析——以北京地区为例. *Teacher Development Research* 教师发展研究 no. 4 (2017): 67–73.

Lin, Xiaoxiao 林潇潇, and Deng, Meng 邓猛. "Meiguo xuexi zhang'ai xuesheng de zhuanxian ji dui woguo teshu jiaoyu de qishi" 美国学习障碍学生的转衔及对我国特殊教育的启示. *Chinese Journal of Special Education* 中国特殊教育 no. 3 (2014): 42–47.

Lindsay, G. "Inclusive Education: A Critical Perspective." *British Journal of Special Education* 30, no. 1 (2003): 3–12.

Lu, Naigui 卢乃桂. "Ronghe jiaoyu zai xianggang de chixu fazhan—jianlun teshu xuexiao de juese zhuanbian" 融合教育在香港的持续发展——兼论特殊学校的角色转变. *Chinese Journal of Special Education* 中国特殊教育 no. 11 (2004): 82–91.

March, J. G. *A Primer on Decision Making*, 37. New York: The Free Press, 1994.

McNay, L. "Agency and Experience: Gender as a Lived Relation." *The Sociological Review* 52, no. 2 (2004): 175–190.

Meyer, J. W., and Rowan, B. "Institutionalized Organizations: Formal Structure as Myth and Ceremony." *American Journal of Sociology* 83, no. 2 (1997): 340–363.

Sannino, A. "Teachers' Talk of Experiencing: Conflict, Resistance and Agency." *Teaching and Teacher Education* 26, no. 4 (2010): 838–844.

Shen, Junhong 申军红, Wang, Yongxiang 王永祥, and Hao, Guoqiang 郝国强. "Jiaoshi peixun xuqiu fenxi moxing jiangou yanjiu—yi haidian qu zhongxiaoxue xinren banzhuren weili" 教师培训需求分析模型建构研究——以海淀区中小学新任班主任为例. *Teacher Education Research* 教师教育研究, no. 6 (2016): 75–82.

Singal, N. "Working Towards Inclusion: Reflections from the Classroom." *Teaching and Teacher Education* 24, no. 6 (2008): 1516–1529.

Tian, Boqiong 田波琼, Shen, Renhong 申仁洪, and Liao, Lili 廖丽莉. "Sugelan zhongxiaoxue ronghe jiaoyu jiaoshi zhiqian peiyang de beijing, tedian ji qishi—yi IPP xiangmu weili" 苏格兰中小学融合教育教师职前培养的背景、特点及启示——以IPP项目为例. *Primary & Secondary Schooling Abroad*外国中小学教育 no. 10 (2017): 39–46.

Tiwari, A., Das, A. K., and Sharma, M. "Inclusive Education a 'Rhetoric' or 'Reality'? Teachers' Perspectives and Beliefs." *Teaching and Teacher Education* 52, no. 12 (2015): 128–136.

Wang, Hongxia 王红霞, Peng, Xin 彭欣, and Wang, Yanjie 王艳杰. "Beijing shi haidian qu xiaoxue ronghe jiaoyu xianzhuang diaocha yanjiu baogao" 北京市海淀区小学融合教育现状调查研究报告. *Chinese Journal of Special Education* 中国特殊教育 no. 4 (2011): 37–41.

Wang, Xiuying 王秀英. "Youxiao jiaoshi peixun de yaosu yu moxing jiangou" 有效教师培训的要素与模型建构. *The Inservice Education and Training of School Teachers* 中小学教师培训 no. 4 (2015): 18–21.

Wei, Xiaomei 魏小梅, and Li, Baoqing 李宝庆. "Xin gaokao jincheng zhong xuexiao biange de kunjing yu yingdui celüe: xin zhidu zhuyi de shijiao" 新高考进程中学校变革的困境与应对策略：新制度主义的视角. *Research on Educational Development* 教育发展研究 37, no. 22 (2017): 16–24.

Westwood, P. "'Differentiation' as a Strategy for Inclusive Classroom Practice: Some Difficulties Identified." *Australian Journal of Learning Disabilities* 6, no. 1 (2001): 5–11.

Xie, Zhengli 谢正立, and Deng, Meng 邓猛. "Lun ronghe jiaoyu jiaoshi juese ji xingcheng lujing" 论融合教育教师角色及形成路径. *Teacher Education Research* 教师教育研究 30, no. 6 (2018): 25–30.

Xu, Shuai 徐帅, and Zhao, Bin 赵斌. "Teshu jiaoyu jiaoshi zhuanye fazhan yuqi peixun xuqiu de guanxi yanjiu" 特殊教育教师专业发展与其培训需求的关系研究. *Journal of Educational Development* 教育导刊 no. 10 (2015): 79–82.

Yan, Jiaping 严加平. "Jiaoshi 'xiangyao de' jiushi 'xuqiu' le ma—OTP moshi jiqi zai jiaoshi xuexi xuqiu fenxi zhong de yunyong" 教师"想要的"就是"需求"了吗——OTP模式及其在教师学习需求分析中的运用. *Shanghai Research on Education* 上海教育科研 no. 12 (2013): 35–38.

Yin, Hongbiao 尹弘飚. "Lun kecheng biange de zhiduhua—jiyu xin zhidu zhuyi de fenxi" 论课程变革的制度化——基于新制度主义的分析. *Journal of Higher Education* 高等教育研究 30, no. 4 (2009): 75–81.

Ying, Xing 应星. "Zhixing yanjiu de fangfalun zai fansi" 质性研究的方法论再反思. *Journal of Guangxi University for Nationalities* (Philosophical and Social Science Edition), no. 4 (2016): 59–63.

Young, K., Mannix-McNamara, P., and Coughlan, B. "Authentic Inclusion–Utopian Thinking? Irish Post-primary Teachers' Perspectives of Inclusive Education." *Teaching and Teacher Education* 68, no. 11 (2017): 1–11.

Yu, Xin 余新. "Youxiao jiaoshi peixun de qige guanjian huanjie—yi 'guopei jihua—peixunzhe yanxiu xiangmu' peixun guanlizhe yanxiuban weili" 有效教师培训的七个关键环节——以"国培计划——培训者研修项目"培训管理者研修班为例. *Educational Research* 教育研究 31, no. 2 (2010): 77–83.

Yu, Xin 余新. *Jiaoshi peixunshi zhuanye xiulian* 教师培训师专业修炼, 90–110. Beijing: Educational Science Publishing House, 2014.

Yu, Yuzhen 余玉珍, and Yin, Hongbiao 尹弘飚. "Xianggang ronghe jiaoyu zhengce xia de jiaoshi zhuanye fazhan" 香港融合教育政策下的教师专业发展. *Journal of South China Normal University* (Social Science Edition) no. 6 (2014): 44–49.

Zeng, Yaru 曾雅茹. "Putong xiaoxue jiaoshi dui suiban jiudu de taidu jiaoxue celüe yu suoxu zhichi de yanjiu" 普通小学教师对随班就读的态度、教学策略与所需支持的研究. *Chinese Journal of Special Education* 中国特殊教育 no. 12 (2007): 5–9.

Zhang, Mengmeng 张猛猛. "Daxue zhangcheng shishi de dangxia kunjing yu pojie zhice—jiyu xin zhidu zhuyi de shijiao" 大学章程实施的当下困境与破解之策——基于新制度主义的视角. *Jiangsu Higher Education* 江苏高教 no. 3 (2019): 37–43.

Zhang, Yuexin 张悦歆. "Puxiao jiaoshi dui canji ertong suiban jiudu de taidu yanjiu" 普校教师对残疾儿童随班就读的态度研究. *Journal of Educational Studies* 教育学报 12, no. 3 (2016): 104–113.

Zhao, Decheng 赵德成, and Liang, Yongzheng 梁永正. "Peixun xuqiu fenxi: neihan moshi yu tuijin" 培训需求分析：内涵、模式与推进. *Teacher Education Research* 教师教育研究 no. 6 (2010): 11–16.

Zhou, Jiaxian 周加仙. "Weile meiwei xuesheng de fazhan: jiyu nao yu renzhi kexue de tongyong jiaoxue sheji" 为了每位学生的发展：基于脑与认知科学的通用教学设计. *Global Education* 全球教育展望 39, no. 1 (2010): 15–20.

Zhou, Xu 周序, and Liu, Qinglong 刘庆龙. "Jiaoshi yu yingshi jiaoyu: cong chongtu zouxiang hejie" 教师与应试教育：从冲突走向和解. *Journal of Educational Science of Hunan Normal University* 湖南师范大学教育科学学报 16, no. 5 (2017): 92–97.

Zhou, Xueguang 周雪光. *Zuzhi shehuixue shijiang* 组织社会学十讲, 77. Beijing: Social Sciences Academic Press, 2003.

Zhu, Xudong 朱旭东, and Song, Huan 宋萑. "Lun jiaoshi peixun de hexin yaosu" 论教师培训的核心要素. *Teacher Education Research* 教师教育研究 25, no. 3 (2013): 1–8.

Zucker, L. G. "The Role of Institutionalization in Cultural Persistence." *American Sociological Review* 42, no. 5 (1977): 726–743.

Zucker, L. G. "Institutional Theories of Organization." *Review of Sociology* 13, no. 1 (1987), 443–464.

7 Action Research into the Improvement of the Competence of Teachers in Inclusive Education

Research into teacher development should go deep into the daily education and teaching life of schools.[1]

During the implementation of inclusive education, the main responsibility of regular schools has been highlighted, and their teachers have proven to be the "cells" to implement inclusive education. The ability of teachers in this regard is bound to be closely related to the school field, and can be generated therein. Therefore, research into the improvement of teachers' inclusive education competence should go deep into the daily education and teaching life of schools. As early as 1995, some researchers proposed that responsible inclusion should be implemented in schools. Responsible inclusion of students with learning disabilities in regular education involves putting the students first, allowing teachers to self-select their involvement in inclusion, providing adequate resources, developing school-based inclusive models, maintaining a continuum of services, offering professional development, developing an inclusion philosophy, and refining curriculum approaches and service delivery to meet all students' needs.[2] When we go into the teachers' workplace—the school—"action" means not only exploration of the improvement path of the competence of teachers in inclusive education, but also confirmation of the aforementioned research into the influencing factors and mechanism of the competence of teachers in inclusive education. Therefore, we chose a regular primary school to conduct action research into the improvement of the competence of teachers in inclusive education.

The American social psychologist Kurt Lewin (1890–1947) put forward the term "action research" in the 1940s, established its basic concept, and openly advocated it, attracting much attention from the academic community. After the 1950s, the idea of action research was introduced into the field of education research, and then used widely. Different researchers gave different definitions to action research.

DOI: 10.4324/9781003432982-8

304 *Action Research into the Improvement of the Competence*

Stenhouse held that the main characteristic of action research was that "teachers become researchers." Elliott regarded "improving practice" as the basic purpose and characteristic of action research, and "constructing and utilizing theory" subordinate to this basic purpose. Kemmis thought that action research was a form of self-reflective inquiry by practitioners in social situations in order to improve the rationality and legitimacy of their practice, enhance their understanding of practice, and improve their social situation.[3]

The *International Encyclopedia of Education* defines action research as

Reflective research conducted by participants in social situations (educational situations) in order to improve their rational understanding of the social or educational practices they are engaged in, and to deepen their understanding of the practical activities and the context on which they depend.[4]

Action Research Scheme

The purpose of this research is to solve the actual problem of teachers' lack of inclusive education competence in the school for case study, and improve the teaching quality of the LRC program in the school from the perspective of teachers, school culture and management, and school-wide and social support, and on, and probe the process and strategies for improving the competence of teachers in inclusive education through reflection, summary, and analysis of the whole action process, so as to provide certain references for the improvement of the competence of teachers in inclusive education in future.

On this basis, this research covers two aspects: First, it analyzes and discusses the process of improving the competence of teachers in inclusive education; and, second, it probes the strategies for improving competence in combination with the theory of teacher professional development.

Selection of Respondents

In this research, all the regular teachers (hereinafter referred to as the "teachers") from T Primary School in Baohe District of Hefei City, Anhui Province are selected as respondents, except the resource teachers therefrom.

Established in 1981 as a full-time general primary school, T Primary School began to enroll children with intellectual disabilities or autism in the district and set up a special class (that is, a class composed of school-age special needs children) in 2005. Since 2012, some special needs children have been enrolled in the school's regular classes. In 2015, the school began to change the function of the special class and build a special education resource room. Currently, there are three resource teachers (also known as special education tutors, a kind of full-time teachers engaged in tutoring special needs children).[5] The resource room is still in the transition period, where the special class is taught collectively and LRC program students are tutored. The resource teachers serve as both subject teachers of the special class and tutors of LRC students.

The reasons for choosing this school as the research object are as follows. First, it is representative of regular primary and middle schools that began to implement the LRC program when there was a lack of sound support and a security system, and the competence of teachers in inclusive education was poor. Although T Primary School has resource teachers, their main responsibility lies in the collective teaching of the special class, and the school has no clear requirements for them to provide guidance and support for the LRC program. What is more, it also lacks professional support in various aspects such as rehabilitation training.

Second, it has pressing problems that need to be addressed. Teachers from this school do not identify with the LRC program, which leads to difficulty in implementation of the program. Their lack of skills in special education causes poor implementation of the program. In order to improve the education and teaching quality of the LRC program, it is necessary to improve the inclusive education competence of the teachers therein.

Third, there is a basis for research in this school. Although its teachers lack inclusive education competence, they have certain sympathy and compassion for the special needs children. In recent years, the administrators of this school have gradually realized the importance of improving the competence of teachers in inclusive education, and introduced a number of professionals in the special education field to improve the implementation of the LRC program.

Fourth, the school has advantages for this research. A major researcher is one of the three resource teachers of this school, maintaining a harmonious relationship with other researchers and the respondents. What is more, he is a middle-level administrator of the school, which is conducive to promoting action to a certain extent.

Research Method

Action research mainly has the following characteristics.

The first characteristic lies in "improvement." To improve the quality of action and practical work is the primary goal of action research. Action research can not only solve the problems arising from educational practice, but also improve the teaching quality and research level of teachers.[6]

The second characteristic refers to "participation." Teachers participate in the research as researchers. The participation is also characterized by "cooperation" and "reflection." The participating teachers who conducted individualized and isolated research in the past come to join the cooperative group research. Such cooperation includes themed dialogues between teachers, and between teachers and other schools' faculty members, as well as collaboration and support among teachers, experts, school administrators, and local education administrators. The teachers that take part in the action research

306 *Action Research into the Improvement of the Competence*

become "reflective practitioners," undertaking active reflection and integrating action and research.[7,8]

This research aims to improve the competence of T Primary School teachers in inclusive education through an action plan, and solve the problem of its teachers' lack of competence in LRC practice. Since action research is more suitable for the exploration of specific activities, this research adopts the method of action research.

Research Steps

Based on previous research into the competence of teachers in inclusive education, this research divides the competence of teachers in inclusive education into four dimensions: professional attitude, professional knowledge, professional skills, and the ability to get support. It first investigates and analyzes the current situation and development needs of the competence of T Primary School teachers in inclusive education, and then designs an action plan for improvement of their competence in combination with other documents, and adjusts the environment for implementation of the plan.

This research is divided into three phases for planning, implementation, and evaluation respectively.

In the first planning phase, we carefully study relevant documents to determine the action research direction. By means of questionnaire survey, teacher interview, and objects collection, we try to get an in-depth understanding of the current situation of the competence of teachers in inclusive education and analyze their original state. Then, according to the current situation as well as the theory of teacher professional development, the researchers join hands with some co-researchers to make an action plan, and prepare for concrete action.

In the second implementation phase, the researchers and co-researchers carry out the action for improvement of the teachers' inclusive education competence in accordance with the action plan. Members of the research team use reflective notes to record important events in the course of action, and conduct personal reflection. The researchers collect various text materials, such as the teachers' study notes and school system-related documents, as well as the teachers' feedback on the action plan in the process of the action, to keep abreast of the improvement situation of the competence of teachers in inclusive education. The researchers also hold continuous and intensive discussions with co-researchers to make constant revisions on the improvement path.

In the third evaluation phase, the researchers collect and analyze the data from the teachers, parents of the LRC students, co-researchers, and so on to evaluate the effect of the action. The main evaluation method is to make a second questionnaire survey of the teachers, and conduct a post-test with the *Scale of Teacher Competence in Inclusive Education* to determine the changes, and then evaluate the effect of the action plan in combination with re-interviews with the teachers, parents of the LRC students, and co-researchers.

Action Research into the Improvement of the Competence 307

Data Collection Methods

Questionnaire Survey

The *Scale of Teacher Competence in Inclusive Education* was used to conduct two surveys of T Primary School teachers. The first survey was conducted before the implementation of the action plan to understand the original state of the competence of teachers in inclusive education. The second survey was made to investigate the teachers' state after the completion of the whole action. Then, a comparison was made to analyze the changes in teachers' inclusive education competence. The scale sheets were issued twice. The pre-test scale sheets were issued in the planning phase . A total of 59 scale sheets were issued, and 43 retrieved, accounting for 72.9 percent of the total. The post-test scale sheets were issued during the evaluation phase. A total of 59 scale sheets were issued, and 48 retrieved, making up 81.4 percent of the total.

Interview Method

This research mainly adopts the semi-structured interview method. Teachers were interviewed in the action planning phase to understand their attitude toward the LRC program and related needs. In the action evaluation phase, semi-structured interviews were also conducted with T Primary School teachers, administrators, resource teachers, and parents of LRC students to collect relevant information. With the consent of the interviewees, the interview content was recorded in the form of written or audio recording. According to the interview outline, the researchers asked questions, hoping to obtain interviewees' real attitudes toward the LRC program and understand some of the teachers' educational and teaching experiences in the LRC program. At the same time, they seized the opportunity to ask more questions to find out whether the competence of teachers in inclusive education had really been improved, as well as the deep reasons for improvement or not. The interview outline is provided as an appendix to this book.

In the planning phase, eight teachers of different ages and subjects were interviewed face-to-face. Their basic information is shown in Table 7.1.

In the evaluation phase, semi-structured interviews were also conducted face-to-face with a total of 16 people with different roles. Their basic information is shown in Table 7.2.

Objects Collection Method

Generally, material objects reflect the way people view some things in a certain context. Collection of these objects can be used to analyze the materialized forms of people's ideas in specific circumstances. The objects collected in this research include the teachers' study notes, school rules and regulations, the

308   *Action Research into the Improvement of the Competence*

Table 7.1 Basic Information on Interviewees in Action Planning Phase

Serial number	Interviewee (teacher)	Type	Subject	Age	Interview duration
1	Wen	LRC program teacher	Physical education	24	15 mins
2	Wang	LRC program teacher	Chinese	40	20 mins
3	Mei	LRC program teacher	Fine arts	39	15 mins
4	Hu	LRC program teacher	Music	26	13 mins
5	Ni	LRC program teacher	English	42	18 mins
6	Jiang	Non-LRC-program teacher	Math	40	21 mins
7	Li	Non-LRC-program teacher	Chinese	37	26 mins
8	Guo	Non-LRC-program teacher	Math	33	16 mins

Note: LRC program teacher refers to the one whose class has special needs students, while non-LRC-program teacher refers to the one whose class has no special needs student.

Table 7.2 Basic Information on Interviewees in Evaluation Phase

Serial number	Interviewee (teacher)	Type	Subject	Age	Interview duration
1	Zhao	LRC program teacher	English	27	17 mins
2	Hu	LRC program teacher	Music	26	14 mins
3	Liang	LRC program teacher	Fine arts	25	16 mins
4	Wang	LRC program teacher	Chinese	40	15 mins
5	Yan	LRC program teacher	Chinese	26	15 mins
6	Mei	LRC program teacher	Fine arts	39	17 mins
7	Duan	Non-LRC-program teacher	Chinese	35	12 mins
8	Cheng	Non-LRC-program teacher	Math	44	13 mins
9	Jin	Non-LRC-program teacher	Chinese	42	15 mins
10	Huang	Non-LRC-program teacher	Math	45	12 mins
11	Yuan	Resource teacher	General teacher	26	20 mins
12	Zhuang	Resource teacher	General teacher	26	15 mins
13	Parent of Little Q	Parent of LRC student	None	36	31 mins
14	Parent of Little T	Parent of LRC student	None	64	30 mins
15	Parent of Little G	Parent of LRC student	None	37	35 mins

Action Research into the Improvement of the Competence 309

homework of LRC students, records of resource teachers' guidance for LRC students, and other relevant text materials.

Data Analysis Methods

The data collected in this research mainly include the data obtained via the two questionnaire surveys, interview data, and physical data.

The data collected via the questionnaire surveys were quantitative data, so SPSS20.0 software was used to perform descriptive statistics on the data. The data were divided into two groups according to the survey time, namely the pre-test group and the post-test group. The paired sample t-test was conducted on the four dimensions—professional attitude, professional knowledge, professional skills, and the ability to get support—for a quantitative analysis of the changes of the competence of teachers after the action.

Interview data and physical data were qualitative data. The researchers converted interview recordings and physical data into text before categorizing and coding them. Based on the theory of teacher professional development and the connotation and structure of the competence of teachers in inclusive education, this research carried out three-level coding of the text data. The first step was to categorize and code according to the dimensions of the competence of teachers in inclusive education. The second step was generic coding, which divided the descriptive properties of the text data into those describing variation and those describing attribution. The third step was open coding of the specific information of the text. The data coding logic of this research is shown in Table 7.3.

Course of the Action for Improvement of the Competence of Teachers in Inclusive Education

"Original State" of the Competence of Teachers in Inclusive Education

In the planning phase, the researchers got a clear picture of the teachers' state before implementation of the action plan through analysis of text data, teacher interviews, questionnaires, and other data.

Implementation of the LRC program out of "Conscience"

When T Primary School set up the special class, there was no clear official document to be followed, or corresponding supporting measures. This was done out of the principal's sympathy for special needs children. As the special class became oversized, the LRC program was implemented to place the excessive special needs students in regular classes. As a full-time regular primary school, T Primary School's main task has always been educating and teaching ordinary students. The target management assessment (a kind of assessment system for school work) by the higher-level government department did not

310   *Action Research into the Improvement of the Competence*

Table 7.3 Data Coding

First-level categorization	Generic coding	Open coding	Examples
Categorization by dimension A. Professional attitude	A-a variation	A-a-1 pre-test	Special needs children should be educated by professionals in special schools or classes, so that they can receive more professional guidance.
		A-a-1 post-test	Whether to enroll the children with special needs in regular classes should be determined according to the degree of their respective disability and the interference of their problematic behaviors with other students. If he can follow the study, I'm willing to accept him.
		A-a-2 pre-test	Some ordinary students look at them with strange eyes, thus causing hurt to them, so they'd better go to specialized institutions.
		A-a-2 post-test	The small classes that undertake the LRC program can influence more ordinary families and other people in society to accept them, so as to truly achieve social acceptance and recognition.
	A-b attribution	A-b-1 emotional interaction	After we got familiar with each other, they often said to me, "You are my good friend," or "I love you!" On festivals, they also sent me small cards made by themselves, which really touched me.
		A-b-2 resource teacher support	Once, the resource teacher told us about the evaluation of special needs children. The diversified evaluation methods also inspired us a lot, and gave us a deeper understanding of inclusive education.

Action Research into the Improvement of the Competence   311

cover the LRC program. The LRC program was started out of the "conscience" of school management, and the higher-level administrative department had neither mandatory requirements nor special commendation for it.

Although T Primary School had run the special class for one decade or more and carried out the LRC program for nearly five years, it was still unknown in the industry. One of its leaders said: "We didn't know what the LRC program meant at first, we just selected the excessive special needs students who didn't interfere with the class order and placed them in regular classes." The principal also confessed, "I had no idea of the Special Education Committee, and never contacted those engaged in special education. We had no access to any special education activities."

With regard to the special needs children's parents, as long as there were ordinary teachers willing to accept their children, they would feel grateful, and go to assist their children in regular classrooms personally, but seldom communicate with the subject teachers for fear of bothering them. In contrast, some parents worried about their children being "looked at strangely" in a regular class, and some had no time to go to the classroom to assist their children, and were thus unwilling to let their children attend the LRC program.

"Implanted" Special Education

The experience of running the special class for over 10 years provided T Primary School a foundation for implementing the LRC program. However, it only broke the spatial separation between ordinary children and special needs children, between teachers and special needs children, and between teachers and resource teachers. With regard to cultural atmosphere, there was still an "invisible wall" blocking them. Most ordinary children had no idea there were special needs students in the school, or held a misunderstanding toward them. As a parent said, "Once, I heard a few children on the playground saying, 'The special class is a group of fools. Don't play with them.' I felt quite sad at that." Teachers had sympathy and compassion for special needs children, but in daily work, they had little interaction with them, and seldom communicated with the resource teachers.

The city where T Primary School is located issued the *Special Education Promotion Plan (2014–2017)*, proposing that preference should be given to teachers who engage in the LRC program in their assessment and professional title evaluation. However, this requirement had not been fulfilled in the schools. There was neither an examination requirement nor institutional recognition for LRC program teachers, so they played an awkward role in the work. Moreover, there was no clear regulation on the guidance and support responsibility of resource teachers in the LRC program. There were only requirements on class hours and routine for resource teachers in the collective teaching. A resource teacher said: "No one has asked us to provide guidance for LRC students. We seldom communicate with general education teachers

312 *Action Research into the Improvement of the Competence*

in daily work. Occasionally, I came across some general education teachers at lunch time, and had a word with them."

In terms of organizational structure, the school only had teaching and research groups in general education subjects, namely the Chinese teaching and research group, the math teaching and research group, and the comprehensive teaching and research group (including English, music, fine arts, and so on). Teaching and research activities did not involve discussion of the knowledge and skills in special education as well as the problems related to the LRC program. The resource teachers were also incorporated into the teaching and research groups in general education subjects according to the main subject they taught, and participated in the seminars on general education. Moreover, the school had no relatively systematic teacher professional growth mechanism, such as the master–apprentice system, and the overall teacher professional development atmosphere was not strong.

School management focused on the majority of ordinary students. However, from 2016, school administrators gradually realized the importance of improving the education and teaching quality of the LRC program. In the new round of the three-year development plan of the school, "inclusive education" was taken as the guiding ideology of the school, and implementation of the LRC program was listed as one of the key tasks. However, no specific action had been carried out.

Teachers in Confusion

The data from the survey of the *Scale of Teacher Competence in Inclusive Education* in the planning phase and the preliminary interviews reflect the state of the competence of teachers in inclusive education in T Primary School. With sympathy and compassion for special needs children, more than 70 percent of teachers agreed that special needs children have the same right to receive education as their ordinary peers, but they were in favor of special education for special needs children rather than inclusive education, believing that those children could receive more professional guidance in a special education school or special class. More than half of teachers could not see the benefits of the LRC program for special needs children, worrying that they might be discriminated against in regular class, and their physical and mental development thus affected. In the actual work of the LRC program, teachers usually ignored LRC students, making no requirements on their studies, and not expecting them to make any academic progress. LRC students were basically tutored by their parents accompanying them in the classroom. If the parents had no tutoring skills, these students could only "idle in the class." A teacher said:

> The special needs student in my [regular] class is well-behaved, basically not disturbing my teaching, so I don't have to pay attention to him in class. I worry that excessive requirements will make him feel pressure in his study,

so he does his homework at will. Since his mother is always with him, I don't have to worry about it.

The general education teachers' inclusive education competence was not high on the whole, with a score of 3.14 (full score: 5). The score for their professional knowledge was 2.65, and that for their ability to get support 3.14. In their professional attitude, they recognized the "equal right to education," but held a poor understanding of the LRC program, which led to their neglect of special needs students.

Arguing that they were not professional special education teachers, unable to undertake the LRC program, the teachers were found inactive in LRC practice. One teacher revealed:

When an autistic student joined my class, I had no idea what to do. Sometimes he made a noise in class, but I didn't know how to deal with it. In fact, I didn't dare to deal with it casually, for fear that it would bring bad influence to him or other students.

When we went deep into the reality of teachers' professional activities in T Primary School, we spotted their poor competence in inclusive education, and numerous obstacles on the road to improvement. Due to the loose requirement of the higher-level administrative department in this regard and the obscurity of the school in the industry, teachers had no enthusiasm to implement the LRC program; the cultural atmosphere of separating the special class from regular classes subtly affected teachers' acceptance of the inclusion concept; the unclear system resulted in teachers' lack of a clear identity in LRC practice, which further affected their autonomy and enthusiasm in improving the quality of inclusive education; the traditional organizational structure hindered effective communication between teachers and resource teachers; and the inactive school management provided no support for the improvement of the competence of teachers in inclusive education. In such an occupational environment, teachers who had no special education background inevitably tended to neglect special needs children in class. It is obvious that the action to improve the competence of teachers in inclusive education was hindered by various obstacles, and that there was a long way to go.

Forging Ahead: Action to Improve the Competence of Teachers in Inclusive Education

Setting Sail on the Ice-breaking Journey

After making clear the "original state" of the competence of teachers in inclusive education and analyzing the obstacles to improvement, the researchers joined hands with various parties to develop and implement an action plan. First of all, they contacted school management to explain the purpose and significance of this research, and won administrative support. Then, they

314 *Action Research into the Improvement of the Competence*

formed a research team with two resource teachers, a vice principal in charge of teaching, and a university researcher. Finally, they carried out this research in two semester-based phases, each lasting four months.

GETTING SUPPORT FROM PARENTS AND PROMOTING THE INTERACTION BETWEEN PARENTS AND TEACHERS

To obtain the support of the parents, the researchers created opportunities for communication between parents and teachers of special needs children by holding mini-lectures for the parents and coaching the accompanying parents. In this process, the psychological journey of the parents and their wishes for attending the LRC program were disclosed to the teachers. Thus, the benefits of the LRC program for special needs children were expounded from the parents' perspective, so that the teachers could empathize with them. One teacher noted:

> I was deeply impressed by a lecture given by a parent. Every child in every family is unique. For the parents of special needs children, they have a peaceful attitude toward treating them, so we teachers should follow suit. We shouldn't look at them with special eyes, which would not be good for their physical and mental development.

The parents accompanying their special needs children in school were guided to communicate with the teachers. "The accompanying parents give me a lot of help in class management, such as dealing with some student accidents when I'm absent. Teachers and parents are in the need of each other," a teacher explained. In this way, the teachers found it more convenient and effective to get the parents' support and know more about the special needs children from their parents, such as their characteristics and learning style.

OPENING UP MULTIPLE WAYS TO CREATE AN INCLUSIVE SCHOOL CULTURE

First of all, the research team won the support of school management; one member of the research team was the vice principal in charge of teaching. The administrative power was thus made use of to ensure the smooth creation of an inclusive school culture and the participation of all teachers in the school-based training for the LRC program.

As the "invisible wall" of the school was pushed down, the researchers organized a variety of student activities on festivals in the school. Teachers and students of the special class invited ordinary children and teachers to join their activities. As a regular teacher said, "Once I attended the birthday party of a student from the special class. Although the activity was over, they greeted me upon seeing me again, which made me very happy." Efforts were also made to create an inclusive atmosphere and enhance mutual understanding. As a result, the teachers sometimes were even reminded by some compassionate ordinary students to pay attention to those special needs children.

The T Primary School launched the "Qinglan Project" to establish a teacher professional growth mechanism featuring "experienced teachers tutoring younger teachers." Through collective lesson preparation, class observation, and open class, the younger teachers' professional level was improved, and the overall atmosphere for individual professional development took shape in the school. As one of the projects for teachers' professional growth, school-based training was carried out to improve the competence of teachers in inclusive education, with resource teachers as trainers. Thanks to the training, all teachers systematically learned related educational concepts, knowledge, and skills.

In addition, a LRC program consultation and guidance plan was worked out. Every Friday afternoon was taken as the offline consulting time for LRC program teachers. Online consultation was also available via QQ at any time. The resource teachers provided consultation services, and delivered LRC program-related knowledge on the WeChat Public Account of the school; they also entered the classes with LRC students to provide guidance. As a teacher noted, "The one-to-one chat with special education teachers is a positive. I can ask them whatever I don't understand."

STIMULATING TEACHERS' INITIATIVE

The active promotion of school leaders, inclusive atmosphere, systematic support of resource teachers, and active communication of the parents of special needs children combined to stimulate the initiative of regular teachers and force them to re-identify their role.

In an inclusive atmosphere, the teachers and special needs children got familiar with each other, so the cognitive bias of the teachers toward those children was corrected. "Before communicating with the special needs children, I thought it was hard for them to control themselves and they would even attack others at will. Now I have more contact with them, I think they are also innocent and lovely," said a teacher. With the support of various parties, LRC program teachers could use appropriate ways to communicate with special needs children and develop emotional interaction. "Little T [an autistic boy] is very cute. The teachers in our office like to give him snacks when they see him, so he often runs to our office after class. He remembers many teachers, including those who don't teach him," said a teacher.

The teachers' correct cognition of special needs children was helpful for them to make correct analysis of LRC practice, so as to recognize the concept of inclusive education. Their emotional connection with the special needs children helped to promote their enthusiasm in learning relevant knowledge and skills in the LRC program.

316 *Action Research into the Improvement of the Competence*

Introspection–Obedience Attempt

At first, teachers were unaware of the importance of improving their inclusive education competence, only passively learning the knowledge and skills in the LRC program due to compulsory promotion via administrative force and the active intervention of resource teachers.

With the progress of the action, the interaction of various external factors promoted a change in teachers' thinking as well as improvement in their knowledge and skills in the LRC program. In terms of professional attitude, they became willing to accept the special needs children and actively guided them to get along with the ordinary children. As a general education teacher said, "In class activities, Little N walks slowly, so I find a student to accompany her." Another teacher added: "In some anniversary commemorations, such as the National Day for Helping the Disabled, we will hold class meetings, teaching the students how to help the special needs children." With regard to professional knowledge and skills, the teachers gained some understanding of the connotation of inclusive education, and learned diversified evaluation methods for special needs children, trying to change the methods for homework and examination for those children. As a resource teacher explained, "After learning that the poor performance of special needs children in the examination may be related to their inability to understand the questions, rather than their inability to understand the knowledge point, some teacher read the questions or substitute the pen and paper tests with other means." With respect to the ability to get support, LRC program teachers began to actively seek support from the accompanying parents, understand the relevant characteristics and learning style of the special needs students to find solutions to specific problems.

However, the inclusive class atmosphere only focused on the inclusion in life instead of classroom teaching. "The teacher generally asks no question for him. Occasionally when Little Q put his hand up to answer a question, he was asked to answer a very simple question, such as reading some words." They were passive in obtaining the support from resource teachers. However, the support provided by resource teachers was an extra workload, which had neither been defined as their responsibility in the form of a system nor been recognized in other ways in their assessment. Thus, the guidance was causally provided by resource teachers.

At the end of the first phase, most of the teachers were willing to accept the special needs children. As a teacher said, "This form of study can make them happier and healthier, and learn more living skills. Why don't we do these meaningful things that will help them to have a better social life in the future?" Moreover, the teachers tried to create an inclusive class atmosphere, and seek support from the parents of special needs children.

Set Sailing Again on a New Journey Forward

After the implementation of the action in the first phase, the research team collected the teachers' views and suggestions on the action plan through an

Action Research into the Improvement of the Competence 317

open questionnaire survey, and undertook self-reflection. On this basis, the action plan was modified and implemented again to further promote the improvement of the competence of teachers in inclusive education.

The parents of children with special needs continued to accompany their children to attend school, and were encouraged to undertake more effective communication with the teachers.

Collective activities were utilized to create an inclusive school atmosphere, and a LRC program guidance system was established, expressly stipulating that resource teachers should provide LRC program guidance for no fewer than two class hours per week, the specific content of each guidance should be recorded, and this work should be included in the assessment of resource teachers. As a resource teacher said:

> The teachers who take the initiative to consult us are usually the class tutors and the main subject teachers, such as Chinese and math teachers. Since the minor-subject teachers teach many classes, they generally don't come to consult us. Now we have more time to enter the regular classes to discuss with the teachers more often. We can talk about some deeper issues.

At the same time, the special teaching and research group was set up to organize teaching and research activities and provide teachers with systematic LRC program knowledge and a skills learning platform in the form of comprehensive teaching and research activity (full participation). In addition, the open classes allowed the teachers to enter the special class and observe the teaching methods adopted by resource teachers for different types of special needs children, so that the teachers could intuitively feel the position of resource teachers in classroom teaching, thus affecting their attitude toward special needs children and their educational needs. "They [resource teachers] are more patient in class, paying attention to each student. I saw some kids crying or yelling, but the resource teacher was still very calm. I really appreciate them," said a teacher.

The comprehensive teaching and research activity focused on the adjustment in the education and teaching of LRC students to improve the teachers' cognition of inclusive classroom teaching. It paid attention to both the life and subject learning problems of the special needs children. In this action, the teachers began to have expectations on the academic performance of the LRC students and get satisfaction from it. They adjusted their teaching objectives and contents according to the ability development of the LRC students, and adopted appropriate teaching strategies. "I will design questions according to the ability of the student, such as asking him to read a paragraph instead of some words. Previously, I asked him mechanical questions, but now, I try to ask him some thoughtful questions." Peer guidance was also encouraged in study. For example, an ordinary student was asked to remind his special needs peer to follow the teacher to draw in a fine arts class. After learning some knowledge and skills in the LRC program, the teachers felt less worried about the teaching of LRC students. When they applied the skills to educational practice,

318 *Action Research into the Improvement of the Competence*

they got positive feedback from the students. This sense of achievement and satisfaction helped them identify with the LRC program, thus stimulating their initiative to improve their competence in inclusive education.

Reconsideration

In terms of winning support from societal forces, this research mainly took measures to obtain support from the parents of special needs children, and stimulate the teachers' desire to improve their competence in inclusive education with the parents' support and positive feedback. Front-line workers cannot directly participate in or influence the formulation or modification of macro policies, and the recognition of administrative departments and insiders cannot be achieved overnight, which requires a process of long-term accumulation. However, front-line workers can attract the attention of social personages through their own efforts, and influence the opinions of others. In the first phase of the action research, T Primary School gradually gained recognition in the industry thanks to its experience and efforts made in special education. It joined the provincial Special Education Committee and delivered a report on the work of the LRC program at the provincial annual meeting on special education, receiving favorable comments. From January 2017, the District Education and Sports Bureau began to take T Primary School as the teachers' moral education base, and carried out the "one-day teaching assistant" activity for nearly 300 beginning teachers in the district. These teachers were invited to special classes to assist resource teachers in teaching for one day so that they could understand special needs children and learn the educational ethos of the resource teachers. Thereby, efforts were made to lay the foundation for the development of the LRC program in the whole district. As a result, school management paid more attention to the improvement of the competence of teachers in inclusive education in the second phase of the action research.

Although the teachers were still worried about their ability to teach LRC students, they became willing to learn and try. As a teacher said, "Special needs children with different types of disabilities have different learning characteristics. I have only taught students with autism, so for other types of children, I still need to learn and explore how to teach." Moreover, they could actively seek support from the available resources to solve the difficulties in the implementation of the LRC program.

What is more, the teachers actively put forward suggestions on the action plan for this research. One teacher suggested providing more one-to-one guidance, and another asked for opportunities to personally experience in the special class. They actively considered how to do a better job in the LRC program. A teacher even consulted her old classmate who taught fine arts in a special school about appropriate teaching methods for special needs students. Full participation in the action made LRC practice a part of the daily work of teachers in the school.

Action Research into the Improvement of the Competence 319

Thanks to the multiple measures and continuous efforts, T Primary School finally saw prospects for improving the competence of teachers in inclusive education.

Prospects Seen after Evaluation and Reflection of the Action

Evaluation: The Dawn Is Coming

After the two phases of the action, the researchers made a further survey with the *Scale of Teacher Competence in Inclusive Education* and post-action interviews to evaluate the competence of teachers in inclusive education. The result showed that the inclusive education competence of teachers was improved, evidenced by an increase in the score from 3.14 before the action to 3.52 after the action.

From the perspective of professional attitude, the teachers improved their attitude toward the LRC program, recognizing the positive effects of the LRC program or inclusive education on the children with special needs. However, they believed that whether to enroll the children with special needs in regular classes should be determined according to the degree of their respective disability and the interference their problematic behaviors caused to other students. One of the teachers said it would be a pain for a special needs child to learn in a regular classroom if he was unable to study at all in the school.

With regard to professional knowledge, teachers got a better understanding of the theory of inclusive education as well as the general physical and mental characteristics and learning style of special needs children. They also learned the educational evaluation methods for special needs children. Some teachers suggested applying as a whole individualized educational plans to each special needs child as well as ordinary students at the same level.

In terms of professional skills, teachers became able to make teaching adjustment and flexible evaluation, carry out group cooperation, seek peer support and find ways to improve the classroom participation of special needs children. As the parent of Little G said, "In this semester, the math teacher asked Little G questions in every class. He was often asked to perform on stage in music class."

The ability of teachers to get support was also enhanced. They actively sought support from accompanying parents and resource teachers. As the accompanying parents stayed with their children all the time in the school, it was more convenient for teachers to strive for their resources and support in teaching. One teacher revealed:

Once, Little T burst into crying in class, so I went directly to ask his grandfather after class. The grandfather told me that it was because his mother was on a business trip, and as long as he was told his mother would come back in a few days, he would stop crying. Then, I knew what to do when he cried.

320   *Action Research into the Improvement of the Competence*

Reflection: Hard-won Result

In retrospect, the research team still had some regrets with regard to obtaining the support of school leaders. For example, there was still no specific and operable document on the role, work scope, and assessment requirements of regular teachers in LRC practice. However, there was a teaching achievement award in the assessment of their performance in teaching ordinary students. Therefore, teachers still concentrated on the education and teaching of ordinary students.

With the progress of the action, the teachers no longer found the LRC program a "meaningless administrative task," but good for both special needs children and themselves. They began to learn the knowledge and skills in the LRC program and applied them into practice. "I follow some public accounts or websites, such as Tencent Public Welfare, to learn relevant knowledge through some activities, such as Autism Day," said one.

For teachers who had special needs students in their classes, they could conduct self-reflection in their own teaching and explore teaching methods for these students. They were no longer "bystanders" but "insiders" in the work of the LRC program. For teachers without special needs children in their classes, they gave no consideration to how to teach such students, but showed confidence in undertaking the LRC program.

The research team modified the action plan based on the changes and feedback of teachers and, in this process, their ability was also improved. They found better ways of communication to facilitate implementation of the action plan. The resource teachers began to gain more knowledge of general education, in order to provide better guidance for general education teachers and apply the knowledge and skills of special education to the teaching of general education courses appropriately.

Implementation of the action fed researchers' and respondents' new thinking and expectations for themselves in inclusive education. Step by step, they saw a bright future.

Analysis of Development Process of Competence of Teachers in Inclusive Education and Strategies to Improve It

Development Process of Competence of Teachers in Inclusive Education

The professional development of teachers is a dynamic, continuous process, with different levels of professional needs, attitudes, beliefs, professional knowledge, and skills at different stages of development. Ye Lan divided the process of teacher professional development into five stages—non-concern, virtual concern, survival concern, task concern, and self-renewal concern respectively— according to the index of "teachers' awareness of self-initiated professional development."[9] As a part of teachers' overall competence, the competence of teachers in inclusive education also shows different attitudes, knowledge, and skills in different stages according to their awareness of self-competence

Action Research into the Improvement of the Competence   321

improvement. Through action research, we divided the improvement of the competence of teachers of T Primary School in inclusive education into four stages according to their self-awareness: "showing disregard–being passive–making attempts–making explorations."

Stage of Showing Disregard

Traditionally, special needs children were isolated in special education schools or institutions and taught by special education teachers. Even though increasing numbers of special needs children were enrolled in regular classes, in the educational concepts of most teachers, the education and teaching tasks of special needs children should still be assigned to special education teachers. In daily life, teachers had some sympathy and compassion for special needs children, but in their own education and teaching, they disregarded the existence of this group, excluding them in their own teaching scope and paying no attention to the improvement of their own inclusive education competence.

Stage of Being Passive

When teachers did not recognize their role in LRC practice, it was difficult to stimulate their initiative to improve their competence in inclusive education, which needed to be promoted by external intervention.

With the help of administrative power, all the teachers at the school were forced to participate in the learning of the relevant concepts, knowledge, and skills in the LRC program in an orderly and smooth way. Under the promotion of this collective action, teachers took the learning as an administrative task to complete passively.

Stage of Making Attempts

With the intervention of administration, an inclusive atmosphere of acceptance, tolerance, and respect gradually took shape in the school. Teachers gradually formed a close emotional relationship with the special needs children and their parents, and developed a better understanding of the physical and mental characteristics and learning style of those children as well as the concept of inclusive education, gradually correcting their cognitive bias toward special needs children. Thanks to the continuous support of various resources, they kept learning the knowledge and skills in LRC practice. In the meantime, teachers also made continuous attempts to apply what they had learned to specific LRC practice.

Stage of Making Explorations

In her book *A New Exploration of Teachers' Role and Teacher Development*, Ye Lan pointed out:

322 *Action Research into the Improvement of the Competence*

The work of teachers is a process full of creation. The activation of know-ledge in the process of education, the keen feeling of students' psychological changes, the timely grasp of educational opportunities, and the ingenious resolution of educational contradictions and conflicts all give expression to teachers' creativity. In this process, teachers can also feel the inherent dignity and joy of the profession.[10]

With the continuous promotion of our action, teachers felt satisfied with the positive emotional feedback given by special needs children and their parents, and the progress of those children brought teachers a sense of achievement. This encouraged teachers to take the initiative to improve their competence in inclusive education, and explore ways of improvement in line with their own development needs and learning habits, so as to carry out more targeted and deeper learning of the knowledge and skills for better education and teaching practice.

With more positive feedback and support from the parents of special needs students, teachers quickly entered the stage of making explorations. However, those who did not undertake LRC program remained in the stage of being willing to make attempts in LRC practice.

Strategies to Improve Competence of Teachers in Inclusive Education

Also in her book, Ye Lan put forward the view that the promotion of teacher development should shift from external motivation to internal motivation. "Due to the traditional emphasis on the social function of the teaching profession, teachers often forge ahead with a heavy social mission. Meanwhile, the society always constrains and guides the development of teachers by external forces, but ignores their subjective initiative as independent individuals." She continued:

> For teachers, education is as important as self-education. Even in a sense, self-education should precede the education of others. On the one hand, teacher development is the prerequisite for the success of education and the development of students. On the other hand, self-development is not only the obligation of teachers, but also the right of teachers. It is an important way to enrich the connotation of teachers' life. From the standpoint of teachers, every teacher has the ability of self-development, and the awareness of professional development is the most important driving force for teacher development.

According to the aforementioned research findings, the inclusive school atmosphere not only directly affects the level of the competence of teachers in inclusive education, but also exerts its influence on competence through teacher agency. Based on analysis of the improvement process of the competence of teachers in inclusive education in T Primary School, we will summarize the

Action Research into the Improvement of the Competence   323

path and strategies to improve the competence of teachers in inclusive education in different periods, and then create a model for improvement of the inclusive education competence of the teachers in the school, and finally put forward a few strategies to improve it.

Making Use of Administrative Power

School administrators dominate the formulation of the school system, and impose great influence on the construction of school culture, the degree of resource support, and the intensity and results of the implementation of organizational decisions. As for our action research carried out in T Primary School, we actively sought the support of its administrators.

Firstly, we got in contact with and kept in communication with school management. After explaining the purpose and significance of this research to them, we won administrative support, and invited a vice principal to be a collaborator of our action research. School management gradually realized the importance of improving the education and teaching quality of the LRC program. In the three-year development plan of the school, "inclusive education" was taken as the guiding ideology of the school, and implementation of the LRC program as one of the key tasks. To this end, the concrete measures it took included adjusting and establishing a series of systems; establishing a professional growth project for teachers to improve their competence in inclusive education, and providing school-based training for all the teachers to systematically learn related educational concepts, knowledge, and skills; adjusting the teaching and research system, setting up special teaching and research groups based on the existing subject teaching and research groups, organizing teaching and research activities with the help of the special teaching and research group, and allowing teachers to enter the special class in the form of open classes to observe the teaching methods adopted by resource teachers for different types of special needs children, thus affecting their attitude toward special needs children and teaching methods; and formulating resource teacher consultation and a guidance plan for the LRC program, and establishing a LRC program guidance system to define the responsibilities and assessment standards of resource teachers in implementation of the LRC program.

Therefore, in the process of improving teachers' inclusive education competence, it is necessary to make use of administrative power to promote continuous improvement under the guarantee of a specific system.

Creating an Inclusive Cultural Atmosphere

T Primary School held mini-lectures and provided guidance for the accompanying parents to strengthen their communication with teachers and promote mutual cooperation. A variety of student activities were held on festivals to strengthen interaction between teachers, ordinary children, and special needs children. These activities, permeated with the concept of inclusive education,

324 *Action Research into the Improvement of the Competence*

helped create a strong cultural atmosphere conducive to the improvement of teachers' inclusive education competence.

Bringing into Play the Pivotal Role of Resource Teachers

Resource teachers played an irreplaceable role in improving the competence of teachers in inclusive education in T Primary School. First, they persuaded school management to change their thinking and provide support for the LRC program. Second, they provided professional services for ordinary teachers, including training in the inclusive education concept, knowledge, and skills, weekly counselling service for teachers, online consultation and inclusive education lectures through the QQ and WeChat platforms, and on-site instruction in classes with special needs students. Moreover, a variety of opportunities were created for ordinary children to have contact with special needs children so as to enhance their mutual understanding and stimulate peer support.

In short, building an inclusive school atmosphere is a path to improve teachers' inclusive education competence. In the action research in the case study school, resource teachers developed resources for the school management by changing their thinking to generate an administrative driving force for the formulation of plans and corresponding systems, teacher professional development projects, and adjustment of the organizational structure. Thus, teachers changed their passive attitude to actively improve their competence in inclusive education. This is the main path to improve competence. Resource teachers not only provided professional support for ordinary teachers and created multi-party connection platforms, but also triggered their emotions and internal motivations to improve their competence in inclusive education. This is another path to improvement in this regard, as shown in Figure 7.1.

Based on the action research findings, the following suggestions are put forward to improve the competence of teachers in inclusive education.

First, develop the resources of school administrators to obtain administrative support. It is advisable to help school administrators recognize the concept of inclusive education, to agree that ordinary schools should bear the main responsibility of inclusive education, that the regular classroom is the main battlefield of inclusive education, that ordinary teachers are the main implementers of inclusive education, and to see the importance of teachers having competence in inclusive education for improvement in the quality of the LRC program. They should also be encouraged to formulate a system and take various measures under the system to improve the competence of teachers in inclusive education, which is the main channel for improvement.

Second, through various means, create an inclusive atmosphere so that the concept of inclusive education can be recognized in the whole school. An inclusive cultural atmosphere is like an invisible hand to stimulate the internal motivation of teachers to improve their inclusive education competence. In

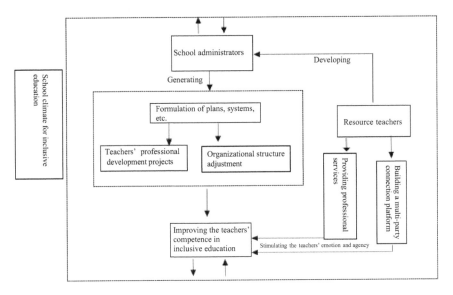

Figure 7.1 Path to Improve Inclusive Education Competence of Teachers in Case Study School.

such an atmosphere, teachers are willing to understand special needs children, actively participate in the training of inclusive education, learn the knowledge and skills of special education, and seek support to solve the problems in LRC practice. This approach is indispensable for the improvement of the competence of teachers in inclusive education.

Third, give full play to the supporting role of resource teachers in the improvement of the competence of teachers in inclusive education. At present, resources teachers are still the only special education professionals in regular schools in China, and many regular schools that have implemented LRC program still lack resources teachers. As evidenced in the case study school, resource teachers did a lot to help create an inclusive atmosphere, and arouse ordinary teachers' initiative to participate in the training of inclusive education and learn the knowledge and skills of special education. The role of resource teachers should never be underestimated in the improvement of the competence of teachers in inclusive education.

Fourth, stimulate teachers' internal motivation and give full play to teacher agency. Administrative power can force all teachers to participate in the learning of inclusive education concepts, knowledge, and skills, but it cannot stimulate their internal motivation. An inclusive atmosphere can gradually impose a positive influence on teachers' cognition and emotion, and encourage them to explore ways of improving their inclusive education competence in line with their own development needs and learning habits, carry out more targeted and deeper inclusive education knowledge and skills learning, and take the

326 *Action Research into the Improvement of the Competence*

initiative to obtain support. Therefore, it is wise to stimulate teacher agency to achieve in-depth improvement.

Fifth, improve the competence of teachers in inclusive education in practice. Ordinary teachers should go to special classes to observe how special education teachers teach special needs children, understand the behavioral characteristics of these children and the classroom management of special education teachers, and learn related skills. It is also necessary for ordinary teachers to undertake the LRC program because positive emotional feedback given by special needs children and their parents will make the teachers feel satisfied, and the progress of the special needs children will give teachers a sense of achievement, which then encourages them to actively improve their competence in inclusive education. Moreover, in-service teachers have different learning styles from those of pre-service teachers. In-service teachers prefer to learn in practice and acquire skills in the process of problem solving. Therefore, even when providing systematic knowledge training, it is necessary to combine theory with practice to make teachers acquire practical skills.

Notes

1 Ye, Lan 叶澜, Bai, Yimin 白益民, et al. *Jiaoshi juese yu jiaoshi fazhan xintan* 教师角色与教师发展新探, 332–333. Beijing: Educational Science Publishing, 2001.
2 Vaughn, S., and Schumm, J. S. "Responsible Inclusion for Students with Learning Disabilities." *Journal of Learning Disabilities* 28, no. 5 (1995): 264–270.
3 Liu, Lianghua 刘良华. *Xindong yanjiu de shi yu si* 行动研究的史与思, 29–30. Shanghai: East China Normal University, 2001.
4 Zheng, Jinzhou 郑金洲. "Xingdong yanjiu: yizhong riyi shoudao guanzhu de yanjiu fangfa" 行动研究：一种日益受到关注的研究方法. *Shanghai Higher Education Research* 上海高教研究 no. 1 (1997): 23–27.
5 Wang, Yan 王雁, and Zhu, Nan 朱楠. *Zhongguo teshu jiaoyu jiaoshi fazhan baogao 2014* 中国特殊教育教师发展报告2014, 259. Beijing: Beijing Normal University Publishing Group, 2015.
6 See note 4 above.
7 See note 3 above.
8 See note 6 above.
9 See note 1 above, 277–302.
10 See note 9 above, 329.

References

Liu, Lianghua 刘良华. *Xindong yanjiu de shi yu si* 行动研究的史与思, 29–30. Shanghai: East China Normal University, 2001.
Vaughn, S., and Schumm, J. S. "Responsible Inclusion for Students with Learning Disabilities." *Journal of Learning Disabilities* 28, no. 5 (1995): 264–270.
Wang, Yan 王雁, and Zhu, Nan 朱楠. *Zhongguo teshu jiaoyu jiaoshi fazhan baogao 2014* 中国特殊教育教师发展报告2014, 259. Beijing: Beijing Normal University Publishing Group, 2015.

Ye, Lan 叶澜, Bai, Yimin 白益民, et al. *Jiaoshi juese yu jiaoshi fazhan xintan* 教师角色与教师发展新探, 332–333. Beijing: Educational Science Publishing, 2001.

Zheng, Jinzhou 郑金洲. "Xingdong yanjiu: yizhong riyi shoudao guànzhu de yanjiu fangfa" 行动研究：一种日益受到关注的研究方法. *Shanghai Higher Education Research* 上海高教研究 no. 1 (1997): 23–27.

Appendix
Interview Outline

Interview Outline Used in Action Planning Phase

1. How do you understand the LRC program (inclusive education)?
2. Are you willing to undertake the LRC program? Why?
3. Do you think you have the ability to undertake the LRC program?
4. What support do you think you need for implementation of the LRC program?

Interview Outline Used in Action Evaluation Phase

The version for general education teachers

1. How do you understand the LRC program (inclusive education)?
2. Are you willing to undertake the LRC program? Why?
3. Do you think you have the ability to undertake the LRC program? Why?
4. What impresses you most in the implementation of the LRC program in your school?

The version for resource teachers
1. What do you think of the school's LRC program?
2. In your opinion, what changes have occurred to general education teachers in the process of the action?
3. What impressed you most in the process of the action?

The version for parents of LRC students

1. What do you think of the school's LRC program?
2. What changes have you found in the teachers' treatment of your child during the year?
3. How do you communicate and cooperate with the teachers?

Index

Note: Page numbers in *italics* indicate figures, **bold** numbers indicate tables, on the corresponding pages.

13th Five-Year Plan for Education 27
13th Five-Year Plan of Zhejiang Province for Development of Special Education 25
14th Five-Year Plan for the Protection and Development of Persons with Disabilities **54**
2020 Guidelines on Enhancing Implementation of the LRC program in Compulsory Education **54**, **71**

Action Plan for Inclusive Education in Beijing Primary and Secondary Schools 24–25
Action Plan for the Development and Improvement of Special Education during the 14th Five-Year Plan Period 247
Action Plan on Inclusive Education in Primary and Secondary Schools of Beijing 138
action research into improving competence: agency, teacher 325–326; concept and definitions 303–304; conscience, implementation of LRC program due to 309; consultation times for teachers 315; creating inclusive school culture 314–315; data collection and analysis 307, **308**, 309, **310**; development process of teachers 320–322; evaluation of competence post-research 319–320; experienced teachers mentoring younger teachers 315; ice-breaking activities 313–315; impact on teachers 320; improving competence 313–319; inclusive atmosphere 324–325; initiative, teachers', stimulation of 315; interviews 307, **308**, 328; introspection-obediance attempt 316; management support 314, 323, 324; method of research 305–309, **308**, **310**; modification of action plan 316–318; original state of teacher competence 309, 311–313; parental support 314; participation of teachers 305–306; poor competence in inclusive education 312–313; practice of inclusive education, improving 326; purpose of 304; recognition of school's achievements 318–319; resource teachers 324, 325; school selected 304–305; selection of respondents 304–305; separation of special needs children and teachers 311–312; steps in 306; strategies to improve competence 322–326, *325*; student activities 314–315
Administrative Measures for Special Education Grant Funds **54**
affective subsystem 151
age, competence of Chinese teachers and 131, *131*, 139–140
agency, teacher 97, 123, 154; constructive participation 172; as influencing factor in teacher competence 145–146, 158–160, **159**, **160**, *162*, 163, **163**, *163*, 164, 167, 168, 169; occupational stress and 167; professional development and 165; school climate and 164;

330 *Index*

stimulation of 325–326; strategies to improve competence 170, *171*, 172
Arnon, S. 76–77
attitude: positive 93–94; of students and teachers re. LRC program 41; teachers' 125–127, 134–135, 218, 222–223, 230, 248–249 *see also* understanding and practice of inclusive education, research into
Australia: attitude, teachers' 222–223; competence cultivation **204, 205, 207, 208, 209, 210, 211, 212**; discrete model of cultivation 198

Bain, A. **204**, 216
Bakker, Arnold 152
behavior, dynamic field theory and 150–152
behavior-oriented advanced model of teacher training needs analysis 267
Beijing: *Action Plan for Inclusive Education in Beijing Primary and Secondary Schools* 24–25; inclusive education in 137–138
Bocala, C. 94, 95
burnout 155

Campbell, E. 143
Canada, competence cultivation in **209, 210, 211**
Carrington, Suzanne 79
Chaiken, S. 94, 97
Chambers, D. **205**
children with special educational needs, definition of term 11
China's Education Modernization 2035 2, 25, **54**, 58
Chinese teachers, competence of: accepting attitude towards special needs children 134–135; agency, teachers, scale for 123; age of teachers 131, *131*, 139–140; compulsory inclusive education courses 228; cooperation between institutions 230–231; current status of competence *129*, 129–130, **130**; data screening 120; demographic factors 138–140; design of 118–125, **121, 122**; educational background of teachers 133–134, 143; evaluation of teachers' attitude 229–230; existing research 125–128; experience teaching 132, *132*, 140; gender 131, 138–139; identity, teacher

133, 142; inclusive education, scale for competence in 123; knowledge and skills 127–128, 135–136; level of competence **129**, 129–144, **130**, *131*, *132*, *133*; practical experience, increase in 229; professional titles of teachers 133, *133*, 142; regional factors 130, *131*; regional variations in competence 137–138; respondents 119–122, **121**, **122**; sampling 119–122, **121, 122**; scale survey 125; school climate, scale for 124–125; school sectors 133, 141; strategies to improve competence 169–174, *171*; stress, teachers', scale of 124; subject taught 133, 140–141; suggestions on cultivation of 228–231; support, ability to get 136–137; teachers' thinking on inclusive education 125–127; training experience of teachers 134, 143–144 *see also* competence of teachers; influencing factors of teacher competence
Cig, O. **212**
Circular of the State Council on Further Improving the Funding Guarantee Mechanism for Urban and Rural Compulsory Education 28
Circular on the Issuance of the Reform Scheme on the Division of Common Financial Authority and Expenditure-related Responsibilities between the Central and Local Governments in the Field of Basic Public Services 28
Circular on the Work of Pilot Counties (Districts) for Establishing a Supporting System for the LRC program 26, **51**, 57, 58, 59, **70**, 72
cognitive crafting 154
cognitive subsystem 151
Colucci-Gray, L. **204**
Common European Principles for Teacher Competences and Qualifications 83
communality 102–103
competence of teachers: Chinese standards **80**; Chinese teachers 84–88; composition of 76–77, 79, 81–88; compulsory inclusive education courses 228; cooperation between institutions 230–231; diversity and pluralism, disability incorporated into 83; evaluation of teachers' attitude 229–230; inclusive education 6–8, 10;

internal motivation for 325; levels of 87–88; policies and plans 2–3, **63–65**; practical experience, increase in 229; regulations 82–88; research into 76–79, **80**, 81–88; standards 77–79; strategies to improve competence 169–174, *171*; suggestions on cultivation of 228–231; United States 79, 81 *see also* action research into improving competence; Chinese teachers, competence of; influencing factors of teacher competence; international experience of competence cultivation; structural model of teacher competence

Compulsory Education Law of the People's Republic of China (PRC) 2, 19, **51**, 56

conceptual framework of teacher competence 89–90, *90*

conceptual subsystem 151

conferences: experiences in LRC practice, exchange of 26; first national conference on special education 21; LRC program, 1994 22; National Conference on the Exchanges of Experiences in LRC Practice 23–24

confirmatory factor analysis 105–106, 108

constructive participation 123, 145, **159**, *162*, 165, *171*, 172

content analysis 47, 56–60

Cooley, P.D. **209**

critical ratio 102

Csikszentmihalyi, M. 174

Cui Youxing 151

cultivation of teacher competence: compulsory inclusive education courses 228; cooperation between institutions 230–231; evaluation of teachers' attitude 229–230; expansion of subjects 62, 66; increase in pre-service 68–69; internal motivation for 322, 325; models 197–202, 214, 221–222; policy analysis 61–62, **63–65**, 66–69; practical experience, increase in 229; pre-service 191; shift to "inclusive" from "special" education 68; standardization and enforcement of 67; suggestions following policy analysis 68–69; suggestions on 228–231 *see also* action research into improving competence; international experience of competence cultivation

cultural-cognitive schema of teachers 259–261

Curriculum Standards for Teacher Education 8, 62, **64**, 67, **71**, 74

Decision of the Central Committee of the Communist Party of China on the Reform of the Education System 19

demographic factors, competence and 138–140

Deng Meng 126

developed/developing countries: inclusive education and 4, 137; pre-service teacher education and cultivation 192–193

disability categories: higher degrees of disability 40–41; increased number of 40–41; number of students in LRC program 31, *33*, 34, *35*

disabled children, use of term 11

discrete model of cultivation 197–198

distance education 59–60

diversity, disability incorporated into 83

Du Lingyu 268

Dutton, Jane E. 154

Du Yuan 269

dynamic field theory 150–152, 168–169

Eagly, A.H. 94, 97

"Early Childhood/Early Childhood Special Education (EC/ECSE)," United States 223–224

ecological approach to professional development 149–150, 167–168

educational background of teachers 133–134, 143 *see also* in-service teacher education and cultivation; pre-service teacher education and cultivation; training for teachers

equal access: and justice as core values 23; LRC system and 20–21; shift from efficiency to fairness 57–58

Europe 83

European Agency for Development in Special Needs Education 78, 83

evaluation: of courses 216, 217–219; in-service teacher education and cultivation 266; international experience 224–225; United States 224–225

exam-oriented schema of teachers 260

experience teaching, competence and 132, *132*, 140

332   *Index*

exploratory factor analysis 103–105, *104*, **105**, *107*

factor analysis 103–105, *104*, **105**, *107*
factor loading 103
female/male teachers 131, 138–139
Feng Yajing 268
financial subsidies 59–60
Fisher, D. 94
Five-Year Work Outline for the Cause of Disabled Persons in China (1988–1992) **49**, 56, 61, **70**
Forlin, C. **205**
14th Five-Year Plan for the Protection and Development of Persons with Disabilities **54**
funding for LRC students 28, 59–60

Gao, W. **206**
Gao Li 127
gender, competence of Chinese teachers and 131, 138–139
Geng Shen 142
Ghana 193
grade, number of LRC students by 36, *38*, *39*
Guidance for the Development of Special Education Resource Teachers in Regular Schools 73–74
Guidelines for Inclusion: Ensuring Access to Education for All (UNESCO) 9
Guidelines on Enhancing Implementation of the LRC program in Compulsory Education 6, 25, 62, **65**, 73
Guidelines on the Construction of Special Education Resources in Regular Schools **53**, **71**
Guiding Opinions on Accelerating the Development of Education in Central and Western China **53**, 57, **65**

Hernandez, K. **209**
home tutoring 59–60
Hong Kong 269
Hopkins, W.G. **213**
Huang Meixian 270
Hwang, Y.S. 142

iceberg model of competency 88–89
identity, teacher, competence and 133, 142
identity schema of teachers 259–260
Implementation Measures for Certification of Teacher Education Programs in Regular Institutions of Higher Learning (Interim) 66
Implementation Plan on Compulsory Education for Children and Adolescents with Disabilities during the Ninth Five-Year Plan 22, **50**, 55, **64**
inclusive education: Beijing 24–25; changes needed for 7; competence of teachers in 6–8, 10; definition 9; developed/developing countries 4; emergence of 1; introduction in provinces and cities 5; laws and regulations around 3–4; LRC program and 9–10, 23–25; origin and impact of 3
Inclusive Practice Project (IPP), Scotland 222
India 262
individualized education plans (IEPs) 258
influencing factors of teacher competence: agency, teacher 145–146, 158–159, **159**, **160**, *162*, 163, **163**, *163*, 164, 165, 167, 168, 169; dynamic field theory 150–152, 168–169; ecological approach to professional development 149–150, 167–168; external factors 146–149; individual factors 145–146; job demands-resources model 152–156, *155*, 169; mechanisms of action 163–169; occupational stress 148, 158, **158**, 159–160, **160**, *162*, 163, **163**, *163*, 164, 165–166, 167, 168, 169; professional development 165; school climate 147–148, 157, **157**, 159–160, **160**, 164, 165–166, 168; strategies to improve competence 169–174, *171*; structural equation model 160, **161**, *162*, 163, **163**, *163*, 164
in-service teacher education and cultivation: case study 272–295, **273–274**, **275–276**, *291*; characteristics of trainees and trainers 266; competence and 143–144; content 265; discrete training elements 271–272; elements of 264; evaluation of 266; foreign teacher training programs 268–270; form 265–266; improvement measures 272; improvements needed 135–136; inclusion of general education teachers 74; inclusive education perspective 74; indigenized training models 270; lack of inclusive education 7–8; multi-level network of

subjects 72–73; needs analysis 266–268, 271; objectives 265; policies and plans 247; policy analysis 69, **70–71**, 72–74; policy documents **70–71**; problems with 271–272; suggestions following policy analysis 74; systematization and institutionalization 73–74; teachers' attitudes towards inclusive education 248–249; training needs analysis 264–265

institutionalism, new 259, 261

institutionalization of inclusive education 249–250

institutional logic 261–262

InTASC Model Core Teaching Standards 77–78, 83, 89, 95, 219–220

integrated model of cultivation 198–200

intellectual disability, students with secondary schools 41–42

Interim Regulations for Special Education Schools **50**, 57

international experience of competence cultivation: attitude, teachers' 222–223; Australia 198, **204**, **205**, **207**, **208**, **209**, **210**, **211**, **212**; Canada **209**, **210**, **211**; challenges faced 226–228; characteristics 219–225; cultivation models 197–202, 214, 221–222; curriculum and content of courses 214–216; defects of curriculum 226; duration of courses 203; educators' lack of competence 227; England **212**; evaluation of courses 216, 217–219, 224–225; Ghana 193; India 262; Ireland 262; lack of cooperation between institutions 227–228; literature research 202–203, **204–213**, 214–219; Mexico 192–193; name/theme of courses 203; practice in inclusive education 223–224; pre-service teacher education and cultivation 192–193; Scotland 200–201, **204**, 222; South Korea 192; standards for teachers 219–221; Tasmania **209**; theory/practice disconnect 226–227; United Kingdom **207**; United States 193–197, 199–200, **206**, **208**, **212**, 222–225

Ireland 262

item-total correlation coefficient 102

Jiang Xiaoying 141

job burnout 155

job crafting 154–155, *155*, 169

job demands-resources (JD-R) model 152–156, *155*, 169

junior high school sector: disability category, number of LRC students by 34, *35*; number of LRC students 36, *37*, *39*

K-6 Elementary Teacher Preparation Standards 220

Key Principles for Promoting Quality in Inclusive Education: Recommendations for Policy Makers (EADSNE) 78

Key Principles for Promoting Quality in Inclusive Education: Recommendations for Practice (EADSNE) 83

Key Work Points of the Department of Basic Education of the Ministry of Education in 2008 51

Key Work Points of the Ministry of Education, 2011–2015 **52**

Key Work Points of the Ministry of Education in 2019 **53**, 56

Killoran, I. **209**

knowledge, necessary for teacher competence 94

knowledge and skills for inclusive education 127–128, 135–136

Lancaster, J. **204**, **208**, 216

Law of the PRC on the Protection of Persons with Disabilities (2008) 2, 22, **49**, 61, 62, **63**, **64**, 67, 144

laws and regulations: competence of teachers 82–88; *Compulsory Education Law of the People's Republic of China (PRC)* 2, 19, **51**, 56; inclusive education 3–4; *Interim Regulations for Special Education Schools* **50**, 57; *Law of the PRC on the Protection of Persons with Disabilities* (2008) 22, **49**, 61, 62, **63**, **64**, 67, 144; *Opinions on Several Issues Concerning the Implementation of the Compulsory Education Law* 20; *Regulations on Education for Individuals with Disabilities* 22, **50**, **53**, 56, 58, 61, **64**, **65**, **71**, 144 *see also* policies and plans

Leader-Janssen, E. **208**

Learning in Regular Classrooms (LRC) program: aim 4, 5; attitudes of students and teachers 41; changes in group composition 29, *30*, 31, *32*, *33*, 34, *35*, 36, *37–39*, 40–41; conscience, implementation due to 309, 311;

334 *Index*

disability categories, number of students 31, *33*, 34, *35*; dominance of 21–22; early practice 2; establishment of 19–21; funding for LRC students 28; further development needs 28–29; higher degrees of disability 40–41; imbalance across school sectors 41–42; inclusive education and 9–10, 23–25; National Conference on the Exchanges of Experiences in LRC Practice 23–24; national demands, changes in 17; national promotion 22; number of students 5–6, 29, *30*, 31, *32*; origins 4–5, 17–21; policies **49–54**; proportion of students in compared to special education schools 40; quality improvement stage 22–29; quality of education 6, 7; school sectors, number of students 36, *37–39*, 40–42; society's attitudes, impact on 6; support systems 25–28; teaching force of 9 *see also* policy analysis
Lewin, Kurt Tsadek 150, 151, 304
Lin, Chongde 76
Li Sen 151
Liu Chunling 126
living space 150–151
Loreman, T. 216
LRC program *see* Learning in Regular Classrooms (LRC) program
Lu Naigui 261

Mager, G. **206**
Ma Hongying 126
Main Work Points of the Ministry of Education in 2010 **51**
Main Work Points of the Ministry of Education in 2018 **53**
Makopoulou, K. **213**
Male, D.B. **207**
male/female teachers 131, 138–139
management support 173, 314, 323, 324
The Measures for the Administration of Special Education Subsidy Fund 28
Mendaglio, S. **210**
merged model of cultivation 200–202
Mexico 192–193
Meyer, John W. 262
Mtika, P. **204**

National Conference on the Exchanges of Experiences in LRC Practice 23–24, **70**, 72, 73

National Special Education Promotion Plan (2014–2016) 2, 56, 57
Neville, R.D. **213**
new institutionalism 259, 261
Nordness, P.D. **208**
Notice on Doing a Good Job in Enrollment of Children and Adolescents with disabilities in Compulsory Education **53**, 56, 57
Notice on Enrollment of Regular Primary and Secondary Schools in 2018 **53**
Notice on Establishment of A Supporting System for the LRC program in all Districts and Counties of Beijing 137–138
Notice on Several Opinions on the Development of Special Education **49**
Notice on the Printing and Distribution of the Teaching Plan of Full-Time Schools (Classes) for the Retarded 20, 48, **49**
Notice Regarding Several Opinions on the Development of Special Education 48
Nuttal, A. **212**, 214–215

occupational stress: agency, teacher 167; evaluation of 174; as influencing factor in teacher competence 148, 158, **158**, 159–160, *162*, 163, **163**, *163*, 164, 165–166, 167, 168, 169; as influencing factor on teacher competence 155–156; reduction of 166–167, 174; school climate and 164, 165–166
occupational stress, teachers', scale of 124
O'Neill, S.C. **211**
onion model of competency 89
Opinions of the State Council on Accelerating the Process of Building a Well- off Society for the Disabled 27–28
Opinions on Further Accelerating the Development of Special Education **51**, 58–59, **64**, 72
Opinions on Further Adjusting and Optimizing Structure to Improve Efficiency in the Use of Educational Appropriations 28
Opinions on Further Promoting the Reform and Development of Special Education during the 10th Five-Year Plan Period **50**, 55, 57, 58, **64**, 67, **70**, 73

*Opinions on Further Strengthening the
Implementation of the LRC program
for Disabled Children and Adolescents
in the Nine-Year Compulsory Education
Stage* 137–138
*Opinions on Several Issues Concerning
the Implementation of the Compulsory
Education Law* 20, **49**
*Opinions on Strengthening the
Development of Special Education
Teaching Force* 2–3, 62, **64**, 66, **71**, 73
organizational structure 152
OTP model of training needs analysis
266–267
*Outline for Reform and Development of
Education in China* 21–22
*Outline of China's National Plan for
Medium and Long-Term Education
Reform and Development (2010–2020)*
23, **51**, 59
*Outline of the Eighth Five-Year Plan for
the Cause of Disabled Persons in China
(1991–1995)* **63**, 66

parents: stigma, inclusive education as
way to avoid 252, 254; support from
314
Parlak-Rakap, A. **212**
Pederson, S.J. **209**
Peebles, J.L. **210**
performance analysis model of training
needs analysis 267
*Plan on Implementation of Compulsory
Education for Disabled Children and
Adolescents during the Eighth Five-Year
Plan Period* **63**, **70**, 73
plans *see* policies and plans
pluralism, disability incorporated into 83
policies and plans: *13th Five-Year
Plan for Education* 27; *13th Five-
Year Plan of Zhejiang Province for
Development of Special Education*
25; *2020 Guidelines on Enhancing
Implementation of the LRC program in
Compulsory Education* **54**, **71**; *Action
Plan for Inclusive Education in Beijing
Primary and Secondary Schools* 24–25;
*Action Plan for the Development and
Improvement of Special Education
during the 14th Five-Year Plan Period*
247; *Action Plan on Inclusive Education
in Primary and Secondary Schools of
Beijing* 138; Administrative Measures

for Special Education Grant Funds **54**;
Beijing 137–138; characteristics of
46–47; *China's Education
Modernization 2035* 2, 25, **54**, 58;
*Circular of the State Council on Further
Improving the Funding Guarantee
Mechanism for Urban and Rural
Compulsory Education* 28; *Circular
on the Issuance of the Reform Scheme
on the Division of Common Financial
Authority and Expenditure-related
Responsibilities between the Central
and Local Governments in the Field of
Basic Public Services* 28; *Circular on
the Work of Pilot Counties (Districts)
for Establishing a Supporting System
for the LRC program* 26, **51**, 57, 58,
59, **70**, 72; competence of teachers
2–3; cultivation of teacher competence
63–65; *Curriculum Standards for
Teacher Education* 8, 62, 67, **71**, 74;
*Decision of the Central Committee
of the Communist Party of China on
the Reform of the Education System*
19; from efficiency to fairness 48,
55–56; *Five-Year Work Outline for the
Cause of Disabled Persons in China*
(1988-1992) **49**, 56, 61, **70**; *Guidelines
on Enhancing Implementation of
the LRC program in Compulsory
Education* 6, 25, 62, **65**; *Guidelines on
the Construction of Special Education
Resources in Regular Schools* 53;
*Guiding Opinions on Accelerating
the Development of Education in
Central and Western China* 53, 57, **65**;
*Implementation Plan on Compulsory
Education for Children and Adolescents
with Disabilities during the Ninth Five-
Year Plan* 22, **50**, 55, **64**; inclusive
education, need for in 74; in-service
teacher education and cultivation
70–71, 247; *Key Work Points of the
Department of Basic Education of
the Ministry of Education in 2008* **51**;
*Key Work Points of the Ministry of
Education, 2011–2015* **52**; *Key Work
Points of the Ministry of Education
in 2019* 56; *Law of the PRC on the
Protection of Persons with Disabilities*
(2008) **49**; *Main Work Points of the
Ministry of Education in 2010* **51**;
Main Work Points of the Ministry of

336 *Index*

Education in 2018 **53**; *The Measures for the Administration of Special Education Subsidy Fund* 28; *National Special Education Promotion Plan (2014–2016)* 2, 6, 56, 57; *Notice on Doing a Good Job in Enrollment of Children and Adolescents with disabilities in Compulsory Education* **53**; *Notice on Establishment of A Supporting System for the LRC program in all Districts and Counties of Beijing* 137–138; *Notice on Several Opinions on the Development of Special Education* 49; *Notice on the Printing and Distribution of the Teaching Plan of Full-Time Schools (Classes) for the Retarded* 20, **49**; *Notice Regarding Several Opinions on the Development of Special Education* 48; *Opinions of the State Council on Accelerating the Process of Building a Well- off Society for the Disabled* 27–28; *Opinions on Further Accelerating the Development of Special Education* **51**, 58–59, **64**, 72; *Opinions on Further Adjusting and Optimizing Structure to Improve Efficiency in the Use of Educational Appropriation*s 28; *Opinions on Further Promoting the Reform and Development of Special Education during the 10th Five-Year Plan Period* **50**, 55, 57, 58, **64**, 67, **70**; *Opinions on Further Strengthening the Implementation of the LRC program for Disabled Children and Adolescents in the Nine-Year Compulsory Education Stage* 137–138; *Opinions on Several Issues Concerning the Implementation of the Compulsory Education Law* **49**; *Opinions on Strengthening the Development of Special Education Teaching Force* 2–3, 62, **64**, **71**; *Outline for Reform and Development of Education in China* 21–22; *Outline of China's National Plan for Medium and Long-Term Education Reform and Development (2010-2020)* 23, **51**, 59; *Outline of the Eighth Five-Year Plan for the Cause of Disabled Persons in China (1991– 1995)* **63**; *Plan on Implementation of Compulsory Education for Disabled Children and Adolescents during the Eighth Five-Year Plan Period* 63, **70**,

73; policy-practice loose coupling 262–263; *Program for Promoting Special Education: Phase II (2017–2020)* **53**, 58, **65**, 73; *Program for Promoting Special Education (2014–2016)* **52**, 62, **65**, 67, **71**; *Several Opinions on the Consolidation and Improvement Work after Acceptance Check of the Realization of "Two Basically" Goal* **50**; *Several Opinions on the Development of Special Education* 2, 21, **63**, 67; *Special Education Promotion Plan (2014–2017)* 311; teachers' attitudes and 135; *Trial Measures for the Development of the LRC program* 22, **49**, 55, 56–57, 62, **63**, 67, 72 *see also* laws and regulations; policy analysis

policy analysis: basis of 46–48; benefits of 46; from bottom-up to top-down 60–61; content analysis 47, 56–60; cultivation policy 61–62, **63–65**, 66–69; from efficiency to fairness 57–58; factual 47; frameworks for 47–48; inclusive education in general education policies 68; increase in pre-service education 68–69; macro policies 48, **49–54**, 55–61; means 58–60; micro policies 48; normative 47; objective of LRC program 57–58; objects, expansion of scope 56–57; outer/middle/core layers 47; preferential policy compensation 59–60; pre-service teacher education and cultivation 61–62, **63–65**, 66; process analysis 47, 60–61; shift to "inclusive" from "special" education 68; standardization and enforcement of pre-service cultivation 67; suggestions following analysis 68–69, 74; support systems 58–60; training policy 69, **70–71**, 72–74; value analysis 47, 48, 55–56

positive attitude 93–94 *see also* attitude

poverty-stricken areas, LRC program in 27

practice in inclusive education: action research into improving competence 326; adjustment rather than innovation 257–258; behavioral guidance as aim 257; classroom order, challenges to 255; cultural-cognitive schema of teachers 259–261; data collection and analysis 250, **251**, 252, **253**;

defective, special needs students seen as 260–261; early 2; exam-oriented schema of teachers 260; experiences in, exchange of 26; extra, inclusive education seen as 255–257; identity schema of teachers 259–260; Inclusive Practice Project (IPP), Scotland 222; individualized education plans (IEPs) 258; institutional logic 261–262; international experience of competence cultivation 223–224; *Key Principles for Promoting Quality in Inclusive Education: Recommendations for Practice* (EADSNE) 83; learning potential of students 254–255; National Conference on the Exchanges of Experiences in LRC Practice 23–24, **70**, 72, 73; normal teaching as priority 258–259; participants in research 250, **251**; policy-practice loose coupling 262–263; research method 250, **251**, 252; school-wide inclusive practices 173; teachers' 248–264, **251**, **253**; teachers' attitudes 248–249; theoretical basis 249–250; theory/practice disconnect 226–227

preferential policy compensation 59–60

pre-service teacher education and cultivation: Australia, discrete model of cultivation in 198; benefits of 192; competence and 143; compulsory inclusive education courses 228; cooperation between institutions 230–231; cultivation models 197–202; cultivation of teacher competence 191; developed/developing countries 192–193; duration of courses 203; evaluation of teachers' attitude 229–230; lack of inclusive education 7–8, 191; literature research 202–203, **204–213**, 214–219; policy analysis 61–62, **63–65**, 66; practical experience, increase in 229; standardization and enforcement of 67; unbalanced development of 137; United States, development of in 193–197 *see also* international experience of competence cultivation

primary school sector: Chinese teachers' competence 133, 141; disability category, number of LRC students by 31, *33*, 34; number of LRC students 36, *37*, *38*

principals, support from 173

process analysis 47, 60–61

professional development of teachers: agency, teacher 165; constructive participation 172; ecological approach 149–150; three-dimensional model of 151–152 *see also* in-service teacher education and cultivation; pre-service teacher education and cultivation; training for teachers

professional standards *see* standards for teachers

Professional Standards for Primary School Teachers 77

Professional Standards for Secondary School Teachers 77

professional titles of teachers 133, *133*, 142

Profile of Inclusive Teachers (EADSNE) 78–79

Program for Promoting Special Education: Phase II (2017–2020) **53**, 58, **71**, 73

Program for Promoting Special Education (2014–2016) **52**, 58, 59, 62, **65**, 67, **71**, 84

Qi Juan 144

Qi Yajing 155

quality of education: LRC practice 6, 7; shift from efficiency to fairness 57–58

Rakap, S. **212**

reform of the education system 19–20, 21–22

regional variations in competence 137–138

regulations *see* laws and regulations

Regulations on Education for Individuals with Disabilities 2, 22, **50**, **52**, **53**, 56, 58, 61, **64**, **65**, **71**, 84, 144

Reichel, N. 76–77

relational crafting 154

reliability testing 102

resource rooms *see* support systems

resource teachers 324, 325

rural areas, LRC program in 27

Rutter, Michael 174

Salamanca Statement 3

Schaefer, Julie 147

school climate 156; agency, teacher 164; creation of inclusive culture 314–315;

338 *Index*

improving teacher competence 172–174; inclusive atmosphere 324–325; as influencing factor on teacher competence 147–148, 157, **157**, 159–160, **160**, 164, 165–166, 168; management system 173; occupational stress and 164, 165–166; principals, support from 173; scale for 124–125; school-wide inclusive practices 173
school culture 152
school field dynamic 152
school sectors: Chinese teachers, competence of 133, 141; imbalance of LRC program across 41–42; number of students in LRC program 36, *37–39*, 40–42
Scotland 200–201; attitude, teachers' 222; competence cultivation **204**; Inclusive Practice Project (IPP) 222
secondary school sector: Chinese teachers' competence 133, 141; LRC program in 41–42
self-development 322
self-efficacy in teaching 123, 145, 170, *171*, 172
Seligman, M.E.P. 174
Several Opinions on the Consolidation and Improvement Work after Acceptance Check of the Realization of "Two Basically" Goal **50**
Several Opinions on the Development of Special Education 2, 21, **63**, 66, 67
Sharma, U. **207**, **210**, **212**, 214–215, 216
Shen Junhong 267
Shi Mengliang 138
Simpson, Alyson 170
skills in inclusive education *see* knowledge and skills for inclusive education
social field dynamic 152
Sokal, L. **210**
Sosu, E.M. **204**
South Korea 192
Special Education Evaluation Report 137
Special Education Promotion Plan (2014–2017) 311
special education schools: as part of inclusive education 58–59; proportion of LRC students to students in 40
standards for teachers: Australia, comparison with China 79; China

80; competence of teachers 77–79; Europe 78–79; inclusive education as integral to 86; international experience of 219–221; *K-6 Elementary Teacher Preparation Standards* 220; *Professional Standards for Primary School Teachers* 77; *Professional Standards for Secondary School Teachers* 77; United States 77–78, 219–220
stress: agency, teacher 167; evaluation of 174; as influencing factor in teacher competence 148, 159–160, **160**, *162*, 163, **163**, *163*, 164, 165–166, 167, 168, 169; as influencing factor on teacher competence 155–156; reduction of 166–167, 174; school climate and 164, 165–166; teachers', scale of 124
structural equation model 160, **161**, *162*, 163, **163**, *163*, 164
structural model of teacher competence: attitude, positive 93–94; communality 102–103; conceptual framework of teacher competence 89–90, *90*; critical ratio 102; dimensions of 99; evaluation of research 109–110; factor analysis 103–105, *104*, **105**, *107*; factor loading 103; iceberg model of competency 88–89; interview survey 90, 92–98, **93**, **98–99**; item-total correlation coefficient 102; knowledge, necessary 94; onion model of competency 89; prediction scale **98–99**; preliminary qualitative research stage 90, 92–98, **93**, **98–99**; reliability analysis 108; reliability testing 102; research framework and approach 88–90, *90*, *91*; scale for evaluation of competence 100–110, **101**, *104*, **105**, *107*, **108**; support, ability to get 95–97; theoretical sources analysis 88–89 *see also* Chinese teachers, competence of; competence of teachers
subject taught, competence and 133, 140–141
subsystems 151–152
Sun Ying 269
support systems: ability to get support 95–97, 109, 136–137; importance of 109; for LRC program 25–28; policy analysis 58–60
suyang (competence) *see* competence of teachers

suzhi (quality): translation of term 10
  see also quality of education
Swain, K.D. **208**, 215
Sweden 4

Taiwan 4
Tan Heping 126
task crafting 154
Tasmania, competence cultivation in
  209
teachers: attitude 41, 125–127, 134–135,
  218, 222–223, 230; definition of term
  9; exam-oriented schema of 260;
  identity schema of 259–260; thinking
  on inclusive education 125–127;
  understanding and practice of
  inclusive education 248–264, **251**,
  253 *see also* competence of teachers;
  cultivation of teacher competence;
  in-service teacher education and
  cultivation; pre-service teacher
  education and cultivation
Thailand 4
13th Five-Year Plan for Education 27
*13th Five-Year Plan of Zhejiang Province
  for Development of Special Education*
  25
Tims, Maria 154
Tiwari, Ashwini 262
Tomlinson, 95
training for teachers: competence and
  143–144; experience of teachers,
  competence and 134; inclusion
  of general education teachers 74;
  inclusive education perspective 74;
  multi-level network of subjects
  72–73; policy analysis 69, **70–71**,
  72–74; suggestions following policy
  analysis 74; systematization and
  institutionalization 73–74 *see also*
  in-service teacher education and
  cultivation; pre-service teacher
  education and cultivation
*Trial Measures for the Development of the
  LRC program* 22, **49**, 55, 56–57, 62, **63**,
  67, **70**, 72, 73
*2020 Guidelines on Enhancing
  Implementation of the LRC program in
  Compulsory Education* **54**

understanding and practice of inclusive
  education, research into: adjustment
  rather than innovation 257–258;
behavioral guidance as aim 257;
classroom order, challenges to 255;
cultural-cognitive schema of teachers
259–261; data collection and analysis
250, **251**, 252, **253**; defective, special
needs students seen as 260–261; exam-
oriented schema of teachers 260; extra,
inclusive education seen as 255–257;
identity schema of teachers 259–260;
individualized education plans (IEPs)
258; institutional logic 261–262;
learning potential of students 254–255;
normal teaching as priority 258–259;
participants in research 250; policy-
practice loose coupling 262–263;
research method 250, **251**, 252;
teachers' attitudes 248–249; theoretical
basis 249–250; understanding,
teachers' 252, 254–257
United Kingdom, competence cultivation
  in **204**, **207**, **212**
United States: attitude, teachers'
  222–223; competence cultivation
  193–197, **206**, **212**; composition of
  teacher competence 79, 81; discrete
  model of cultivation 197; diversity and
  pluralism, disability incorporated into
  83; "Early Childhood/Early Childhood
  Special Education (EC/ECSE)"
  223–224; evaluation of courses
  224–225; inclusive education in
  4; *InTASC Model Core Teaching
  Standards* 219–220; integrated model
  of cultivation 199–200; *K-6 Elementary
  Teacher Preparation Standards* 220;
  standards for teachers 77–78, 83, 89,
  219–220

Wang Hongxia 126, 141
Wei Xiaoman 126
West Africa 193
will subsystem 151
Woronko, D. **209**
Wrzesniewski, Amy 154
Wu Yang 144

Xiong Qi 127, 141
Xu Li 126

Ye Lan 76, 170, 320, 321–322
Yuan Wende 126
Yu Meifang 155
Yu Xin 267

340 *Index*

Zaretsky, H. **209**
Zeng Yaru 126
Zhang Hong 126
Zhang Hui 10
Zhang Lili 147
Zhang Na 145

Zhang Xiaodong 139, 143
Zhao Fujiang 142
Zhejiang Province 25
Zhou Dan 147
Zundans-Fraser, L. **208**